THE WAY
IT WAS
in the U.S.A.

THE WAY IT WAS

in the U.S.A.

Clarence P. Hornung

A PICTORIAL PANORAMA OF AMERICA

1850 TO 1890

Abbeville Press

NEW YORK

Grateful acknowledgment is made to the following for permission to reprint selections included in this book:

James Truslow Adams. *The Epic of America*. Copyright © 1931, 1933. Copyright renewed © 1959 by James Truslow Adams. Reprinted by permission of Little, Brown and Co.

Edwin P. Alexander. *The Pennsylvania Railroad: A Pictorial History*. Copyright © 1947 by E.P. Alexander. Copyright renewed © 1975 by E.P. Alexander. Selection is reprinted with the permission of W.W. Norton & Company, Inc.

The American Guide. Copyright © 1977. By permission of Hastings House Publishers.

Stephen Vincent Benet. "John Brown's Body" from *Selected Works of Stephen Vincent Benet* published by Holt, Rinehart and Winston, Inc. Copyright © 1927, 1928, by Stephen Vincent Benet. Copyright renewed © 1955, by Rosemary Carr Benet. Reprinted by permission of Brandt & Brandt Literary Agency.

Henry Beston. *The Outermost House* by Henry Beston. Copyright © 1928, 1949, 1956 by Henry Beston. Copyright © 1977 by Elizabeth C. Beston. Reprinted by permission of Holt, Rinehart and Winston, Publishers.

Gene M. Brown. *Wall Street: Men and Money*. Copyright © 1952. Reprinted by permission of the author.

Henry Collins Brown (ed.). *Valentine's Manual of Old New York*. Copyright © 1926.

John Burroughs. *The Heart of Burroughs's Journals*. Copyright © 1928. Reprinted by permission of Houghton Mifflin Company.

Nathaniel Burt. *The Perennial Philadelphians: The Anatomy of an American Aristocracy*. Copyright © 1963 by Nathaniel Burt. Reprinted by permission of Little, Brown and Co.

Carl Carmer. "The Susquehanna" from the *Rivers of America* series. Copyright © 1955 by Carl Carmer. Reprinted by permission of the estate.
———. *Stars Fell on Alabama*. Copyright © 1934 by Carl Carmer. Reprinted by permission of the estate.

Frank Cousins and Phil Riley. *The Colonial Architecture of Philadelphia*. Copyright © 1920.

Hart Crane. The lines from "To Brooklyn Bridge" are reprinted from *The Complete Poems and Selected Letters and Prose of Hart Crane*, Brom Weber (ed.), with the permission of Liveright Publishing Corporation. Copyright © 1933, 1958, 1966 by Liveright Publishing Corporation.

John T. Cunningham. *New Jersey*. Copyright © 1966, 1976, by John T. Cunningham. Reprinted by permission of Doubleday and Company, Inc.

Marshall B. Davidson. *Life in America*. Copyright © 1951 by Marshall B. Davidson. Reprinted by permission of Houghton Mifflin Company.

Arnold Ehrlich (ed.). *The Beautiful Country*. Copyright © 1970 by the Viking Press Inc. Reprinted by permission of the Viking Press, Inc.

Edward Robb Ellis. *The Epic of New York City*. Copyright © 1966 by Edward Robb Ellis. Reprinted by permission of the author.

Norman Foerster (ed.). *American Poetry and Prose*. Copyright © 1957. Reprinted by permission of Houghton Mifflin Company.

G. Fox & Company. *Highways & Byways of Connecticut*. Copyright © 1947 by G. Fox & Company. Reprinted by permission of G. Fox & Company.

William Francis Guess. *South Carolina*. Copyright © 1947.

John Gunther. *Inside U.S.A.* Copyright © 1946, 1947 by John Gunther. Copyright © 1947 by the The Curtis Publishing Company. Reprinted by permission of Harper & Row Publishers, Inc.

Frederick Gutheim. *The Potomac*. Copyright © 1949, 1977 by Frederick Gutheim. Reprinted by permission of Holt, Rinehart and Winston, Publishers.

Walter Havighurst. *Land of the Long Horizons*. Copyright © 1960 by Walter Havighurst. Reprinted by permission of Coward, McCann and Geoghegan, Inc.
———. *Ohio, A Bicentennial History*. Copyright © 1976 by American Association for State and Local History. Reprinted with the permission of W.W. Norton & Company, Inc.

Holiday Magazine (eds.). *American Panorama, East of the Mississippi*. Copyright © Travel Magazine, Inc. Reprinted with the permission of Travel Magazine, Inc.

Clarence P. Hornung. *Wheels Across America*. Copyright © 1959 by A.S. Barnes & Company.
———. *The Way It Was: New York, 1850-1890*. Copyright © 1977 by Schocken Books, Inc.

Henry F. Howe. *Massachusetts, There She Is—Behold Her*. Copyright © 1960 by Henry F. Howe. Reprinted by permission of Harper & Row, Publishers, Inc.

Henry James. *The American Scene*. Copyright © 1907. Reprinted by permission of the publishers, Indiana University Press.

Gerald W. Johnson. *Pattern for Liberty*. Copyright © 1952 by McGraw-Hill Inc. Used with permission of McGraw-Hill Book Company.

Harnett T. Kane. *Gone are the Days: An Illustrated History of the Old South*. Copyright © 1960 by Harnett T. Kane. Reprinted by permission of the publishers, E.P. Dutton & Co., Inc.

Alfred Kazin. *Brooklyn Bridge*. Copyright © 1946. Reprinted by permission of the author.

Edgar Lee Masters. *The Sangamon*. Copyright © 1942 by Edgar Lee Masters. Copyright © 1970 by Ellen Coyne Masters. Reprinted by permission of Holt, Rinehart and Winston, Publishers.

Samuel E. Morison. *The Oxford History of the American People*. Copyright © 1965 by Samuel Eliot Morison. Reprinted by permission of Curtis Brown, Ltd.

Lloyd Morris. *Incredible New York*. Copyright © 1951 by Lloyd Morris. Reprinted by permission of Random House, Inc.

Lewis Mumford. *Sticks and Stones*. Copyright © 1924. Reprinted by permission of Dover Publications, Inc.
———. "The Metropolitan Milieu" from *America and Alfred Stieglitz*. Copyright © 1934. Reprinted by permission of the author.

Barrows Mussey. *Vermont Heritage*. Copyright © 1975. Reprinted by permission of the author.

David McCord. *About Boston*. Copyright © 1948, 1973 by David McCord. Reprinted by permission of Little, Brown and Co.

Carson McCullers. *Brooklyn Is My Neighborhood*. Copyright © 1941. Reprinted by permission of Houghton Mifflin Company.

James Oppenheim and Robert Haven Schauffler. *Romantic America*. Copyright © 1913.

Jacqueline Overton. *Long Island's Story*. Copyright © 1929.

The Pageant of America series. Copyright U.S. Publishers Assn. Reprinted by permission of the publishers.

Neal R. Peirce. *The New England States*. Copyright © 1976, 1972 by Neal R. Peirce. Selections are reprinted with the permission of W.W. Norton & Company, Inc.

William T. Polk, *Southern Accent*. Copyright © 1953. Reprinted by permission of William Morrow & Company, Inc.

Louise Dickinson Rich. *The Coast of Maine*. Copyright © 1956, 1962 by Louise Dickinson Rich. Reprinted by permission of Curtis Brown, Ltd.

Kenneth Roberts. *Trending Into Maine*. Copyright © 1938. Reprint, Down East Books, 1977.

Romance of North America. Copyright © 1958 by Houghton Mifflin Company. Reprinted with the permission of Houghton Mifflin Company.

Carl Sandburg. California" and "Red Iron Ore" from *The American Songbag*. Copyright © 1927.
———. "Chicago" in *Chicago Poems*. Copyright © 1916 by Holt, Rinehart and Winston, Inc.; copyright © 1944 by Carl Sandburg.
———. "Prayers of Steel" from *Cornhuskers*. Copyright © 1918, by Holt, Rinehart and Winston, Inc.; copyright © 1944 by Carl Sandburg.
  All selections are printed by permission of Harcourt Brace Jovanovich, Inc.

Mark Schorer. "Wisconsin" from *American Panorama*. Copyright © 1947. Reprinted by permission of Harper & Row, Publishers, Inc.

John Steinbeck. *Travels with Charley in Search of America*. Copyright © 1961, 1962 by The Curtis Publishing Co., Inc. Copyright © 1962 by John Steinbeck. Reprinted by permission of The Viking Press.

Bayrd Still. *Mirror for Gotham*. Copyright © 1956. Reprinted by permission of New York University Press.

Anselm L. Strauss (ed.). *The American City*. Copyright © 1968. Reprinted by permission of the editor.

Harold W. Thompson. *Body, Boots & Britches*. Copyright © 1939 by Harold W. Thompson. Copyright © renewed 1967 by Dr. Marian Thompson. Reprinted by permission of J.B. Lippincott Company.

Paul A.W. Wallace. *Pennsylvania, Seed of a Nation*. Copyright © 1962 by Paul A.W. Wallace. Reprinted by permission of Harper & Row, Publishers, Inc.

Harry Emerson Wildes. *Twin Rivers*. Copyright © 1943, 1971 by Harry Emerson Wildes. Reprinted by permission of Holt, Rinehart and Winston, Publishers.

William E. Wilson. *Indiana*. Copyright © 1966. Reprinted by permission of the publisher, Indiana University Press.

Edwin Wolf, II. *Philadelphia, Portrait of an American City*. Copyright © 1975. Reprinted by permission of Stackpole Books.

Thomas Wolfe. *You Can't Go Home Again*. Copyright © 1934, 1937, 1938, 1940 by Maxwell Perkins as Executor; renewed 1968 by Paul Gitlin. Reprinted by permission of Harper & Row, Publishers, Inc.

Library of Congress Cataloging in Publication Data

Hornung, Clarence Pearson.
    The way it was in the U.S.A.

    Includes index.

    1. United States—Social life and customs—19th century.   1. Title.
E169.H794   973.9   78-15246

ISBN 0-89659-001-1

A TRIBUTE TO
DAVID STOFF
1877—1978

*Arriving from Austria—young,
penniless, and full of dreams—
he found good fortune in America*

Books by Clarence P. Hornung

BOOKPLATES OF HAROLD NELSON

TRADE-MARKS OF CLARENCE P. HORNUNG

HANDBOOK OF DESIGNS & DEVICES

LETTERING FROM A TO Z

EARLY AMERICAN ADVERTISING ART (2 Vols.)

WHEELS ACROSS AMERICA

GALLERY OF THE AMERICAN AUTOMOBILE (Portfolio of 100 Prints)

PORTRAIT GALLERY OF EARLY AUTOMOBILES

ANTIQUES AND JEWELRY DESIGNS

OLD FASHIONED CHRISTMAS in Illustration & Decoration

TREASURY OF AMERICAN DESIGN (2 Vols.)

WILL BRADLEY: HIS GRAPHIC WORK

ALLOVER PATTERNS FOR DESIGNERS AND CRAFTSMEN

200 YEARS OF AMERICAN GRAPHIC ART
    (in Collaboration with Fridolf Johnson)

BACKGROUND PATTERNS & TEXTURES

THE WAY IT WAS: NEW YORK, 1850-1890

THE AMERICAN EAGLE IN ART AND DESIGN

GEOMETRIX: THE INFINITY OF DESIGN (in Preparation)

FOREWORD

IN TODAY'S WORLD OF SATELLITE broadcasts and multi-hued illustrated magazines, pictorial journalism is accepted as commonplace. The world watched, spellbound, the exciting Apollo takeoff and, later, witnessed the astronauts' first faltering steps on the moon. What greater thrills await on the television screen?

Yet, a little over a century ago, the concept of simultaneously picturizing and reporting current events was entirely new. The idea of tying words and pictures together on a printed page was introduced in the famous *Nuremberg Chronicle* almost four hundred years earlier. This was considered revolutionary at the time, even though it was overlooked that, in many instances, the same picture was repeated for several personalities.

The popular press of the 1850s—forerunner of today's picture magazine or tabloid—scored a dramatic breakthrough when the American illustrated weeklies—notably *Gleason's, Ballou's, Harper's,* and *Leslie's*—featured large wood engravings, illustrative of scenes and events that were reported at the same time in the paper. In this way, the Eastern Establishment responded to the public hunger for news beyond urban centers on the Atlantic seaboard.

This book endeavors to re-create a picture of the United States of over a century ago—to capture and reanimate the vast, almost limitless continent then being tamed and conquered every step of the way. A canvas of such gigantic proportions, like the panoramic paintings of those days, must be rendered in broad strokes—sketched in detail where possible—and moving swiftly on to other regions, to reach the outermost limits of this vast land of ours.

The desire to know more of the far reaches of the West was so insatiable that any form of graphic expression, promising to fill in the gaps, won ready acceptance. A popular form of entertainment, not unlike the traveling circus or dramatic troupes going from town to town, was the illustrated panorama—a continuous length of muslin cloth painted with a succession of scenes or a historical narrative. Often, a panorama was arranged to be exhibited around the walls of a circular hall or auditorium. Others, mounted on double rollers and manually operated, traveled along slowly to the accompaniment of a lecturer's recital, with all the attendant sound effects: bells, whistles, Indian hoots and war cries, cannon shots and explosions—and a musical background designed to thrill the audience and make the impression more memorable. John Banvard traveled up and down the length of the Mississippi, painting the epic of the Father of Waters—a spectacle that was exhibited extensively throughout the United States and Great Britain. Another panorama of the "Monumental Grandeur of the Mississippi" was drawn by Professor M. W. Dickeson and painted by I. J. Egan, "covering 15,000 feet of canvas!" Others, featuring the gold rush, were popular; among them was the forty-thousand-foot canvas called "Overland Route to the Pacific" from St. Joseph, Missouri, to California—the work of Minard Lewis who made the journey in 1849. These "moving pictures" of the day reached the principal cities where larger audiences gave some assurance of success. The moving panorama could produce pictures of distant places—it could not record news events.

Here was a vacuum at the midway mark of the nineteenth century, and the publishers of the illustrated journals saw their opportunity. Photography had already burst upon the scene. Pictures of people, places, and cities were shown, but there was no way by which candid shots could be printed in the popular press. It required another forty years before Stephen Horgan developed the halftone plate. Yet the eager public—its appetite whetted by tales of the open plains, the westward expansion, the confrontation with the (understandably) hostile Indians, the saga of the goldfields in California and Colorado, the thrust of the iron rails and the meeting of East and West at Promontory Point, the wonder and grandeur of the Rockies—hungered for news and views of every small town and big city, and all points between.

While Mark Twain regaled the nation with tales about life on the Mississippi, the published pictures of palatial river queens best depicted the frenzied activity at the levees, when gangplanks came alive and whistles shrieked the last minute, "All Aboard"

To match the stirring words of Longfellow's *Wreck of the Hesperus,* poignant engravings of the forbidding coastline of Norman's Woe added their graphic powers to public understanding of the disaster. Reports of numerous exploring expeditions sponsored by the government of the Yellowstone and Grand Canyon regions were published as ponderous tracts before they were enlivened by colorful sketches and paintings of Thomas Moran.

Threading through the pages of America's vanished past, the romantic national legend attained its greatest glamor through the work of its painters—to be viewed only at public exhibits—and its illustrators—to be seen in weekly journals or in illustrated books.

The years covered in this book reach from 1850 to 1890, an infinitesimal span measured against America's age. It is not an arbitrary period. It covers the era when topical events began to be reported by wood engravings, until their gradual disappearance with the advent of halftone printing. During those years, the popular press perfected rapid machinery and, at the same time, developed the technique of printing from large blocks or engravings—at first directly, and later through the medium of electroplates.

The "candid camera" of the second half of the nineteenth century was in the hands of artist-journalists, often sent by their journals to sketch distant places, injecting a new dimension in reporting feature stories. These men were sometimes dispatched on special assignments to sketch newsworthy scenes; at other times they acted as roving reporters, roaming the land and sending their drawings in to the publisher's office, there to be transferred to the box-wood block.

Highly technical skills were required of the wood-engraver, to render without distortion, to maintain tonal values and the textual grains called for by the illustrator. This competence was so specialized that various engravers were assigned specific tasks: one engraved only faces and figures; others landscapes; others architectural subjects, while still others cut in the sky effects, using graining tools for parallel incisions that covered the areas before cloud effects could be introduced. Speed was essential in covering current events, to meet publishers' deadlines and "scoop" competitors. An ingenious, time-saving method—attributed to Frank Leslie—was to cut huge blocks into as many as thirty-two pieces, each part assigned to a single engraver, after which all parts were bolted securely together, forming the large illustration. Though the public was unaware of this miracle of production, competitors were

astounded by the feat until they, too, mastered the technique.

The best American illustrators were in Boston and New York—centers where the leading magazines and books were published. Here the country's finest artists were concentrated—their names a roster of the nation's topmost talent: Winslow Homer, A. R. Waud, Thomas Nast, Arthur B. Frost, Frederick Remington, Edwin Abbey, C. A. Reinhart, and many more. The gradual improvement in reproductive processes, plus the constant betterment in the engraver's craft, combined to attract ever-widening audiences and markets for the illustrators' finest efforts. Today, pages of some of these weeklies—costing only pennies when published—command over a hundred dollars a print for the work of some of these artists, especially that of Winslow Homer.

A regional sequence is followed in this volume, starting with the northern limits of New England, and traveling south along the Atlantic coast. Inland, we journey to the more important riverways—natural highways for exploration and transportation—across the Alleghenies to the Ohio Valley and Great Lakes regions. Here, our course follows, north and south, the mighty Mississippi, before venturing across the plains to the Rockies. Thence, crossing the Sierras to the Pacific coast, our itinerary terminates in the Northwest—a kaleidoscopic sweep of the continent in arbitrarily selected areas, compacted within the limits of a single volume. This compendium of a vast territory—not strictly a geographic study nor a gazetteer—certainly not socio-historical in purpose—hastens from ocean to ocean, omitting entire areas so sparsely settled and so seldom visited that the editors of the weeklies ignored them in their coverage. The long-established and well-known eastern regions were featured in greater detail than now seems to have been warranted. Obviously, this created an uneven picture, the heavy emphasis on population centers giving readers a distorted view. Each new issue unfolded many new pictures, revealing fresh facets of the country's magnitude, yet leaving many questions unanswered. A reader was able to learn more about a diminutive New England town than about the great state of Texas.

We have found it necessary, where the illustrated publications were weak, to turn, after prolonged research, to other sources. Two volumes, titled *Picturesque America*—published 1872-1874, under the distinguished

editorial guidance of William Cullen Bryant—
contained the supreme expression of fine-line
engraving by a notable staff of artists and the
country's most superlative wood-engravers.
Among the landscapists enlisted in this
monumental project were Thomas Moran,
J. D. Woodward, Granville Perkins, James D.
Smillie and, especially, Harry Fenn, its principal illustrator, whose travels and sketch-pad
took him across the land when stagecoaches
and railways presented hazards, even in the
best weather. These drawings, dispatched to
the home publishing office of D. Appleton &
Company, were delivered to the engraver for
execution on the woodblock. Fidelity in
transferring the illustrator's art, the boldness
of salient features, the flashing contrasts of
blacks and whites, reached the finest expression in reproductive engraving in America.

Many of these engravings appear on the
pages which follow, along with those from the
illustrated periodicals.

In the preface to the original edition of *Picturesque America,* editor Bryant announced his
intention "to present full descriptions and
elaborate delineations of the scenery characteristic of all the different parts of the country."
Bryant continued: "The wealth of material for
the purpose is almost boundless. It will be admitted that our country abounds with scenery
new to the artist's pencil, of a varied
character, whether beautiful or grand, or
formed of those sharper but no less striking
combinations of outline which belong to
neither of these classes . . . In the Old World
every spot remarkable in these respects has
been visited by the artists; studied and
sketched again and again; observed in sunshine
and in the shade of clouds, and regarded from
every point of view that may give variety to
the delineation. Both those who see in a landscape only what it shows to the common eyes,
and those whose imagination, like that of
Turner, transfigures and glorifies whatever
they may look at, have made of these places,
for the most part, all that could be made of
them, until desire is felt for the elements of
natural beauty in new combinations, and for
regions not yet rifled of all that they can yield
to the pencil. Among our White Mountains,
our Catskills, our Alleghenies, our Rocky
Mountains, and our Sierra Nevada, we have
some of the wildest and most beautiful scenery
in the world. On our majestic rivers—among
the largest on either continent—and on our
lakes—the largest and noblest in the

world—the country often wears an aspect in
which beauty is blended with majesty; and on
our prairies and savannas, the spectator, surprised at the vastness of their features, finds
himself, notwithstanding the soft and gentle
sweep of their outlines, overpowered with a
sense of sublimity."

I subscribe to the Confucian dictum as to
the value of pictures, but the literary-visual
form enhances a presentation. There is here no
intent to be textually descriptive, but rather to
supplement pictures with words from
distinguished writers of the nineteenth and
twentieth centuries. A conscientious effort has
been made to associate the quotations so that
they are contemporary with the visual material,
though this has not always been possible.

An anthology is particularly valuable when
the quotations are pertinent to the pictures,
serving as a spur to further study. The narrow
margins, dictated by the format of these pages,
have necessarily reduced many extracts to mere
snippets of their original sources. It is hoped,
however, that each is sufficient to stir the imagination and inspire the reader to search
for—or reacquaint himself with—the original
sources. You will find each regional section introduced by a brief essay and, on every page,
a capsular comment that endows the pictures
with deeper meaning.

Such a book makes heavy demands on time
and talents, eliciting the efforts and skills of
many people. It has been my good fortune to
have such assistance. On the sectional essays, I
am particularly indebted to Irene Sickel Sims
whose aid has been invaluable. Mark Green-
berg has been most helpful in countless ways,
including writing and other vital support. I
owe much to Fridolf Johnson, my esteemed
collaborator on many projects; also to
Hayward Cirker, Peter Helck, and young
David Stoff. On the publisher's staff, Cindy
Parzych has been a dependable and intelligent
co-worker. Free access to the shelves of the
Nassau County Library System has been
graciously accorded to me, and librarians in
nearby branches of Garden City and Malverne
have been exceedingly helpful.

To Harry Abrams and Bob Abrams of
Abbeville Press, I am deeply indebted for their
inspiring and generous cooperation. And, to
my wife Sara, I pay heartfelt appreciation for
her invariably calm forebearance during the
long months of the book's creation.

Clarence P. Hornung

CONTENTS

PART THREE

THE SOUTH

PART FOUR

LAKE STATES

MIDWEST & SOUTHWEST

PART FIVE

MOUNTAIN STATES & WEST COAST

PART SIX

THE WAY
IT WAS
in the U. S. A.

Along Maine's Rock-bound Coast

MOUNT DESERT ISLAND . . . "THE OVENS" . . .

GREAT HEAD . . . EAGLE LAKE . . . SOMES'

POND . . . CADILLAC MOUNTAIN . . . PORTLAND

. . . CASCO BAY . . . AUGUSTA . . . OLDTOWN . . .

PENOBSCOT, KENNEBEC AND ANDROSCOGGIN

RIVERS . . . CAMDEN AND VICINITY . . .

PORTSMOUTH AND THE ISLES OF SHOALS,

NEW HAMPSHIRE

CASTLE HEAD, MOUNT DESERT

Along Maine's Rock-bound Coast

WITH A JIGSAWED COASTLINE of 2,500 miles, and countless offshore islands, Maine is the most spectacular—as well as the largest—of the New England states. Bounded on the east by Canada's provinces of Quebec and New Brunswick, with the St. John and the St. Croix rivers forming part of the international boundary, Maine shares its state-side boundary only with New Hampshire. To the east lies the Bay of Fundy; to the south, the vast Atlantic.

Ancient ages laid down a bedrock of sandstone, shale, and limestone, crystallized by molten granite. While the softer rock generally eroded into valleys, the most resilient formed Maine's mountainous west, and, on the east, the mountains of Mount Desert. Long drift ridges, deposited by the receding glaciers, dammed the valleys and created Maine's amazing endowment of more than 2,200 lakes, etching out rugged waterways.

In Frenchman's Bay, just off the coast of Maine southeast of Bangor, Mount Desert Island stands in breath-taking majesty, surrounded by seas, crowned with mountains—the only area along the Atlantic coast where mountains stand close to the sea. Ever since the end of the 1880s, Mount Desert has been one of New England's most famous tourist resorts as well as a leading fishing and lumbering area. Acacia National park occupies the greater part of the island. Among numerous harbors, those best known are Southwest and Northeast, with—on the eastern shore—Bar Harbor, so named for the sandy bar which connects it with the northernmost island in the Porcupine group.

The village, East Eden, is the tourist center. Most visitors booked for a holiday at East Eden set themselves to explore the rocks along the shore, then ascend the Green Mountain for its "thunder-smitten" view. After these tributes to island scenery, hunting and fishing compete with the allure of coastal bays and inlets for the yachtsman's delight—"A yachting party might spend an entire summer in threading the mazes of hundred-harbored Maine," as Whittier described it.

Points of exceptional interest are the "ovens," about seven miles up the bay, and "Schooner Head," "Great Head," and "Otter Creek Cliffs" on the seaward shore. While some of the Ovens are only slight indentations, others are large enough to hold thirty to forty people. At low tide, the shore at the "Ovens" is a favorite picnic ground for summer visitors. They lunch in the caves, saunter through the forests on the cliffs, gather harebells and roses, and search the rocky shore for weird sea creatures brought in by the waves.

It was Champlain, landing here in 1604, who named the island. In 1613 a French Jesuit mission and colony were established, but in the same year the British destroyed the settlement, claiming the land because of earlier explorations made by Cabot.

Human occupation of the peninsula, now known as Maine, goes back to prehistoric times, as burial mounds of the Red Paint people—found in the south-central part of the state—indicate. Afterward, the Indians came and left tremendous heaps of shells, said to

date back 1,000 to 5,000 years. When the white explorers arrived, there were friendly Abnaki Indians settled on certain coastal and inland sections. Norsemen may have known Maine's coast long before the arrival of British, French, and Spanish mariners, who preceded Champlain's settlement at the mouth of the St. Croix.

From the extreme southwestern tip of the state to its northeastern boundary, the land is threaded with rivers—the Kennebec, Penobscott, Androscoggin, Saco, and the St. Croix being the most important. They trace their intricate courses over the land and pour into the Atlantic. The St. John, after meandering through northern Maine, flows into New Brunswick.

Maine's generally poor soil and short growing season operate against a prosperous agriculture, and the lack of coal and steel is a handicap to extensive manufacturing. But the matchless majesty of Maine's seacoasts and mountains, and its fish and wild game, hold an irresistible lure for visitors, creating a lucrative tourist industry. The protected harbors, which serve as fishing ports, the rapid rivers providing power for factories, and the still-extensive lumber resources are factors important to Maine's economy.

From the days when her straight white pines provided masts for the British navy, lumbering has dominated Maine's industry and export trade. Although the virgin timber now is largely cut, and forest fires have taken a devastating toll, conservation and reforestation enable Maine to still manufacture pulpwood and paper. Maine gained her name of the "Pine Tree State" from the once-great stands of white pine which are now almost extinct. Forests of spruce, fir, hemlock, and hardwoods are still to be found in most parts of the state. Especially in the lesser populated northern counties that are sheltered by lakes and woods, moose, deer, black bears, and smaller game abound. Fowl and fish are plentiful, and Maine lobsters are famous across the nation. There is heavy concentration on market gardening, poultry raising, and dairying to meet the needs of local and New England markets. The cultivation of potatoes, especially in Aroostook County, has spread Maine's fame far beyond New England. A highly profitable timber trade is carried on with Europe and Asia.

4

There's no getting away from the fact—Mt. Desert Island really is a fabulous place. Those who love it claim that it is one of the most dramatically beautiful spots in the world; and I'm forced to admit that they could be right. It's a big island, sixteen miles long and about twelve miles wide, connected with the mainland by a bridge. It is cut almost in two by Somes Sound, the only true fjord on the Atlantic coast—a deep, narrow, seven-mile stretch of water between high cliffs, penetrating to the very heart of the island. In addition, Mt. Desert has twenty-six fresh-water lakes and ponds, and I don't know how many salt-water coves and harbors. Cadillac Mountain, the highest mountain on the whole Atlantic coast, rises fifteen-hundred and thirty-two feet from the eastern half of the island; and there are seventeen other hills which the inhabitants call mountains as well. All around the shore are scores of smaller islands in the waters of Blue Hill Bay and Frenchman Bay. Although the name of the island, and especially of the town of Bar Harbor, has for decades been a household word connoting a playground for the very wealthy, actually by far the larger part of it is wild land, covered by unspoiled forest and open to anybody to enjoy. There are excellent roads all over the island, and you can drive scarcely a hundred feet without having a new and stunning view revealed to you.

LOUISE DICKINSON RICH
The Coast of Maine

THE CLIFFS NEAR "THE OVENS"

*. . . dotted with hundreds of isles and inlets
as the swift-flowing Penobscot, Kennebec, and
Androscoggin rush to greet the sea*

THE "SPOUTING HORN" IN A STORM

They say here that great waves reach this coast in threes. Three great waves, then an indeterminate run of lesser rhythms, then three great waves again. On Celtic coasts it is the seventh wave that is seen coming like a king out of the grey, cold sea. The Cape tradition, however, is no half-real, half-mystical fancy, but the truth itself. Great waves do indeed approach this beach by threes. Again and again have I watched three giants roll in one after the other out of the Atlantic, cross the outer bar, break, form again, and follow each other in to fulfillment and destruction on this solitary beach. Coast Guard crews are all well aware of this triple rhythm and take advantage of the lull that follows the last wave to launch their boats. It is true that there are single giants as well. I have been roused by them in the night. Waked by their tremendous and unexpected crash, I have sometimes heard the last of the heavy overspill, sometimes only the loud, withdrawing roar. After the roar came a briefest pause, and after the pause the return of ocean to the night's long cadences. Such solitary titans, flinging their green tons down upon a quiet world, shake beach and dune. Late one September night, as I sat reading, the very father of all waves must have flung himself down before the house, for the quiet of the night was suddenly overturned by a gigantic, tumbling crash and an earthquake rumbling; the beach trembled beneath the avalanche, the dune shook, and my house so shook on its dune that the flame of a lamp quivered and pictures jarred on the wall.

HENRY BESTON

The Outermost House

6

*Majestic Cadillac crowns Mount Desert Island,
highest peak on the long Atlantic seaboard from
downeast Maine to the Florida Keys . . .*

I never knew, or had forgotten how much of Maine sticks up like a thumb into Canada...We know so little of our own geography. Why, Maine extends northward almost to the mouth of the St. Lawrence, and its upper border is perhaps a hundred miles north of Quebec...As I drove north through the little towns and the increasing forest rolling away to the horizon, the season changed quickly and out of all proportion. Perhaps it was my getting away from the steadying hand of the sea, and also perhaps I was getting very far north. The houses had a snow-beaten look, and many were crushed and deserted, driven to earth by the winters. Except in the towns there was evidence of a population which had once lived here and farmed and had its being and had been driven out. The forests were marching back, and where farm wagons once had been only the big logging trucks rumbled along. And the game had come back, too; deer strayed on the roads and there were marks of bear.

JOHN STEINBECK
*Travels with Charley
in Search of America*

GREAT HEAD

EAGLE LAKE

. . . where forest-clad headlands and granite cliffs, side by side, unite to create vistas of unparalleled beauty and unforgettable drama

THUNDER CAVE

Mount Desert has a unique combination of mountain and sea that sets it apart from all other resorts. Unique, too, is Bar Harbor's strange combination of mountainous social elegances and shaggy simplicity, which leads summer visitors to build magnificent mansions in which to entertain admiring friends; then to build log cabins far off in the deep woods to which they sulkily retire to escape the social activities made necessary by their mansions. From Champlain, who first gave the island its name, down to John Greenleaf Whittier, men have spoken as highly of the beauties of Mount Desert as it's possible to speak. "From the summit of Green Mountain," wrote an anonymous visitor in 1866, "the view is one of unparalleled wonder. Half ocean, half land, and the middle distance a bright mosaic of island and bay, it stretches from far Katahdin at the north, a hundred and twenty miles as the crow flies, to an unlimited distance over the sea."

KENNETH ROBERTS
Trending Into Maine, 1938

EAGLE CLIFF, SOMES' SOUND

VIEW FROM VIA MALA, AT "THE OVENS"

Beyond Cape Elizabeth and Portland Head Light, the blue waters of Casco Bay beckon, studded with islands—one for every day in the year . . .

In the long, covered walk that bridged the gorge between the lighthouse and the house, we played in stormy days; and every evening it was a fresh excitement to watch the lighting of the lamps, and think how far the lighthouse sent its rays, and how many hearts it gladdened with assurance of safety. As I grew older I was allowed to kindle the lamps sometimes myself. That was indeed a pleasure. So little a creature as I might do that much for the great world! But by the fireside our best pleasure lay,— with plants and singing birds and books and playthings and loving care and kindness the cold and stormy season wore itself at last away, and died into the summer calm. We hardly saw a human face beside our own all winter; but with the spring came manifold life to our lonely dwelling,—human life among other forms. Our neighbors from Star rowed across; the pilot-boat from Portsmouth steered over, and brought us letters, newspapers, magazines, and told us the news of months. The faint echoes from the far-off world hardly touched us little ones. We listened to the talk of our elders, "Winfield Scott and Santa Anna!" "The war in Mexico!" "The famine in Ireland!" It all meant nothing to us. We heard the reading aloud of details of the famine, and saw tears in the eyes of the reader, and were vaguely sorry; but the fate of Red Riding-Hood was much more near and dreadful to us.

EVERGREEN LANDING.

WHITE HEAD.

PORTLAND HEAD LIGHT.

PORTLAND HARBOR AND ISLANDS

EVERGREEN LANDING, WHITE HEAD, PORTLAND HEAD LIGHT

. . . while just across Maine's southernmost Kittery Point, Portsmouth remembers her past, John Paul Jones, and its glorious naval victories

APPLEDORE ISLAND.

STAR ISLAND.

PORTSMOUTH AND ISLES OF SHOALS

APPLEDORE ISLAND, WHALE ROCK LIGHT, CHURCH STAR ISLAND

Often, in pleasant days, the head of the family sailed away to visit the other islands, sometimes taking the children with him, oftener going alone, frequently not returning till after dark. The landing at White Island is so dangerous that the greatest care is requisite, if there is any sea running, to get ashore in safety. Two long and very solid timbers about three feet apart are laid from the boat-house to low-water mark, and between those timbers the boat's bow must be accurately steered; if she goes to the right or the left, woe to her crew unless the sea is calm! Safely lodged in the slip, as it is called, she is drawn up into the boat house by a capstan, and fastened securely. The lighthouse gave no ray to the dark rock below it; sending its beams far out to sea, it left us at its foot in greater darkness for its lofty light. How sweet the summer wind blew, how softly splashed the water round me, how refreshing was the odor of the sparkling brine!

CELIA THAXTER

Phoenixlike, Portland has risen many times from Indian raids, British bombardment, and catastrophic fires to become Maine's largest city

Still, I'd like to tell you about a few things in Portland that you shouldn't miss. One of them is a very simple pleasure, that of walking along State Street. State Street is considered by many to be one of the really famous and outstandingly beautiful streets in America. It isn't spectacular. It's wide and quiet, with brick sidewalks and a roof of murmuring boughs; and the houses that face onto it are gracious and simple and dignified. A favorite of mine is the old Shepley House, now the Portland Club, which has an especially lovely doorway, with leaded fanlight and sidelights and a very nice Palladian window over it. This house has a public dining room, so if you are interested in fine old interiors, you can inspect this one. State Street starts down at Deering's Oaks, which is the Deering's Woods of Longfellow's poem, "My Lost Youth." You remember:

> And Deering's Woods are
>   fresh and fair,
> And with joy that is almost
>   pain
> My heart goes back to
>   wander there . . .

Deering's Oaks is now the largest of the city's public parks, but it's still fresh and fair. It's almost like a well-groomed forest, with a pond where you can go boating in summer or skating in winter; and you can play tennis there, or bowl on the green, while your children take advantage of the excellent playground facilities.

LOUISE DICKINSON RICH

The Coast of Maine

CITY OF PORTLAND, FROM THE HARBOR

CITY HALL, MARKET SQUARE, PORTLAND

Native son Longfellow sings Portland's praises, writing in My Lost Youth: *"Often I think of the beautiful town that is seated by the sea . . ."*

VIEW IN CONGRESS STREET, PORTLAND

JUNCTION OF FREE AND CONGRESS STREETS, PORTLAND

She was doing all right until the great fire of July 4, 1866, which we have mentioned before. Again the city was laid waste with a financial loss amounting to millions, but miraculously without the loss of a life. Again the city groggily pulled itself together and started rebuilding immediately. The result was an improvement. Streets were straightened and widened, areas of congestion were removed, and the park system that makes Portland so beautiful today was inaugurated. The city fathers, with a wisdom and vision a little unusual in that era, set aside certain sites of great commercial value as public squares and parks for "protection against the spread of fire and to promote the general health." These parks, twenty-six in number, range in size from small, tree-shaded plots to Deering's Oaks's beautiful fifty-four acres; and they are scattered all through the city. You are always within easy walking distance of one or another, so you never can forget about trees and grass and nesting birds. That's one of the reasons I like Portland.

LOUISE DICKINSON RICH
The Coast of Maine

*State-of-Mainers point pridefully to their Capitol,
whose building by noted architect
Charles Bulfinch was started back in 1829*

A whole fleet of schooners and packets plied regularly between Augusta and Boston, and a healthy commercial traffic developed. It was not at all unusual to see twenty-five or more ships docked at the Augusta wharves, even though she did seem to be an inland city. This lasted until the arrival of the railroad, which competed so successfully with the shipping that now no boats go to Augusta. However, by this time (1827) Augusta had become the capital of the state; and although she is an industrial city with over forty enterprises, it is as the capital that she is best known today. The Capitol was begun in 1829. It's a noble and beautiful edifice designed by Charles Bulfinch of Boston and constructed of Hallowell granite, which is unusually fine—a clear gray marked with black tourmaline specks and bearing very little mica. The gold figure on top of the dome represents Wisdom, a hopeful choice for any building housing a governing body, I would say. The Capitol contains a Hall of Flags, as well as the very excellent State Library, which performs an unusually good and efficient service in supplying books to people in isolated areas away from the ordinary sources. I used to live in the backwoods myself, and I don't know how I would have got through the long, snow-bound winters without the book boxes from the State Library.

LOUISE DICKINSON RICH

The Coast of Maine

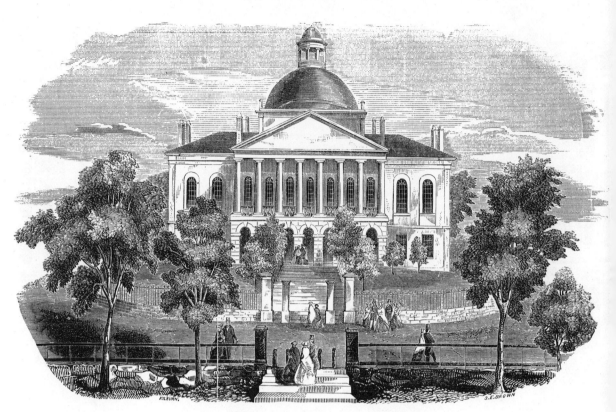

STATE HOUSE AT AUGUSTA, MAINE

UNITED STATES ARSENAL, AUGUSTA

Besides lumbering and logging, the Penobscot's fame derives from its ancient Indian tribes, whose annual powwow and palaver are a cherished tradition

OLDTOWN, ON THE PENOBSCOT RIVER, MAINE

Within a dozen miles of Bangor we passed through the villages of Stillwater and Oldtown, built at the falls of the Penobscot, which furnish the principal power by which the Maine woods are converted into lumber. The mills are built directly over and across the river. Here is a close jam, a hard rub at all seasons; and then the once green tree, long since white, I need not say as the driven snow, but as a driven log, becomes lumber merely. Here your inch, your two- and your three-inch stuff begin to be, and Mr. Sawyer marks off those spaces which decide the destiny of so many prostrate forests. Through this steel riddle, more or less coarse, is the arrowy Maine forest, from Ktaadn and Chesuncook, and the headwaters of the St. John, relentlessly sifted, till it comes out boards, clapboards, laths and shingles such as the wind can take, still perchance to be slit and slit again till men get a size that will suit. There were in 1837, as I read, two hundred and fifty sawmills on the Penobscot and its tributaries above Bangor, the greater part of them in this immediate neighborhood, and they sawed two hundred millions of feet of boards annually. To this is to be added the lumber of the Kennebec, Androscoggin, Saco, Passamaquoddy and other streams.

HENRY DAVID THOREAU
The Maine Woods, 1864

SAW-MILLS ON THE PENOBSCOT RIVER, OLDTOWN

About halfway up the Maine coast lies Camden, near Rockland and Rockport—names descriptive of the rugged terrain—overlooking Penobscot Bay and its many islands: Vinalhaven, its largest

It is customary to speak of Maine as a rugged state. The adjective is deserved, as this witness can testify. I have met her rugged yeomanry and I have skirted her rugged shore line; have viewed her rugged mountains and ranged her rugged forests...A few years of Maine politics would make almost anyone indifferent to the rigors of the climate and the hardships of the wilderness.

IRVIN S. COBB

We were standing where there was a fine view of the harbor and its long stretches of shore all covered by the great army of the pointed firs, darkly cloaked and standing as if they waited to embark. As we looked far seaward among the outer islands, the trees seemed to march seaward still, going steadily over the heights and down to the water's edge.

SARAH ORNE JEWETT

CAMDEN AND VICINITY

Boston ...
Cradle of Liberty ...
Athens of America

THE COMMON . . . FANEUIL HALL . . .

STATE HOUSE . . . CUSTOM HOUSE . . .

BOSTON HARBOR . . . CHELSEA . . .

EAST BOSTON . . . QUINCY MARKET . . .

BACK BAY . . . BLACKSTONE SQUARE . . .

LOUISBURG SQUARE . . . TREMONT STREET . . .

AMAICA POND . . . BOSTON NECK . . .

LOWELL RAILROAD DEPOT . . .

BOSTON AND CAMBRIDGE RAILROAD . . .

CAMBRIDGE . . . HARVARD UNIVERSITY

Boston ...
Cradle of Liberty ...
Athens of America

BREWER FOUNTAIN, BOSTON COMMON

I T WAS A "BOLD, BALD, BLEAK, TRIPLE-hilled peninsula" to which the Elder, John Winthrop, came in 1630, seeking a site for the main colony of the Massachusetts Bay Company.

One effusive Pilgrim, wandering about in the neighborhood where Charlestown and Bunker Hill now are, declared that the land possessed "rare endowments, dainty hillocks, plains delicate and fair, streams jetting jocundly," but another report described the promontory as "bleak and drear, a hideous wilderness, possessed by barbarous Indians, very cold, sickly, rocky, barren, unfit for culture, likely to make the people miserable."

The newcomers called the area "Tri-Mountain"; the Indians—more poetic—named it "Shawmut," or "Sweet Waters." The earliest settlers, coming from the old Boston of the fens in British Lincolnshire, named the new colony "Boston." Settlers in Charlestown—"suffering from exceeding want of water"—found allure in the Indians' name of

"Sweet Waters" and moved to Boston. They bought land from the owner Reverend, Blackstone, for thirty pounds and, as *Picturesque America* told its readers in 1872, "Boston began to exist with its teeming memories, its dramatic history, steady growth, and its picturesque and romantic aspects."

Certainly few American cities can boast such a rich background, such devotion to learning, such pride in natural endowments, such lusty commercial and industrial development.

Boston's notable ministers and statesmen—the vanguard in American Puritanism as, later, their successors were the ardent champions of Abolition—contributed immeasurably to Boston's intellectual life, until the town became known as the "Athens of America."

The Congregational organization of churches allowed almost every man a say in religious affairs, just as he had in the town meeting in local government. Following the Massachusetts Bay Charter, the legislature and the magistrates gave the colonists a representative system, embodying the seeds of democracy and nationalism.

The city's proud "firsts" are the *Boston Public Latin School,* established in 1630; *Harvard University,* founded in nearby Cambridge in 1636; a *Free Public Library* in 1653; and the first newspaper in the Thirteen Colonies, the *News-Letter,* in 1704. The Boston Public Latin School—attended by many famous men—produced five signers of the Declaration of Independence and four Presidents of Harvard.

Every United States history book is starred with outstanding events from Boston's early days: Boston Massacre, Boston Tea Party, Battle of Bunker Hill; and names like Faneuil Hall, Old North Church, the Old South Meeting House, are equally etched in the nation's memory. Boston's revolutionary heroes—John and Samuel Adams, Paul Revere, Benjamin Franklin, John Hancock, Josiah Quincy, Artemas Ward, and others, are interwoven with the nation's history.

Wooden ships built in Boston carried its name around the world; innumerable fisheries flourished, and the manufacture of shoes and textiles prospered. The port's advantageous location gave Boston supremacy over other New England colonial towns. Just as great Boston fortunes were made in textiles and in boots and shoes, the young clipper boat captains in the China trade often made sizeable fortunes after no more than two or three voyages. Their turnover was immediate and enormous.

There is great charm to Boston Common, for more than two centuries a promenade for grown-ups and playground for children. Occupying nearly 50 acres between Beacon and Boylston Streets, with its lawns as velvety and green as those of boasted London parks, its rows of elms on the Great Mall dating back 150 years, the Common reveals both venerable age and the care with which it is maintained by modern Boston.

Prominent Boston families—Cabots, Lowells, Lodges, and others—made fortunes from shipping, and from mills and factories built on New England rivers. They built substantial homes on Beacon Hill and in the Back Bay sections, and patronized the arts and letters. Despite the conservative tone of their culture, they backed reformers, notably the Abolitionists. Their influence persisted long after the growth of industry brought many immigrants—chiefly Irish at first—and Boston changed from a farm-surrounded commercial city to an industrial metropolis. Where other European settlers in America—from Canada to the Caribbean— thought of themselves as French, English, Dutch, or Spanish, with an expectation of eventually returning "home," the New England settler regarded America as home, convinced that his service to God and English-speaking people was vitally important, and bringing liberty, democracy, and universal education. Cotton Mather, in 1684, is reputed to be the first to apply the name "American" not only to the Indian, but to the colonists.

The water view shows Boston's industrial and commercial character: large, many-windowed factories...tall, smoke-stained chimneys...above the thickly-settled streets from City Point, to South Boston and Chelsea. As in most cities—dating back several centuries—beautiful, modern avenues run into the narrow, crooked streets of colonial days. *Picturesque America* informed its readers: "The almost-mathematically cone-shaped city is actually the most uneven and jagged; its general plan is no plan at all. Many of its thorofares run so crazily that he who travels by them comes almost to his starting point, while others run into 'No thorofare'."

In words somewhat less than transcendental Ralph Waldo Emerson is credited with the comment: "We say the cows have laid out Boston. Well, there are worse surveyors."

In the heart of Boston, noted for its Beacon Hill, Back Bay, Louisburg Square and many other residential sections of the city . . .

Yet the old charm lingers on. You will find it in the lovely old red brick homes of Beacon Hill, with cobblestoned Acorn Street and Louisburg Square, where a little green park is ringed by stately 19th-century houses and gas lampposts. Historic Boston can be seen in an hour or two along the mile-and-a-half Freedom Trail in this most walkable of all American cities: the State House with its 23-carat gold dome, begun from designs by Charles Bulfinch in 1795; the pleasant expanse of the Boston Common, which the town bought as a "trayning field" for the militia and for the "feeding of Cattell" back in the 17th century, and where pirates, witches, and Quakers were hanged from an elm near the Frog Pond; Park Street Church, where William Lloyd Garrison delivered his first antislavery speech in 1829; the Old Granary Burying Ground with the graves of John Hancock, Samuel Adams, and Paul Revere; the Boston Athenaeum, the literary *sanctum sanctorum* of old Boston; King's Chapel, which was the Episcopal place of worship of early British governors and later the first Unitarian church in America; the Old State House and scene of the Boston Massacre; the Old South Meeting House where Bostonians met to protest the British tea tax before staging their famous Tea Party; Faneuil Hall, where Sam Adams and James Otis delivered the fiery speeches that led to Revolution; the Paul Revere House, Boston's oldest wooden frame building (1677); and the Old North Church, immortalized by Longfellow's poem about Revere's midnight ride.

PANORAMIC VIEW (

NEAL R. PEIRCE

The New England States,
1976

*. . . steep, staggered side streets criss-cross with
dead-end lanes where unpredictable, classic mansions
are often flanked by drab, depressing lodging houses*

CITY OF BOSTON

There is nothing in New England corresponding at all to the feudal aristocracies of the Old World. Whether it be owing to the stock from which we were derived, or to the practical working of our institutions, or to the abrogation of the technical "law of honor," which draws a sharp line between the personally responsible class of "gentlemen" and the unnamed multitude of those who are not expected to risk their lives for an abstraction,—whatever be the cause, we have no such aristocracy here as that which grew up out of the military systems of the Middle Ages. What we mean by "aristocracy" is merely the richer part of the community, that live in the tallest houses, drive real carriages, (not "kerridges,") kid-glove their hands, and French-bonnet their ladies' heads, give parties where the persons who call them by the above title are not invited, and have a provokingly easy way of dressing, walking, talking, and nodding to people, as if they felt entirely at home, and would not be embarrassed in the least, if they met the Governor, or even the President of the United States, face to face. Some of these great folks are really well-bred, some of them are only purse-proud and assuming,—but they form a class, and are named as above in the common speech.

OLIVER WENDELL HOLMES
*The Autocrat of the
Breakfast-Table, 1858*

Architecturally, Boston was a living museum of America's changing styles expressed in public buildings from the days of native-born Charles Bulfinch and his influence . . .

The Boston Custom House—the work of Ammi Young—was the first-magnitude star in the galaxy of Boston's Greek Revival buildings. The monolithic columns weigh forty-two tons each. It stood, in 1849, facing the waterfront, but its original charm is entirely lost today under the great tower rising above it. A few of its inner columns now form a kind of modern Stonehenge out in Franklin Park. The old Tremont House, with a Greek facade of white Quincy granite, was the first of many impressive American hotels which appeared during the Greek Revival. It is one of the vanished buildings of Boston which I would like most to have seen. It must have been a noble affair with that great dining room seating two hundred diners at once, its whale-oil lamps, and bathing rooms in the basement. Dickens said of it that "it had more galleries, colonnades, piazzas, and passages than he could remember or the reader believe." It was built by Isaiah Rogers in 1829 and was torn down in true American fashion in the mid-1890's. It was Rogers who designed the Howard Athenaeum, a granite Gothic building off Scollay Square which burned in 1846 and was rebuilt by the same man. A theater where Joseph Jefferson once played, it is known today the world over as the Old Howard. Another example of Rogers's Gothic style is the Unitarian Church in Harvard Square. Such are the beginning of the architectural history of our city.

DAVID MC CORD
About Boston, 1948

THE STATE HOUSE, BOSTON

BOSTON ATHENAEUM

. . . on through the period of Greek Revival when, as Kilhan so charmingly noted, "Boston shed its provincial attitude and began to assume the airs of a metropolis"

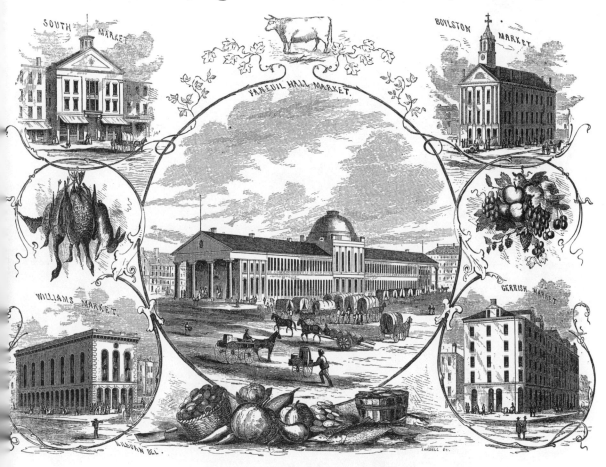

PUBLIC MARKET HOUSES IN BOSTON

"No matter what the period, the style was fixed then, as now, purely and simply by fashion and nothing else. No distinctively American style was ever really in evidence, and quite possibly none ever will be, for as long as people lack definite religious and political convictions, and particularly as long as a lagging philosophy fails to catch up with runaway science, just so long will Americans be unable to create a style of their own as distinctive as the Grecian or the Gothic." This opinion I take verbatim from a remarkable little book of one hundred pages called *Boston after Bulfinch*, by Walter H. Kilham—a book which every Bostonian who cares about his city should find time to read. Mr. Kilham laments the fact that an architect's name is not likely to live long after his death. This is a sad truth indeed. Christopher Wren is the one architect of London that the world at large remembers; Bulfinch is *the* architect of Boston, at least so far as the general public goes. Even one with so assertive a name as Ammi Young is forgotten, though his Greek Revival Custom House has since soared to a height unchallenged till this present moment of renewed and noisy building activity.

DAVID MC CORD

About Boston, 1948

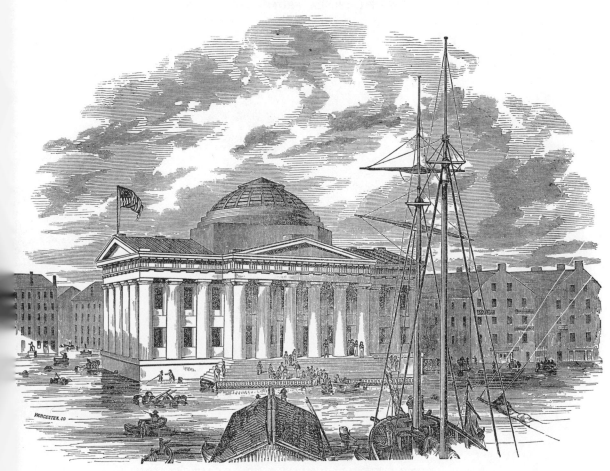

BOSTON CUSTOM HOUSE

Rivers, bridges, docks and wharves mark the maritime complex that is Boston, interlaced with peninsulas and an endless, labyrinthian shoreline . . .

The familiar phrase of one if by land and two if by sea gives numerical emphasis to the Atlantic Ocean. So through the greater part of three centuries the emphasis of Boston has been on the sea that washes almost to her door. By reason of her long, deep-channeled, and intricate harbor, Boston is a riparian city without really enjoying in the larger sense an actual outlook on the ocean; and because of this fact we sometimes forget that she is a seaport city first of all. New York is so very nearly encircled by ships and tugs and barges and ferries, and San Francisco so plainly indented by the Pacific, that we think of them in the maritime sense first and last. Many of us in Boston today can and do go about our business without so much as a sight of any part of the waterfront for months at a time. We know that the waterfront is there.

DAVID MC CORD

About Boston, 1948

VIEW OF CHELSEA FROM EAST BOSTON

LOOKING TOWARD CHELSEA FROM EAST BOSTON

. . . recalling to residents and visitors alike that the city's growth stems from shipping and distributing its harvest of the seas

SCENE ON SOUTH BOSTON BRIDGE

The first area of permanent settlement in the present City of Boston was in the Dock Square section, which is now part of the North End. By the time when the large stream of Irish immigration began, in the eighteen-forties, this area was already solidly build up, and the social leaders of the city were moving from it to outlying parts. This great wave of immigration changed the North End rapidly into a congested tenement district. By 1850 half of the 23,000 inhabitants were Irish, and the proportion increased steadily until 1880, when this was a predominantly Irish district. Soon afterward, however, the Irish population declined rapidly before a new wave of immigration, which came largely from Italy and Russia. In 1880 there were fewer than a thousand Italians in the district, but fifteen years later, the state census listed 7700 Italians, 6800 Irish, 6200 Jews (all but 400 coming from Russia), 1200 British or British Americans (immigrants from England, Scotland, and Canada), and 800 Portuguese. Throughout the early nineteen-hundreds the Italian immigration continued, while the Irish moved out in increasing numbers, and the Jews, though they retained their clothing stores on Salem and Hanover Streets, also sought other places to live.

WILLIAM FOOTE WHYTE,
New England Quarterly, 1939

LAUNCHING OF THE U.S.S. MERRIMAC, FROM THE CHARLESTOWN NAVY YARD

As the principal port on the Atlantic coast, Boston harbor brought prosperity to the Colonies, until Britain's wartime blockade temporarily bottled up its seaborne commerce

The seaports of Massachusetts have turned their backs to the element that made them great, save for play and for fishing; Boston alone is still in the deep-sea game. But all her modern docks and terminals and dredged channels will avail nothing if the spirit perish that led her founders to "trye all ports." *Sicut patribus...* We can ask no more here. But in that unknown harbor toward which we all are scudding may our eyes behold some vision like that vouchsafed our fathers, when a California clipper ship made port after a voyage around the world. A summer day with a sea-turn in the wind. The Grand Banks fog, rolling in wave after wave, is dissolved by the perfumed breath of New England hayfields into a gentle haze that turns the State House dome to old gold, films brick walls with a soft patina, and sifts blue shadows among the foliage of the Common elms. Out of the mist in Massachusetts Bay comes riding a clipper ship, with the effortless speed of an albatross. Her proud commander keeps his skysails and studdingsails past Boston light...

VIEW IN BOSTON HARBOR—ENGLISH MAIL STEAMER GOING TO SEA

*In the heyday of the clipper ships, wealthy merchants
sent their swift vessels sailing the seven seas
to bring back aromatic spices, tea, coffee and rum*

...After the long voyage she is in the pink of condition. Paintwork is spotless, decks holystoned cream white, shrouds freshly tarred, ratlines square. Viewed through a powerful glass, her seizings, flemish-eyes, splices, and pointings are the perfection of the old-time art of rigging. The chafing-gear line has just been removed, leaving spars and shrouds immaculate. The boys touched up her skysail poles with white paint, as she crossed the Bay. Boom-ending her studdingsails and hauling a few points on the wind to shoot the Narrows, between Georges and Gallups and Lovells Islands, she pays off again through President Road, and comes booming up the stream, a sight so beautiful that even the lounging soldiers at the Castle, persistent baiters of passing crews, are dumb with wonder and admiration.

SAMUEL ELIOT MORISON,
*The Maritime History
of Massachusetts, 1921*

26

*Genre scenes of neighborhood and ethnic blend
added a bit of spicy divertissement to otherwise
dull street settings . . .*

There is one week of October, indeed, when I never fail to recapture a certain boyhood remembrance of the color of Halloween. It comes at the close of evening—usually near a fruit store or a flower shop—just when the office buildings pour their life stream into the streets and people for the moment seem uniformly gay and animate and kindly, and the lights come on with a special brightness and twinkle. This above all is the time not only to talk about but to walk about Boston. It is never again so tranquil in the early morning, when the sun puts a pale bright film across the rooftops and chimneys over the Basin, softening in deep purple-blue the aristocratic outline of the Hill. It is the one time when the dark of evening flows quietly in, as sadness will sometimes drift in and out of a human face. It is the season of the end of something and the promise of something else that is not winter. I think perhaps above all that it is the season of dignity, when unconsciously we tend to match ourselves against the brilliance of nature; when our city, old and new, seems even better than she is—as though she were suddenly housecleaned and painted, and aired by all the winds that blow across her from the land and the sea.

DAVID MC CORD
About Boston, 1973

CORNER OF WINTER, WASHINGTON AND SUMMER STREETS, BOSTON

BOSTON STREET SHOWMEN AND MUSICIANS

. . . and provided top-notch illustrators, like Winslow Homer, the opportunity to depict the everyday happenings in the busy metropolis

THE FOUNTAIN ON BOSTON COMMON

TREMONT STREET, OPPOSITE BOSTON COMMON, JULY 4, 1857

We were a cosmopolitan gang. There were Italians, Scotch, Irish, Bohemians, Jews and nondescripts. Here we received our first lessons in languages. We could curse, for example, in all these idioms, and babble a bit in tongues. Demark, McGovern, Kovar, Donovan...these were as often my companions as were the Wolfsons, Fritzes, Levis and Golds. We knew nothing of racial prejudice; one touch of Nature— usually a top seat in the gallery of the burlesque houses—made us all kin. Later, our education would be completed by our parents; we would learn to hate one another as befits members of a Christian civilization. But in those days we were still savages. Indeed, we were so hopelessly retrograde that we cherished only the usual prejudices against girls. The ones we knew were for the greater part tomboys. I don't remember— memory, of course, is a trickster—a single shy girl out of my entire childhood. It is possible that I myself was shy, and that the boldness of the lasses was simply a relative deduction. We were, I recall, a distinctly sophisticated group. We were crammed with misinformation, it is true, thereby resembling the sophisticates of our adulthood. But we knew that there were things that we were not supposed to know, and we acted as if we knew them. That is almost a formula. And before we realized it, we really knew them...

ISAAC GOLDBERG

American Mercury, 1929

In key cities along the Atlantic seaboard, but especially in Boston—citadel of periodical publishing, landmark areas were singled out and illustrated in detail

Anyone who presumes to write about Boston runs the risk of being branded a literary poacher. You see, the city has been sequestrated as a kind of game preserve by the author of *H.M. Pulham, Esq.* Anecdotal rights are fiefed out (in a manor of speaking) to Mr. Cleveland Amory, and thus Boston has become a strictly posted property with seignorial dues payable at the end of every royalty period. I have no wish to disturb this highly profitable arrangement between two fellow authors—but look, I saw the place first. May I not be permitted (just this once) to mention Beacon Street, Commonwealth Avenue and Scollay Square without risking a plagiarism suit? I'll take the chance anyway. To paraphrase Van Wyck Brooks' remark about Bronson Alcott: "Who can expel a man from the Garden of Eden that exists behind his own brow?"

MERCANTILE LIBRARY, SUMMER STREET, BOSTON

HENRY MORTON ROBINSON
Massachusetts, in
American Panorama, 1960

CORNER OF COURT AND TREMONT STREETS, WITH NEW IRON BUILDING

*Not restricted to buildings and relics of the past,
pictures of hotels and theatres provided readers
with a stimulating familiarity with the contemporary scene*

ENTRANCE TO THE NEW BOSTON THEATRE, WASHINGTON STREET

BLACKSTONE SQUARE, BOSTON

The city attracted architects (H.H. Richardson), gave birth to painters (Winslow Homer), created music ("the Boston classicists"), and nourished thinkers and writers—William Dean Howells, the Adams clan, John Boyle O'Reilly, who made *The Pilot* into an international paper, Robert Grant the conservative, B.O. Flower the radical, Borden Parker Bowne, Edgar Brightman, Dallas Lore Sharp, and others. Across the Charles was the brilliant Harvard faculty. The *Atlantic Monthly* continued to be prestigious. The tradition of Emerson and Thoreau still flourished—in the Free Religious Association with its two magazines, in Benjamin R. Tucker, philosophical anarchist and writer for the *Globe,* in B.O. Flower's *The Arena Magazine,* humorless but radical, in a performance of an upsetting foreign play, *A Doll's House,* in 1889, and an upsetting native play, *Margaret Fleming* (in Lynn, 1890) by James A. Herne. Young Hamlin Garland, penniless, came out of the West to read strong literature in the Boston Public Library, the director of which admitted that of course he had anarchist books on his shelves that any mature person could borrow. Flower brought out his *Progressive Men, Women and Movements* in 1914, the year the Twentieth Century Club, founded as that century dawned, published a survey of movements from 1884 to 1914. Nor should it be forgotten that Boston during these years nourished the Mugwumps and the Anti-Imperialist League.

*The Athens of America,
from The Many Voices of
Boston, 1975*

At the midway point in the 19th century, publishers were issuing street and mercantile directories, enlarged annually to keep pace with the city's growth

EAST AND WEST SIDES, FROM COURT STREET TO THE COMMON

When I got into the streets upon this Sunday morning, the air was so clear, the houses were so bright and gay, the signboards were painted in such gaudy colours, the gilded letters were so very golden, the bricks were so very red, the stone was so very white, the blinds and area railings were so very green, the knobs and plates upon the street doors were so marvellously bright and twinkling, and all so slight and unsubstantial in appearance, that every thoroughfare in the city looked exactly like a scene in a pantomime. It rarely happens in the business streets that a tradesman—if I may venture to call anybody a tradesman where everybody is a merchant—resides above his store; so that many occupations are often carried on in one house, and the whole front is covered with boards and inscriptions. As I walked along, I kept glancing up at these boards, confidently expecting to see a few of them change into something; and I never turned a corner suddenly without looking out for the Clown and Pantaloon, who, I had no doubt, were hiding in a doorway or behind some pillar close at hand.

CHARLES DICKENS
American Notes, 1842

PANORAMIC VIEW OF TREMONT STREET, BOSTON

Some popular weekly journals went a step further, offering their readers graphic illustrations of important downtown buildings clearly identified

TREMONT TEMPLE.   MONTGOMERY PLACE.   GLEASON'S PUBLISHING HALL.   BROMFIELD STREET.

DE

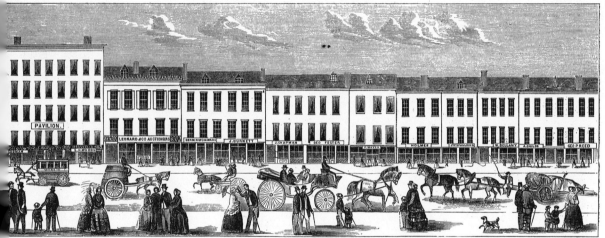

PAVILION HOTEL   REED'S MUSIC STORE.

TREMONT HOUSE.   BEACON STREET.   ALBION HOTEL.

E

Since America has become as famous for plumbing as for liberty, it is astonishing to find how little progress had been made in sanitary engineering before the Civil War. The lack of city water systems and a crude system of sewers were responsible. Philadelphia, generally reckoned the cleanest North American city, set up the Fairmount waterworks, pumping water from the Schuylkill river with wooden pipes bored out of solid logs, as early as 1801; it was gradually improved to a point when, in 1830, six million gallons could be delivered daily. Low-lying New Orleans followed, of necessity, in 1833. But New York City did not complete her Croton aqueduct until 1842, and prior to the present century the principal city reservoir was on the site of the Public Library at Fifth Avenue and 42nd Street. Boston tapped Lake Cochituate, whose water was introduced with a great display of fountains in the Frog Pond in 1848. Boston's four-story Tremont House, built in 1829 of native granite in the Greek revival style, with columns, capitals, and other details faithfully copied from James Stuart's *Antiquities of Attica,* had numerous public rooms and private parlors, 170 guest rooms, and eight "bathing rooms" in the basement, supplied with cold water only from rainwater cisterns. The Tremont House's rival for "America's best hotel" was the Astor House in City Hall Square in New York, built in 1836. This had 309 guest rooms and was the first building to have running water laid on above the ground floor.

SAMUEL ELIOT MORISON
The Oxford History of the American People, 1965

32

*Long periods of severe winter weather gave
New Englanders, youngsters and oldsters alike, a
chance to enjoy the thrills of sleighing and skating*

A hard, dull bitterness
    of cold,
That checked, mid-
    vein, the circling race
Of life-blood in the
    sharpened face,
The coming of the
    snow-storm told.
The wind blew east: we
    heard the roar
Of Ocean on his wintry
    shore,
And felt the strong
    pulse throbbing
    there
Beat with low rhythm our
    inland air...
In starry flake, and
    pellicle,
All day the hoary meteor
    fell;
And, when the second
    morning shone,
We looked upon a world
    unknown,
On nothing we could call
    our own.
Around the glistening
    wonder bent
The blue walls of the
    firmament,
No cloud above, no earth
    below,—
A universe of sky and
    snow!

JOHN GREENLEAF WHITTIER

Snow-Bound, 1866

A SLEIGHING SCENE NEAR BOSTON

SKATING ON JAMAICA POND, NEAR BOSTON

*The tinkle of sleigh-bells on city streets
sounded a joyous note as both private sleighs and
public conveyances took to their runners*

SLEIGHING SCENE ON BOSTON NECK

We are glad to present for our readers the spirited winter scene of one of the old landmarks of the city, a classic locality happily termed "Parnassus Corner" by noted essayist N. P. Willis. All our citizens will recognize it at once as the bookstore of Messrs. Ticknor & Fields, the well-known Athenian publishers. There are not many of these old buildings left, though fortunately Washington Street possesses some... How many changes we, who do not reckon many Olympiads, can recall in the city of our birth! How many fine old mansions razed! How many home sanctuaries profaned! It is very consoling, however, to reflect that this is all right, and that we are accomplishing our "manifest destiny"; and it is refreshing to know that if Washington Street, from Cornhill to School Street, has undergone many changes, it has not fallen into the hands of Goths and Vandals. On the contrary, it has become a Paternoster Row; it numbers its busy presses by the hundreds, and sends forth its books by the millions to gladden hands and hearts throughout our wide continent.

*Ballou's Pictorial
February 21, 1857*

ANCIENT BUILDING, CORNER OF SCHOOL AND WASHINGTON STREETS, BOSTON

Boston's sobriquet "The Hub" was well earned: stage, omnibus and private coach brought the traveler to the railroad depot for trains leaving in all directions

Though it was hoped that Boston and its suburbs would soon be connected by the horse railway, doubts were expressed that such transit could ever enjoy a solid success because, as *Ballou's Pictorial,* June 7, 1856, said: "The founders of this village, never dreaming of its possible magnitude, were excessively economical in laying out the town throughfares, now too contracted for the vehicular tide which flows through them already." New York's broad and spacious streets were referred to with open envy. Boston's Tremont Street track had been laid experimentally; if the system did not work to the public satisfaction, the tracks were to be removed. Yet the obvious advantages of the horse cars were glowingly set forth: "Street surfaces are full of irregularities...passage over them in an ordinary conveyance reminds one of a run across a 'chop' sea. All this jolting is avoided on the rail. The cars glide as smoothly as a rowboat over a quiet stream." By 1857, Boston was making horse car fashion news with an open car on the Metropolitan Horse Railroad. The month was April; the car, "very pretty, with elaborate paintings," and the passengers' attire were well described:

THE NEW LOWELL RAILROAD DEPOT, CAUSEWAY STREET, BOSTON

TRAINS TAKING ENGINE FOR TRIP TO NEW YORK FROM BOSTON

The streets of Boston were among the first to bear steel tracks, in 1855, for newly organized urban transit by horse-drawn cars

THE BOSTON AND CAMBRIDGE NEW HORSE RAILROAD

"The new open car offers a very novel appearance as it moves through our streets filled with ladies and gentlemen, presenting a variety of costumes, black coats alternating with gaily colored silks and satins, collapsed frocks contrasting with expanded crinolines." Though the cars had been running for two years, each new one attracted crowds of on-lookers along its routes.

The Metropolitan Horse Railroad—with 500 horses, about 50 open and top-seated cars, 50 omnibuses, and 80 closed and open sleighs—announced its intention to provide enough cars, each of which seated 24, for every passenger to have a seat. Added allurements were offices in the Metropolitan Hotel, "fitted up very liberally with a complete suite of apartments for the ladies, provided with all modern conveniences." So short a time before, people who lacked private carriages had been forced to walk, even to the suburbs. Then came the Omnibus "Hourly" on wheels or sleigh-runners according to season.

CLARENCE P. HORNUNG
Wheels Across
America, 1959

THE METROPOLITAN HORSE RAILROAD, TREMONT STREET, BOSTON

Not long after the Pilgrims landed at Plymouth, Harvard started "in a small house in a cow-yard," the gift of a wealthy benefactor who endowed his estate for higher learning

But of course the heart of the University is the old College, and that lies to the north of the river, fenced in by the swirl and jangle of traffic which unfortunately makes Harvard Square one of the busiest arteries in the Greater Boston area. Here, however, withdrawn from all the noise and sick hurry of the day, the stranger may enter the Harvard Yard. Other American colleges have campuses, but Harvard has always had and always will have her Yard of grass and trees and youth and old familiar ghosts. There in the northwest corner, the oldest group of Harvard buildings links the fabulous past with the incredible present. These buildings are arranged, as the architectural fashion was, with "free form in Euclidean space." Massachusetts Hall, built at the public charge in 1720, has seen the nation and Harvard through ten wars. Designed as a residential hall, it quartered six hundred and forty soldiers during the Revolution. It was earlier the site of the first laboratory of experimental physics in America, and has served in turn as a dormitory, a theater workshop, and lately as an administration center, including the offices of the president. The original Harvard Hall was burned in 1764, but a new one was built in 1766. A lecture hall today, it, too, has in other centuries given various services: the college kitchen was there; so was the buttery; so was the Chapel. Just beyond Harvard Hall is the little gem of Georgian architecture called Holden Chapel, built in 1744, gift of the widow of a rich London merchant.

DAVID MC CORD

About Boston, 1975

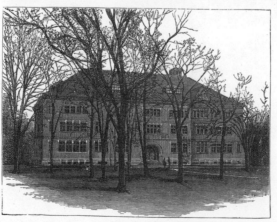

HARVARD UNIVERSITY BUILDINGS

AUSTIN HALL, THE COLLEGE YARD, SEVER HALL, MEMORIAL HALL

A Cluster of Towns
Surrounds the Hub

WALTHAM . . . BRIGHTON . . . COHASSET . . .

NAHANT . . . ROXBURY . . . MEDFORD . . .

LONGWOOD . . . BROOKLINE . . . LOWELL . . .

MANCHESTER . . . SPRINGFIELD . . . WORCESTER

. . . PROVINCETOWN . . . PLYMOUTH . . . LYNN

. . . NEW BEDFORD . . . GLOUCESTER . . .

ROCKPORT . . . MARBLEHEAD

MAIN STREET, WALTHAM

A Cluster of Towns
Surrounds the Hub

YOU NEED ONLY GLANCE AT A MAP of Massachusetts to appreciate the conglomeration of towns and villages that clusters around Boston. They sprang up on or near the dancing rivers, and a number are nearly as old as Boston itself. A few examples: Charlestown antedates Boston by a year; Arlington was founded in the same year as Boston (1630); Waltham followed in 1634; Brookline in 1638; Newton before 1640; Winchester in 1640; and Worcester in 1648.

Boston's city limits have expanded to include a number of cities and towns, some with traditions like those cherished by Boston. In a number of the surrounding towns, historic buildings are still well preserved. Charlestown, where the Battle of Bunker Hill was fought on June 17, 1775, is the site of a naval shipyard where the U.S.S. *Constitution* is moored.

Arlington is an important residential suburb with some interesting seventeenth-century buildings. The residential town and suburb of Brookline was a part of Boston known as "Muddy River," until it was separated in 1705. It was in Brookline that Amy Lowell made her home. Newton, west of Boston on the Charles River, is notable for its large number of handsome homes and several villages focused on industry. Here Nathaniel Hawthorne and Mary Baker Eddy had homes.

Roxbury and West Roxbury (with the Roxbury Latin School), Dorchester, Brighton, and Hyde Park are other towns that neighbor Boston and reflect its traditions.

Certain towns witnessed the early development of specific industries: Lowell for textiles, for example, and Roxbury for boots and shoes. Lowell, at the confluence of the Merrimack and Concord rivers, was settled in 1653. When its great mills were built in 1822, Lowell became one of the country's greatest textile centers.

Farmers in surrounding towns, attracted by the convenient and ready market, raised sheep for wool and hides; farmers' daughters welcomed the opportunity for gainful employment. The long hours—from six in the morning to six or seven in the evening—met with little objection: work on a farm was more strenuous and required even longer hours. To these girls, who had driven cattle to pasture, milked cows, worked in the fields, and scrubbed floors at home, mill work afforded an attractive alternative and tangible rewards.

Francis Cabot Lowell had made studies of conditions in English mills, and the mills at Lowell were regarded as models for their time.

Charles Dickens, who had visited the English mills and declared that the workers were living in deepest gloom, also visited Lowell on his American tour in 1842, and recorded his impressions in *American Notes.*

As the vast influx of foreign workers came to New England, conditions changed, and the labor force became predominantly Irish, followed by Greek, Polish, and Spanish.

It was in New England that organized industry began. Many of the settlers possessed crafts and skills gained from their English, Scottish, and Welsh backgrounds, which enabled them to start similar industries in Massachusetts. In *The Oxford History of the American People,* Samuel Eliot Morison writes:

> "Fullers from Rowley in Yorkshire set up a fulling mill in the Bay Colony, where home woven cloth could be shrunk and sheared. John Winthrop, Jr., later Governor of Connecticut, set up an ambitious and, for a time, a successful ironworks at Saugus, near Lynn. Here iron ore dug out of swamps and ponds, smelted with oak charcoal and flux from nearby rocks, was fashioned into pots and pans, anchors, chains, and other hardware for local needs."

Later, the men who ran the ironworks established others, and it is to these beginnings that the United States owes its stupendous iron and steel industry.

One evidence that the small towns shared the rich mental and spiritual resources that blessed Boston was to be found in the Reverend John Eliot. He lived in Roxbury and devised the first equivalent in Roman letters of the hitherto unwritten Algonquin language, making it possible for the entire Bible to be printed in Algonquin. This was the first Bible to be printed in the New World and its first translation into a "barbarous" language. (Another "first": the printing was done on the first press to be set up in the English colonies, in Harvard College Yard.)

Many of Boston's outlying towns—Chelsea, Revere, Somerville, Everett, Medford, Malden—are little different from Boston itself. A large percentage of their residents commute to jobs in Boston; others work in local factories. All these towns have a large admixture of first-generation Americans. Situated north and northwest of the hub, they have the closest ties to the city and are the most industrialized.

Less dominated by Boston, but well within its geographical area, are a number of old towns along the north shore and extending west to the valley of the Merrimack. These pursue their own existence, while enjoying the advantages of a proximity to Boston's culture and economy.

A distinctive aura seems to hover over Salem and Beverly, through tales of witch trials and histories of clipper captains and the fortunes made from voyages in the China trade.

Gloucester, though not in the Boston perimeter, remains a fishing port of great importance and is rimmed with fashionable summer resorts and private cottages.

Between the towns closest to Boston and those most distant, there are many small residential towns. A number of elegant suburbs encircle Beverly—towns like Wenham, Topsfield, Hamilton, and Manchester—where there are great estates, the homes of some of the wealthiest of Massachusetts families.

Only five miles from the heart of Boston, in the little town of Brighton, droves of cattle and sheep clogged the roads . . .

Brighton—originally a part of Cambridge—is five miles from Boston, and is one of the pleasantest towns in Massachusetts. Its natural boundary, the Charles River, provides a graceful and picturesque setting, affording lovely vistas from every angle. The chief interest in the town, at present, is in its celebrated Cattle Market, which originated during the Revolution, through the enterprise of Jonathan Winship, who bought cattle for the army; and thus from a limited trade, the market has become a very important feature of the business of the place. Sales for several years run to between two and three million dollars per annum, and the number of cattle to several hundred thousand. The importance of the market draws strangers from various parts of the country, and they are provided with comforts at the finest suburban hotel in the vicinity of Boston. This hotel is kept by Mr. Wilson, and stands in the first rank of "out-of-town" hotels. It is a pleasant summer resort, and thousands prove, by their frequent visits, its very great superiority to other hotels in the vicinity. Thursday is market day, and, for several days previous, the roads are thronged with droves of cattle and sheep. At one time, Brighton was the residence of Peter Faneuil, the donor of Faneuil Hall to the city of Boston.

Gleason's Pictorial Drawing-Room Companion, June 26, 1852

GOING TO BRIGHTON

WILSON'S HOTEL AT BRIGHTON

. . . on their way to market and abattoir, a reminder of the brisk livestock trade dating back to Revolutionary times

DRIVING TO MARKET

Boston became the great colonial market for live animals and meat. In 1663 the spot where the old state house stands was officially designated as a market place, and in 1742 Faneuil Hall became the gathering place for buyers and sellers. During or soon after the French and Italian War of 1756, Brighton sprang into prominence as a center for the cattle and meat trade, beginning with the activities of one butcher contractor, Jonathan Winship by name, who supplied the British army with meat. During the Revolution, Brighton continued its interest in the business and soon after the was over was the recognized market town in New England for cattle, hogs and sheep on the hoof, as well as for slaughtering and slaughter-house products. The Brighton Market was a magnified town fair held weekly. The peaceful village was for a day densely thronged with herds, drovers, and buyers. The trading done, Brighton reverted to its normal sleepy quiet. Brighton Market served as a model for many others, first in the east and afterward in the west; and Brighton itself continued to do a flourishing business until the growth of western packing houses killed most of its picturesque activities. To the present day, however, meat packing is one of its means of livelihood.

Pageant of America, 1926

CATTLE MARKET AT BRIGHTON

*Seaside watering places attracted urban dwellers
by offering ''every modern comfort'': bathing cabanas,
and endless verandas for sea-gazing*

It would be a curious and entertaining study to trace the evolution of our great hotels, from the cheerful roadside taverns and country inns, beloved of all travellers, to more pretentious road houses, to coffee houses, then to great crowded hotels. We could see the growth of these vast hotels, especially those of summer resorts, and also to their decay. In many fashionable watering-places great hotels have been torn down within a few years to furnish space for lawns and grounds around a splendid private residence. But the average American of means in the Northern states would spend a few weeks or even months at the big hotels at Saratoga, Niagara Falls, or the White Mountains. Along the Eastern coast, the chief resorts are to be found at Atlantic City, Old Point Comfort, and in New England, along Cape Cod and the environs of Boston.

ALICE MORSE EARLE

Stage Coach & Tavern

Days, 1900

ROCKLAND HOUSE, COHASSET

NAHANT HOTEL

*In nearby Roxbury and Medford, in addition to taverns
"affording entertainment and food for man and beast,"
modern hostelries were built that accommodated hundreds*

NORFOLK HOUSE, ROXBURY

As travel quickened—in 1826 Josiah Quincy, this time in a public stage, traveled from Boston to Washington in eight days—more specialized institutions took over the various functions of the tavern at key points on the road. Some served as tippling houses, some as boarding-houses, and others as hotels. In the larger cities where the concentration of travelers was greatest the city hotel burgeoned into a peculiarly American establishment where every need and convenience of the guest was anticipated, including many he was slow to recognize. Englishmen were astonished to learn that in some of these public places they could have their shirts washed and ironed while they bathed. The tinkling of ice was heard everywhere in every season of the year.

MARSHALL B. DAVIDSON
Life in America, 1951

FOUNTAIN HOUSE, MEDFORD

"Gentlemen's residences" and "elegant and tasteful private dwellings" appeared in the better and more quiet districts of the smaller towns . . .

We now present our readers with some accurately drawn views of gentlemen's residences in the adjoining city of Roxbury and the town of Brookline. They will revive pleasant memories among those familiar with the spots; they will also show the variety of tastes and styles exhibited in domestic architecture, and afford hints to those about to erect dwellings for themselves. In the variety of the examples shown are included cottages in the Elizabethan style of English architecture, those of Italian villa influence, the neo-Gothic style, the French chateau style and many others. It is evident that Americans have a wide choice of eclectic styles from which to choose when planning their residences.

Ballou's Pictorial

Drawing-Room Companion,

June 16, 1855

RESIDENCE AT ROXBURY

ITALIAN COTTAGE, ROXBURY

GENERAL WARREN HOUSE, ROXBURY

GOTHIC COTTAGE, HIGHLANDS

GOTHIC COTTAGE, ROXBURY

. . . displaying a composite of prevailing architectural styles, mostly of eclectic influence, then in vogue

CARNES' VILLA, HIGHLANDS

RESIDENCE AT LONGWOOD, BROOKLINE

In designing residential cottages, we have aimed rather at producing beauty by means of form and proportion, than by ornament; hence, it is not unlikely that those who have only a smattering of taste, and think a cottage cannot possess any beauty unless it is bedizened with ornaments, will be disappointed with the simplicity of most of these plans. But we trust, on the other hand, that persons of more information and more correct taste, and especially those who have followed us in our development of the true sources of interest in rural architecture, will agree with us that tasteful simplicity, not fanciful complexity, is the true character for cottages.

A.J. DOWNING
The Architecture of Country Houses, 1850

HOUSE AT LONGWOOD

GOTHIC COTTAGE, LONGWOOD

COTTAGE AT LONGWOOD

By dam and millrace, the swift-flowing rivers gave motive power to New England's rapidly growing textile industry . . .

We were thus entering the State of New Hampshire on the bosom of the flood formed by the tribute of its innumerable valleys. The river was the only key which could unlock its maze, presenting its hills and valleys, its lakes and streams, in their natural order and position. The Merrimack, or Sturgeon River, is formed by the confluence of the Pemigewasset, which rises near the Notch of the White Mountains, and the Winnepisiogee, which drains the lake of the same name, signifying "The Smile of the Great Spirit." From their junction it runs south seventy-eight miles to Massachusetts, and thence east thirty-five miles to the sea. I have traced its stream from where it bubbles out of the rocks of the White Mountains above the clouds, to where it is lost amid the salt billows of the ocean on Plum Island beach. At first it comes on murmuring to itself by the base of stately and retired mountains, through moist primitive woods whose juices it receives, where the bear still drinks it, and the cabins of settlers are far between, and there are few to cross its stream; enjoying in solitude its cascades still unknown to fame; by long ranges of mountains of Sandwich and Squam, slumbering like tumuli of Titans, with the peaks of Mossehillock, the Haystack, and Kearsarge reflected in its waters; where the maple and the raspberry, those lovers of the hills, flourish amid temperate dews.

HENRY DAVID THOREAU

A Week on the Concord and Merrimack Rivers, 1852

JUNCTION OF THE CONCORD AND MERRIMACK RIVERS, LOWELL

MERRIMACK STREET, LOWELL

*. . . where the hum of shuttle, loom, and bobbin
meant work for willing hands and the creation
of a new labor force—the "Lowell girls"*

MANCHESTER PRINT WORKS, MANCHESTER, N.H.

BOOT COTTON MILLS, LOWELL

Each new mill erected by the Associates copied Francis Lowell's boarding house plan. While the number of girls in all boarding house mills were never a majority of the employees in cotton textiles, the Lowell girls became far more famous than any other group. Foreign visitors regarded Lowell as one of the sights that must not be missed, and famous Americans lectured there to audiences composed mainly of mill girls. For daughters of back country New England farmers, the mills of Lowell were a finishing school or college where they could learn the ways of the world and make money in the process. The companies made the change from farm to factory easy by sending agents in long black covered wagons to explain the rules to hesitant parents, and to bring the girls and their baggage direct to the boarding houses. No doubt the agents talked more of lectures and libraries, clothes and smart shops than of the twelve to thirteen-hour work day. Or they held out the goal of four dollars a week, two dollars and seventy-five cents more than the cost of board, without mentioning that few girls ever worked fast enough to achieve such pay. But to girls used to hard work on poor farms, to big families in little houses, the realities were not too bad. Six girls sleeping in a small room might seem crowded to an upper class visitor, but to the girls it was just like home.

T.C. COCHRAN

*The Factory Comes to
New England*

On the important east-west turnpike from Boston to Albany, in the state's midlands, Springfield developed into a diversified industrial center . . .

Establishment of the United States Armory at Springfield in 1777 set in motion a beginning of industry. Pittsfield had a woolen mill by 1801. The establishment of Williams College in 1793 and Amherst College in 1821 began to provide trained leadership for a new generation. Stimulated in the beginning by the British blockade, by 1825 more than twenty turnpike corporations and an equal number of bridge-building companies were hard at work surveying and building east-west highways to carry regular stagecoach service from Boston to Albany. In 1839 a new steam railroad began to provide service between Worcester and Springfield, and by 1855 western Massachusetts was covered by a network of fifteen railroads, letting inhabitants out from behind their mountain barriers and letting summer visitors in. Still more important, freight traffic now made possible a full participation of these western counties in the burgeoning industrial revolution, that rapidly made of the Springfield-Westfield-Holyoke-Chicopee area an industrial complex rivaling those of Fall River-New Bedford, Lawrence-Haverhill, and the Greater Boston region. Springfield's population grew to 10,000 by 1840, and its textile, paper and machinery factories soon mushroomed into the expanding cities of Westfield, Chicopee and Holyoke, to produce an industrial region today populated by almost 300,000 people.

HENRY F. HOWE

Massachusetts, There She Is—Behold Her 1960

COURT HOUSE, SPRINGFIELD

SPRINGFIELD, FROM THE LONGMEADOW ROAD

. . . as the first steam railroad, in 1839, extended service to new areas around Worcester and previously isolated villages

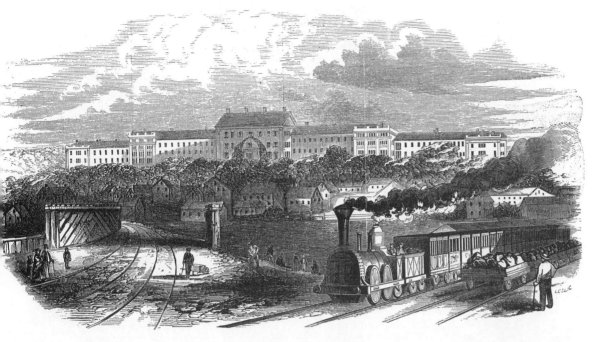

STATE INSTITUTION, WORCESTER

LINCOLN SQUARE, WORCESTER

You have seen, I think, W---, the distant village in New England, where I spent nearly the last half of the last century. Perhaps, however, you have merely looked at it as a passing traveller, and did not remark its simple beauty. To memory, every tree, every green pasture and humble dwelling, are as familiar as the room I sit in. It was distant about two miles from the ocean, and scattered on both sides of a small but tranquil and beautiful river, which was crossed by a wooden bridge in the centre of the village. On the north side rose gentle hills gracefully from the river, and on the south spread out level meadows, dotted with buttonwood trees and weeping elms. The meeting-house and parsonage were on the north side, overlooking on the south the village, whose houses were scattered about the bridge, and ascended, at least the better sort, towards the church. Beyond the hills on the north, stretched out, as if to shelter us, the protecting forest. The meeting-house was the square, barn-like structure, common at that period to all New England. Ours, however, was adorned with a steeple and belfry, and graced with a most sweet sounding bell.

ELIZA BUCKMINSTER LEE

Sketches of a New England Village, c. 1850

Due south of Boston lies New Bedford, on a well-protected harbor that accounted for more whale fishing than any other American port on the Atlantic coast . . .

In the latter half of the century more than a third of the nation's woolens were produced in Massachusetts. Fall River, Lawrence, Lowell, and New Bedford led all other cities in cotton manufacture. By 1890 Lawrence was third and Lowell fourth among American cities in the manufacture of woolens. By 1900 Massachusetts produced almost half the shoes in the United States, a quarter of these coming from Lynn, and large fractions from Brockton, Haverhill, Marlborough and Worcester. Shoe machinery from Beverly, Boston and Waltham and paper-mill machinery from Lowell, Pittsfield, Lawrence and Worcester were world-famous. All this prodigious and bustling prosperity rested, once the machines had been built and paid for, on the shifting base of a labor surplus provided by unceasing immigration through Boston's port, which remained a good immigrant port because it also furnished the shortest commercially practical route for sending the British mails to Canada.

HENRY F. HOWE

*Massachusetts,
There She Is—Behold Her
1960*

COURT HOUSE, NEW BEDFORD

CITY HALL, NEW BEDFORD

*. . . while to the north lies Lynn, a coastal city
whose origins may be traced to its early tanneries
and their subsequent growth into a great shoe industry*

THE EXCHANGE, LYNN

THE COMMON, LYNN

ATLANTIC BEACH, LYNN

The town of Lynn, first settled in 1629 and incorporated the following year, was originally called by its Indian name, Saugus. By 1850 it became a city with a population of over 13,000. Lynn's first inhabitants were farmers, but gradually they turned their attention to the manufacture of ladies' shoes, which flourished to become the city's principal business. The stock for the shoes is cut in larger buildings; the uppers are tied in bundles and given to females to be bound at home. They are then returned to the manufactories where they are sewn to the soles by men. The shoe workmen are called cordwainers, more properly cordovaniers; the word being derived from Cordovan leather, originally made in Cordoba, Spain from goat skins brought over from Morocco, in Africa. When the shoes are finished, they are packed in large wooden crates, sixty to a box. It is estimated that there are about 150 factories, employing 10,000, more than half of whom are females. In addition to Lynn's major shoe industry, there are vessels engaged in whaling, cod and mackerel fishing and coastwise shipping.

Ballou's Pictorial

Drawing-Room Companion,

January 10, 1857

On Cape Ann, in Gloucester and Rockport, fishing was the grim business of men who ventured to "go down to the sea in ships" . . .

Then up and spoke the orator of the occasion, another pillar of the municipality, bidding the world welcome to Gloucester, and incidentally pointing out wherein Gloucester excelled the rest of the world. Then he turned to the sea-wealth of the city, and spoke of the price that must be paid for the yearly harvest. They would hear later the names of their lost dead—one hundred and seventeen of them. (The widows stared a little, and looked at one another here.) Gloucester could not boast any overwhelming mills or factories. Her sons worked for such wage as the sea gave; and they all knew that neither Georges nor the Banks were cow-pastures. The utmost that folk ashore could accomplish was to help the widows and the orphans; and after a few general remarks he took this opportunity of thanking, in the name of the city, those who had so public-spiritedly consented to participate in the exercises of the occasion.

RUDYARD KIPLING

For Those in Peril on the Sea

GLOUCESTER AND ROCKPORT

. . . reminding us, as have many poets, that tragedy always lurks in New England's "stern and rock-bound coast"

In the hush of the autumn night
I hear the voice of the sea,
In the hush of the autumn night
It seems to say to me—
Mine are the winds above,
Mine are the caves below,
Mine are the dead of yesterday
And the dead of long ago!

And I think of the fleet that sailed
From the lovely Gloucester shore,
I think of the fleet that sailed
And came back nevermore;
My eyes are filled with tears,
And my heart is numb with woe—
It seems as if 'twere yesterday,
And it all was long ago!

THOMAS BAILEY ALDRICH
The Voice of the Sea, 1907

SWALLOWS' CAVE, NAHANT

NORMAN'S WOE, GLOUCESTER

Colder and louder blew the wind,
  A gale from the Northeast,
The snow fell hissing in the brine,
  And the billows frothed like yeast.

Down came the storm, and smote amain
  The vessel in its strength;
She shuddered and paused, like a frighted steed,
  Then leaped her cable's length....

Such was the wreck of the Hesperus,
  In the midnight and the snow!
Christ save us all from a death like this,
  On the reef of Norman's Woe!

HENRY WADSWORTH LONGFELLOW
The Wreck of the Hesperus, 1839

Marblehead's first settlers were hard-bitten fishermen from Britain's Cornwall who, in 1629, "came not for religion but to catch fish"

Just before reaching Salem one is called off by the lure of Marblehead. Wonderful old houses remain here, there being at least three or four of great distinction which are all available for examination. The bay of Marblehead is a gem of beauty and one who loves at once natural scenery and old America finds them both in this town at their best. One is here away from the bustle of the city, yet by no means distant from the attractive features of American outdoor life. Marblehead is a yachting center; its harbor gay with snowy winged craft; its streets uneven, winding, full of surprises, and its back country appealing from its variety of roadsides.

WALLACE NUTTING

Massachusetts Beautiful

1923

TOWN HALL, MARBLEHEAD

MARBLEHEAD AND HARBOR

A glimpse of the harbor appears between weather-beaten houses that shoulder one another, on narrow streets and winding lanes

Tribute needs to be paid to the fishing industry, which was the perpetual work horse that kept the other enterprises going. In good years such ports as Gloucester, Wellfleet, Hingham and Cohasset each packed more than 40,000 barrels of mackerel. Four or five voyages were commonly made each summer following the mackerel northward as their "schools" migrated. Often the first voyage in May found mackerel off Cape May, New Jersey, and a June voyage off Block Island. The midsummer voyages were short, in New England waters, but fall frequently found the schooners traveling as far as Bay of St. Lawrence. In port, the wharves were busy as the already split, gibbed and salted fish were packed in barrels by boys in their early teens at 25 cents per day. Local cooper shops made the barrels, and local saltworks evaporated much of the salt from sea water. Each schooner had a crew of about ten men and boys. Originally these were all New England born: by mid-century a considerable immigration of Portuguese seamen were prospering in the fishing trade, many of them becoming masters of schooners with the encouragement of Yankee owners.

HENRY F. HOWE
Massachusetts, There She Is—Behold Her, 1960

CURING FISH

WEIGHING FISH

MARBLEHEAD SCHOONER

GLOUCESTER HARBOR

At the northern tip of Cape Cod's hook stands Provincetown —across the bay from Plymouth, where the Mayflower's *Pilgrims landed, in 1620, to establish the Massachusetts Bay Colony*

Cape Cod wears its heart on its sleeve; and wears it like a Christian on the very end of its sleeve in lieu of a fist. For where the arm of earth gathers protectingly about Cape Cod Bay, and its fingers enfold a harbor of a thousand ships, there is concentrated in a league of shore, village and dune the quintessence of the Cape's beauty and romance and dear, naive humanity. Provincetown is the natural climax of the Cape. You work up to this climax from Plymouth, past the quaint town halls, meeting-houses, fan-light portals, water-mills and wind-mills of places with such well-flavored names as Sand-wich (where the Cape proper begins), Barnstable, Hyannis, Yarmouth, Har-wich, Chatham, Well-fleet and Truro. You cross wide-swelling uplands from which you may look down, as at a map modeled in relief, upon the curve of the Cape's gold and green and wine-red arm, and see how the stacklike towers of the wireless station are like a bit of Pittsburgh that has strayed by accident to spotless climes; and notice how the sand-spit out toward Provincetown gleams like a horizontal ex-clamation point of gold.

ROBERT HAVEN SCHAUFFLER
Romantic America, 1913

PLYMOUTH, FROM THE BURYING GROUND

PROVINCETOWN HARBOR

High Peaks & Highlights in Scenic New Hampshire

SHELBURNE FALLS . . . MOUNT WASHINGTON . . .

COG WHEEL RAILROAD . . . GORHAM . . .

DIXVILLE NOTCH . . . CONCORD . . .

HILLSBOROUGH . . . LAKE WINNIPESAUKEE

. . . PORTSMOUTH . . . MEREDITH BRIDGE

SHELBURNE FALLS

High Peaks &
Highlights in Scenic
New Hampshire

ITS LAND AREA IS MODEST, ITS AGRICUL--tural terrain limited; but its mountains are magnificent, its water courses tumultous and beautiful, and its lakes numerous and of an incredible loveliness. The White Mountains of New Hampshire are the highest in New England and —excepting only the Black Mountains of North Carolina—the highest east of the Mississippi. With the Province of Quebec as its northern boundary, the Connecticut River defining its western border, Massachusetts on the south, and Connecticut on the east—New Hampshire has just 18 miles of shoreline on the Atlantic Ocean. Its largest lake, the Winnipesaukee, has an almost incredible number of habitable islands—274—in its 44,000 acres of silvery waters. The White Mountains form a great plateau, with a score of peaks of various heights, traversed by deep, narrow valleys. In the branches of the Connecticut River valley are the Androscoggin, Saco, and Pemigewasset rivers. Countless little streams dance down steep glens from mountain springs, forming waterfalls and pathways.

"Starting from Centre Harbor, a summer resort of considerable celebrity...the regular stagecoach for Conway and the mountains is soon among high hills...winding in and out among them, the stage passes now under the dark, frowning brow of a cliff, and afterward by some deep ravine, and then comes upon a lofty plateau... till at Eaton the summit of Mount Washington is often distinctly seen....Driving on the mountain road...one watches the great hill-tops come up, like billows, one after another, from the sea of mountains round out, as the coach winds and twists among them....Not only the mountains, but the village itself, and the gentle meadows of the Saco, add to the soft charm of this very Arcadia of the White Hills." wrote Susan N. Carter, in *Picturesque America*.

Historic Portsmouth—New Hampshire's only seaport—with flagstone streets and gracious homes dating from the great whaling days, is located on an estuary of the Pistaguu, at Salmon Hills. The state's abundance of streams and lakes has been extensively harnessed, manufacturing being concentrated in the lower valleys of the Connecticut and the Merrimack Rivers. Manchester, Nashua, Concord, and Keene are the largest cities. While the ocean tempers the coastal climate, the inland areas are subject to great extremes—with as much as eight feet of snowfall in the mountains.

The rocky topography and stony soil prohibit commercial agriculture, but second-growth fir, spruce, and hardwoods cover much of the land, making lumber, pulp, and paper important industries, especially in the north. Poultry and poultry products, and livestock, apples, and nursery and dairy products are the chief sources of farm income.

Although New Hampshire is known as the Granite State, granite is no longer extensively quarried. Leather and leather products are important industries in the southern part of the state, in addition to the manufacture of textiles, electrical equipment, and machinery. New Hampshire is noted for its efforts to revive native crafts: pottery-making, weaving, wood carving; and it is the site of two Shaker communities, famous for their handcrafted furniture and home accessories.

From the early 19th century, the resort and vacation-related industry has been a primary source of income. The cog railway held great fascination for tourists in the early 1870s, ascending into the clouds, to the top of Mount Washington. The railway was scarcely less a feat of engineering than a test of patience, for the New Hampshire legislature was highly scornful of the plan, and the short summer season, while it was a-building reduced working days to a minimum.

With the largest legislature of any government in the world, numbering 443, every local community in New Hampshire has its own representatives. Martin Pring (1605) and Captain John Smith (1614) gave the first accounts of the region now known as New Hampshire. The Council of New England—successors to the Plymouth Colony—issued a Royal Grant. Settlements were made and abandoned, until a group of Anglican farmers and fishermen founded Portsmouth in 1630. Massachusetts annexed south New Hampshire in 1641, claiming misrepresentation. By 1679, New Hampshire was proclaimed a royal colony, with appointees of the Crown in authority. It was only in 1741 that one man, Benning Wentworth, became governor exclusively for New Hampshire. The French and Indian War had prevented colonization in the inland areas but, as Indian hostility lessened, a land rush started. Lumber camps were set up and sawmills were built along the streams. When the king's deputies blazed the tall white pines with arrows, to mark them for the Royal Navy, much resentment was aroused. As the American Revolution started, many in the populace were eager for independence. A committee of safety was organized, and it is claimed that the Sons of Liberty in Portsmouth raised the first liberty pole in the colonies. The people met on January 3, 1776, and formed a new government, with a legislature, council, and governor (called the president).

New Hampshire's beauty and serenity have long attracted artists and writers. Hawthorne, Whittier, and Longfellow spent summers here. Thomas Bailey Aldrich was a native of the state. In the work of Robert Frost, the poet's own words declare that there is not one of his poems "but has something in it of New Hampshire."

On one wintry occasion, as we are told in Drake's *Heart of the White Mountains*, the wind rose to such a fury that the inmates of the station, expecting every moment that the building would be blown over, wrapped themselves in blankets and quilts, binding them tightly with ropes, to which were attached bars of iron, so that, as one of the men said in relating the story, "if the house went by the board, we might stand a chance—a slim one—of anchoring somewhere, somehow."...

...But had the house gone, they would probably have been lifted from their feet like bags of wool, "dashed against the rocks, and smashed like eggshells," as one of the men coolly remarked to his visitor.

*Harper's Weekly
January 14, 1882*

CARRIAGE ROAD, MOUNT WASHINGTON

PANORAMA OF THE WHITE MOUNTAINS

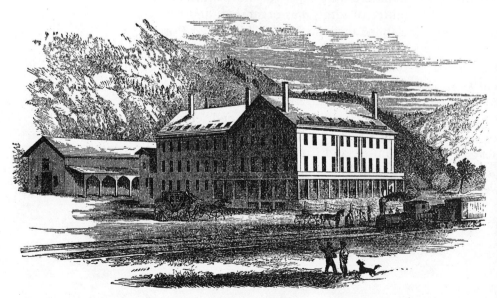

ALPINE HOUSE, GORHAM

METEOROLOGICAL STATION, MT. WASHINGTO

Long before the Civil War, thousands of vacationers braved the rigors of mountain climbing to enjoy the scenic beauties celebrated by poets and painters . . .

FOOT OF THE MOUNTAIN

MOUNT WASHINGTON RAILROAD

JACOB'S LADDER

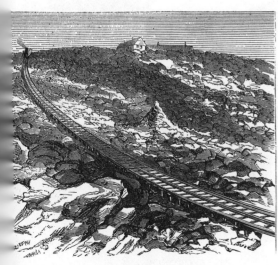

TIP-TOP HOUSE

AMONG THE CLOUDS

The road is really as steep in some places as a flight of stairs...But we think of the atmospheric brakes, of the friction brakes, of the ratchet wheel, and the cogs...The stoutest of the party looks a little pale; but we feel the firm grip of cog upon cog; we remember that the wheel is so clamped upon the pin-rigged middle rail that neither the engine nor the car can be lifted or thrown off; that the pawl that dropped into the ratchet-wheel would hold us in the steepest place; that the shutting of a valve... in the atmospheric brakes effectually stops the wheels from turning...We seem to go up from the middle of a great valley; there are no level places. The mountains about us shrink into small hills. Now, no trees. Now, only rocks. Now, we are at the top, cloud-wrapped.

Harper's Weekly
August 21, 1869

Not any drift boulders in Green and White Mountains, because the old ice-sheet plucked them from these mountains and dropped them over the landscape to the south; here they lie like a herd of slumbering elephants with their calves, sleeping the sleep of geologic ages. The view of the White Mountains very impressive. We came through the Crawford Notch, down and down and down, over a superb road, through woods, with these great rocky peaks shouldering the sky on each side. Simply stupendous!

JOHN BURROUGHS

The state's capital at Concord, on both sides of the Merrimack, where as early as 1818 its famed Concord coaches were shipped throughout the world

If I must choose which I
would elevate—
The people or the already
lofty mountains,
I'd elevate the already
lofty mountains.
The only fault I find with
old New Hampshire
Is that her mountains
aren't quite high
enough.
I was not always so;
I've come to be so.
How, to my sorrow, how
have I attained
A height from which to
look down critical
On mountains? What has
given me assurance
To say what height
becomes New Hamp-
shire mountains,
Or any mountains? Can it
be some strength
I feel as of an earthquake
in my back
To heave them higher to
the morning star?

ROBERT FROST

TOWN OF CONCORD

BIRTHPLACE OF PRESIDENT PIERCE, HILLSBOROUGH

Lake Winnipesaukee, so named by the Indians, means "Smile of the Great Spirit." One of the largest lakes, boasts 183 miles of shoreline and 274 islands

One of the most travelled routes to the White Mountains is by railroad to Concord, and thence to Lake Winnipesaukee (pronounced by the Indians Win-ne-pe-sock-e, with the accent on the penultima), an excellent point of departure for the mountain region. It signifies the poetical feeling of the aborigines, and their appreciation of the beauties of nature. No one who has lingered by the magnificent shores of this sheet of water, who has gazed upon its broad expanse dotted with numerous islands, and gleaming in the rays of the rising and setting sun, will deny the appropriateness of the Indian name...

...The lake stretches into seven large bays, three on the west, three on the east, and one on the north. Its waters are of crystalline purity, and its depth in some places is said to be unfathomable. The islets that gem its bosom are said to number three hundred and sixty-five, the largest of them containing five hundred acres of fertile soil, yielding heavy crops of corn and grain.

Ballou's Pictorial Drawing-Room Companion
June 12, 1855

RED HILL FROM LAKE WINNIPESAUKEE

LAKE WINNIPESAUKEE

CENTER HARBOR, LAKE WINNIPESAUKEE

First settled in 1623, early Portsmouth grew rapidly from interests in fishing, shipbuilding, and privateering, but settled down to enjoy the glory of its naval shipyard

The town of Portsmouth, N.H., the state's only seaport on a short strip of Atlantic coast, is located on the south side of the Piscataqua River, three miles inland from the sea. Its defense built to protect both the town and its historic naval base are Fort Constitution and Fort McClary, the latter in Kittery, opposite. It was here on Navy Island that the *North America,* the first line-of-battle ship was launched, during the Revolution. Portsmouth has long been proud of the skill of its naval architects and builders. Machine shops, iron foundries and saw mills are manned by highly skilled craftsmen for which the town is celebrated. In 1850 the population of Portsmouth was nearly ten thousand.

UNITED STATES NAVY YARD, PORTSMOUTH

Gleason's Pictorial   July 23, 1853

MARKET SQUARE, PORTSMOUTH

Meredith is situated in the center of the state between lakes Winnipesaukee and Waukewan, a region noted for exquisite lake and mountain scenery

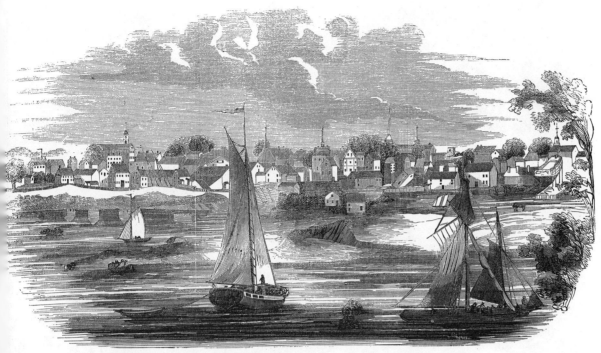

PORTSMOUTH, FROM THE NORTH

Gleason's Pictorial   October 30, 1852

Meredith Bridge is located in the neighborhood of exquisite lakes, studded throughout with small green islands, burdened with rich foliage and surrounded with lofty mountains on every side. The fertility of its soil and the general wholesomeness of the area form the nucleus of attraction which gives the town preference for its annual agricultural fair under state auspices. The many huge tents erected within the grounds provide ample space for the exhibition of farm implements, machinery and fancy articles of every description. The judging of horses, cattle and hogs culminates in keen competition from entries from all corners of the Granite State.

NEW HAMPSHIRE STATE FAIR, MEREDITH BRIDGE

*The Granite State—noted for the grandeur of its mountains
—has but a tiny outlet to the sea, where the New England
coastline continues with its jagged, rocky formations*

Unafraid, too, we watched the summer tempests, and listened to the deep, melodious thunder rolling away over the rain-calmed ocean. It was fine indeed from the lighthouse itself to watch the storm come rushing over the sea and ingulf us in our helplessness. How the rain weltered down over the great panes of plate glass,—floods of sweet, fresh water that poured off the rocks and mingled with the bitter brine. I wondered why the fresh floods never made the salt sea any sweeter. Those pale flames that we beheld burning from the spikes of the lightning-rod, I suppose were identical with the St. Elmo's fire that I have seen seen described as haunting the spars of ships in thunder-storms. And here I am reminded of a story told by some gentlemen visiting Appledore sixteen or eighteen years ago. They started from Portsmouth for the Shoals in a whaleboat, one evening in summer, with a native Star-Islander, Richard Randall by name, to manage the boat. They had sailed about half the distance, when they were surprised at seeing a large ball of fire, like a rising moon, rolling toward them over the sea from the south.

CELIA THAXTER

*Among the Isles of Shoals,
1873*

ALONG NEW HAMPSHIRE'S ATLANTIC SHORES

Amid Vermont's Green Hills

LAKE MEMPHREMAGOG . . . MOUNT

MANSFIELD . . . CORDUROY ROAD . . .

GREEN MOUNTAINS . . . SMUGGLER'S

NOTCH . . . MONTPELIER . . . SUGAR

MAPLE HARVEST . . . ON THE

MISSISQUOI RIVER . . . MARBLE QUARRIES,

WEST RUTLAND . . . PROCTOR

OWL'S HEAD LANDING, LAKE MEMPHREMAGOG

Amid Vermont's Green Hills

VERMONT'S GENTLE, GREEN-covered hills conceal a granite foundation, resembling the stern, rocklike character of its natives. *Vert:* green; *mont:* mountain; so the state reveals the source of its name. Samuel de Champlain is the first white man known to have reached the area. He had laid the founda-

tions for Quebec and then, in 1609, journeyed south with a Huron war party to the beautiful lake that now bears his name. Not until 1724 was the first permanent settlement built near what is now Brattleboro. In 1741, the commission of the Royal Governor of New Hampshire, Benning Wentworth, declared New Hampshire's boundary to extend across the

Merrimack, "until it met with our [i.e., the king's] other governments"—the eastern limits of the colony of New York. Violent disputes erupted, but New York's claim, to what is now Vermont, was upheld by the British.

The Revolution brought border battles to a temporary halt. In 1777, Vermont declared itself an independent state, but due to New York's opposition the Continental Congress refused to give Vermont recognition as a colony or state. Vermonters reaffirmed their independence and adopted a constitution. For ten years after the American victory at Yorktown, Vermont remained an independent state, performed all the services of a sovereign government, coined money, established post offices, naturalized citizens, and appointed ambassadors to foreign countries. In 1791, Vermont entered the Union.

Limited arable land and abundant rainfall make grazing a major industry, and the famous breed of Morgan horse was developed here. Hay is the state's chief crop. Dairy farming dominates agriculture, and milk is shipped in great quantities to the metropolitan markets of Boston and New York.

John Gunther, in *Inside America,* tells us: "Vermont has smooth and gentle dulcet hills—yes, but underneath is slate, marble, granite. This granite is solid in the state character. . . .The triumph of Vermont is a certain richness of character—richness that is nevertheless stern. The typical Vermonter is rugged, reticent, suspicious of outsiders, frugal, individualistic, and with great will to survive. . . .

"The basis of life in Vermont remains agriculture; this in turn is based on fluid milk. Most Vermont dairy farms are small, worked by their own owners, and held in the same family for generations. The farmers are well organized; most belong to the Grange.
. . .Though the typical Vermont farmer may be poor, he will go through almost any hardship to educate his children."

Vermont, said to have more cattle than people, is also known for maple syrup, apples, and potatoes. In Rutland and Proctor, industry is concentrated on the quarrying and finishing of marble; in Barre, Vermont's famous granite is quarried and processed. From the self-sufficient farms of pioneer days, Vermont agriculture developed commercially to beef cattle and grain. When the growth of the West supplied these at lower prices, and wool textile mills sprang up in New England, Vermont farmers turned to sheep-raising. After the Civil War, with competition from west Australia and South America, farmers turned to an easier life in the cities or migrated west. Abandoned farms became a common sight but, through a transition to dairy farming, Vermont's agriculture was saved from a permanent decline.

The most truly rural of the New England states, Vermont lies between the granite masses of the White Mountains on one side, and the Adirondacks on the other. Its soil is mellower than its neighbors; its water courses gentler. Forested Green Mountains traverse the state from north to south in four groups: the Green Mountains (proper), from Canada to the Massachusetts line, rising to Mount Mansfield which is Vermont's highest peak; the Taconic Mountains, an important source of marble; the Granite Hills, named for their valuable stone; and the Sandrock Hills. There are also scattered hills, called monadnocks.

Crawford's Notch in the White Mountains and Smugglers' Notch in the Green Mountains would be called canyons in the far West. Although the Eastern notches are not so ruggedly grand, they are more beautiful. Mosses and ferns cover them, and, in some places, ancient roots twine around the rocks like boa-constrictors. Huge gnarled roots encircle the rocks like giant anacondas. Abundant moisture has led to the luxuriant growth of lichens and ferns and has painted the rocks with delicate tints.

The unspoiled beauty of quiet towns and wooded mountains draws many thousands of vacationers each year; and climbers and hikers are attracted to the Long Trail,—which runs along the Green Mountains the entire length of the state—to make tourism a leading industry and major source of state income.

The serene Vermont countryside—intricately interlaced with soft mountain slopes, tilled fields, and gentle brooks—suddenly erupts in its Green Mountains . . .

ROCK OF TERROR

Mount Mansfield, the highest of the Green Mountain range, is situated near the northern extremity, about twenty miles, in a direct line east, or a little north of east, from Burlington, on Lake Champlain. This mountain has been less popular among tourists and pleasure seekers than the White Mountains and the Catskills principally because its attractions have been little known. Of recent years, it has been more visited than formerly; and a good hotel at Stowe, five miles from its base, has now every summer its throng of tourists. There is also a Summit House, situated at the base of the highest peak known as the Nose, where travellers may find plain but suitable accommodation if they wish to prolong their stay on the mountain top overnight. Mansfield is conveniently reached by rail from Burlington; and thence by Concord coaches ten miles to Stowe. From Stowe a carriage road reaches to the summit of the mountain. . . This mountain is, moreover, not without the usual number of faces and resemblances to familiar objects, among the most notable of which is that described as the "Old Woman of the Mountain," represented herewith.

ROSSITER JOHNSON

Picturesque America, 1872

VIEW FROM MOUNTAIN ROAD

. . . where, in granite boulders, sharp cliffs, and forest-clad escarpments, Nature sculpts her time-worn shapes and forms

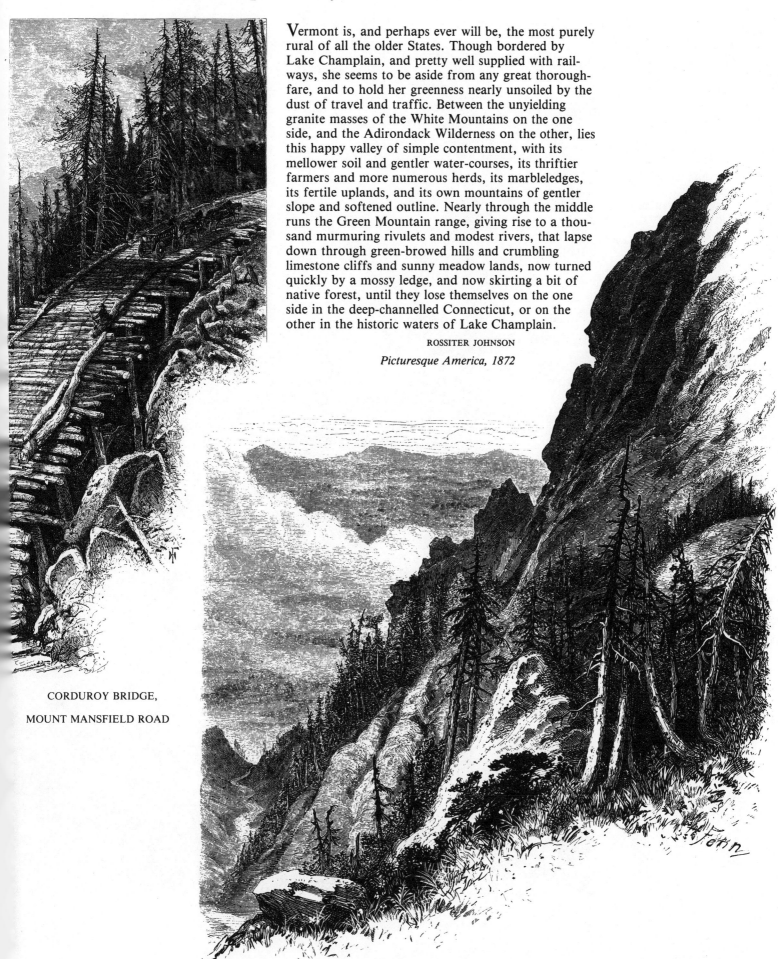

Vermont is, and perhaps ever will be, the most purely rural of all the older States. Though bordered by Lake Champlain, and pretty well supplied with railways, she seems to be aside from any great thoroughfare, and to hold her greenness nearly unsoiled by the dust of travel and traffic. Between the unyielding granite masses of the White Mountains on the one side, and the Adirondack Wilderness on the other, lies this happy valley of simple contentment, with its mellower soil and gentler water-courses, its thriftier farmers and more numerous herds, its marbleledges, its fertile uplands, and its own mountains of gentler slope and softened outline. Nearly through the middle runs the Green Mountain range, giving rise to a thousand murmuring rivulets and modest rivers, that lapse down through green-browed hills and crumbling limestone cliffs and sunny meadow lands, now turned quickly by a mossy ledge, and now skirting a bit of native forest, until they lose themselves on the one side in the deep-channelled Connecticut, or on the other in the historic waters of Lake Champlain.

ROSSITER JOHNSON

Picturesque America, 1872

CORDUROY BRIDGE,

MOUNT MANSFIELD ROAD

THE OLD WOMAN OF THE MOUNTAIN

At Smuggler's Notch, "giant trees find nourishment in crevices, and huge, gnarled roots encircle the rocks like immense anacondas"

Another view shows us the mountain cliffs looming through the mists of what is known as Smuggler's Notch. In the far West this notch would be called a canyon, but it differs mainly from the canyons of the Sierra in being more picturesque—not so ruggedly grand as those rocky walls, but the abundant moisture has filled it with superb forest growths, has covered all the rocks with ferns and lichens, has painted the stone with delicious tints. The sides of the Notch rise to an altitude of about a thousand feet, the upper verge of the cliffs rising above the fringe of mountain trees that cling to their sides. The floor of the Notch is covered with immense boulders and fallen masses of rocks, which in this half-lighted vault have partly crumbled, and given foothold for vegetation. Mosses and ferns cover them, and in many instances great trees have found nourishment in the crevices, sometimes huge gnarled roots encircling the rocks like immense anacondas. Smuggler's Notch has a hundred poetical charms that deserve for it a better name. It is so called because once used as a hiding place for goods smuggled over the Canada border.

ROSSITER JOHNSON

Picturesque America, 1872

VIEW TOWARD SMUGGLER'S NOTCH

Vermont's vast Lake Memphremagog, most of which projects into bordering Canada, affords vistas of striking beauty from every perspective

LAKE MEMPHREMAGOG, NORTH FROM OWL'S HEAD

We are fast nearing Owl's Head. The boat winds in and out between the cedar-robed islands, and the golden haze vanishes into the clear and breezy day. We do not land during the journey down the lake, but pass Owl's Head, with only a glimpse of its magnificent height. At one place the shore is almost perpendicular, and on the southern side there is an extraordinary granite boulder, balanced on a natural pedestal, named Balance Rock. Hereabout, too, are the villas of some wealthy Montreal merchants, enclosed in magnificent parks on the banks. Owl's Head is the most prominent mountain, and is cone-shaped. But in our passage to the head of the lake, we see other heights that do not fall far below it. Here is Mount Elephantus, now faintly resembling an elephant's back, afterward changing, as we proceed further north, into a horse-shoe form. In the morning we ascend Owl's Head. The pathway from the hotel is in good condition, overarched by pines and cedars, bordered by pleasant fields. The air is filled with the fragrance of wild flowers, mosses and ferns. Occasionally, through the green curtain that shelters us from the mounting sun, we catch a glimpse of the untroubled, azure sky. The summit reached, we have such a view as rewards our toil. Looking south, we see the lake from end to end, its island and villages, the near rivers flashing in the sunlight.

W.H. RIDEING

Picturesque America, 1872

At maple-sugar time, Vermonters get out their giant kettles and sap yokes to harvest maple sugar, at one time their sole sweetener

At this season of the year sugar orchards become places of much resort, especially for those who love the sweet things of life. In this village parties are frequently formed, who take a trip to some maple orchard in the vicinity, and there regale their palates with maple molasses. These maple sugar manufactories are generally located in romantic spots—in some beautiful valley or on some delightful hillside, where the air is pure and invigorating, and the landscape views enchanting and picturesque. Vermont contains thousands of such delightful retreats; and at this season of the year, when the crystal waters of the brooks are released from their frozen bands and come leaping down the mountain sides, waking the beautiful trout from his winter's sleep, and filling the valleys and groves with sweet music, it is pleasant to visit these sugar orchards, drink sap, lap maple molasses, and make love! Let the Vermont ladies beware; for in such places they may fall in love, while they would not dream of such a thing in their homes.

A BURLINGTON
CORRESPONDENT
The Boston Atlas, 1852

SUGAR MAPLE TIME, VERMONT

MONTPELIER, CAPITAL OF VERMONT

Deep in the woods, Vermont's mountain streams beckon the angler to cast his fly with lures for brown and rainbow trout

ON THE MISSISQUOI, NORTHERN VERMONT

"Only an idle little stream,
Whose amber waters softly gleam,
Where I may wade through
woodland shade,
And cast the fly, and loaf,
and dream."

An angler's wish.

HENRY VAN DYKE

There is no joy like that of the deep woods. The woods have a power over the mind and a serenity of their own. No wonder we are always getting ready to go. No wonder we anxiously meet in the business offices of the men who are to make up the party, and discuss every detail of our anticipated pleasures...They are the woods of God—all right! They open to one vistas of sunlight falling slantwise through tall trees silent as the cathedral and almost as musical. The ripple of the falling water is musical. Weariness is not of the flesh alone. It is to the mind as well. These heal all the elements of a man, mind, soul and body. As I go along after having written some story of the woods—a trip up the Missisquoi for instance, I long to go back. It is the growing hope of the age, this love of the hills and forests.

ARTHUR G. STAPLES
A Tribute to the Woods

When the sugar-boilers get hungry, said a magazine of 1850, "as people are apt to do on occasions like this, a slice of brown bread, thickly covered with half-boiled sap, forms a very satisfying luncheon." Every step in sugaring is fun, but the big jollification comes at the end of the season. "The farmers take turns in inviting their neighbors to a sugaring-off, when the most interesting and fascinating of the population gather around the boiling sweetness and make merry while the hours slip away. It is estimated that the sugar-making season does more to encourage marriage than almost any other phenomenon in nature."

BARROWS MUSSEY
Vermont Heritage, 1975

Besides the lush greenery of its hills and dales, Vermonters are proudest of their native products: maple sugar, blue and white grained marble and granite—quarried in Barre, Proctor, Rutland and Graniteville

The quarries of New England have little gold in them, but the gnomes who dwell in the rock-ribbed hills of Vermont evidently possess the secret of wealth, for wherever the pickaxe strikes those quarries gold fills the coffers of those who develop the mines of marble and granite. Indeed the working of those quarries has become one of the most important industries of the eastern states, and is attracting a thrifty class of immigrants. This is especially true of the marble quarries of Vermont, which extend along the basin of Otter Creek. Marble of several varieties is found from Dorset to Burlington and beyond, and blue marble abounds east and west of the Green Mountains. But the veins of pure white fine-grained marble extend chiefly from Dorset to Middlebury. There is a watershed in Dorset where two streams arise within a few feet of each other. The Battenkill chooses a southerly course and enters the Hudson. The Otter Creek prefers a northerly direction, and meandering through a valley of surpassing loveliness, dominated by the imposing heights of Killington Peak, flows into Lake Champlain, and mingles its waters with the Gulf of St. Lawrence.

HARPER'S WEEKLY,
November 15, 1890

MARBLE QUARRIES AND MARBLE DRESSING, WEST RUTLAND AND PROCTOR

Rhode Island's Busy Towns & Seaports

PROVIDENCE . . . ITS OLD LANDMARKS

. . . WESTMINSTER STREET . . . MARKET

SQUARE . . . ROCKY POINT . . . PAWTUCKET

MILLS . . . WOONSOCKET . . . NEWPORT . . .

ON THE BEACH

OLD HOMESTEAD. / OLD LANDMARK. / CITY MONUMENT.

IN PROVIDENCE

Rhode Island's Busy Towns & Seaports

NEATLY ALIGNED WITH THE SOUTHERN boundary of Massachusetts, flanking the eastern border of Connecticut, with waters of the Atlantic invading the state for 30 miles by way of Narragansett Bay—Rhode Island is the nation's smallest state and, from some viewpoints, the most extraordinary.

Providence, the capital, is also the largest city. Tiny as Rhode Island is, it possesses inestimable riches in Narragansett Bay, which is directly south of Providence and stretches for 30 miles to the Atlantic.

As early as 1524, the area is said to have been visited by Giovanni da Verrazano and, in 1614, by the Dutch Adriean Block. But it was not until 1636 that Roger Williams—having been banished for his freedom of thought by the Massachusetts Bay Colony in 1635—established the first settlement near Providence. He traveled on foot from Salem to Seekonk Plains and spent the winter with Indians there, becoming their advocate and friendly protector for as long as he lived. The next spring, Williams and five companions went by log-canoe on the Seekonk River, landing at what is today Slate Rock. Some Narragansett Indians, then the most powerful tribe in New England, were watching from a neighboring shore. Tradition has it that they greeted Williams with a friendly *"What Cheer!"*—words that later came to be the name of banks, public buildings, and various societies in the state.

A settlement was established near what is now Providence, which attracted a population notable for varied opinions, eager to think and speak as they wished.

In 1638, William Coddington, John Clarke, and Anne Hutchinson bought, with Williams's aid, the island of Aquidneck (now Rhode Island) from the Narragansetts, and established the settlement of Portsmouth. Factional differences developed and Coddington left the settlement. In 1638, he founded Newport, on the southwest side of the island.

The name of Providence reveals the spirit of its founders, and many street names indicate their ideals: Happy Street, Hope Street, Joy Street, Benefit Street.

By 1873, Providence had become New England's second city, one of the wealthiest—in proportion to its size—in the entire country.

From a sleepy town in the middle 1600s—a colony of idealists and freethinkers—to the most aristocratic and glamorous watering place less than two centuries later—Newport attracted the elite of Europe and America. Until the American Revolution, Newport was the commercial center, made vastly prosperous by the "Triangular Trade"—in rum, Negro slaves, and molasses.

Two hundred years ago, Newport had only one rival as the leading port in the Atlantic colonies: two hundred vessels were engaged in foreign trade; three hundred to four hundred more distributed the products unloaded on the docks to the coastal towns from Massachusetts to Virginia, providing merchants in Boston, New York and Philadelphia with their stocks. There was a line of packet ships running regularly between Newport and London.

Rhode Island's Bishop Berkeley wrote in 1728: "Newport is the most thriving in all America for bigness. I was never more agreeably surprised than at the sight of the town and the harbor." New Yorkers were admonished that, if they would only emulate the enterprise of Newporters, they might in time become formidable rivals.

What Newport became in the mid-1800s is too well known to require detailed description. Once more, Newport drew people from towns and cities, not for industry but for recreation. People of culture and wealth, foreign ministers, titled families, authors, actors, clergymen, politicians, highbred and fashionable women—Newport was the magnet that attracted them all. Great mansions—always called cottages—lined the avenues. Every morning the world's greatest steamships landed their elegant passengers; every afternoon a parade of luxurious equipages added to the splendor of the scene. Merchants built stately mansions on the water side, and their wainscoted walls, mahogany stairways, marble mantels, and tiled fireplaces still inspire awe.

At Rocky Point on Warwick Neck, passing from the Bay to Narragansett Pier, on what had been a waste with fishermen's old houses, thousands of bathers were to be seen. By the late eighties not fewer than eighteen hotels had been erected along the shore, some elegant and costly, of vast dimensions.

Samuel Slater, with the financial backing of Moses Brown, was a pioneer in establishing cotton textile mills built at Pawtucket in 1790.

From the turn-of-the-century grandeur of the mansions in Newport, to the crowded streets of factory towns, Rhode Island was a microcosm of all that was once most aristocratic, and also most typical of a thriving industrial state.

The nation's smallest state, with the longest name "The State of Rhode Island and Providence Plantations," is unique in many ways . . .

In the winter of 1636 Williams made his way to Narragansett Bay and there, having bought the land from the Indians, he and his followers built the town of Providence. There they founded their society on the principles for which Williams had fought. Each head of a family was to have an equal voice with all the others in the government. In religion, every individual was to be completely free to worship as he thought best; and there was a complete separation of church and state. The activities of the state were strictly limited to civil affairs.

In 1647, when the town of Providence united with the towns of Warwick, Portsmouth, and Newport to form the colony of Rhode Island, these principles were written into the constitution of the colony, establishing "a government held by the free and voluntarie consent of all, or the greater part of the free inhabitants," and providing for freedom of conscience and separation of church and state. Thus Rhode Island, under the inspiration and guidance of Roger Williams, became the great pilot experiment in American democracy and religious toleration.

C. BRIDENBAUGH

William Penn, Founder of Colonies

WESTMINSTER STREET.

MARKET SQUARE AND "WHAT CHEER" BUILDING, PROVIDENCE

*. . . having had two capitals, both Newport
and Providence, as late as 1900 when the new
state capitol was built in the latter city*

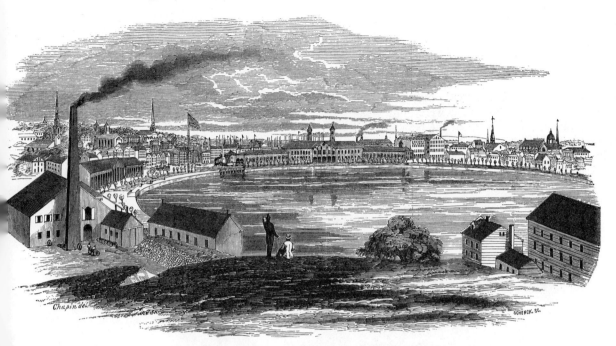

PROVIDENCE, FROM SMITH'S HILL

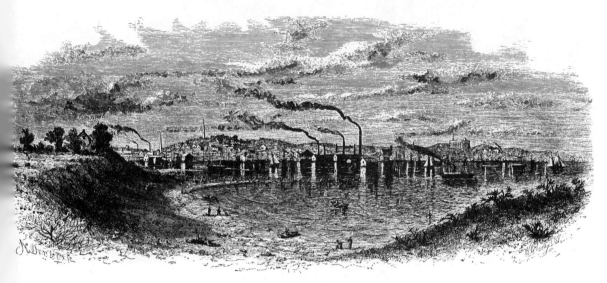

PROVIDENCE, FROM SOUTHERN SUBURBS

BREAKWATER, NARRAGANSETT PIER

"Little Rhody" is a
unique world. Physically,
it ranks as America's
smallest state. Until New
Jersey surpassed it recently, it was the most densely
populated of all the states,
and can safely be called
the "most ethnic." Final-
ly, it is the most con-
sistently Democratic state
in its voting habits. The
compactness is illustrated
by Rhode Island's mea-
surements: only 48 miles
from north to south, and
an even more modest 37
miles from east to west.
These 1,214 square miles
could be contained in New
York State 41 times, in
Texas 227 times, in Alaska
almost 500 times. . . . A
word should be said about
Providence's watery site
and its port. The city is
located on the Providence
and Seekunk Rivers, which
flow into and form the
head of Narragansett Bay.
This was traditionally Providence's window to the
world, and the history
books are replete with
romantic references to the
era when tall-masted In-
diamen and other ships
crowded the harbor. One
important improvement of
recent years was the con-
struction of a hurricane
barrier, a sensible in-
surance against disasters
which have plagued the
city in the past.

NEAL R. PEIRCE
The New England States,
1976

Pawtucket owes its fame as the birthplace of America's cotton industry, in 1790—to a young British mill apprentice, Samuel Slater . . .

Simultaneously with the sudden rise of the Cotton Kingdom in the South, Samuel Slater, a cotton-mill operative from England, was in Rhode Island trying to remember how the textile machinery which he had tended in the old country had been built, for England prohibited the export of any of the machines lest the industry might be set up elsewhere. Slater was successful, machines were built here, and the foundations laid for the growth of the New England textile mills. Great as the differences between the sections had already been, they were to be increasingly emphasized during the next half century.

JAMES TRUSLOW ADAMS
The Epic of America, 1931

OLD SLATER MILL, PAWTUCKET

With some justification, Rhode Island claims to be the birthplace of the American factory system. And it was at Pawtucket in 1790 that Samuel Slater—financed by Moses Brown of the famous Rhode Island merchant family—reproduced the Arkwright machines of England, starting the young country's first mechanized cotton mill. Within 25 years of Slater's coming, according to one account, Rhode Island Mills were turning out more than 27 million yards of cloth a year and providing jobs for 26,000 operatives (including many child laborers). Together with cotton milling, the woolen and worsted industry flourished in 19th-and early 20th-century Rhode Island. Until the 1940s, when the exodus of mills to the South hit its peak, spinning and weaving was the dominant industry of Rhode Island. It was also the state's Achilles heel, because the ethnic stock workers were paid appallingly low wages; the image of the old textile industry, as one labor leader described it to me, was of dim 25-watt lighting and creaking old elevators in rambling, often decrepit mill buildings. In the 1920s, 90,000 men and women—three-fifths of the Rhode Island factory employment—were in textiles; in the last few years, the total has been scarcely 18,000.

NEAL R. PEIRCE
The New England States, 1976

THE FALLS AND MILLS ON THE PAWTUCKET RIVER

DUNNELL MILLS, PAWTUCKET

. . . whose successful operation in cotton spinning was duplicated in neighboring Woonsocket, a town off in the extreme northeast corner of the state

MAIN STREET, PAWTUCKET

"New England," wrote Bernard DeVoto nearly twenty years ago, "is a finished place...it is the first American section to be finished, to achieve stability in the conditions of its life. It is the first old civilization and the first permanent civilization in America." Obviously this comment suffers somewhat from exaggeration, but it does point up the fact that there are areas in the nations that have become comparatively old economically—and as such, despite their prestige, raise special problems. These areas are not limited to the six northeastern states, nor even to the Middle Atlantic area...

POST OFFICE SQUARE, WOONSOCKET

WOONSOCKET COMPANY'S MILL

...But the impact of economic maturity and economic stability in industrial development without a corresponding stability in employment is to be found primarily in an area such as New England, where industrialization has been more pronounced and more continuous. The results are that machinery is old, methods are perforce old, and too frequently management is old. Community after community has relied for years upon one or two industries, and a decline in the world market for the products of these industries may take place. Some fast-growing industries have settled elsewhere, leaving areas of serious unemployment and of economic stagnation in our generally prosperous country.

JOHN F. KENNEDY

New England Industry, 1953

Before the Revolution, Newport prospered as its skippers plied the infamous triangular trade: slaves from Africa; molasses and rum via the Caribbean. In the Gilded Age socialites built their "cottages" here

The great event in the fashionable world was a Newport ball. A lady who had married a man of cultivation and taste, a member of one of New York's oldest families, who had inherited from her father an enormous fortune, was at once seized with the ambition to take and hold a brilliant social position, to gratify which she built one of the handsomest houses in this city, importing interiors from Europe for it and such old Spanish tapestries as had never before been introduced into New York; after which she went to Newport and bought a beautiful villa on Bellevue Avenue and there gave, in the grounds of that villa, the handsomest ball that had ever been given there....All Newport was present to give brilliancy to the scene. Everything was to be European; so one supped at small tables as at a ball in Paris all through the night.

WARD MC ALLISTER

Society As I Have Found It,
1890

ON THE BEACH

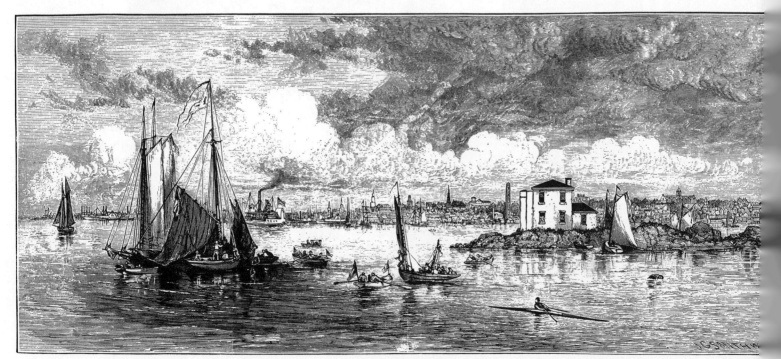

NEWPORT, FROM THE BAY

The Connecticut Valley & Villages

WINDSOR LOCKS . . . SAYBROOK . . .

THE CONNECTICUT . . . MIDDLETOWN . . .

HARTFORD . . . STATE HOUSE . . .

TRINITY COLLEGE . . . PUTNEY . . .

SUGAR LOAF MOUNTAIN . . .

BELLOWS FALLS . . . GREENFIELD . . .

SUNDERLAND . . . NEW HAVEN . . .

YALE COLLEGE . . . SALISBURY . . .

ALONG THE SOUND . . . NEW LONDON . . .

NORWALK . . . BRIDGEPORT . . .

STRATFORD . . . MILFORD

WINDSOR LOCKS, CONNECTICUT RIVER

The Connecticut Valley & Villages

OFTEN CALLED "QUEEN OF NEW England rivers"—the Connecticut flows from a trio of small lakes in northeast New Hampshire for nearly 400 miles, to empty in Long Island Sound. Along its course, it gathers waters of many small, sparkling streams, and provides water power for countless industries. Creating a rich, alluvial valley and prosperous farmlands, and inspiring the settlement of many villages and towns, the Connecticut River defines the boundaries of New Hampshire and Vermont, flows all across Massachusetts, and bisects Connecticut, enriching the land every mile of the way.

Three men—Thomas Hooker, Samuel Stone, and John Haynes—the first two "reverends," the third a wealthy landowner who was elected governor of Massachusetts Bay, felt cramped in the Massachusetts Bay Colony and declared that "the bent of their spirits" prompted them to leave. They marched across country, guided only by a compass, and reached the Connecticut river, settling three towns: Hartford, Windsor, and Wethersfield.

Previously, the Dutch navigator, Adriaen Block, had sailed into Long Island Sound, and discovered the mouth of the Connecticut river in 1614. The Dutch built a fort in 1633 but, constantly harried by the English, abandoned the settlement in 1654.

The fertile valley inspired glowing reports,

and a second group of Puritans set forth from Cambridge, numbering about a hundred men, women, and children. One chronicle recounts their hardships: "On foot, through a hideous, trackless wilderness, over mountains, through swamps, thickets, and rivers, with no cover but the heavens, nor any lodgings but what simple nature affords, subsisting en route on milk from the cattle they drove with them. They carried packs, arms, and some utensils, and were nearly a fortnight on the journey." This group also settled in Hartford. The report summarizes: "This adventure was the more remarkable, as many of this company were persons of figure, who had lived in affluence and honor in England, and were strangers to danger and fatigue."

A third group of Puritans—these from London—came seeking a site for a trading town to compete with New York and Boston. Their leaders, Theophilus Eaton and the Reverend John Davenport, selected New Haven. This colony spread along the river and crossed Long Island Sound. A written constitution, called the Fundamental Orders of Connecticut and New Haven, was evolved in 1639 and served until 1662, when Charles II issued a corporate charter which remained the law for colony and state until 1818. Representatives from three Connecticut river towns—Hartford, Windsor, and Wethersfield—had adopted the fundamental orders for "an orderly and decent government according to God." Any householder of "honest conversation" was admitted to town meetings. The desire for more and better land, rather than religious differences, prompted many of the migrations to Connecticut. A number of settlements burgeoned along the river and the sound. The government functioned smoothly, except for a brief period during the administration of Sir Edmund Andros. On his royal appointment as Governor General of New England, he sent word that Connecticut must surrender its charter. This request being ignored, Sir Edmund journeyed to Hartford with sixty British troops. The assembly was in session. The governor general was greeted courteously. The charter was laid on a table. Suddenly, the lights were extinguished, a Captain Wadsworth of the assembly snatched the charter and disappeared into the night. This led to the tale, still told, of Hartford's famous "charter oak." Like the great elm of Boston Common, Hartford's oak is said to have been of fabulous age, a thousand years, with a diameter of seven feet. In a hollow root of the old tree, Captain Wadsworth is reputed to have secreted the precious charter.

The Connecticut River separates the state in almost equal—east and west—sections, generally referred to as the east and west "highlands." Artists and craftsmen were drawn to Connecticut early in colonial days, and small manufacturing projects sprang up, attracted by the plentiful water power. Villages were settled all along the river shores and throughout the fertile valley. But, although it is known for its rural beauty, Connecticut's wealth is derived overwhelmingly from its industry. Alexis de Toqueville's summary is widely known: "Connecticut...the little spot ...that makes the clock peddler, the schoolmaster, and the senator. The first, gives you time; the second, tells you what to do with it; the third, makes your law and your civilization."

Famous for making firearms and ammunition since the American Revolution, Connecticut—often called the "gadget" state—produces many manufactures requiring special skills: revolvers, clocks and watches, silverware, auger bits, ball bearings, typewriters, electrical products, as well as hats, saddlery, coffins, and submarines.

Chicopee is another charming river town on the route to Holyoke—early famous for the Mount Holyoke "female seminary." Here are enchanting glimpses of Northampton on the right and, more distant, Amherst with its prestigious college, founded in 1821. One of the most beautiful cities on the river is Brattleboro, in Vermont, where the water earned such a reputation for purity that it inspired the establishment of several "water-cure" sanitariums. In the heart of the mountains—where the White River empties into the Connecticut, at White River Junction—the distance is short to Hanover, noted for Dartmouth College, chartered by royal grant in 1769. Dartmouth has many distinguished graduates, among them Daniel Webster.

From Saybrook on Long Island Sound, to Stewartstown on the Canadian border, hundreds of settlements owe their beginnings and steady growth to the Connecticut River and the many little rivers that flow into it. With the Connecticut, the Housatonic and the Naugatuck merit mention. Each in its meanderings collects a multitude of smaller rivers and streams. Together, richly, they fertilize and power the state.

Flowing purposefully from near the Canadian border due south to the Long Island Sound, the Connecticut River divides New Hampshire and Vermont . . .

This isn't a piece about Middletown or Anyburg or Sauk Center. The country towns here in New England all bear a family resemblance to one another, but they also have individual characters that can be learned only by living in them. They are more or less united as communities, more or less friendly to newcomers, more or less dominated by cliques that are more or less conservative and sometimes corrupt. But all of them are different from small towns in other parts of the country, and I suspect that all of them have been rapidly changing since the war, in fashions that are not always apparent to their own inhabitants...Sheridan is a town only in the New England sense; in New York it would be an unincorporated village, in Pennsylvania a township and farther west nothing more than a school district. It consists of about twenty-five square miles of land shaped like a narrow slice of pie—a valley ten miles along with a lake in the south, farmland in the north and a range of wooded hills on either side. The back roads are full of abandoned farms like those described in Slater Brown's novel, "The Burning Wheel." North of the village, locally called the Center, there are twenty fairly prosperous dairy farms. Summer cottages are clustered along the shores of the lake and scattered through the hills. The winter population is about 450.

MALCOLM COWLEY *Town Report: 1942*

SAYBROOK

THE CONNECTICUT, ABOVE MIDDLETOWN

. . . the entire length of each state, continuing through Massachusetts and Connecticut. Its valley of enchanting beauty . . . famous for many history-rich towns

MAIN STREET BRIDGE, HARTFORD

The Indian word *Quinnehtukqut* meant: "Beside the long tidal river." The state of Connecticut, as now constituted, is well served by rivers—7600 miles of them; but the one from which it takes its name, along which it was originally settled, and which is still its central axis, is the Connecticut. "The Great River," the early settlers called it. Perhaps this was partly because the Indian word was too much of a mouthful, but it was also an honest evaluation. It is indeed a Great River, the longest in New England. Up at the Canadian border, where it rises, it is just a trickle, but it picks up force and volume all the way down its 360-mile course between New Hampshire and Vermont, through Massachusetts, and then through Connecticut to Long Island Sound. Dropping some 1600 feet en route, it provides the water power on which are based many of New England's cities—Bellows Falls, Brattleboro, Turners Falls, Greenfield, Holyoke, Springfield, Windsor Locks, Hartford, Middletown. These are important cities in the economic life of New England, and the Great River made them so.

The broad central valley through which the river flows for two thirds of its course through Connecticut is the heart of the state, a rich, busy, self-sufficient middle ground between an extended New York suburbia to the west and a hilly hinterland to the east. Some of the state's greatest industrial cities are here—though one hardly thinks of them as river towns; and the center of population of the state is only slightly to the southwest of the valley. Here, too, are the state's richest agricultural lands.

ARTHUR BARTLETT
American Panorama, 1947

HARTFORD, FROM EAST SIDE OF THE RIVER

At Connecticut's capital, Hartford, sternwheelers once transported luxuriant produce of the region— especially leaf tobacco—downriver to New York markets

The river traffic consisted mostly of flatboats, occasionally with sails and poling devices to get them back upstream, but more commonly the flatboats were broken up for their timber when they arrived at Hartford. A few small steamboats managed to cope with the rapids above Springfield, the earliest one on the Connecticut River invented and built by Samuel Morey in 1793, six years after John Fitch's original invention, of which Morey was unaware, and fourteen years before Robert Fulton's. Stern-wheelers built by Thomas Blanchard thrived briefly on the Connecticut after 1826. Charles Dickens wrote a deprecatory account of riding a small steamboat downriver among February ice-cakes from Springfield to Hartford during his American tour. But the most active steamboating on the Connecticut River was not in Massachusetts, but rather below Hartford, where service to New York by the Connecticut Steamboat Company persisted long after the railroads arrived. In Massachusetts most Connecticut River traffic was of the canalboat type. Tobacco, potatoes, celery and onions were the agricultural products, especially leaf tobacco for cigar wrappers, on which Connecticut valley farmers grew wealthy from 1830 on.

STEAMERS ON THE CONNECTICUT, HARTFORD

HENRY F. HOWE
Massachusetts:
There She Is—Behold Her, 1960

HARTFORD, FROM COLT'S FACTORY

While various industries developed, as early as the eighteenth century, Hartford prospered as the center for underwriting, especially of casualty insurance

STATE HOUSE, MAIN STREET, HARTFORD

TRINITY COLLEGE, HARTFORD

The lamps which lined the streets of Hartford sent forth an icy breath-like light. Here, there could be no sympathy, no tenderness, no mood to warm a passing stranger. The night was young—but it had settled as if to stay forever. Such a night was March 5, 1860. It was when Abraham Lincoln came to Hartford, gaunt and tall, and supperless, but fired by a greater appetite—into the state where once lived John Brown, who now "lay mouldering;" and Harriet Beecher Stowe, whose battlecry for freedom was fanning flames across the eastern horizon. This great and really rended heart must surely have opened wider beneath the soot-stained, loosely-draping coat as he rode down Main Street in his carriage and perceived the strength of his support. Yankee men and women had forsaken warming hearths this cold and winter-ending evening to blend their sense of right with his. For he had spoken— this gentle, worn and weary man—and Yankee hearts went out to him. The torchlights swept around him like a sudden gust of flaming wind, and Lincoln spoke again. "The boys are wide awake," he said; "let's call them Wide-Awakes." The name spread through the nation. That's how the Wide-Awakes first formed—to gird themselves to battle for what they considered right. "Right, Eternal Right, makes might, and as we understand our duty, so do it."

Highways & Byways of Connecticut, 1947

Along the river's winding course, every town had its grist mill, where the plunging waters were dammed to provide needed water power

OLD MILL, PUTNEY

The mills were everywhere. The town where I have spent the pleasantest of my summers is far to the north; it has 500 inhabitants and a single woodworking mill. A century ago it had 1200 inhabitants and the two creeks powered a gristmill, a sawmill, a planing and turning mill, a fulling mill, a fanning mill, and one of those primordial "machine shops" that would do anything the surrounding market wanted done. What ended this happiest period of the industrial revolution was not only the spread of steam and, later on, of electric power that made industrial concentrations economical, but even more the development of the railroad network. Massachusetts and Connecticut, with their greater railroad mileage, developed the mill town as we now know it—and learned the vulnerability of a one-industry economy when later shifts came.

BERNARD DE VOTO

New England, from

The Romance of North America, 1958

BELLOWS FALLS

With the passing years, old mill sites display only a pile of stones, half-rotted wheels and timber, relics of a civilization that has passed

For the Yankees who turned to the glacial waterfalls had found the genius of their breed. We may now return to those masonry dams that are the vestiges of another age. They are on all rivers and creeks and on some brooks so small that you can hardly believe the evidence. Beside them are brick walls it would take high explosives or a vagabond hurricane with its torrents of rain to demolish, though roofs and windows have been gone for two generations or more. The walls are those of little mills that were powered by the dams, the mills to which the Yankee genius brought precision, versatility, and unsurpassed craftsmanship. The Yankees were predestined smiths, mechanics, artificers, contrivers, innovators. The direct and orderly progression of machine processes was their intellectual idiom. Indeed it was their spiritual well-being, for what is the logic of machines if it is not the identical economy, exactness, propriety and neatness that I have already called elegance? At the village green, the exquisite steeple and the scrubbed stoop with a pumpkin on it; in the shipyards, the lines of the clippers; in the shop, a turret lathe or a drop forge growing ever more complex and automatic as Yankee logic works out its functions.

BERNARD DE VOTO
New England, from
*The Romance of North
America, 1958*

STEVENS BROOK, BARNET

WHETSTONE BROOK, BRATTLEBORO

Upstream, where the river narrows, its mood changes from a placid stream, feeding fertile meadows, to plunge precipitously between granite boulders . . .

Tinkling rills of the hills,
Rippling down the trails,
From the crags of mountain-tops
Into wooded dales,

Joining brooks in lily nooks
Flashing foamy white,
Purling round the stony pools
In a wild delight!

On-swirling, upward-curling,
Plumed with tossing spray,
Dancing, teasing, frolicking,
And wandering away.

Into streams deep in dreams,
Curved in slender grace,
Shadow-flecked and glimmering
In veils of leafy lace!

Thus the waters, sparkling, darkling,
Like our myriad lives—
Brooks a-play, streams a-dream,
While the river strives.

Toward the free, unbounded sea
They rush victoriously;
Like human souls, merged into great
Unfathomed unity.

MILDRED HOBBS
Little Rivers

THE WEST BRANCH OF BELLOWS FALLS

CONNECTICUT VALLEY, FROM ROCKY MOUNTAIN, GREENFIELD

. . . where wooden structures spanned the river, including quaint covered bridges, many of which are still in service a century and a half later

SUGAR LOAF MOUNTAIN, FROM SUNDERLAND

WHITE RIVER JUNCTION

This elegance is the swept and garnished New England countryside, the houses and town halls and meetinghouses whose white paint is spiritual dignity, the fanlights of the mansions, the scrubbed stoops (with a pumpkin on them at harvesttime) of the farmhouses themselves, sited not only so that they are sheltered from the prevailing wind but so that they take in the vista of the creek curving toward the fold in the hills. It is almost inconceivable now that the hill farms were once a wheat country and a sheep country. That period could not possibly last; the upland soil washed into the creeks long ago. . . The farmers who did not go west moved to the valleys and to whatever flatland New England has, mainly in Connecticut, Down East in Maine, and along the Connecticut River. Sometimes they moved their town halls and meetinghouses with them. Valley soil, truck gardening, and dairy farming saved the stricken agriculture. Commercial farming, with the increased efficiency of specialized one-crop agriculture but also with its greater risks, took the place of subsistence farming. . . In summer the Connecticut Valley is wonderfully pleasing striations of green and white, the onion fields and the cheesecloth tents that shade the tobacco fields. But the truth is that not many of the original Yankees were talented farmers; their genius was of a different kind.

BERNARD DE VOTO

The Romance of North America, 1958

*Long Island Sound has a hundred towns and villages—
each an entity, important industrially, or
as a seaport or summer resort . . .*

THE VILLAGE GREEN, NORWALK

The flames which once had glowed on Norwalk slopes, like falls of crimson water, as all the city was destroyed by foreign soldiers, had long since paled. A new and prosperous city had sprung up from rubbled ashes, a city filled with industry and pride...And yet, what's this we see? A large, impressive concourse of grim, determined people is gathered on the village green. No human tears fall here. Their heavy clothes are gathered warmly against the winter's cold. Small children snuggle safely in their rugged parents' arms. And quiet lies on every side, as silently as midnight on a desert. But time for everything relentlessly arrives— and time has come. The last farewells are spoken— the last endearing glances interchanged....The same mute gleam of inquiry and question fills the eye and trembles on the lips of everyone there. But no one words it—no one whispers —the thought in every mind. Instead, we hear the somber strains of a Doxology, as voices rise in ever-growing chant. And, slowly, the long cavalcade of prairie wagons joins the file of wagons rolling by. And many Norwalk families wind Westward towards Ohio's Firelands— their new home to be. A grateful nation's gift of homage for their gallant sacrifice in war, when all homesteads burned. New lands for old—new worlds to conquer. And thus Norwalk in Ohio was founded —by pioneers from ravaged Norwalk in Connecticut.

*Highways & Byways of
Connecticut, 1947*

MAIN STREET, NORWALK

. . . where the joys of sailing, swimming, oystering and fishing combine the aspects of both land and sea, providing abundant year-round pleasures

NORWALK from RIVER.

OYSTER BOATS. ROTON POINT.

My life is like a stroll
  upon the beach,
As near the ocean's edge
  as I can go;
My tardy steps its waves
  sometimes o'erreach,
Sometimes I stay to let
  them overflow.

My sole employment 'tis,
  and scrupulous care,
To place my gains beyond
  the reach of tides;
Each smoother pebble, and
  each shell more rare,
Which ocean kindly to my
  hand confides,

I have but few companions
  on the shore,
They scorn the strand who
  sail upon the sea;
Yet oft I think the ocean
  they've sailed o'er
Is deeper known upon
  the strand to me.

The middle sea contains no
  crimson dulse,
Its deeper waves cast up
  no pearls to view;
Along the shore my hand
  is on its pulse,
And I converse with many
  a shipwrecked crew.

HENRY DAVID THOREAU

VIEW FROM WILSONS POINT.

NORWALK, ROTON POINT AND WILSONS POINT, ON THE SOUND

*The coastal towns of Bridgeport, Stratford, and Milford
are steeped in antiquarian lore—their current charm intermixed
with ancient adventures, bloody battles, defeats and victories*

We are going to weave our tale from all the worn but still glossy threads from the life of P.T. Barnum. It is only fitting that we visit Bridgeport, to think of this great showman and explore the many unexpected facets which historic light casts on his name. For Barnum, founder of "The Greatest Show on Earth," is rightly Bridgeport's most loved son. With him as leader, Bridgeport grew to present size with all her vast and teeming, thriving industry which makes her name renowned throughout the world.

Settled in 1639, the town of Stratford, first known as Cupheag, with its shading elms and old white houses, became a constant center of startling events. For this was the home of the Johnsons—the Reverend Doctor Samuel Johnson, and his erudite son, William Samuel. Dr. Johnson became a president of King's College in New York, and one of Columbia University's founders. His son became Connecticut's first senator and a celebrated lawyer.

Milford was also settled in 1639 and became a favorite recreation spot for people who value gastronomical delights. Milford—land of oysters—Indians from many miles around came each year for "salting" as they called it. This consisted solely of downing as many oysters as the sated appetite could hold. And, though times have changed, Milford is still proud of her succulent, juicy seafood.

*Highways & Byways of
Connecticut, 1947*

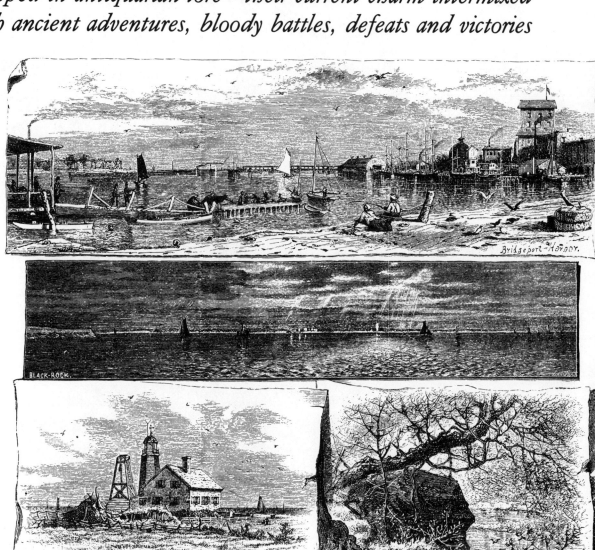

SCENES IN BRIDGEPORT, STRATFORD, AND MILFORD

In New London, a privateers' rendezvous during the Revolution
—partially burned in 1781, blockaded by the British in 1812
—shipping, shipbuilding and whaling brought maritime prosperity

NEW LONDON, FROM THE SHORE ROAD

STATE STREET, NEW LONDON

What tempestuous threads of history she has woven in the over-all pattern of romance! To wander on her crowded, crooked water-front byways or view the silent walks on now stilled captains' homes is to bring to mind a hundred different memories of excitement and adventure. The air is redolent with salt and spices—mingled with molasses and the sharper tang of tar and hempen ropes. New London is the cradle of all men who brave the deep. Rendezvous of privateers, port of pirates—graceful sloops and white-rigged schooners once bobbed where submarines and ships of war now lie at anchor. For centuries her never-quiet streets have echoed to the roystering gayness of heart-free, sea-bound men. In 1847, whaling ships rocked restlessly, tugging at their hawsers—for New London, then, was at the peak of her great and prosperous whaling trade. Seventy some odd ships and barks, brigs and schooners, sailed the seven seas in search of gold and danger. The gushing flow of whale and sperm oil, the floundering seals and sea-elephants which slithered from the decks of ice-caked ships, were only mute reminders of the perils they had faced. From the Southern seas to Greenland and the regions east of Cape Horn. To the Arctic where the freezing floes closed in like whitened, death-trap jaws. For, as the old Gazette enthusiastically exhorted: "Now, my horse jockeys, beat your cattle and horses into spears, lances, harpoons and whaling gear, and let us all strike out; many spouts ahead."

Highways & Byways of
Connecticut, 1947

*In Connecticut's northwest corner, at Salisbury,
busy blast furnaces gave valuable aid to the
struggling colonies in the Revolutionary War*

Salisbury! Salisbury once was the Birmingham of this vast country. Salisbury, where Mt. Riga stands in all her humble majesty and lonely splendor. If we had traveled here in 1847 we would have seen an awesome sight. The last long, flickering flame of ruddy light on Old Forge Pond, which must have glowed among the mountain fastnesses like a bowl of ruby wine, as stillness fell once more across the rugged peaks. The only burning forge gone out when progress moved the thriving trade to Salisbury streets beneath. In 1847 railroads came to shift the source of industry to more accessible spots. But progress could not change the fame which earlier days had brought— when Salisbury men climbed heavily up these hills to seek the ore and bring it into light. The elevated hills. The deep, extensive limestone valleys. If we had been there then, we would have seen the last full saddle bags of ore going down those rocky lanes on teams of oxen— the same dirt road which bore the weight of cannon ball and cannon—of anchor chains and anchors. For here it was they forged the anchor of the "Constitution," and six strong, straining yoke of oxen bore it down beneath the shadow of the western ridges of the Hudson. But now you see, instead of belching flame and cinder, the white little houses standing forth against the stain of forest green on hill-tops. The forges in the hills lie dormant as time moves on—but Salisbury is a proud and prosperous town.

Highways & Byways of

Connecticut, 1947

SITE OF REVOLUTIONARY FOUNDRY, SALISBURY

TWIN LAKES, SALISBURY

New Haven—which boasts a beautiful green and Yale's elm-shaded campus—is notable for Yankee inventiveness. Here Eli Whitney helped spark the industrial revolution

YALE COLLEGE, NEW HAVEN

RAILROAD STATION, NEW HAVEN

New Haven—beehive of industry, amidst whose teeming streets, incongruously, sleep vestiges of venerable grandeur and hoary nostalgic stories of the past—remnants of a most prodigious history. New Haven—settled in 1638—what a fabulous wealth of romance and great deeds lies here where Yale presents the benefits of faultless culture to students garnered from the whole wide world. Her solid red hills stand sentinels, in lofty meditation, above the still-unfolding mysteries of her elm-lined streets. The West and Mill and Quinnipiac Rivers flow mutely by. New Haven fairly reeks of histrionic lore. There are episodic portraits of redskins in the forest—of colonial courage and ingenious acts of skill. Bravery and treason walk hand in hand through the hushed shadows of the alleys. Shades of Roger Sherman and Benedict Arnold, of Baldwins, Davenports, and Hookers haunt the narrow byways where inventiveness has lodged since early days. Here came into being the first type foundry, and the first successful milling machines. The first engine lathes, and the first polished copper—the first commercial switchboard and the first machine for dipping wooden matches. This is the town for erudition, for Winchester rifles and Sargent locks—for New Haven clocks and numerous other manufactures. From 1701 to 1875 New Haven was the joint capital of the state and through the panorama of her iridescent past float images of all America's elite.

Highways & Byways of Connecticut, 1947

Inspired by the Romanesque tradition of southern France, H. H. Richardson—one of the true geniuses of American architecture—gave Yale a new face, many years before it acquired Wrexham and Harkness Memorial

It was typical of America that nobody thought of founding a new college in the same town where one already existed; local and sectarian feelings were too strong to follow the example of Oxford and Cambridge. By 1840, over 150 small denominational colleges, each located as far distant as possible from the others, were in existence. The driving impulse for secondary and higher education in the United States prior to the Civil War, and a principal motive to this day, has been religious, not secular; and these slenderly endowed sectarian colleges educated the whole man and maintained a standard of excellence in the liberal arts that has seldom been attained in wealthy, tax-supported state universities. The older colonial and early federal colleges were now being transformed into proper universities by adding faculties of law, medicine, theology, and science to the original arts and letters. But the idea of a university being a center for scholarly and scientific research lay far in the future.

SAMUEL ELIOT MORISON

The Oxford History of the American People, 1965

RECITATION HALL AND NEW LIBRARY, YALE COLLEGE, NEW HAVEN

New York . . . Gateway to a Continent

NEW YORK BAY . . . THE EAST RIVER . . .

VIEW FROM TRINITY CHURCH STEEPLE

. . . ON THE BATTERY . . . IMMIGRATION

AND CUSTOMS SCENES . . . TENEMENTS

. . . WASHINGTON MARKET . . .

GRAND CENTRAL STATION . . .

TRAIN SHED . . . STREET DOCKS . . .

BROOKLYN BRIDGE . . . WALL STREET . . .

STOCK EXCHANGE . . . BLIZZARD OF 1888 . . .

SLEIGHING IN CENTRAL PARK . . .

PARK SCENES . . . CONEY ISLAND

. . . FIREWORKS CELEBRATIONS

. . . STEAMBOAT TRAVEL

NEW YORK BAY

New York ... Gateway to a Continent

WITH THE WATERS OF THE lordly Hudson on one side, the swift tides of the East River on the other, and their meeting in a spacious bay at the south, New York City is blessed beyond most cities of the world with a landlocked harbor that, by a narrow channel, flows into the Atlantic Ocean. The Hudson comes down from the north for over 150 miles, its mighty mouth inviting entrance to the continent. The East River, a virtual arm of the sea, pours into Long Island Sound—a ready approach to New England and its rivers.

Several explorers, from two directions, approached New York state. Giovanni da Verrazano sailed into New York Bay in 1524; Samuel de Champlain, in 1609, traveled by the lake that now bears his name, reaching the western boundaries of the state. Henry Hudson, in service of the Dutch, sailed up the Hudson, almost to what is now Albany. Verrazano anchored in the Narrows, now named for him. He and his men admired the kindly, feather-clad natives who came down to the shores in welcome, showing where to land safely. But, "a contrary flow of wind coming from the sea, we were enforced to return to our ship, leaving this land, to our great discontentment...."

From Canada, the French continued to penetrate New York state in the north and west. Jesuit missionaries labored to bring Christianity to the Indians. But the friendship of the French with the Huron tribe led to ceaseless hostility with the Iroquois, who controlled western New York. The West India Company, chartered in 1621, established its New Netherland colony, with two settlements: New Amsterdam on the southern end of what is now Manhattan Island, and Nassau, at present-day Albany. The Dutch traded trinkets worth about twenty-four dollars for the New Amsterdam area. The most capable of the Dutch administrators, Peter Stuyvesant, was also the last. The English, who, since Lion Gardner's arrival in 1639, had been settling on Long Island and in southeastern New York, were claiming the entire region, based on John Cabot's explorations. Minor wars developed and, in 1664, the English defeated the Dutch. New Netherland was renamed the "Colonies of New York and New Jersey," and an effort was made to combine them with New England, under Sir Edmund Andros. This failed, but, until the American Revolution, New York remained English, with Dutch settlers sharing in the limited self-government which the Royal laws allowed. As the revolutionary war developed, the British invaded New York City, holding it until the war's end. But the patriots held most of the state. In 1734, when Alexander Hamilton established the first bank in New York, the city became the nation's financial capital. It was made the capital of the nation, from 1789 to 1791, and was also the capital of the state, until Albany, in 1797, became the capital.

The largest city in the United States, New York is also one of the three largest cities in the world. Approaching New York by way of the sea, the visitor sails over the lower bay, the Narrows—which is formed by the projection of Long Island on one hand, and Staten Island on the other.

The inner bay opens from the Narrows and centered in the view, New York City appears dramatically. On the right, the city of Brooklyn spreads an endless panorama of spires, towers, and homes. On the western rim of the inner bay, New Jersey's shores appear. Every imaginable type of waterborne craft gathers here: steamers, all sizes, some off for distant ports; white-sailed sloops, skiffs, and beautiful yachts. "The prospect," said Walt Whitman, "off toward Staten Island, or down the Narrows, or the other way, up the Hudson—what refreshment of spirit such sights gave me years ago (and many times since)."

Viewing New York City from the inner bay, a circular, fortlike building appears near a fringe of trees, on the lower shore. Here is a pleasure promenade with a fine seawall. The building is the famed Castle Garden, through which vast numbers of immigrants arrived in America. Once a fort, then a summer garden, then a music hall, by the mid-1800s Castle Garden served the commissioners of emigration as headquarters. The Battery was once New York City's only social promenade, where belles and beaux and sturdy Knickerbockers of social and political importance strolled in pleasant weather. On the East River boundary, not far from the Battery, where the wharves were, sailing ships from far-off ports discharged their cargoes, and old tars congregated, and a steamship was regarded as a profanation. In the heart of the city, on Broadway, less than a mile from the Battery, the beautiful tower of Trinity Church rises above its historic graveyard with tumbling tombstones. The church, comparatively new, faces down Wall Street on the site of a Colonial edifice. Looking south from Trinity's spire, the small green patch of Bowling Green appears at the end of Broadway.

Fifth Avenue—from its southern extremity at Washington Square to the entrance of Central Park at Fifty-ninth Street—was given over to wealth and elegance. Extending north to One hundred-tenth Street, paralleling Central Park, Fifth Avenue continued to be the preferred site for millionaires' residences. The park—once an area of rough rocks, brushwood, and ash heaps, a deposit for city refuse—had become the pride of the city.

A contemporary account says: "There were no forests, no groves, no lawns, no lake, no walks. It was simply a forest of rocks and rubbish. The ground was excavated for lakes; trees were planted; paths laid out; bridges built. The result is a pleasure-ground that is already famous. In its union of art with nature, it is unapproached in this country, and unexcelled abroad. For the children, there are nurseries, goat-carriages, camel-rides, swings, 'run-arounds,' and other devices."

Its rich historical background, cosmopolitan atmosphere, cultural and educational advantages, colorful neighborhoods, exotic foods, smart shops, parks, gardens, and diversity of entertainment drew hundreds of thousands of visitors to New York City annually.

"Rich, hemm'd, thick all around with sailships and steamships"—Whitman, poet of Mannahatta, "saw clearly through mist and fog . . .

Looking down south from the Battery, one views the large bay, New York harbor. Due west is Jersey City, and southwesterly, Staten Island, known to the Indians as Squehonga Manackmong...extending some fourteen miles in length. The island, within half an hour's sail of the metropolis, and possessing great and varied topographical advantages, has become a favorite resort for summer residence, and many stately chateaux crown its beautiful heights or nestle in its peaceful glens.

T. ADDISON RICHARDS

New York Circumnavigated,

1861

VIEW FROM TRINITY CHURCH STEEPLE

SCENE ON THE EAST RIVER

" . . . an island sixteen miles long, solid founded, numberless crowded streets, high growths of iron, slender, strong, light, splendidly uprising toward clear skies . . . "

NEW YORK RIVER FRONT AND SOUTH STREET

The countless masts, the white shore steamers, the lighters, the ferry-boats, the black sea-steamers well model'd,
The down-town streets, the jobbers' houses of business, the houses of business of the ship-merchants and money-brokers, the river-streets,
Immigrants arriving, fifteen or twenty thousand in a week,
The carts hauling goods, the manly race of drivers of horses, the brown-faced sailors,
The summer air, the bright sun shining, and the sailing clouds aloft,
The winter snows, the sleigh-bells, the broken ice in the river, passing along up or down with the flood-tide or ebb-tide,
The mechanics of the city, the masters, well-form'd, beautiful-faced, looking you straight in the eyes,
Trottoirs throng'd, vehicles, Broadway, the women, the shops and shows,
A million people—manners free and superb—open voices—hospitality—the most courageous and friendly young men,
City of hurried and sparkling waters! city of spires and masts!
City nested in bays! my city!

WALT WHITMAN
Mannahatta, 1855

Edwin Abbey pictured the view at the Battery—a point where all immigrants arrive—capturing the nostalgic longings for their homelands

"The New York waterfront, Battery included, was lined by dreaming landsmen as well," wrote Herman Melville, "posted like silent sentinels all around the town...thousands upon thousands of mortal men fixed in ocean reveries. Some leaning against the spiles; some seated upon the pier-heads; some looking over the bulwarks of ships from China; some high aloft in the rigging, as if striving to get a still better seaward peep. But all these landsmen, of week days pent up of lath and plaster—tied to counters, nailed to benches, clinched to desks... Strange! Nothing will content them but the extremest limit of the land...They must get just as nigh the water as they possibly can without falling in. And there they stand—miles of them— leagues. Inlanders all, they come from lanes and alleys, streets and avenues—north, east, south, and west. Yet there they all unite." When Melville wrote, New York was a city of ships, hemmed by masts and ever conscious of the salty lick of the sea at the end of every short crosstown street.

MARSHALL B. DAVIDSON

Life in America, 1951

THE BATTERY AND NEW YORK HARBOR

BAGGAGE INSPECTION BY CUSTOM HOUSE OFFICIALS

The returning traveler, after making his European "grand tour," was often treated with indignities— sufficient to discourage future trips abroad

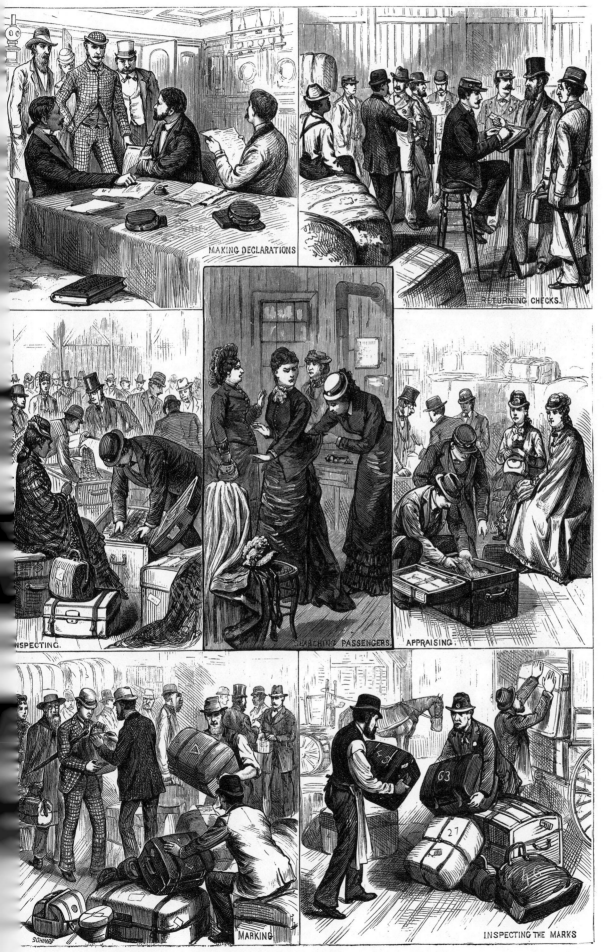

NEW YORK CITY—TRAVELERS FACE THE TERRORS OF CUSTOM INSPECTION

The hordes of immigrants entering the New York port area, the main point for almost 90 per cent of European travelers, taxed the customs inspectors to irritable degrees. It has been estimated that between 1880 and 1884 some two million people headed for the United States. During the mid-year months of greatest activity, there were weeks when well over 15,000 were handled on Ellis Island, in New York harbor. Customs officials, in their processing on the docks, had to bear the brunt of this wild disorder, as resultant scenes of confusion with disgruntled passengers were commonplace. Generally, arrivals fell into four main categories: 1) immigrants, who made up the vast majority; 2) commercial travelers with interests abroad; 3) returnees, those who had come a few years before and made return visits to the homeland; 4) the wealthy, whose European junkets meant the Grand Tour and profligate spending. Inspectors were alerted to spot contraband carried by immigrants, and this meant minute inspection of clothes and personal effects. Temper flare-ups were frequent when zealous inspectors pried into every nook and cranny of trunks and carpetbags stuffed with assorted belongings.

CLARENCE P. HORNUNG

The Way It Was: New York, 1850-1890

Shocking conditions prevailing in New York's tenement slums, prompted Charles Dickens, on his 1842 visit, to observe: "Debauchery has made the very houses old . . .

New York life among the poor has one central distinguishing feature—namely, the fact that all live in tenements or in houses built on much the same principle. This principle is about as bad as it can possibly be. In the typical tenement house the staircase passes up a well in the centre of the house. It has no light from the open air, no ventilation; it is absolutely dark at midday, except for such glasses over the doors of the flats, and possibly from a skylight at the top of the house. It is a well for all the noxious gases to accumulate in; it cannot be aired; the rays of the sun never penetrate to it; in the worst houses it is foul with the coming and going of the innumerable denizens of the tenements. On its steps play the pale, unhealthy children who even allowing for the enormous death rate, still swarm in these horrible dwellings. Can a more frightfully unwholesome system be imagined? Yet this is not the worst. The tenements, opening in flats off these stairs, may be constituted of more or fewer rooms, but as a rule the bedrooms never have direct access to the open air. They open into the living rooms, and their windows open on to the stairs, so that not alone can the bedrooms never be properly aired, but they are so constructed that they receive all the impure gases that accumulate in the central well.

CHARLOTTE G. O'BRIEN

The Emigrant in New York,
1884

TENEMENT LIFE IN "BOTTLE ALLEY"

" . . . as though the world of vice and misery had nothing else to show . . . all that is loathesome, drooping and decayed is here"

IN THE TENEMENTS OF NEW YORK

This is the place, these the narrow ways diverging to the left and right, and reeking everywhere with dirt and filth. Such lives are led here, bear the same fruit here, as elsewhere. The coarse and bloated faces at the doors have counterparts at home and all the world over. Debauchery has made the very houses old...Open the door of one of these cramped hutches full of sleeping Negroes. Bah! They have a charcoal fire within, there is a smell of singeing clothes on flesh, so close they gather round the brazier; and vapours issue forth that blind and suffocate. From every quarter, as you glance about in these dark streets, some figure crawls half-awakened, as if the judgment hour were near at hand, and every obscure grave were giving up its dead. Where dogs would howl to lie, men and women and boys slink off to sleep, forcing the dislodged rats to move away in quest of better lodgings. Here, too, are lanes and alleys paved with mud knee-deep; underground chambers where they dance and game; the walls bedecked with rough designs of ships, of forts, and flags, and American Eagles out of number; ruined houses, open to the street, whence through wide gaps in the walls other ruins loom upon the eyes, as though the world of vice and misery had nothing else to show...all that is loathesome, drooping and decayed is here.

CHARLES DICKENS
American Notes, 1842

Every day was market day, as fish and fowl, meats and produce to feed Manhattan's huge population were trucked in from upstate farms and New Jersey to Washington Market

Washington Market on the lower West Side waterfront was the scene of bedlam, of struggling masses, carts and drays tangled together, and the cacophony of shouts and sounds creating a din that was indescribable. It was the largest point of entry for fish and fowl, meats and produce, that poured in from across the river daily to provision a hungry city. Established on this site since 1813, it replaced the original Bear market. During the dark hours of early morning the heavily laden wagons arrived by nearby ferry from Jersey, choking the thoroughfares for blocks around. A fee of twenty-five cents was charged each waggoner, but many avoided the payment due the clerk of the market. As reported in *Harper's Weekly:* "The tax is often exacted at the expense of ugly language freely spilt by the elusive brutes who man the trucks. They have to be pursued in many cases into the lowest dives before the reluctant quarter satisfies the toll. When the waggoner cheats the city it costs his employer nothing and means drink-money." The entire market site has been cleared only within the last decade.

CLARENCE P. HORNUNG
The Way It Was:
New York, 1850-1890

WASHINGTON MARKET ON THE WEST SIDE, NEW YORK

On the same site since 1813, when the Bear Market was superseded by the vast complex of stalls and sheds, divided into many irregular lanes and alleys

The reportorial talents of the magazine illustrators were often at their best when called upon to depict a scene of melee and confusion. While the early photographer had to set his cumbersome box camera and tripod at a given spot and then hope for a lucky moment, the artist, employing his best judgment, could arrange his people and setting for the composition that best told his story. Only through the artist's innate sense of journalism could such a scene be made available to the public. His drawing was then transcribed onto a block of wood for an engraver (in this case Lagarde) to prepare for printing in the illustrated weeklies. Their vast circulation reached out to every corner of the country, the only medium of communication then available to all. There was a popular song of the day: "He went to the Washington Market one day, And there he stole a big ham. He got three months in the penitentiary, Along with the rest of the gang."

CLARENCE P. HORNUNG

The Way It Was:
New York, 1850-1890

The huge railroad depot for Commodore Vanderbilt's New York Central, at Forty-second Street, became the focus for elevated and horsecar surface lines

One of the most imposing buildings in the city is the new Grand Central Depot, on Forty-second Street and Fourth Avenue. It was projected by Commodore Vanderbilt and ground was broken for it on the 15th of November, 1869; it was ready for occupancy by October 9th, 1871. The depot is constructed of red brick, a mansard roof, with iron trimmings painted white, in imitation of marble. The south front is adorned with three and the west front with two massive pavilions. The central pavilion of each front contains an illuminated clock. The entire building is 696 feet long and 240 feet wide. The train shed is 610 feet long, and 200 feet wide, and is covered with an immense circular roof of iron and glass. The principal entrance is on Forty-second Street. There are included accommodations for offices, waiting rooms, baggage rooms, etc. The Hudson River and New York Central using the depot are the only lines entering the city, and they are provided with a common terminus in the very heart of the metropolis. About eighty trains enter and depart from this depot every day. The running of these is regulated by the depot-master, who occupies an elevated position at the north end of the car-house, from which he can see the tracks for several miles. A system of automatic signals governs the running of the trains through the city.

JAMES D. MC CABE

*Lights and Shadows of
New York Life, 1872*

GRAND CENTRAL STATION

OUTSIDE GRAND CENTRAL STATION, NEW YORK

Following the terminal's opening, in 1871, intensive building in nearby upper East Side sections resulted in development of residential and business properties

ELEVATED RAILROAD, NEW YORK

INTERIOR—GRAND CENTRAL STATION

In the 'seventies, elevated railroads were built; and for miles and miles, on each side of these ill-designed iron ways, which contrasted so unfavorably with those Berlin built only slightly later, tenement houses were planted. Thousands of people lived under the shadow of the elevated, with the smoke of the old-fashioned locomotives puffing into their windows, with the clank and rattle causing them to shout in daily conversation to overcome the roar outside. The obliviousness to low sounds, the indifference to cacophony which makes the ideal radio listener of present-day America, was part of the original acquisition of Manhattan in the Brown Decades. This torment of noise-troubled sleep, lowered the waking efficiency, depleted vitality; but it was endured as if it were an irremediable fact of nature. In the lull of the elevated's thunder, the occasional tinkle of the cowbells of the ragman on a side street, or the solemn *I-l-l-l cas'clo's* of the second-hand clothing buyer, would have an almost pastoral touch; while *Carmen,* on an Italian's clanking hand organ, could splash the sky with color.

LEWIS MUMFORD

The Metropolitan Milieu,

1934

New York was the nation's financial capital, and Wall Street its very citadel, where fortunes ebbed and flowed with daily fluctuations of the economy . . .

Here is the building of the New York Stock Exchange, which has an ornate, pillared facade on Broad Street. The Stock Exchange is the financial heart of the nation, and it has transformed trading into a science. It is the direct descendant of a group of men who met daily under an old buttonwood tree on Wall Street to trade in securities.... Trading on the Exchange today is a highly formalized, complicated activity. To become a member, one has to buy a 'seat'—probably the most costly chair in the world, since it has no physical existence. The main trading floor is a huge, domed hall, with a grove of 'trading posts' which are a modern equivalent for buttonwood trees. From the visitors' gallery, the floor makes a bewildering impression. Men are running about without apparent direction. Clacking noises issue from two great call boards at the north and south ends of the hall. There is a constant flashing of ticker tape on large screens, recording the latest transactions. Every company listing its securities on the Exchange receives a coded designation, and to read the ticker you have to master the Exchange's codebook.

GENE M. BROWN

Wall Street: Men and Money, 1952

NEW YORK STOCK EXCHANGE

. . . creating cyclical disturbances that threw traders into a wild panic of disorderly selling whenever bad news broke on the ticker

WALL STREET—SCENES DURING A PANIC

The narrow canyon of Wall Street was ill prepared to handle the huge crowds and traffic that accumulated during periods of sudden stress on the securities market. When the news circulated that commodity values were plunging, thousands of brokers and bankers as well as the frenzied citizenry descended upon the financial houses to learn of their fate. Caught up in the milling throngs were the horsedrawn omnibuses that turned off Broadway at Trinity Church to make their way through the street. The favorite vantage point, as always, for viewing the tumult, was the steps of the Sub-Treasury Building as crowds hovered around the statue of Washington. On this very site (now called Federal Hall) stood the first seat of the United States Government. From its steps the Declaration of Independence was first read to New Yorkers, and from its balcony George Washington took his oath of office when inaugurated as the country's first president, in 1789. The huge bronze statue was the work of John Q.A. Ward, who modeled this likeness from portraits by Gilbert Stuart and the head by Jean Antoine Houdon. It was unveiled in 1883, just a year before the tumultuous scene depicted herewith.

CLARENCE P. HORNUNG

The Way It Was: New York, 1850-1890

The great blizzard of 1888 set memorable records for second-story-high snow drifts, ice-covered power lines, and disrupted traffic conditions . . .

Walls of snow blocked all the streets west of Seventh Avenue. Traffic halted. Horse-drawn streetcars bogged down, and although first four horses, then six horses, and finally eight horses were hitched to one car, the cars couldn't be budged. Steam trains were immobilized in the suburbs, some plowing to a stop in a deep railroad cut at Spuyten Duyvil just north of the city limits. A New York Central locomotive tried to butt through snow packed in the Fourth Avenue tunnel, only to topple off its rails. Some idiot asked Chauncey M. Depew, president of the New York Central, if the line could maintain its train service. Depew snorted, 'Trains! Why, we don't even know whether we've got a railroad left!' Vehicular traffic on the Brooklyn Bridge was halted, and police warned pedestrians not to walk across in the shrieking storm. Now Brooklyn was entirely cut off from Manhattan. After various adventures, ferryboats gave up trying to reach Manhattan; thus, Staten Island and New Jersey almost became inaccessible. A few brave and greedy cabdrivers still slogged through the streets. Some poured whiskey into their horses to keep them from freezing to death, and the price of a cab ride rose to thirty dollars, then forty dollars, and ultimately to more than fifty dollars.

EDWARD ROBB ELLIS

The Epic of New York City,
1966

DURING NEW YORK'S BLIZZARD

. . . as scenes of citywide devastation and misery proved so much grist for the mill of journalist and artist-reporter

NEW YORK CITY—SNOWBOUND IN 1888

There have been a good many tempestuous snow storms in New York since then, and certain statistics have been referred to by wiseacres, in the way of inches of snowfall and velocity of wind in subsequent storms to at least rival if not surpass that classic hurricane, but nothing that New York has experienced since has been a marker to it in spectacular devastation. Some of its details are worth recalling. The Staten Island ferryboats had their flagstaffs snapped off the instant they put out their noses in the morning. A Sixth Avenue elevated train loaded with passengers consumed six hours and twenty minutes in covering a distance of two blocks. Many of the passengers effected their escape after hours of waiting by means of a ladder reared against the 'L' structure by private enterprise. It cost fifty cents a head to go down the ladder into the comparative freedom of the blizzard and the drifts. The electric lights had failed and the great thoroughfare was in total darkness. Mr. Barremore, a merchant, was found dead of cold and exhaustion the next morning, within four blocks of his home.

HENRY COLLINS BROWN, ED.
Valentine's Manual of Old New York, 1926

Not all of winter's vicissitudes brought the blizzard's terrors, as seen in this pleasant setting in Central Park, recalling the delights of sleighing . . .

Snow laid in our streets for a long time in these days and every vehicle took to runners. The uptown drives and Central Park were alive with sleigh riders. In the early morning and all through the forenoon happy fathers might have been seen taking an airing behind the staid family horse, harnessed to the family sleigh. The fair young lady with the bang-tailed pony, russet harness and 'natty' cutter was also noticeable. The 'swell' young man with his Russian drosky drawn by three horses decorated with red plumes was the observed of all observers, while the fashionable man reclined lazily in the regulation sleigh with the English 'tiger' drawing the lines over the prancing steeds. In the afternoon and evening the butcher, the baker, and all kinds of tradesmen who possessed horses that worked through the working days helped make the holiday gathering. The proprietors of the road houses were joyous, and as they went to bed with the prospect of a continued run of sleighing, they dreamed of fortunes that the best of modern Utopias could not hope to realize.

HENRY COLLINS BROWN, ED.

Valentine's Manual of Old New York, 1926

SLEIGHING IN NEW YORK'S CENTRAL PARK

. . . in horse-drawn cutters, to the tinkling tune
of sleighbells and bright laughter, as sleighs pass
near Daniel Webster's statue and the Dakota apartments

Authors William Cullen Bryant and Washington Irving, and public servant Andrew Green—called "Central Park's Godfather"—who met with a group of concerned citizens . . .

To the park, accordingly, and to the Park only, hitherto, the aesthetic appetite has had to address itself, and the place has therefore borne the brunt of many a peremptory call, acting out year after year the character of the cheerful, capable, bustling, even if overworked, hostess of the one inn, somewhere, who has to take all the travel, who is often at her wits' end to know how to deal with it, but who, none the less, has, for the honor of the home, never once failed of hospitality. It has had to have something for everybody, since everybody arrives famished; it has had to multiply itself to extravagance, to pathetic little efforts of exaggeration and deception, to be, breathlessly, everywhere and everything at once, and produce on the spot the particular romantic object demanded, lake or river or cataract, wild woodland or teeming garden, boundless vista or bosky nook, noble eminence or smiling valley.... You are perfectly aware, as you hang about her in May and June, that you *have,* as a travelled person, beheld more scenery and communed with nature in ampler or fairer forms; but it is quite equally definite to you that none of those adventures have counted more to you for experience, for stirred sensibility—inasmuch as you can be, at the best, and in the showiest countries, only thrilled by the pastoral or the awful, and as to pass, in New York, from the discipline of the streets to this so different many-smiling presence is to be thrilled at every turn.

HENRY JAMES

The American Scene, 1907

SCENES IN CENTRAL PARK

. . . are to be credited with urging the city fathers "to create a park and playground for family picnic parties and gregarious pleasures for the enjoyment of all"

THE DRIVE IN CENTRAL PARK AT FOUR O'CLOCK

THE CHILDREN'S SWINGS—CENTRAL PARK

The best place to see the driving is at a point not far from the Egyptian obelisk which the Khedive gave us some years ago. . . . As the tide of dissatisfied and weary wealth rolls by its base here, in the fantastic variety of its equipages, does the needle discern so much difference between their occupants and the occupants of the chariots that swept beneath it in the capital of the Ptolemies two thousand years ago? . . . . They pass in all kinds of vehicles, and there are all kinds of people in them, though at times there are no people at all, as when the servants have been sent out to exercise the horses. . . . A gentleman driving a pair, abreast or tandem, with a groom on the rumble, for no purpose except to express his quality, is a common sight enough; and sometimes you see a lady illustrating her consequence in like manner. A lady driving, while a gentleman occupies the seat behind her, is a sight which always affects me like the sight of a man taking a woman's arm in walking, as the man of an underbred sort is apt to do. . . . But these stylish turnouts form only a part of the spectacle in the Park driveways. . . . There are family carryalls, with friendly-looking families, old and young, getting the good of the Park together in a long, leisurely jog; and open buggies with yellow wheels and raffish men in them behind their widespread trotters. . . .

WILLIAM DEAN HOWELLS
Impressions and Experiences, 1896

*New Yorkers could avail themselves of many excursion lines
for daily trips to seashore resorts and trips up the Hudson
to Albany, or coastal steamers to points north and south*

Such was the growing popularity of Coney Island that it became necessary to schedule regular sailings from downtown Manhattan to reach the beaches of Coney and West Brighton. The new Iron Pier extended out into deep water, and was several hundred feet long. Now, the Iron Steamboat Line could disgorge its weekend crowds as they poured in by the thousands. "For one end of Coney Island had been transformed into the most pretentious of Atlantic watering places, and the other end had been made into a popular amusement park. You could go down to Coney by railroad, from Brooklyn, or take a steamboat at the Battery and sail down the harbor. Prosperous New Yorkers who formerly sent their families, for the summer, to Long Branch and joined them only over week-ends, were now able to have their nights at the shore and return to the city, every day, refreshed for business. The splendid new resort had been brought within an hour's journey of New York. Manhattan Beach, at the far eastern end of the Island, was the most exclusive and expensive section of the resort. Two enormous, ornate wooden hotels—the Manhattan Beach and the Oriental—had broad piazzas that looked, over lawns and flowerbeds, to the beach and the sea...."

LLOYD MORRIS
Incredible New York, 1951

THE SUMMER EXODUS—LEAVING BY STEAMBOAT

CONEY ISLAND EXCURSIONISTS

By far the most popular trip, from lower Manhattan, was the hour-long ride to Coney Island, which boasted amusements and attractions for every taste

ON THE BEACH, CONEY ISLAND

Coney Island, the American Brighton, grew in popularity as the city increased in size and congestion in the seventies. On a hot Sunday, half a million people (making a 'carpet of heads') might crowd its wide stretch of sand in a few hours, a traveler of 1887 reported in the London *Times*. "They spread over the four miles of sand strip, with...bands of music...in full blast; countless vehicles moving; all the miniature theatres, minstrel shows, merry-go-rounds, Punch and Judy enterprises, fat women, big snakes, giant, dwarf, and midget exhibits, circuses and menageries, swings, flying horses, and fortune telling shops open; and everywhere a dense but good-humored crowd, sightseeing, drinking beer, and swallowing 'clam chowder.' " Fireworks enlivened the scene at night until time to go home, when 'the swelling torrents of humanity,' flowing out upon station and pier, emphasized the 'vast magnitude of a Coney Island Sunday.' While the 'masses' frequented Coney Island, the 'classes,' in this city of increasing contrast, spent a more extended 'season' at such resorts for the wealthy as Long Branch, New Jersey, and Newport, Rhode Island.

BAYRD STILL

Mirror for Gotham, 1956

To celebrate the centennial of our independence, in 1876, and the opening of the Brooklyn Bridge, in 1883, New Yorkers were treated to unforgettable fireworks displays

As a young lad, Frank Weitenkampf recalls, in his *Manhattan Kaleidoscope,* "being awestruck by the pyrotechnic displays in Tompkins Square, in the seventies, the chief set piece being a heroic-size equestrian portrait of George Washington." On other occasions "Pyrotechnic spectacles, notably those staged by Henry J. Pain at Manhattan Beach from 1879 on. In a promotional brochure issued at a later date, Pain describes his shows as 'brilliant and spectacular.' Among his most memorable shows were those commemorating the Centennial Exhibition, in 1876, and especially a most elaborate spectacle staged for the opening of the Brooklyn Bridge, in 1883. Later, his repertoire included *The Last Days of Pompeii* (1886), *The Burning of Moscow* (1886), *Sebastopol* (1887), *The Eruption of Vesuvius* and others."

CLARENCE P. HORNUNG

*The Way It Was:
New York, 1850-1890*

CENTENNIAL CELEBRATION, UNION SQUARE, NEW YORK

CELEBRATING THE OPENING OF THE BROOKLYN BRIDGE IN 1883

On Long Island...New York Reaches Out to Sea

MONTAUK POINT . . . BROOKLYN BRIDGE

. . . NEW YORK HARBOR . . . FULTON

STREET FERRY . . . PROSPECT PARK . . .

BROOKLYN SCENES . . . EASTERN LONG

ISLAND . . . SAG HARBOR . . . SHELTER

ISLAND . . . EAST HAMPTON WINDMILLS

. . . "HOME, SWEET HOME" COTTAGE

MONTAUK POINT

On Long Island... New York Reaches Out to Sea

Fɴᴏᴍ ᴛʜᴇ ʜᴇᴀᴠɪʟʏ ɪɴᴅᴜꜱᴛʀɪᴀʟɪᴢᴇᴅ city of Brooklyn on its western end, to Montauk Point of spacious dude ranches and sprawling white beaches at the extreme edge of its easternmost peninsula, Long Island is a fascinating diversity of large and small towns, elegant estates and country houses, modest farms, horse and cattle ranches, great poultry farms, and glamorous seaside resorts.

Long before the arrival of white settlers, Indians occupied the island. Both Dutch and English colonies had sprung up in several localities when, in 1664, the English gained control. Hollanders and Walloons had settled near Gowanus Bay, followed by Dutch farmers, who established the hamlet of *Breucklen*. Under the English, this became Brooklyn—chartered as a village in 1816, as a city in 1834. When Brooklyn absorbed Williamsburg in 1855, it was the third largest city in the United States. Taking in Flatbush, Utrecht, Gravesend—until it occupied all of Kings County—Brooklyn became a borough of

New York City in 1898. With the huge market of New York, the building of railways and highways, Brooklyn attracted a great influx of residents. Variously referred to as the "City of Homes," the "City of Churches," Brooklyn also is often called New York's "dormitory." Those who know Brooklyn praise its handsome streets, beautiful Prospect Park, its fascinating views of ocean, sound, and harbor, as well as the excellence and extent of its educational institutions. The noteworthy *Brooklyn Daily Eagle,* founded in 1841, had Walt Whitman as editor in 1846-1847. Long Island is notable for summer resorts on both shores—richly wooded on the north, and long, smooth beaches on the south. Jones Beach, one of the two state parks, is a favorite of thousands.

Many evidences of Long Island's history remain: the Protestant Dutch Reformed Church in Flatbush, built in 1654, restored in 1786; the Lefferts homestead, erected in 1777; the home of the author of *"Home, Sweet Home,"* John Howard Payne, who, like the famous preacher, Henry Ward Beecher, lived in East Hampton. Readers of *Picturesque America,* in the mid-1800s, learned of Sag Harbor's whaling days: "When Sag Harbor was first settled [1730], whales were common visitors to its shores . . . When the land was first purchased from the Indians, the sachems were allowed, by the terms of the purchase, to fish in all the creeks and ponds, hunt in the woods, and to have the 'finnes' and 'tayles' of all whales caught on the coast."

Granting that Sag Harbor is old, quaint, the article continues:

"But Sag Harbor has a measure of newness by the side of East Hampton, the most easterly town on Long Island. This township was settled in 1649, by thirty families from Lynn and adjacent towns in Massachusetts. The land was purchased from the famous Montauk tribe. This part of the country does not seem to have the bloody Indian record of so many other selections . . . Instead of making the red man their determined enemy, measures seem to have been taken to secure his kindly cooperation; and the remainder of the ancient tribe now upon the island, fishing in the same seas and hunting on the same ground as their fathers did,

bear witness to the forethought and humanity of the first settlers of this region . . . East Hampton has just one wide street, nearly three hundred feet wide. There are no hotels, no shops, no manufactures. The residences are principally farmers' houses, congregated in a village after the French method, with their farms stretching to the ocean shore on one side, and to the pine plains that lie between the town and the bay on the other. Perhaps no town in America retains so nearly the primitive habits, tastes, and ideas of our forefathers. It is rapidly becoming a favorite summer resort, visitors finding no accommodation save that offered by private families."

East Hampton and Southampton—on the southern fork of Long Island—from the viewpoint of more than two centuries, regarded Greenport—on the north fork—dating only from 1827, as a newcomer. Greenport, however, the terminus of the Long Island Railroad, had the aspect of an ideal New England village, green and quiet.

At Orient Point a summer hotel attracted many vacationers. With the Sound on one side, the Bay on the other, there was an incessant pageant of steamers, sailing vessels, fishing boats, yachts, and smaller pleasure craft, plus the incomparable ocean air!

From East Hampton, the road to the sandy cliffs of Montauk Point follows the shore. The gentle, grass-grown hills offered lush grazing for the herds of sheep and cattle pastured there. Sunken in the sands, wrecks of ships continue as gruesome reminders of the sea's toll in wild weather. At the edge of the land, where the tumultuous Atlantic sweeps in unbroken force, stands Montauk lighthouse, built in 1795.

Eastern Long Island, with its vast bays and surrounding seas, is noted for its fisheries: bluefish, mackerel, and a small fish called the mossbunker, or the menhaden or bonyfish. This fish, less than a pound in weight—comparable in size to a whale as a fly is to a bull—was valued for its oil and caught in seines along the shore in enormous quantities. Often a single haul netted a million fish, which yielded fifteen hundred gallons of oil, in days untroubled by the search for sources of energy.

Ample waterways at the western tip of Long Island—"the oceanic amplitude," according to Walt Whitman—made Brooklyn an extension of the port of New York

Brooklyn Heights itself is a window on the port. Here, where the perspective is fixed by the towers of Manhattan and the hills of New Jersey and Staten Island, the channels running between seem fingers of the world ocean. Here one can easily embrace the suggestion, which Whitman felt so easily, that the whole American world opens out from here, north and west. It is no accident that the four remarkable men who found here the richest symbols of their lives—Whitman and Hart Crane, the poets, John and Washington Roebling, the bridge-builders—should have been stirred so deeply by it to the epic sense.

ALFRED KAZIN
Brooklyn Bridge, 1946

SEA-BEAUTY! stretch'd and basking!
One side thy inland ocean laving, broad, with copious
    commerce, steamers, sails,
And one the Atlantic's wind caressing, fierce or gentle
    —mighty hulls dark-gliding in the distance,
Isles of sweet brooks of drinking-water
    —healthy air and soil!
Isle of the salty shore and breeze and brine!

NEW YORK HARBOR, FROM A BROOKLYN BRIDGE TOWER, UNDER CONSTRUCTION

FULTON STREET, FROM THE FERRY, BROOKLYN

The city's real growth developed from the seemingly limitless land areas . . . a series of separate villages: Flatlands, Flatbush, New Utrecht, Gravesend, and Bushwick

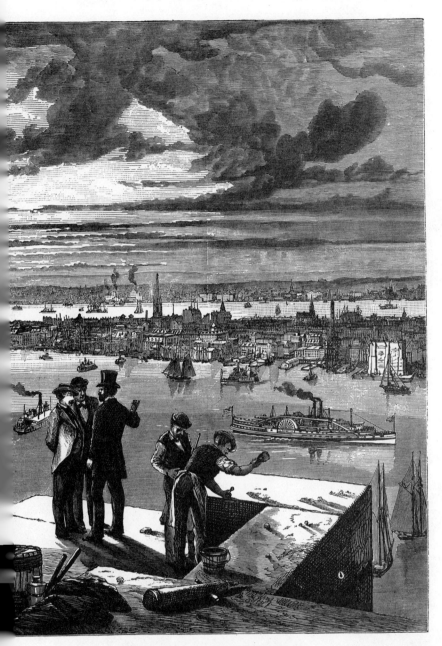

Manhattan is the nub of the city and the smallest of its five boroughs. Within its tight confines buildings must go skyward if they go anywhere. It is possible to live on this narrow island, hemmed in and buffered by brick and mortar, and remain unaware of the lick of the tide at the ends of the short cross-town streets, not to realize the immensity of the ocean traffic that on every tide swarms about its fringe of docks. But it is also possible, and infinitely more rewarding, to view from the tops of its taller buildings one of the largest natural harbors in the world and to note how the tip of lower Manhattan reaches into the upper end of the harbor like a beckoning finger to the commerce of the world; a summons, it might be added, that is heeded by more than twelve thousand ocean-going vessels in any one year. New York is a seaborne city, split into islands and parts of islands by salty currents that run in all directions, sometimes contradicting one another in angry patches of water, as they do at Hell Gate where the tides meet in a sort of syncopated rhythm.

MARSHALL B. DAVIDSON
New York, from
Romance of North America, 1958

I STAND as on some mighty eagle's beak,
Eastward the sea absorbing, viewing,
   (nothing but sea and sky,)
The tossing waves, the foam, the ships in the distance,
The wild unrest, the snowy curling caps—that inbound
   urge and urge of waves,
Seeking the shores forever.

WALT WHITMAN
from *Montauk Point*

FULTON FERRY SLIP, BROOKLYN

Unlike densely populated downtown Manhattan, Brooklyn offered sylvan solitude—"a city of cottages and villas . . . among cultivated fields and miniature groves"

Brooklyn, in a dignified way, is a fantastic place. The street where I live has a quietness and sense of permanence that seem to belong to the nineteenth century. The street is very short. At one end, there are comfortable old houses, with gracious facades and pleasant backyards in the rear. Down on the next block, the street becomes more heterogeneous, for there is a fire station; a convent; and a small candy factory. The street is bordered with maple trees, and in the autumn the children rake up the leaves and make bonfires in the gutter. It is strange in New York to find yourself living in a real neighborhood. I buy my coal from the man who lives next-door. And I am very curious about the old lady living on my right. Comparing the Brooklyn that I know with Manhattan is like comparing a comfortable and complacent duenna to her more brilliant and neurotic sister. Things move more slowly out here (the street-cars still rattle leisurely down most of the main streets), and there is a feeling for tradition.

CARSON MC CULLERS

Brooklyn Is My Neighborhood, 1941

BROOKLYN STREET SCENES

Brooklyn's civic consciousness and Manhattan's fine example led to the creation of Prospect Park—"to lay out a public garden and parade ground for the city of Brooklyn"

PROSPECT PARK, BROOKLYN

A park fairly well managed near a large town, will surely become a new centre of that town. With the determination of location, size, and boundaries should therefore be associated the duty of arranging new trunk routes of communication between it and the distant parts of the town existing and forecasted. These may be either narrow informal elongations of the park, varying say from two to five hundred feet in width, and radiating irregularly from it, or if, unfortunately, the town is already laid out in the unhappy way that New York and Brooklyn, San Francisco and Chicago, are, and, I am glad to say, Boston is not, on a plan made long years ago by a man who never saw a spring-carriage, and who had a conscientious dread of the Graces, then we must probably adopt formal Park-ways. They should be so planned and constructed as never to be noisy and seldom crowded, and so also that the straightforward movement of pleasure-carriages need never be obstructed, unless at absolutely necessary crossings, by slow-going heavy vehicles used for commercial purposes. If possible, also, they should be branched or reticulated with other ways of a similar class, so that no part of the town should finally be many minutes' walk from some one of them.

FREDERICK OLMSTED

For 120 miles, out to Montauk Point, most of Long Island was low-lying farmland, valued and convenient source of produce for New York. Toward the north shore, rolling hills . . .

The broad beach,
Sea-wind and the sea's
  irregular rhythm,
Great dunes with their pale
  grass, and on the beach
Driftwood, tangle of
  bones, an occasional
  shell,
Now coarse, now carven
  and delicate—whorls of
  time
Stranded in space, deaf
  ears listening
To lost time, old oceanic
  secrets.
Along the water's edge,
  in pattern casual
As the pattern of the stars,
  the pin-pointed air-holes
Left by the sand-flea under
  the receding spume
Wink and blink out again.
  A gull drifts over,
Wide wings crucified
  against the sky—
His shadow travels the
  shore, upon its margins
You will find his signature:
  one long line,
Two shorter lines curving
  out from it, a nearly
Perfect graph of the bird
  himself in flight.
His footprint is his image
  fallen from heaven.

JOHN HALL WHEELOCK
Afternoon: Amagansett Beach

SCENES ON EASTERN LONG ISLAND

. . . marked the terrain which rose to a height of over 400 feet around Huntington. On the south shore, narrow strips of flatland and dunes bordered the sea for miles

SAG HARBOR

VIEW FROM WHITE HILL, SHELTER ISLAND

In its Golden Era, Sag Harbor had sixty-three vessels engaged in whaling, though meanwhile New Bedford had pulled far ahead of the other whaling ports. It has been estimated by Dr. E.P. Hohman that in 1847 there were about 900 whaling vessels in the entire world, of which the United States owned some 722, ships or barks, ranging from 200 to 500 tons. In that year New Bedford claimed 254; Nantucket, 75; New London, Connecticut, 70; and Sag Harbor, 62. Whale-oil was used for illumination and in the curing of leather; whale-bone was used in women's clothing (corsets, basques, hoop skirts, bodices, and hats), for the ribs of umbrellas, for carriage whips, and even (when scraped) for the stuffing of furniture. There was money in the business for the owners of ships and their captains.

HAROLD W. THOMPSON
Body, Boots & Britches, 1939

SHIPS'S GRAVEYARD

The Long Island countryside was so dotted with windmills that it took on the look of Holland. Many served as gristmills, others pumped water for irrigating farmlands and cranberry bogs

Herman Melville says in *Moby-Dick* that "islanders seem to make the best whale-men." It was certainly Paumanok, Isle of Shells, and the far eastern stretches of its one hundred and twenty miles that turned hardy English farmers into men renowned in song and legend. The Yorkshiremen who founded Southampton in 1640 and the Kentishmen who settled East Hampton in 1649 certainly came to Long Island with no thought of whale-oil and baleen; but the storms on the "south fluke" of the great eastern tail washed up leviathan, and the Shinnecock Indians could show the art of the wooden harpoons in off-shore fishery. When the Red Men sold East Hampton in 1648 for twenty coats, twenty-four hoes, and other goods, they specified that they were to have the "fynnes and tayles of all such whales as shall be cast up, and desire that they may be friendly dealt with in the other parte." I hope that they had their wish. It is evident that their skill was used to profit the whites, just as the Mohawks' craft in hunting was the source of Albany's wealth.

HAROLD W. THOMPSON

Body, Boots & Britches, 1939

GRIST WINDMILLS AT EAST HAMPTON

East Hampton's people love their traditions and cherished landmarks: Clinton Academy, the Mulford House, and especially John Howard Payne's "Home, Sweet Home"

HOME OF JOHN HOWARD PAYNE

PAYNE'S "HOME, SWEET HOME"

'Mid pleasures and palaces
  though we may roam,
Be it ever so humble, there's
  no place like home;
A charm from the skies seems
  to hallow us there,
Which sought through the world
  is ne'er met with elsewhere.
An exile from home splendour
  dazzles in vain,
Oh give me my lowly thatched
  cottage again;
The birds singing gayly, that
  came at my call,
Give me them, and that peace
  of mind dearer to all.

JOHN HOWARD PAYNE
Home, Sweet Home

The eastern end of the island has been described as the flukes of a whale, divided by Peconic Bay—with Shelter Island and Gardiner's Island blocking entrance to the open seas

The second whaling boom began on Long Island in the latter half of the Eighteenth Century. Close by East Hampton was the town of Sag Harbor caught in the crook of the sheltering arm of Gardiner's Bay, an ideal whaling port. Men began to drift over there from the Hamptons, and, with a fleet of three vessels, the *Good Luck, Dolphin,* and *Success,* Sag Harbor's fame as a whaling town began. Then in 1817 fire swept the entire town; hardly a store in the business section was left standing. Poor Sag Harbor, it seems to have had a troubled history. Sadly buffeted by the war, it was just beginning to reestablish itself when this disaster occurred. But "a whaler's life is one long gamble" and by 1820 the town was rebuilt and more vessels added to the fleet. By this time New Bedford, Mass., and New London, Conn., were rival whaling centers as well as Nantucket. For the next twenty-five years the industry flourished; Long Island whaling was at its height and great changes had come since the days when the whale watch had sounded his call from off the crest of the dunes." Instead of creeping along the stormy waters off Fire Island Beach, Sag Harbor whalers set out for a voyage that often encircled the globe. Sometimes, if luck was good, he came back in two years. More often, however, the time was three or more.

JACQUELINE OVERTON
Long Island's Story, 1929

LONG ISLAND FISHERMEN—"DIVIDING UP"

WHALING OFF LONG ISLAND

The Hudson ...
Renowned in History ...
Revered for Beauty

THE PALISADES . . .PEEKSKILL . . .

STORM KING . . .ANTHONY'S NOSE . . .

CROW'S NEST . . .LONG ISLAND . . .

WEST POINT . . .SLEEPY HOLLOW . . .

TARRYTOWN . . .BUTTERMILK FALLS . . .

THE WALLKILL . . .NEWBURG . . .

POUGHKEEPSIE . . .KINGSTON . . .THE

RONDOUT . . .ESOPUS CREEK . . .SCENES

IN THE CATSKILL MOUNTAINS . . .

CATSKILL FALLS . . .ON THE

HUDSON RIVER BOAT

THE PALISADES

The Hudson...
Renowned in History
Revered for Beauty

ANCIENT TRAIL OF THE INDIANS, path of the fur traders, highway of the Dutch and English settlers—the magnificent Hudson River is one of the great waterways of the world. One, also, of the most beautiful. Its origin is in Lake Tear of the Clouds, in the Adirondacks. Flowing generally south for over three hundred miles, it empties into the upper New York bay at New York City. As far north as Albany the waters are tidal, and navigable to that point for ocean-going vessels. At its mouth, in the vicinity of New York City, the Hudson is over 4,000 feet in width, serving as a boundary between New York and New Jersey. The George Washington Bridge, the Holland and Lincoln vehicular tunnels, a railway tunnel, the Hudson Tubes, and ferries connect the two states. Upriver, the next wide expanse of water is the Tappan Zee, in the

Sleepy Hollow country where, according to Washington Irving, the Headless Horseman rides, and Rip Van Winkle awakes from his long sleep. Here, on the west shore, the New Jersey side, are the majestic palisades, which enhance the Hudson's beauty. The Storm King Highway, passing the United States Military Academy at West Point, affords breath-taking views of the Hudson far below. The Catskill Mountains to the north send fascinating reflections over the river valley. On the east shore, the Roosevelt estate on Hyde Park and other mansions share glorious river views. In its upper reaches there are falls that supply water power. Parts of the New York State barge canal unite the Hudson with the Great Lakes, and with Lake Champlain and the St. Lawrence River.

A delightful way to appreciate the Hudson's beauty is to start near the highlands, at Poughkeepsie. Here the river's course is a broad expanse for more than twenty miles, its northern point Crom Elbow—the *Krum Elleboge* of the early Dutch. Its southern extremity is Newburg. Washington's headquarters were nearby, during some of the stormiest days of the Revolution. On the east bank, about two miles below the town, was the home of Samuel Morse, of telegraph fame. A mile or so beyond, the blacksmith Theophilis Antony, lived. It was he who forged the great chain that formerly guarded the Hudson at Fort Montgomery. Newburg presents some of the most spectacular views of the Hudson—preparatory to the even grander aspects ahead. The old toll road runs along the western bank of the river, within the highlands, alongside the glorious peaks of Storm King and Crow's Nest and their everchanging beauty in sunlight and shadow. Just beyond, on a bold promontory jutting into the river—a spot often called the Hudson's most perfect—is West Point. The steep shore rises to form sharp precipices and rough terraces, between which are smooth cliffs where the names of famous victories have been chiseled. West Point was one of the country's most important military posts during the American Revolution, commanding the entrance to the upper Hudson. It served as a deposit for munitions and quartered troops within its fortifications, to be sent to various fields of the war. Here, from Gee's Point to Constitution Island (not now surrounded by water), the mighty chain made by the neighboring blacksmith was stretched.

The importance of West Point to the young colonies made the magnitude of Benedict Arnold's treason all the more shocking. This brilliant officer, one of the heroes of Fort Ticonderoga, once the commander of the revolutionary forces at Philadelphia, later the commandant at West Point, had been passed over by congress, despite Washington's protests, and others promoted above him. Did he turn traitor for this reason? The visitor to the Point may remember the history books—how Arnold's plans went awry, how he fled, later living in England and in Canada, and provoking Washington's tragic comment: "Whom now can we trust?"

As Storm King dominates the northern highlands, Anthony's Nose is the chief peak in the southern group, descending sharply into the river at one of the most perfect bends in its course. The promontory juts out into the stream so boldly that it seems to close the channel, and it is said that Henry Hudson thought for a time that his progress was brought to a close, and that the "arm of the sea," up which he assumed he was sailing, had ended here among the hills.

As we reach the quieter aspects of the Hudson valley, on the western shore, near Haverstraw, the enormous escarpments of the palisades appear, a natural barrier between the river and the fertile farms beyond it. The palisades, cut by deep and narrow ravines, show through their fissures exquisite views of river and land. The west and east shores present the widest contrasts: on the west, quiet farming country; on the eastern shore, every kind of dwelling, from great country estates to the smallest suburban cottage, where occupants spend the greater part of their days "in town." All over the Hudson's banks, from Newburg to New York, there are clustered villages and little cities. To the south, the river flows in a broader stream until, on the eastern side, the city begins. The river now changes its aspect and passes between crowded shores that send across it the thunder of their busy life. At the palisades, long reaches of tranquil stream come to an end, as the Hudson sweeps grandly and smoothly into the sea.

The voyage of the *Experiment* had immediate results. It popularized the Hudson River sloop as no other agency could have done. Hundreds of the single-stickers with big mainsails dotted the river throughout the first fifty years of the nineteenth century. Many of them were famous for their furnishings, their size, their achievements. Around 1795 Captain Andrew Brink built the "very large and splendid" *Maria,* which for many years carried passengers and cargo from Livingston Manor and the upriver towns. The *John Jay* was her Poughkeepsie rival. Among the first of the distinguished upriver families to own their own sloop were the De Windts who had made their money out of a sugar plantation in the Virgin Islands. The *Caroline,* named after the daughter who married the famous landscape architect Andrew Jackson Downing, performed many errands for the new aristocracy of Fishkill.

CARL CARMER
The Hudson, 1939

THE HUDSON, NEAR PEEKSKILL

STORM KING AND CROW'S NEST

Though lacking in castles and ruins, America's "Great River of the Mountains" compares favorably with Germany's glorious Rhine

The Hudson, however, is larger and grander. It is not to be devoured in detail. No region without association, is, except by science. But its spacious and stately character, its varied and magnificent outline, from the Palisades to the Catskill, are as epical as the loveliness of the Rhine is lyrical. The Hudson implies a continent behind. For vineyards it has forests. For a belt of water, a majestic stream. For graceful and grain-goldened heights it has imposing mountains. There is no littleness about the Hudson, but there is in the Rhine. Here every thing is boldly touched. What lucid and penetrant lights, what broad and sober shadows! The river moistens the feet, and the clouds anoint the heads, of regal hills.

ANTHONY'S NOSE, FROM IONA ISLAND

Of all our rivers that I know, the Hudson, with this grandeur, has the most exquisite episodes. Its morning and evening reaches are like the lakes of dreams. Looking from this garden, at twilight, toward the huge hills, enameled with soft darkness, that guard the entrance of the Highlands, near West Point, I "would be a merman bold," to float on the last ray through that mysterious gate to the softest shadow in Cro' Nest, where, if *I were* a merman gold, I should know the culprit fay was sleeping. Out of that dim portal glide the white sails of sloops, like spectres; they loiter languidly along the bases of the hills, as the evening breeze runs after them, enamored, and they fly, taking my fascinated eyes captive, far and far away, until they glimmer like ghosts and strand my sight upon the distance.

GEORGE WILLIAM CURTIS

Lotus-Eating: A Summer Book, 1852

AT THE FOOT OF THE PALISADES

At West Point, the majestic Hudson winds its way through gaps between towering heads, following the mighty channels of the highlands . . .

Rounding Dunderberg and reaching out again for three miles northwest we run, on the east side, close under Anthony's Nose, not at all disagreeable but certainly massive and Roman. Here, at Fort Montgomery (west), we reach the end of the first section of the Hudson Highlands, and now run but little east for north for six miles to West Point (west side). Both banks are very lofty, and midway of this stretch, Sugarloaf Hill stands (east). At Highland Falls (west), we reach the point where the land traveler must swing away from the river, unless he can gain favor with West Point officials. Garrison, on the east, is the point of departure of a ferry to West Point. The termination of this ferry under the bastions of the military school is the most striking American view to remind us of the Old World and its castles, especially since the rising grade through the tremendous gateway suggests or surpasses the approach to old Carcassonne. West Point, just below Constitution Island, juts into the river and must be rounded on our way to the village of Cold Spring (east), a mile to the north. Crow's Nest rises directly west of Cold Spring and is followed in a mile more by Storm King Mountain, the climax of the Highlands. But let not the traveler be fooled here, for Storm King is on the east bank and directly opposite the mountain! The village lies between Bull Hill to the south of it and Breakneck Ridge to the north of it, both of which fine elevations are shown in our pictures from Storm King Mountain opposite.

WALLACE NUTTING

New York Beautiful, 1927

WEST POINT, AND SCENES IN VICINITY

. . . passing Dunderberg, Crow's Nest, Anthony's Nose,
Bear Mountain, and other peaks given wide renown by
famous painters of the Hudson River School

Over tunnels—for trains, for vehicles—under the mighty span of the last great bridge to go up, we sail up the Hudson. The Palisades are on the Jersey shore, as bold and fine a bank as any river boasts. The cliffs, on the Manhattan side, with their looming towers, the homes of men, afford a fine foil to set off the natural cliffs on the western shore. A little north of Yonkers, and opposite Hastings, we pass the Jersey line and have New York counties on both sides of us. But the cliffs are continuous to Nyack and the new Cliff Drive is an alternate means of observation. On the right, above Hastings, is old Dobbs Ferry, Irvington, and Tarrytown in order—fair hills covered with fair estates, the best combination of natural and cultural features in America. From broad Tappan Bay (three miles across), we pass north on a long curve westward into Haverstraw Bay, first skirting, on the west, Hook Mountain and its long cliffs. Directly behind it hides Rockland Lake, fronted on the shore by a village of the same name.

SOUTH FROM WEST POINT'S ACADEMY GROUNDS

ANTHONY'S NOSE, FROM THE WESTERN SHORE

Opposite is Ossining, with its one prison and many palaces. We face, just above it, nosing half way across the broad stream, Croton. Croton River empties what is left of its waters into the Hudson. Haverstraw (west side) ends for the time the near approach of the western hills, but on the east the landscape is ever rolling, tossing outlines, ideal for estates and mostly preempted for them. Thus, the Palisades, while ending as to name shortly after passing out of New Jersey, really continue with a shore generally as bold and with loftier background for many miles.

WALLACE NUTTING
New York Beautiful, 1927

Settled by Dutch burghers, famed by Washington Irving, the historic village of Sleepy Hollow lies on the east bank of the Tappan Zee, where the Hudson is its widest

From the listless repose of the place, and the peculiar character of its inhabitants, who are descendants from the original Dutch settlers, this sequestered glen has long been known by the name of SLEEPY HOLLOW, and its rustic lads are called the Sleepy Hollow Boys throughout all the neighboring country. A drowsy, dreamy influence seems to hang over the land, and to pervade the very atmosphere. Some say that the place was bewitched by a high German doctor, during the early days of the settlement; others, that an old Indian chief, the prophet or wizard of his tribe, held his powwows there before the country was discovered by Master Hendrick Hudson. Certain it is, the place still continues under the sway of some witching power, that holds a spell over the minds of the good people, causing them to walk in a continual reverie. They are given to all kinds of marvelous beliefs; are subject to trances and visions; and frequently see strange sights, and hear music and voices in the air. The whole neighborhood abounds with local tales, haunted spots, and twilight superstitions; stars shoot and meteors glare oftener across the valley than in any other part of the country, and the nightmare, with her whole nine fold, seems to make it the favorite scene of her gambols.

WASHINGTON IRVING

The Legend of Sleepy Hollow, from *The Sketch Book, 1822*

OLD DUTCH CHURCH, SLEEPY HOLLOW

THE MILL AT SLEEPY HOLLOW, TARRYTOWN

*A few miles inland to the west, hidden behind
the Hudson highlands, the Wallkill's waters near Mohonk
and Minnewaska create settings of unsurpassed beauty*

BUTTERMILK FALLS, WALLKILL RIVER

Almost every fair day of an autumn in the middle 1820's a delicate, melancholy, blue-eyed young man played on his flute in a forest mottled by the shadows of the Catskills. Before him an easel held a little canvas; beside him lay a palette and brushes. To travelers of the river road who were curious enough to seek the source of liquid echoes in the rocky glens above them he said in gentle British accents that he was Thomas Cole, an artist, and that after two years of peripatetic trading of flute solos and oil landscapes for bread he had at last found in the Hudson valley the subjects which, of all subjects in the world, he most wanted to paint. "From the moment when his eye first caught the rural beauties clustering around the cliffs of Weehawken," wrote the young man's biographer a few years later, "Cole's heart had been wandering in the Highlands and nestling in the bosom of the Catskills."

CARL CARMER
The Hudson, 1939

ARNOLD'S FALLS, ON THE WALLKILL

Newburgh, on the Hudson's west shore, is the gateway to Orange County's fertile farmlands and vineyards, supplying produce for the cities to the south

THE HUDSON RIVER, NEAR NEWBURGH

Of the Hudson it may be said that it is a very large river for its size—that is, for the quantity of water it discharges into the sea. Its watershed is comparatively small—less, I think, than that of the Connecticut. It is a huge trough with a very slight incline, through which the current moves very slowly and which would fill from the sea were its supplies from the mountains cut off. Its fall from Albany to the bay is only about five feet. Any object upon it, drifting with the current, progresses southward no more than eight miles in twenty-four hours. The ebb tide will carry it about twelve miles, and the flood set it back from seven to nine. A drop of water at Albany, therefore, will be nearly three weeks in reaching New York, though it will get pretty well pickled some days earlier. Some rivers by their volume and impetuosity penetrate the sea, but here the sea is the aggressor and sometimes meets the mountain water nearly halfway.

JOHN BURROUGHS
A River View, from
Signs and Seasons, 1886

NEWBURGH, ON THE WEST SHORE OF THE HUDSON

Upstream at Poughkeepsie, site of Vassar College, the landscape for miles around is rich in dairy farms and noted for cattle-raising

MAIN ST., POUGHKEEPSIE

VIEW OF POUGHKEEPSIE FROM COLLEGE HILL

Both Poughkeepsie and Newburgh had smelled rich cargo passing their wharves. Newburgh had a whaler on the way to the Pacific in 1832 before the Poughkeepsie Whaling Company was organized "for the purpose of engaging in the whale fisheries in the Atlantic and Pacific oceans and elsewhere and the manufacture of oil and spermacetti candles." Among the directors of the enterprise were the wealthy brewer, Matthew Vassar—who founded a college; euphoniously named Paraclete Potter, and Alexander J. Coffin (no whaling company could be complete without a Nantucketer). A crowd at the dock cheered lustily and a cannon, booming from a high rock overhead, made the echoes fly back and forth between the October-tinged banks of the Hudson, as the 300-ton *Vermont,* first Poughkeepsie whaler, set sail.

CARL CARMER
The Hudson, 1939

For a time in 1777, when the Continental army was being harried by the British, New York's state senate met at the temporary capital, Kingston . . .

"You could depend upon the *Mary Powell,*" the river families say. "She was always on time." They laugh and say the Military Academy used to time its formations by the sound of her bell because it was always nearer right than the West Point clocks. Even on the day the cyclone hit her, twisting her broadside against the rushing wind and tumbling her stacks overboard, pilot Guernsey Betts brought her into Rondout on schedule. On ordinary days she had minutes to spare. She never wasted effort at a landing. Sometimes Guernsey Betts did not bother to make fast her landing lines—just held her up against the dock while the gangway was run ashore and the passengers came abroad. He knew how to take advantage of every tide, every whorl and eddy on her course. Once he had given the boys in the engine room the jingle she would be off like a race horse. She could slip into top speed while other boats were casting off. The only time she ever gave him trouble, he used to say, was when he would try to pass the mouth of Rondout Creek on one of his few trips to Albany. She was so accustomed to turn in there that she would bear to the left no matter how firm he held the wheel—as if she had some sort of curvature.

WALLACE NUTTING
New York Beautiful, 1927

CELEBRATING NEW YORK'S CENTENNIAL, KINGSTON

EDDYVILLE, RONDOUT CREEK, NEAR KINGSTON

. . . an important river point where the Rondout and Esopus meet the Hudson. In July 1877, all of Kingston turned out to celebrate the centennial

RONDOUT CREEK EVENING OF CELEBRATION. 1877.

KINGSTON.

HOUSE IN WHICH THE FIRST CONSTITUTION WAS FRAMED.

Yet, as Aldous Huxley has observed, a countryside and its people are to a very large extent the inventions of its poets and its novelists. To the degree that this may be true, New York State is the creation of Washington Irving and James Fenimore Cooper. The whimsies of the one and the romances of the other, both culled from the lore of the land, may disturb the modern historian and anthropologist looking for measurable facts. But these legends have been indelibly stamped on New York soil and we are all the richer for them. New Yorkers, whatever their origin, are the spiritual heirs of Diedrich Knickerbocker and Natty Bumpo. As Irving wove its magic into his stories, the Hudson River became one of the world's enchanted waterways. To this day one cannot pass the Dunderberg (Thunder Mountain) at the southern entrance to the Highlands, without harking for the voice of Mein Heer, the bulbous-bottomed Dutch goblin with his sugar-loaf hat, bawling his orders for wind and lightning. And who ever visited the Catskills without sensing the abiding presence of Rip Van Winkle and his troop of small folk?

MARSHALL B. DAVIDSON

The Romance of North America, 1958

Where! why, up on the Catskills. I used often to go up into the mountains after wolves' skins and bears; once they bought me to get them a stuffed painter; and so I often went. There's a place in them hills that I used to climb to when I wanted to see the carryings on of the world, that would well pay any man for a barked shin or a torn moccasin. You know the Catskills, lad, for you must have seen them on your left, as you followed the river up from York, looking as blue as a piece of clear sky, and holding the clouds on their tops, as the smoke curls over the head of an Indian chief at a council fire. Well, there's the High-peak and the Round-top, which lay back, like a father and mother among their children, seeing they are far above all the other hills. But the place I mean is next to the river, where one of the ridges juts out a little from the rest, and where the rocks fall for the best part of a thousand feet so much up and down that a man standing on their edges is fool enough to think he can jump from top to bottom.

JAMES FENIMORE COOPER

The Pioneers, 1823

RONDOUT BRIDGE, KINGSTON

Discovery of the sublime Catskill scenery by such famed artists as Thomas Cole, George Inness, Asher Durand, and others of the Hudson River school . . .

From the Mountain House the busy and all-glorious Hudson is seen winding half its silver length,—towns, villas, and white spires, sparkling on the shores, and snowy sails and gaily-painted steamers specking its bosom. It is a constant diorama of the most lively beauty; and the traveller, as he looks down upon it, sighs to make it a home. Yet a smaller and less-frequented stream would best fulfil desires born of a sigh. There is either no seclusion on the Hudson, or there is so much that the conveniences of life are difficult to obtain. Where the steamers come to shore (twenty a day, with each from one to seven hundred passengers) it is certainly far from secluded enough. No place can be rural, in all the *virtues* of the phrase, where a steamer will take the villager to the city between noon and night, and bring him back between midnight and morning. There is a suburban look and character about all the villages on the Hudson which seems out of place among such scenery. They are suburbs, in fact; steam has destroyed the distance between them and the city. The Mountain House on the Catskill, it should be remarked, is a luxurious hotel. How the proprietor can have dragged up, and keeps dragging up, so many superfluities from the river level to the eagle's nest, excites your wonder. It is the more strange, because in climbing a mountain the feeling is natural that you leave such enervating indulgences below.

NATHANIEL P. WILLIS

The Catskill Mountains, 1867

SCENES IN THE CATSKILL MOUNTAINS

. . . helped publicize the mountain scene, and the Mountain House as a premier resort, inspiring Thomas Nast to sketch these in 1866

DEPARTING.

IN THE CLOUDS.

THE ARTIST IN THE MOUNTAINS.

THE BEAR AT THE LAUREL HOUSE.

VIEW FROM SUNSET ROCK

LAST ON NORTH MOUNTAIN

NEARING THE MOUNTAIN HOUSE

HAINE'S FALL.

FAWNS LEAP

DREAM AFTER A DAY'S ADVENTURE

GOOD-BY

UNDER THE KAUTERSKILL FALL

Midst greens and shades
   the Cauterskill leaps,
From cliffs where the
   wood-flower clings;
All summer he moistens
   his verdant steps,
With the sweet light spray
   of the mountain springs;
And he shakes the woods
   on the mountain side,
When they drip with the
   rains of autumn tide.
But when in the forest
   bare and old,
The blast of December
   calls—
He builds in the starlight
   clear and cold,
A palace of ice where his
   torrent falls;
With turret, and arch, and
   fretwork fair,
And pillars blue as the
   summer air.
. . . Too gentle of mien he
   seemed, and fair,
For a child of those rugged
   steeps;
His home lay down in the
   valley where
The kingly Hudson rolls
   to the deeps;
But he wore the hunter's
   frock that day,
And a slender gun on his
   shoulder lay.

WILLIAM CULLEN BRYANT
The Cauterskill Falls, 1887

The scenic grandeur of the Hudson—the majestic Palisades, Tappan Zee, West Point, the Highlands and the many towns that line both banks—could best be viewed from the boat decks of the ever-popular Day Line

Almost every fair day of an autumn in the middle 1820's a delicate, melancholy, blue-eyed young man played on his flute in a forest mottled by the shadows of the Catskills. Before him an easel held a little canvas; beside him lay a palette and brushes. To travelers of the river road who were curious enough to seek the source of liquid echoes in the rocky glens above them he said in gentle British accents that he was Thomas Cole, an artist, and that after two years of peripatetic trading of flute solos and oil landscapes for bread he had at last found in the Hudson valley the subjects which, of all subjects in the world, he most wanted to paint.

CARL CARMER

The Hudson, 1939

ON THE OPEN DECK OF THE HUDSON RIVER BOAT

UP THE HUDSON

From Saratoga ... North
to the St. Lawrence

THOUSAND ISLANDS . . .LAKE GEORGE

. . .SARATOGA . . .CALDWELL VILLAGE . . .

BLACK MOUNTAIN . . .SABBATH DAY POINT . . .

FORT TICONDEROGA . . .LAKE CHAMPLAIN . . .

PLATTSBURG . . .WHITEFACE MOUNTAIN . . .

LAKE PLACID . . .SARANAC LAKE . . .

ST. REGIS LAKE . . .AUSABLE CHASM . . .

OPALESCENT FALLS . . .FISHING

IN THE ADIRONDACKS . . .

From Saratoga .. North to the St. Lawrence

ENTRANCE TO THOUSAND ISLANDS

PLAIN OLD "YORK STATE" HAD BE-come the "Empire State"—with nearly one-and-a-half million population, by 1820. Between 1830 and 1860, the state had about one-seventh of all the population in the United States. The Hudson River was the colonial highway, and Dutch colonists still formed the elite class, financially and socially. Only a few miles from Albany, the famous American spa of Saratoga Springs had become the social and sporting center for mid-Victorian America. Here, for a "modest room-and-board of two dollars a day, it was possible to meet everybody who was anybody," and enjoy curative baths and waters. Passengers from the Hudson River steamboats and schooners, the trains from the New York Central, and those of the Boston railroad, all poured into Albany. Travelers going west crossed the Hudson by ferry in summer and by sleigh in winter.

New York, a state of lakes, has countless beautiful expanses of water—miniature inland seas such as occur nowhere else. Pennsylvania has none "above the dignity of ponds;" New Jersey has two fine lakes, one of which extends into New York, but all the vast territory in Virginia, East Tennessee, and North Carolina is without lakes. Of all the lakes in New York, Champlain and George are best known, most important in history, the most beautiful, and most visited by tourists. About sixty miles north of Albany the waters of Lake George flow into Lake Champlain, whose surface is dotted with many small islands—"there's one for every day in the year," local residents tell the visitor. Travelers came by the Saratoga railway to Glen's Falls, then by stagecoach to the lake.

James Fenimore Cooper peopled the shores of Lake George with creatures of his imagination, as Walter Scott had the Highlands of Scotland.

There are striking differences between the shores of Lake George and those of Champlain. At Lake George, the mountains come down to the edge of the waters; on Lake Champlain, the mountains in parallel lines, to the left and right, leave between them lovely stretches of country fields and orchards and farmhouses. The history-rich towns of Ticonderoga and Crown Point are on the lake, and at its widest area is Plattsburg. At Saranac, a group of three lakes, linked by the Saranac River, go to swell Lake Champlain.

The northeast part of New York state has some of the most beautiful lakes, the highest mountains, and the wildest country. Here are the towering Adirondacks, and lakes that can be counted by the hundreds. A tract, called the Wilderness, was known only to a few trappers, hunters, and lumbermen for many decades, after other portions of the Adirondacks had become famous resort areas. It lies between the lakes George and Champlain on the east, the St. Lawrence on the northwest,

extends to Canada on the north, and nearly to the Mohawk River on the south. In its fastnesses are five ranges of mountains that terminate on the shore of Lake Champlain. Geologists consider the area the oldest land on the globe, or the first that showed itself from the waters. In the valleys, between the mountain ranges, are beautiful lakes and ponds said to number more than a thousand. A labyrinth of lakes is connected by rivers, brooks, and rills. The Saranac, Ausable, Boquet, and the Racket rise in and flow through the Wilderness, where in its distant recesses flow the springs of the Hudson. A writer in the 1850s declared:

Thirty years ago, Adirondack was almost as unknown as the interior of Africa. There were few huts or houses, and very few visitors. But of late the number of sportsmen and tourists has increased, and taverns have been established in some of the wildest spots. In summer, the lakes swarm with the boats of travellers in search of game or health, or mere contemplation of beautiful scenery. All travelling is done by small boats of light build, rowed by a single guide, and made so light that they can be lifted from the water, and carried on the guide's shoulders from pond to pond, or stream to stream.

Competent guides, steady, intelligent, and experienced men, can be hired at all the taverns for two or three dollars a day, who will provide boats, tents, and everything requisite for the trip. Each traveller should have a guide and a boat to himself, and the cost of their maintenance in the woods is not more than a dollar for each man in the party. The fare is chiefly trout and venison, of which there is generally an abundance, procured by rod and gun.

Vivid contrast to the picturesque Adirondack country—with its famous spas, falls, chasms, glens, and lakes—are the tightly clustered industrial towns and cities to the south, many antedating the American Revolution. Amsterdam built a reputation for carpets; Gloversville for gloves; Schenectady for electrical products—the list is almost endless. Every map shows the towns; almost every home enjoys their products.

World-renowned Saratoga spa and its medicinal waters, first discovered in 1767 by General William Johnson, has since attracted visitors in increasing numbers

Within a few miles is Saratoga, memorable for the decisive check that really spelled, under Burgoyne, the beginning of another era. Bennington, Oriskany, Crown Point are near, and "from the river to the ends of the earth" the movements of the nations swing wide from this fulcrum. The neighborhood of Saratoga itself, however, is a plain, and the place must derive its main attraction from the waters and from historic aspects. The state has taken praiseworthy action in cleansing Saratoga from the tawdry circuslike atmosphere of the past. This process of getting rid of the unsightly is an enlightened and continuous policy on the part of the state. It has worked transformations. The best of it is the example and stimulus it affords private improvements. Some small cities are making good capital of their "parlor" appearance. Naturally any family retiring from the great city will select if possible a "parlor" town.

WALLACE NUTTING

New York Beautiful, 1927

STANWIX, UNION, AND CONGRESS HALLS, SARATOGA

HIGH ROCK, EMPIRE, AND IODINE SPRINGS, SARATOGA

CONGRESS SPRING

UNITED STATES HOTEL

Nearby Lake George, a vacationer's paradise, is famed for its bounteous climate, scenic grandeur, and the palatial Fort William Henry Hotel at its southern tip

SCENES ON LAKE GEORGE

The lake is just large enough to be beautiful. Were it broader the fine effect of channel between mountains would be lost. Beginning at its southern end, almost directly under French Mountain, it shows its charm with no delay. Between that elevation and Rattlesnake Cobble nestle the villages of Caldwell and Lake George, and the ruins of at least three old forts, Henry, George, and Gage. Not without significance, Bloody Pond lies just to the south, for this fairest region in the east was also the region most stubbornly contested. A lake not too lengthy to be conquered from end to end by a swimming champion, despite its cold floods, is comprehensible and lovable. The whole state of New York is almost too large to fall in love with, like an elephant. But Lake George we can love—no, we cannot help loving it. Now we come to what is the unchallenged climax of beauty, in the Narrows. They are scattered with many islands and dominated by fine steep banks in the form of Shelving Rock Mountain on the right and the aptly named Tongue Mountain on the left, which, ending in Montcalm Point, reaches for miles into the lake forming Northwest Bay to the west.

WALLACE NUTTING

New York Beautiful, 1927

The village of Caldwell, since renamed Lake George, stands at its lower edge, with a commanding view northward. Here one boards the lake steamer for a delightful sail . . .

The land that is New York has played an important part in the strategy of nations. It has been a coveted land, for it promised abundance and authority to those who could invest and command it. On maps of America it looks like a horn of plenty thrust down towards the sea from the north and west to receive the wealth of the continent and funnel it to the extreme limit of the land at Manhattan Island. Thus the English viewed it when they quietly and firmly took over Holland's claim from Peter Stuyvesant in 1664. And thus also did the French, who for a century and a half held a counterclaim to the largest part of the present state, as the names of some of its counties and villages—St. Lawrence and Orleans, Montcalm, Chateaugay, and Raquette—continue to remind us. If in the summer of 1609 Samuel de Champlain had chosen to follow the Indian trails that led to the south, instead of doing battle with the Iroquois beside the lake that bears his name, Henry Hudson might have found the lilies of France waving a greeting on Manhattan Island when he arrived later that same season; and the history of New York and of all North America would have been quite different.

MARSHALL B. DAVIDSON

The Romance of North America, 1958

CALDWELL VILLAGE, LAKE GEORGE

CALDWELL VILLAGE

. . . heading north, crisscrossing from shore to shore, touching numerous islands enroute to pick up vacationers or picnickers

DAVIS'S HOLLOW, SABBATH DAY POINT

BLACK MOUNTAIN, FROM THE NARROWS

LAKE GEORGE, FROM PROSPECT MOUNTAIN

If one were seeking a nearly perfect site, one of the islands in the Narrows would supply the demand. The lofty peak of Erebus (2,533 ft.) to the right, and Black Mountain, somewhat higher, still north, all dominate this channel of ecstatic splendor. The islands continue, though less thickly strewn, for several miles. Deer Deep and Bloomer Mountain, to the right, are minor peaks protecting Sabbath Day Point, named as by inspiration, as any eye will admit which has gazed on the lake when no ripple stirred it. Friends Point and Indian Kettles, next on the left, are not too lofty to be familiar. The kettles are named from remarkable potholes in the ledges near the lake, which mark a time when the water line was higher. Here is probably the finest contrast on the lake, for on the right (east shore), thrusting its vast bulk well out into the waters, is Record Hill, and directly on the margin, Anthony's Nose, very likely named in reminiscence by early voyagers who had passed the mountain of the same name on the Hudson. The land sickles about these peaks and stretches away, north by east, with Roger's Rock and Roger's Slide on the west shore (left) and all lovely Stone's Bay, where the village of Baldwin clings under Cook's Mountain, opposite to and north of Roger's. Passing on, we face the virtual end of the lake, at the heights above Fort Ticonderoga, which is hidden from this view by these heights. The lake now becomes a narrow stream, makes a half circle to the right about the village of Ticonderoga, and empties, at length, under the ruins of the fort into Champlain.

WALLACE NUTTING
New York Beautiful, 1927

A mere four miles from Lake George is Lake Champlain,
a broad expanse of water extending over a hundred miles
to the north between the states of New York and Vermont

RUINS OF FORT TICONDEROGA

SPLIT ROCK, LAKE CHAMPLAIN

BURLINGTON BAY

Champlain's past is enriched by many historical episodes, including the great naval battle of 1814, when the British were trounced by an American fleet under MacDonough

- DISTANT VIEW OF ST. ALBANS.
- BALL I.
- HEN I.
- BOW & ARROW & LONG POINT.
- PLATTSBURG FROM CUMBERLAND PT. R.
- GREEN MTS. FROM PLATTSBURG.
- CUMBERLAND BAY.
- CUMBERLAND POINT.

LAKE CHAMPLAIN, FROM PLATTSBURG TO ST. ALBANS

The tail of the lake (South Bay) lies between Vanderburg Mountain and the heights on the opposite (north) side, singularly called The Diameter. The Champlain Canal, however, enters the lake some six miles from its end, at Whitehall. Death Rock, a height above Whitehall, affords a view for miles due north along the exceedingly narrow portion of the lake, a mere channel to Snody Dock and little wider all the way to Benson's Landing, about twenty miles from the extreme south end. Whitehall itself is most picturesque huddled under Skene Mountain. Mettawee River, joining Wood Creek, passes Whitehall, unites with East Bay, then South Bay and then reaches off to the fascinating twist of waters, passing, on the right, Bald Mountain, four miles from Whitehall. The stream is narrow enough for small boats and timid sailors, provided one does not choose the steamer. It is a pleasure to be able to stop at will. The lighthouses marking the dangerous channel are so numerous as to be a considerable feature of the scenery. No lofty crests appear near the lake for many miles, yet the hills are bold enough to be fine;, and they lend much variety to our progress. At Ticonderoga we pass a point no more easily defended than many others, but chosen for defence because it protects also the outlet of Lake George. Champlain, the crucial point here, is a quarter mile across, and the scenery, while not magnificent, is perhaps better, enthralling in beauty.

WALLACE NUTTING
New York Beautiful, 1927

*The Adirondacks, New York's loftiest mountains, lie in the
sector between Lake Champlain and the St. Lawrence, with
towering Mt. Marcy, or Tahawus, its highest peak . . .*

"An Adirondack mountain is thickly fir clad,"
writes Stephen Birmingham, "with a smoothly rounded top, but some offer steep slides, jagged cliffs,
ledges, and tall rockfaced precipices with cascading
waterfalls. At the feet of the mountains lie the lakes,
many of them approachable only on foot, and a few
that can be seen only from the air. From the valleys
and lake shores below, the surrounding mountains
form a stern horizon, dark green and brooding." The
Adirondacks woods are still full of spruce, balsam,
hemlock, ash, cedar, and birch; trout and bass and
pike and pickerel match wits with thousands of
fishermen; deer flash through the trees. The wilderness, although no longer "forever wild," as the great
conservationists of the 1890s hoped it would be, has
enough primitive quality to bring lasting enjoyment to
campers, sturdy hikers, walkers, sedentary nature
lovers, or flower pickers. Saranac, Lake George, Lake
Placid, the Tupper Lake chain, are largely spoiled,
but in the surrounding lonely woods and in those of
Long Lake, Blue Mountain Lake, Raquette Lake, and
the lakes of the Fulton chain there exists a backwoods
feeling that repays the wanderer. The Ausable Chasm,
overbilled as the "Grand Canyon of the East," is
famed for its eroded, sculptured sandstone cliffs, two
hundred feet high; and at the High Falls Gorge at
Wilmington, the Ausable River drops more than a
hundred feet over turbulent waterfalls.

The Beautiful Country, 1970

WHITEFACE, FROM LAKE PLACID

BIRMINGHAM FALLS, AUSABLE CHASM

"New York State has everything" is a familiar
boast among New Yorkers, and sometimes they
add, "even two kinds of mountains." North of
the Catskills lie rolling hills and the river plain
of the east-flowing Mohawk, and beyond that
lies rising land again—the foothills of the
Adirondacks. Steeper and higher than the Catskills, the tree lined slopes of the Adirondacks offer silence, the companionship of nature, the
shade of balsam, spruce and hemlock, and hidden lakes where the only sounds are those of
fish jumping and the whisper of wind riffling
the water. While the Adirondacks are not high
compared with Western mountains, more than
two score of their countless peaks rise above the
four-thousand-foot level. The highest, to which
the Adirondack Indians gave the name of
Tahawus (the cloud splitter), is over five thousand feet and provides on its steep sides not only
a level nook for Lake Tear-of-the-Clouds where
the Hudson rises, but also an iron mine.

CARL CARMER

New York, 1949

. . . surrounded by many others: Whiteface, Dix Peak, Seward, Colden and McIntyre—their valleys said to contain over a thousand lakes and ponds of great beauty

LOWER SARANAC LAKE

ST. REGIS LAKE

SAND POINT, LITTLE TUPPER LAKE

The Ausable affords some of the wildest and most impressive scenes east of the Rockies, plunging precipitously between huge columns of rock . . .

Three hundred miles from the Atlantic Ocean, the Hudson River flows out of a secretive little body of pure water in the Adirondack Mountains. Below the heights of Mount Marcy, standing at 5,344 feet as the highest peak in New York, known long ago as *Tahawus,* the Cloud Splitter, the source of the Hudson River is Lake Tear-of-the-Clouds. Mirroring the sky of the Adirondacks, surrounded by balsam fir, spruce, and white cedar and the small blossoms of the north, the lake lies at an altitude of 4,322 feet. It was a long time being discovered. It lies in remote wilderness still. Deer drink at its shallows. The hermit thrushes chime in the firs. Black bears in August eat blueberries and wild raspberries on its uplands. The quietness of the northern year dwells calmly around the lake and the infant river that flows from it. A small, clear, cold mountain stream called Feldspar Brook runs out of the lake. Joined by other small tricklings, they become great enough to create the Opalescent River, which, in turn, gathering power and with water enough to merit the honor, becomes the Hudson River, well on its way to downstream destiny and greatness.

VIRGINIA S. EIFERT

Of Men and Rivers, 1966

OPALESCENT FALLS

THE AUSABLE CHASM

. . . creating the Great Falls, one hundred and fifty feet high, and forming spectacular chasms between mountainous walls that narrow to a mere five-foot passage

CLEARING A LOG JAM, GREAT FALLS OF THE AUSABLE

We entered the rocky gorge between the steep slopes of Mount McIntyre and the cliffs of Wallface Mountain. There we encountered enormous masses of rocks, some worn by the abrasion of the elements, some angular, some bare, and some covered with moss, and many of them baring large trees, whose roots, clasping them on all sides, strike into the earth for sustenance. One of the masses presented a singular appearance; it is of cubic form, its summit full thirty feet from its base, and upon it was quite a grove of hemlock and cedar trees. Around and partly under this and others lying loosely, apparently kept from rolling by roots and vines, we were compelled to clamber a long distance, when we reached a point more than one hundred feet above the bottom of the gorge, where we could see the famous Indian Pass in all its wild grandeur. Before us arose a perpendicular cliff, nearly twelve hundred feet from base to summit, as raw in appearance as if cleft only yesterday. Above us sloped McIntyre, still more lofty than the cliff of Wallface, and in the gorge lay piles of rocks, chaotic in position, grand in dimensions, and awful in general aspect. Through these the waters of this branch of the Hudson, bubbling from a spring not far distant (close by a fountain of the Ausable), find their way. Here the headwaters of these rivers commingle in the spring season, and, when they separate, they find their way to the Atlantic Ocean at points a thousand miles apart.

BENSON J. LOSSING

The Hudson from the Wilderness to the Sea,

1866

The vast Adirondack Forest Preserve—a wooded wonderland—paradise for hunters and fishermen—contains 45 mountain peaks towering above 4,000 feet, including Mount Marcy, highest in the Empire State

There is no joy like that of the deep woods. The woods have a power over the mind and a serenity of their own. No wonder we are always getting ready anxiously to go. They are the woods of God—all right! They open to one vistas of sunlight falling slantwise through tall trees silent as the cathedral and almost as musical. The winds blow up high but not here below. The ripple of the falling water is musical. The distances come up near and ask you to come along. Weariness is not of the flesh alone. It is to the mind as well. These heal all the elements of a man, mind, soul and body. As I go along the street after having written some story of the woods— a trip up the Allagash for instance, strange men, whom I have never met, stop me and beamingly tell of their plans for going into the woods. It is the growing hope of the age, this love of the hills and forests.

ARTHUR G. STAPLES

A Tribute to the Woods

BLACK-BASS FISHING IN THE ADIRONDACKS

Upstate New York... from Albany... West to Buffalo

ALBANY SCENES . . . CITY HALL AND

STATE CAPITOL . . . LITTLE FALLS . . .

CANAL SCENE . . . VALLEY OF THE

MOHAWK . . . FORT PLAIN . . . UTICA . . .

OSWEGO . . . TRENTON FALLS . . .

SYRACUSE . . . ROCHESTER . . . FALLS

OF THE GENESEE . . . ITHACA . . .

CAYUGA LAKE . . . AURORA . . .

. . . WATKINS GLEN . . . PORTAGE . . .

RAILROAD BRIDGE . . . BUFFALO SCENES . . .

ERIE CANAL, BUFFALO . . . LIGHT HOUSE

. . . NIAGARA FALLS . . . WHIRLPOOL . . .

SUSPENSION BRIDGE . . . AND RAPIDS . . .

CAVE OF THE WINDS

HIGH FALLS

Upstate New York... from Albany... West to Buffalo

THE OLDEST SETTLEMENT IN THE original thirteen colonies—excepting only Jamestown, Virginia—Albany had become the chief point of departure for emigrants from the Eastern seaboard to the region of the Great Lakes and the upper Mississippi valley. Tourists poured into Albany, to entrain for Buffalo, where, by 1845, west-bound travelers numbered about 100,000 annually. Settled in 1609, where Henry Hudson had moored the *Half-Moon,* Albany was now a great railroad and steamboat terminus. The Mohawk River—emptying into the Hudson at Cohoes, north of Albany—called the "water level" route, was paralleled by the old Mohawk Trail, the most accessible road through a gap in the mountains. During the colonization period, the river road was a series of turnpikes, from Schenectady to as far as Rome, with lesser trails stretching west.

Yankees were leaving the stony fields of New Hampshire and Vermont for the rich Mohawk valley—some to farm, some to grow wealthy by promoting a bank or a store, or by floating stock for a turnpike or canal. True to their New England antecedents, the newcomers set up preparatory schools and colleges: Presbyterians built Union College at Schenectady; Congregationalists—Hamilton College at Clinton; the Episcopalians—Hobart College at Geneva; the Baptists—Colgate at Hamilton, and, also the Baptists—the University of Rochester. These denominational colleges of the typical New England sort in time developed into nonsectarian universities.

To the south of the Mohawk, the great Allegheny plateau slopes gently to the central part of the state, while to the east it rises in the beautiful Catskill Mountains, in sight of the Hudson. Some of the peaks are over 4,000 feet in height—not so grand as the Adirondacks, but studded with delightful holiday resorts overlooking a great panorama of hill and valley. Row upon row of peaks, tumultuous cataracts, enchanting cascades, cool glens, sharp precipices—with intriguing names like Pudding-Stone Hall, Rip Van Winkle's House, Druid Rocks—delight countless thousands of vacationers.

Wearing its 250 years of American history lightly, the Mohawk Valley is a region of deep peace, despite bloody battles fought there during the French and Indian War, and the Revolution. At its source a gentle stream, the Mohawk is fed by important tributaries until it reaches the city of Utica. Tranquility vanishes at Little Falls, where, in primordial days, river and mountains battled. "Rocks are strewn everywhere . . . between the houses, in the gardens, cropping out from the green hills." The river descends 40 feet, creating small falls of great value to the town—furnishing power for many factories. From this point to Schenectady is the heart of the valley. Once it did a great business in dairy produce and with the Indian fur traders.

The Erie Canal, which opened in 1825, followed the river's course. The New York State Barge Canal—begun in 1905—extends the old Erie Canal, connecting the Great Lakes with the Hudson River. The large industrial cities of Buffalo on Lake Erie and Rochester near Lake Ontario and—to the east—Syracuse, Binghamton, and Utica—owe much of their lusty growth to the canals. Although it was almost destroyed by fire in the War of 1812, Buffalo grew rapidly when the Erie Canal was opened. A major Great Lakes port—made accessible to ocean-going vessels by the St. Lawrence Seaway—Buffalo is one of the greatest grain-distributing ports in the United States. Between the populous industrial cities are areas of rich agricultural land, with luxuriant apple orchards and vineyards. Contributing to New York's fame as the "state of lakes and rivers," the west-central section sparkles with numerous lakes, among which the Finger Lakes are particularly notable. These long, narrow glacial lakes, of which Cayuga is the largest, are famed for beauty, resorts, and state parks. Cornell University, Ithaca College, and Wells College overlook Lake Cayuga. In addition to its rich endowment of lakes, the valley is drained by the Allegheny River and the Susquehanna and Delaware network.

What the Himalayas are to other mountain ranges, Niagara Falls is to other falls. "Not only the grandest, but so greatly preeminent as to be without rivalry" wrote one observer. He continues: "Over the ledge of limestone rocks, the accumulated waters of four vast inland lakes hurl themselves madly on their way to the ocean."

Although there are falls that exceed the height of Niagara, none equals its volume and beauty. . . awesome in its impact.

Cities in the southern section of the state, near the Pennsylvania boundary—like Binghamton and Elmira—differ as much from those in the north—like Lake Placid—as Dallas in Texas differs from San Antonio. Cohoes, where the Mohawk joins the Hudson, is the *Lowell* of New York, completely concentrated on manufacturing, with cotton mills, woolen mills, paper factories, and iron foundries. The state that leads the nation in manufacturing is also one of the chief agricultural states. More grain is milled in Buffalo than in Minneapolis; more milk products are shipped from New York than from Wisconsin, the dairy state of the Midwest.

At the crossroads of rail lines, and the confluence of canals and rivers, the Empire State's capital at Albany became a busy port at the headwaters of the Hudson . . .

OLD DUTCH HOUSE, ALBANY

BLEECKER HALL, ALBANY

STANWIX HALL, ALBANY

No one who has ever seen wide State Street rise from the Hudson River docks to the Capitol Building is likely to forget the sight. It is a sweeping and majestic approach to ornate nothingness—to the three-acre, $25,000,000 gingerbread castle in whose facade the period influences come and go as raggedly as do political influences within. But politics aside—and architecture, too, for most of Albany's other streets are lined with dull look-alike houses of dark red brick or brownstone—Albany has one surpassing distinction. That is Keeler's, the best year-round city restaurant in all upstate, an eating house that feeds sophisticated Manhattanites, rural politicians, foreign diplomats whose palates can be weaned from exotic dishes—and all come away singing the praises of the food.

CARL CARMER
New York, 1949

WINTER SCENE, ALBANY

. . .gateway to a chain of cities leading westward:
Schenectady, Utica, Rome, Syracuse, Rochester, Niagara
Falls, and Buffalo—links that bind the Mohawk valley

OLD CAPITOL OF THE STATE OF NEW YORK, ALBANY

Three roads leave Albany, the York State capital, in an east-west course across the rolling hills and river flats that separate the Catskills from the Adirondacks. The northernmost is the Schenectady-Utica-Syracuse turnpike, which runs along the north bank of the historic Mohawk. The southernmost is the Cherry Valley Pike, one of the world's most beautiful highways, which sweeps up and down milelong hills as if it were the track of a magnificent out-sized roller coaster. Between the two, at least part of the way, runs the new Thruway, the comfortable speedway that unhappily bypasses the fine old towns and buildings and the restaurants that serve the distinctive foods and wines of the region. This is the upstate area. Only the inhabitants, legend claims, can define its boundaries, and they are not given to exactitude in matters of geography. The late Samuel Hopkins Adams, the distinguished author who lived all his years in this area, once said, "Upstate is west of Albany," and considered the subject closed.

CARL CARMER
New York, 1949

NEW CAPITOL, ALBANY

With the opening of the Erie Canal, in 1825, after ten years of building, many who had ridiculed De Witt Clinton's "mighty ditch" came to reverse their hasty opinion . . .

Improved transportation was the first condition of this quickening life. Canals, roads, and railroads not only took people west but connected them with markets when they got there. In 1826, when Charles Vaughan made a trip on the newly opened Erie Canal, the country on each side of it between Utica and Rochester had been cleared to a width of not more than one mile. Yet only next year the governor of Georgia was complaining that wheat from central New York was being sold at Savannah more cheaply than wheat from central Georgia. By bringing the Great Lakes within reach of a metropolitan market, the Erie Canal opened up the hitherto neglected northern regions of Ohio, and of Indiana and Illinois. At the same time it made New York City the principal gateway to the Northwest. The Erie Canal forced Boston, Philadelphia, and Baltimore into rival activity. Philadelphia was shocked to find that her cheapest route to Pittsburgh was by way of New York City, Albany, Buffalo, and wagon road or canal from Lake Erie. Pennsylvania then put through the "portage" system of canals to Pittsburgh, surmounting the Alleghenies at an elevation of 2300 feet by a series of inclined planes, up which canal boats or railroad cars were hauled by stationary steam engines. Pennsylvania had almost 1000 miles of canal in operation by 1840. In twenty years time the railroads had rendered most of them obsolete.

SAMUEL ELIOT MORISON

The Oxford History of the American People, 1965

CANAL BOAT AT LITTLE FALLS, HERKIMER COUNTY

FORT PLAIN, ON THE MOHAWK RIVER

. . .as they witnessed an immediate and dramatic upsurge in two-way traffic—golden harvests towed in all manner of mule-drawn barges

LITTLE FALLS, ON THE MOHAWK

VALLEY OF THE MOHAWK

A good bit of the stuff that legends are made of went into New York's first great corporate effort, the building of the Erie Canal. The idea of cutting such a water passage three hundred and sixty-odd miles through a wilderness of forest and swamp seemed at the time, even to such a far-seeking mind as Thomas Jefferson's, "little short of madness." It did take vision and determination just short of madness to realize the job. But it was finished in good season, in the fall of 1825, and the Irish bogtrotters whose brawn had dug the way—whose very presence in these parts blazed a trail for millions of compatriots and co-religionists—were free for other heavy work that now needed doing. Nothing before or since has so dramatically emphasized New York's vital place in the Union. The "mighty ditch" was only four feet deep but it quickly floated a tremendous burden of traffic. Within barely a score of years the canal business concentrating at Albany was greater than that derived by New Orleans from the trade of the whole Mississippi River basin. The original canal has long since been replaced by broader and quicker channels of communication. The fact remains that it left an imperishable impress on the land. Most of the major cities of the state have grown from frontier villages that sprang to sudden life at the magic touch of the canal.

MARSHALL B. DAVIDSON
The Romance of North America, 1958

*Utica, on the Mohawk, and Oswego, on Lake Ontario,
typified towns that grew along with the canal era,
flourishing from the flow of east-west traffic*

Upstate cities follow a pattern too. Through the old part of town runs the chief residential thoroughfare. Here, in lawn-girt rows, stand the sprawling dark Victorian piles built by the old families who made their money early—the tribes referred to, with some awe, as Old Amsterdam, Old Herkimer, Old Rome. Inevitably, some of the elegant mansions have been converted to funeral homes and others have been sold to enterprising immigrant families—and their colorful alterations of conservative facades sometimes startle their neighbors. On the side streets, near this major aisle of aristocracy, stand the expensive new residences of the well-to-do come-latelies whose ranking is less sacrosanct. And on the "other side" of town, in thousands of homes varying little in design, live the employees of the big industries. Of the smaller upstate cities, many are identified with a single industry.

CARL CARMER
New York, 1949

NEW YORK STATE FAIR GROUND, UTICA

PANORAMIC VIEW OF UTICA

Oswego, Owego, Otsego, Otego—place names of pleasant euphony, though often confusing—recalled the heritage of Iroquois predecessors throughout the upstate region

STATE INSTITUTION, UTICA

Owego appeared, a town say of about five thousand, nestling down by the waterside amid a great growth of elms, and showing every element of wealth and placid comfort. A group of homes along the Susquehanna, their backs perched out over it, reminded us of the houses at Florence on the Arno....Then we entered the town over a long, shaky iron bridge and rejoiced to see one of the prettiest cities we had yet found. Curiously, I was most definitely moved by Owego. There is something about the old fashioned, comfortable American town at its best—the town where moderate wealth and religion and a certain social tradition hold—which is at once pleasing and yet comfortable—a gratifying and yet almost disturbingly exclusive state of affairs. At least as far as I am concerned, such places and people are antipodal to anything that I could ever again think, believe or feel.

THEODORE DREISER
A Hoosier Holiday, 1943

OSWEGO, ON LAKE ONTARIO

As if to mimic Niagara's thunder, at a hundred places throughout the state there are falls and cataracts of awesome beauty . . .

And, moreover, this vague sense of old-world romance, which I am trying to describe, is a completely different thing from the startling natural grandeur of virgin forests, great prairies, vast deserts and towering mountains. It can only appear under particular conditions in the history of any landscape and it requires a particular kind of landscape for it to reveal itself at all. These conditions are precisely fulfilled in the hilly regions of "up-state" New York of which I am speaking. The hills are not too high, the woods are not too continuous. Grassy slopes, park-like reaches, winding rivers, pastoral valleys, old walls, old water-mills, old farmsteads, old bridges, old burying-grounds give to the contemplative imagination that poetic sense of *human continuity,* of the generations following each other in slow religious succession, which is what the mind pines for, if it is to feel the full sense of its mortal inheritance. Where, moreover, by an incredible piece of luck I was allowed to settle, the actual earth-strata is peculiarly harmonious to my exacting taste. Grey slaty boulders lie in every direction, covered with the loveliest mosses and lichens, and intersected where the pines and hemlocks and birches grow by rich black earth-mould where the most delicate of wild flowers and ferns appear in their seasons.

JOHN COWPER POWYS
Autobiography, 1962

ALHAMBRA FALLS

TRENTON FALLS

. . . some a delicate ribbon of silvery mist, others a treacherous cascade— each a marvel considered alone

TRENTON FALLS, FROM EAST BANK

It is possible that after one of the tremendous thunderstorms which burst upon this climate sometimes in summer, the glory of the cataract may, for a few hours, renew, and so unite the splendor of full foliage with the flashing of mighty waters: but this is a chance which the traveller for pleasure will scarce hit or wait for. The frowning walls on either side, driven asunder by the plunges of the torrent in more "yeasty moods," present a sufficient scale by which to measure its slumbering power. Those who live in climes where snow seldom falls, and more seldom lies through one sunny day unmelted, can have but a faint idea of a spring *freshet* in America. After the first heavy snow in December, each successive fall adds solidity to the heap upon the earth's bosom, and the alternate thawing and freezing consolidates the bottom into ice, and cuts off the heat of the soil from the flakes added almost daily to the surface. Till the middle of March, or later, the sleighing is hard and crisp. Then the sun draws toward the line, and with the equinox come soft southern winds, with sharp changes to the north, pouring sleet and rain upon the crusty covering of nature; and, first of all, the small streams begin to trickle under the ice, smothered and faint; the roads across the hard-frozen rivers crack and grow treacherous. As the days grow longer, the snow gets clammy and heavy, and drops to the ground, an acre at a time, clicking like a troop of morris-dancers.

NATHANIEL P. WILLIS

American Scenery, 1840

For more than a century, Syracusans have had to watch New York Central's trains pass through their main streets, evoking bitter denunciations

The first great railroad objective was to close the gaps in the rails between Albany and the Lakes. By 1839 the Mohawk Valley was joined to Auburn on the west, by the Utica and Syracuse Railroad as far as Syracuse, and then to Auburn, by the Auburn and Syracuse Railroad. The first trip from Utica to Syracuse was recorded in the rhapsodic vein the "annihilator of space" seemed always to bring forth: "Syracuse is now within nine hours of Albany and within nineteen hours of New York. W....was at Syracuse at half-past eight o'clock yesterday morning, remained until four o'clock and was at home this morning, breakfasting on a salmon taken from Lake Ontario night before last, having traveled 300 miles, passing a night at Utica, nearly a whole day at Syracuse and being absent only forty-two hours.

CODMAN HISLOP

The Mohawk, 1948

SALINA STREET, SYRACUSE

RAILROAD DEPOT, ROCHESTER

MARKET SQUARE, SYRACUSE

RAILROAD YARDS, ROCHESTER

ERIE CANAL ACQUEDUCT, ROCHESTER

With the coming of the Erie Canal and the railroads, and with many flour mills situated on the Genesee, Rochester billed itself "the nation's breadbasket"

The heart of Rochester lies on the Genesee, and swift running water is the reason for the city's being. In its earliest character it was a milltown, whose economy depended upon a double service from the Genesee. The river made a highway for the flatboats that carried wheat to the Rochester mills and river water turned the mill wheels that ground the wheat into flour. But the business was of limited promise. The early millers produced good flour, but the trick was to get it to good markets. These were in the East. Days were required to move a barrel of flour even as far as Albany, and wagoners were expensive. When the Erie Canal reached Rochester and crossed the Genesee by aqueduct less than a dozen years after the village was founded, there was great rejoicing. Here was the dreamed-of outlet for the product of Rochester mills. Profits soared. Industry was immensely stimulated. New mills sprang up along the river. They stood cheek to jowl in the vicinity of the Upper Falls, and there were mills at the Middle and Lower Falls as well. Rochester's boast that it was the breadbasket of the nation was not pure puffery, and its title, the Flour City, was widely flaunted.

HENRY W. CLUNE
The Genesee, 1963

FALLS OF THE GENESEE, ROCHESTER

The Genesee and its deep ravines that had to be bridged, as rail lines crisscrossed the state in the 1850s, presented a genuine challenge . . .

At a time when the public was more ingenuous than it is today, the High Bridge was considered so wonderful a thing that excursion trains were run to Portage, a hamlet on the right, and to Portageville, on the left bank of the river, and taverns at these places did a bang-up business entertaining bridge gazers. No longer the cynosure it once was, the bridge is still more than an incidental attraction at Letchworth Park, and a person on the ground, gazing up at it as a train moves across its long, lacy span, knows the tingle of apprehension one experiences watching a man ride a bicycle on a high wire in a circus. The first bridge has more history than the second. Besides the spectacular fire that destroyed it, a workmen's riot, which required the threat of a milita company's cannon to quell, attended its building, and several persons died from eating roast ox at a barbecue that celebrated its opening.

HENRY W. CLUNE
The Genesee, 1963

RAILROAD BRIDGE ACROSS THE GENESEE, PORTAGE

GENESEE FALLS, ROCHESTER

. . . that was solved in this awkward, towering structure of timbered trusses which attracted tourists from nearby Letchworth Park, "Grand Canyon of the East"

The Genesee River was on its springtime rampage. It had overflowed its banks and flooded the cellars of houses in three small communities a short distance south of the city of Rochester, New York. It had washed over porches and eddied into the downstairs rooms of dwellings in the most depressed areas of these settlements. It was creeping higher by the hours. This was an old story to the residents of Riverdale, of Ballantyne, an adjoining community to the north, and to a handful of suburbanites on the east side of the river. With the certainty of the vernal equinox, they expected, sometime each March, to be menaced by floodwaters or actually flooded out. They were fatalists. Eleven months out of the twelve they lived in peace and security; then, with greater resignation than Job, they suffered not only the inconvenience of having to store their household chattels in places beyond the river's highest reach but often the indignity of being rescued by police boats.

HENRY W. CLUNE
The Genesee, 1963

LOWER FALLS

HIGH BANKS, PORTAGE

At the foot of Lake Seneca and its land-locked waters of deep blue and emerald lies spectacular Watkins Glen—noted for its steep chasms, gorges, and cascading waterfalls

MOUNTAIN HOUSE

We are now in Glen Alpha, as it has been somewhat fantastically called. Inside the great rock barrier, which we have just succeeded in passing, a narrow but secure bridge crosses the chasm; and from this bridge a fine view is had of the first cascade, as it pours swirling through a rift in the rocks, and falls, roaring and foaming, into a deep basin, scooped out of the solid rock-bed by the constant fret and chafe and turmoil of the waters. Quitting the bridge, and clambering up a series of steps, we gain presently a narrow foot-path, cut out from the face of the cliff, and follow its fantastic windings until all further progress is barred by a transverse wall, over which the waters of the long cascade fall from a great height into the dark pool below. At this point the rugged and lofty walls of the gorge draw close together.

O. B. BUNCE

Picturesque America, 1872

GLEN ALPHA

*Located in the state's central region, roughly running
north and south, in an area of rolling hills are the
Finger Lakes: Keuka, Seneca, Cayuga, Owasco and Skaneateles*

RAINBOW FALLS

Before us is what is called the Glen of Pools, from
the variety and extent of its water-worn basins. Standing on the bridge, and looking up the gorge, the eye
falls upon a series of cascades and rapids, low and
broad, but very beautiful. The enclosing walls are
again sufficiently broken to allow the growth of trees
in some places, and to let the light in freely. Beyond
these, again, cascades of greater breadth drop from
one rocky ledge to another, foaming and seething;
while over the southern wall, and the pathway that
clings to it, a thin stream, falling from a great height,
spreads itself out like a veil of silver mist, and mingles
its waters with those in the rockbound channel far
below. At certain seasons of the year the sun is at an
angle which...

...sends glancing lights through the gorge, which
break in prismatic colors on this thin fringe of a
waterfall, and hence give it the name of Rainbow
Falls. For the nomenclature of the glen is hopelessly
free and confusing, each season giving a new series of
designations to its various falls and aspects. "Glen
Cathedral" is a term that seems to have adhered with
some tenacity, but the other water-falls and pools
have almost as many terms as there are tastes and
fancies among the visitors; and names, at best, apply
to one feature only of the scene they describe,
whereas in each picture there are usually a hundred
phases that rival each other in beauty and interest.

O. B. BUNCE

Picturesque America, 1872

ENTRANCE TO WATKINS GLEN

186

Buffalo, *the Empire State's second great city—a transportation hub located on Lake Erie—is a giant complex of milling and manufacturing activities . . .*

It was my felicity to catch a grain steamer and an elevator emptying that same steamer. The steamer might have been two thousand tons burden. She was laden with wheat in bulk; from stem to stern, thirteen feet deep, lay the clean, red wheat. There was no twenty-five per cent dirt admixture about it at all. It was wheat, fit for the grindstones as it lay. They maneuvered the fore-hatch of that steamer directly under an elevator —a house of red tin a hundred and fifty feet high. Then they let down into that fore-hatch a trunk as if it had been the trunk of an elephant, but stiff because it was a pipe of iron-clamped wood. And the trunk had a steel-shod nose to it, and contained an endless chain of steel buckets.

RUDYARD KIPLING

The Selected Works of Rudyard Kipling, 1900

ERIE CANAL BASIN AND GRAIN ELEVATOR, BUFFALO

SHIP CANAL, BUFFALO

. . . an important inland port receiving huge shipments of ore and grain from the West, and processing these for distribution to all parts of the world

---

187

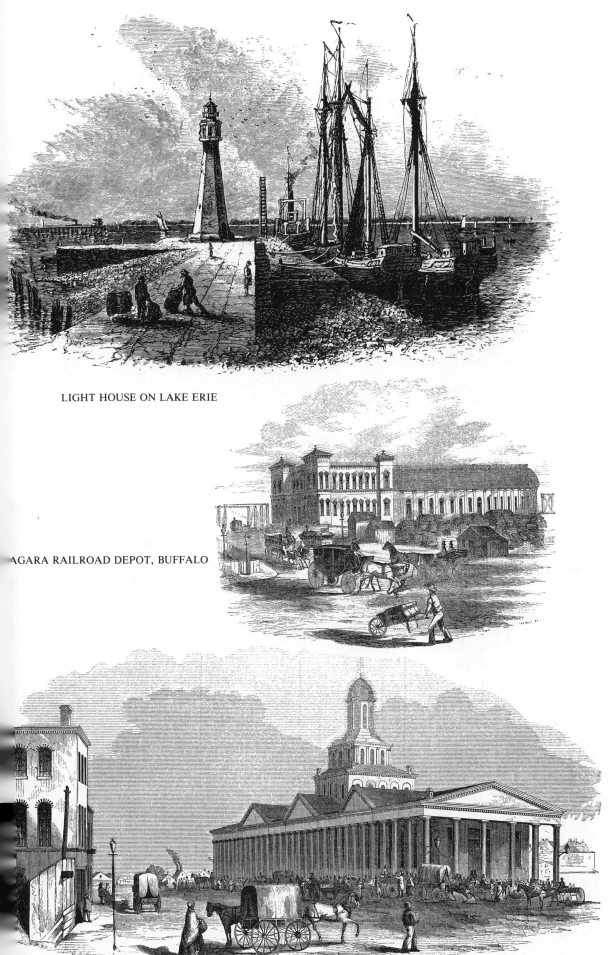

LIGHT HOUSE ON LAKE ERIE

AGARA RAILROAD DEPOT, BUFFALO

MARKET HOUSE, BUFFALO

Buffalo, at the end of the century's first decade, was a small giant of a city, for the most part as ugly as the sin it sheltered. It flowered in the vast chateux of Delaware Avenue Avenue and Chapin Parkway out of the east-side slums. The shops and stores of downtown—Main Street, Court Street, and Lafayette Square—were nothing remarkable but still able to furnish all the appurtenances of civilization. The city illustrated the best and worst of industrial America. It was pushing, inventive, and vigorous; but it was also disordered, corrupt, and hideous. Like Cleveland, Detroit, and Chicago, farther west on the Lakes, it was run by its businessmen; and its businessmen had no ambitions other than making money and retreating to their palaces with it. Cereals from the northern plains and iron ore from the Superior ranges came plowing down the Lakes in the huge bulk carriers—hogbacks—and the Buffalo mills turned the grain into flour and feedstuffs and the ore into pig iron. In its harbor, heavy midwestern cargoes were transshipped to the Erie Canal or the East-going railroads; and in the hundreds of grimy, greasy slips of South Buffalo, canalboats were emptied into ships for passage West. All down the Niagara to the Falls, through Black Rock, the Tonawandas, La Salle, and on into the Falls city itself, the mills and factories smoked, steamed, and fumed through the days and flamed through the nights.

REXFORD G. TUGWELL
The Light of Other Days,
1962

New York's most spectacular natural wonder is, of course, Niagara Falls, first seen and described by Father Hennepin, in 1678, as "a vast and prodigious cadence of water . . .

For more than ten years, men have been spinning like spiders the iron web that connects Canada with the Union: have tried with great labour various experiments, and when their work has been destroyed by the powers of Nature, have begun again; and at length triumphed over all obstacles. As the river here is almost as deep as it is broad, the erection of piers was out of the question, and since the river runs at the Narrows with fearful velocity, there could be no bridge of boats. . . . Nothing remained, therefore, but to adopt the plan of the spider, when he flings his fine thread from tree to tree through the air. Paper kites were prepared, and, when the wind was fair for the attempt, sent across, loaded with the first thin wires. . . and now from the first thin, almost invisible wire, we have arrived at a grand and beautiful suspension bridge, that is, perhaps, unequalled in the world. The chains on which it hangs are as thick as ship's masts, and more than a thousand feet long, and the towers that support them are masterpieces of modern architecture. They are about 250 feet high, and divided into two stories; through the upper one runs a railroad, and through the lower a broad and spacious roadway for passengers, horsemen, and carriages.

J.G. KOHL

SUSPENSION BRIDGE, TWO MILES BELOW NIAGARA FALLS

THE WHIRLPOOL

. . . which falls after a surprising and astonishing manner.''
This "thundering water" of the American Indian has been a
mecca for tourists ever since its discovery, three centuries ago

BELOW AMERICAN FALLS

After wandering on some of our great lakes for many months, I bent my course towards the celebrated Falls of Niagara being desirous of taking a sketch of them, for the amusement of my family.

RAPIDS ABOVE AMERICAN FALLS

Returning as I then was from a tedious journey, and possessing little more than some drawings of rare birds and plants, I reached the tavern at Niagara Falls in such plight as might have deterred many an individual from obtruding himself upon a circle of well-clad and perhaps wellbred society.

JOHN JAMES AUDUBON

Delineations of American Scenery and Character, 1926

Behold Niagara! The accumulated waters of four vast inland seas tumble over its limestone ledge on their wild dash to the wide Atlantic

THE CAVE OF THE WINDS

Still I had not half seen Niagara. Following the verge of the island, the path led me to the Horseshoe, where the . . . broad [river], rushing along on a level with its banks, pours its whole breadth over a concave line of precipice, and thence pursues its course between lofty crags towards Ontario. A sort of bridge, two or three feet wide, stretches out along the edge of the descending sheet, and hangs upon the rising mist, as if that were the foundation of the frail structure. Here I stationed myself in the blast of wind, which the rushing river bore along with it. The bridge was tremulous beneath me, and marked the tremor of the solid earth. I looked along the whitening rapids, and endeavored to distinguish a mass of water far above the falls, to follow it to their verge, and go down with it, in fancy, to the abyss of clouds and storm. Casting my eyes across the river, and every side, I took in the whole scene at a glance, and tried to comprehend it in one vast idea. After an hour thus spent, I left the bridge, and, by a staircase, winding almost interminably round a post, descended to the base of the precipice. From that point, my path lay over slippery stones, and among great fragments of the cliff, to the edge of the cataract, were the wind at once enveloped me in spray, and perhaps dashed the rainbow round me. Were my long desires fulfilled? And had I seen Niagara?

FRANCES WRIGHT

The Dolliver Romance and Other Pieces, 1876

The Garden State . . . from the Atlantic . . . to the Delaware

JERSEY CITY . . . COMMUNIPAW . . .

THE HUDSON . . . HOBOKEN . . . NEWARK . . .

ELIZABETH . . . RAHWAY . . . PASSAIC FALLS

. . . THE RAMAPO . . . TRENTON . . . STATE

HOUSE . . . PRINCETON . . . RED BANK . . .

NEVERSINK HIGHLANDS . . . FAIRHAVEN . . .

DELAWARE WATER GAP . . . BUSHKILL FALLS

. . . THE UPPER DELAWARE

DELAWARE WATER GAP

The Garden State... from the Atlantic to the Delaware

NEW JERSEY WAS ONCE TWO JERSEYS: East Jersey and West Jersey. Settled by Scottish and New England Dissenters, East Jersey wore the somber cloak of Calvinism. In West Jersey, the Quakers developed a landed aristocracy, powerful both politically and economically.

The state's history goes back to Dutch and Swedish communities which were established before settlements by the English. Dutch claims to the Hudson and Delaware valleys were based on the voyages of Henry Hudson, who sailed into what is now Newark Bay in 1609, and on explorations of the lower

Delaware made by Cornelis Jacobsen May in 1614. Patroonships were offered by the Dutch West India Company, and small colonies were located where Hoboken, Jersey City, and Gloucester City now stand. New Sweden, established by Swedes and Finns in 1638, was annexed in 1655 to the New Netherland Colony. In 1664, Richard Nicolls—acting for James, Duke of York (later James II)—seized New Netherland for the English. Nicolls had encouraged New England Dissenters to buy Indian land in the Elizabethtown and Monmouth regions.

Free lands and a liberal charter attracted settlers, but confusion resulted from an unwieldy number of land owners. Strife developed, dividing the area. In 1664, William Penn purchased the West Jersey area and, in 1677, Penn and eleven other Quakers bought East Jersey. Its independence from New York was recognized, but authority remained with New York governors until 1738. The Provincial Congress, in 1776, adopted a constitution and declared New Jersey a state. In 1790, Trenton became the capital.

During the War of Independence, New Jersey played a strategic role. George Washington, after his daring attack on the Hessians at Trenton, went on to win important battles at Princeton and Monmouth, adding immeasurably to the confidence of the patriots. Four times Washington moved his army across the state, wintering twice at Morristown.

New Jersey's population had grown from an estimated 15,000 in 1700, to approximately 184,000 in 1787—the year New Jersey ratified the Constitution. Only four states in the nation are smaller in size than New Jersey, yet it ranks eight in population. Despite its small size, the state is an industrial giant, a major transportation terminus, and a year-round commuter area for thousands who work in New York City and Philadelphia.

From the time when dogwood and rhododendrons show their first buds until the maples "put on their dresses of red and gold," visitors flock to New Jersey—appropriately known as the *Garden State*— to enjoy its ocean shores, lovely lakes, state parks, and forests. South New Jersey's urban centers are Atlantic City—famed for its white sands and boardwalk—now renowned as a convention city and amusement center; and Camden—thought of as an outpost of Philadelphia—a manufacturing complex, and the largest Jersey port on the Delaware River. Newark, the state's largest city—a hub of industry—creates a vast variety of products. The important textile industry, powered by the falls of the Passaic—was initiated at Paterson.

New Jersey is noted for potteries, glassworks, shoe factories, and brickworks, as well as for mining and processing of iron and copper. The pattern of the state's development was molded by 1865. The roads were improved, the Morris Canal and the Delaware and Raritan canals, were rechartered, and the Camden and Amboy Railroad completed a line from New York to Philadelphia. From the landed aristocracy, the enormous economic expansion brought an industrial democracy.

New Jersey's moderate climate creates a good growing season and farms are richly productive, concentrating chiefly on dairying, poultry raising, and field crops, especially tomatoes and apples. The southern inland region, the scrub-pine area, cultivates cranberries and blueberries. Acres of tidal marshes, east of Newark and Hackensack, have been converted to commercial use. The state's major rivers—the Passaic, Hackensack, and Raritan—provide drainage. The Atlantic Coast is dotted with resort towns and commercial fishing. Stretching across the northwest corner, from New York's border to the spectacular Delaware Water Gap, are the Kittatinny Mountains—a region of exceptional beauty, popular with vacationists. Across the Delaware River, many toll and free bridges link New Jersey with Pennsylvania and Delaware. The Garden State Parkway, the New Jersey Turnpike, and the Pulaski Skyway are among New Jersey's great network of toll roads and freeways. Several ferries, the facilities of the Port of New York Authority: double-decked George Washington Bridge, the Lincoln and Holland vehicular tunnels, and three bridges to Staten Island add to New Jersey's accessibility. The state's best-known institutions of higher learning, established during the eighteenth century, are Princeton University, at Princeton, as the College of New Jersey, in 1746; and Rutgers, the state university, chiefly at New Brunswick, as Queen's College, in 1766.

Jersey City—variously known as Paulus Hook, Pavonia, and Communipaw—has, since the days of its settlement by the Dutch in 1629, always lived in the shadow . . .

Ships came first. Stevens used Nicholas Roosevelt's foundry at Second River (Belleville) to build a 60-foot steamer, *Polacca,* getting technical advice from Josiah Hornblower who had brought the first steam engine to America, almost half a century before. On October 21, 1798, the *Polacca* took its trial trip down the Passaic. She made three and a half miles per hour and actually voyaged to New York, but the engine was poorly bedded and the vibration opened the ship's seams. Further experimentation followed and in 1804 Stevens, with his two sons, Robert and John, launched the *Little Juliana,* a small twin-screw craft, which ran for a brief time as ferryboat between Hoboken and New York. He built a hundredfooter, the *Phoenix,* but in 1807, Robert Fulton's *Clermont* made its successful trial on the Hudson, and Fulton and Livingston secured a monopoly to operate steamships in New York waters. Although the *Phoenix* ran a bootleg trip from New Brunswick to New York, forty-five miles in nine and a half hours, Stevens sent the vessel to the Delaware.

HARRY EMERSON WILDES

Twin Rivers, 1943

JERSEY CITY, FROM THE HUDSON

COURT HOUSE

RAILROAD YARDS, JERSEY CITY

NEW RAILROAD DEPOT, JERSEY CITY

. . . *of its great neighbor, a ferry ride across the Hudson.*
An important seaport in its own right, it is also
a terminus for rail lines leading west

195

COMMUNIPAW

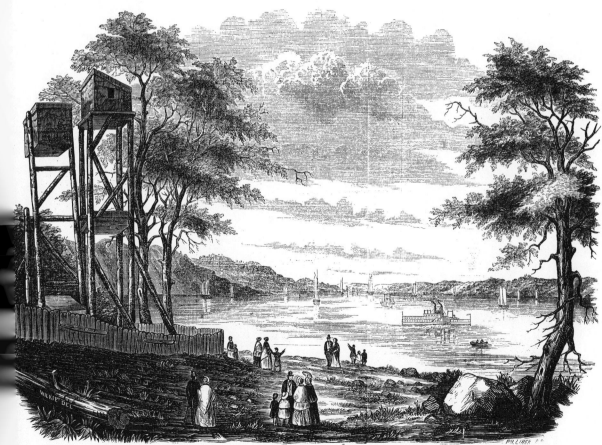

HUDSON RIVER, FROM ELYSIAN FIELDS, HOBOKEN

Stevens himself boiled in protest against New Jersey's backwardness. Other states boasted smooth, privately built turnpikes, over which, at low tolls, a carriage could run at seven miles an hour. New York had thirteen such roads, Pennsylvania five; in the New England states, capitalists had built no fewer than forty-eight. New Jersey had none. Stevens argued vainly that turnpikes cheapened freight, cut costs of goods and boosted realty values by granting more accessibility to markets, schools and churches, but Twin Rivers farmers refused to listen. "Pikes," they said, "are aristocratic; for democratic people, the common road is good enough." Twin Rivers remained conservative. Travelers from New York ferried in an open boat to Paulus Hook, paying sixpence for the privilege, and then took the stage to Newark across salt marsh that "trembled underfoot." This section of the journey particularly annoyed Stevens for the cross-log corduroy caused continuous bumping and sometimes made women travel-sick. In summer, stagnant pools bred millions of mosquitoes which, in addition to their cruel torment, "infected the air," it was said, "with epidemical fever." Seasoned travelers swathed themselves in thick sailcloth or bundled up in cloaks, but these were stifling hot and gave no protection to the face and hands. Stevens envied the ferryhouse proprietors and tavern hosts who kept wetwood fires smoldering all summer to smoke the insects out.

HARRY EMERSON WILDES
Twin Rivers, 1943

In May 1666, Robert Treat and thirty followers from Connecticut sailed into Newark Bay, where the pious band landed to settle the west bank of the river . . .

When it came to proving the value of industrial diversity, Newark topped all New Jersey rivals by 1860. Newark had the Morris Canal, good railroad connections and a wide bay for shipping. Newark's emergence as a city of industrial variety began early. Dr. Jabez G. Goble, "an eminent and public-spirited citizen," took a careful look in 1836, when Newark officially became a city. Dr. Goble pridefully declared no city of "similar extent and population" exceeded Newark in the "number, variety and beauty of workmanship" in manufactures. He then documented an impressive variety: leather, hats, carriages, clothing, saddles, coach axles, coach lace, bowie knives, malleable iron, patent leather, silver plating, jewelry, cutlery, buggy railings, statuary, lathes, mechanics' tools, looking glasses, bellows, and so on through several more pages. Jacob Wiss, on his way from Switzerland to Texas with two St. Bernard dogs, tarried in Newark in 1848 to make cutlery (using his dogs on a treadmill to supply power). His reputation for fine scissors mounted; he never left the city by the Passaic. Edward Balbach, who arrived from Germany the same year, let others seek gold in California; he found his on the floors of Newark's jewelry houses. Opening a small refining plant in 1851 to handle jewelry floor sweepings—the only such place in the Untied States—Balbach drew trade from cities throughout North America. By 1875 Balbach handled more gold and silver than the U.S. Mint.

JOHN T. CUNNINGHAM
New Jersey, 1966

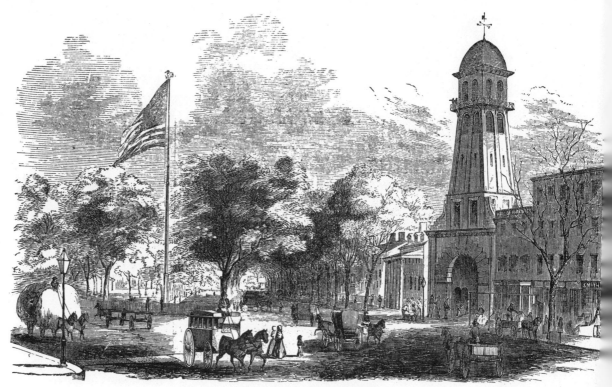

PARK PLACE, NEWARK

BROAD AND MARKET STREETS, NEWARK

*. . . founding what became Jersey's largest city, Newark—
a thriving metropolis with varied activities: milling,
brewing, metal crafts, paints, and varnishes*

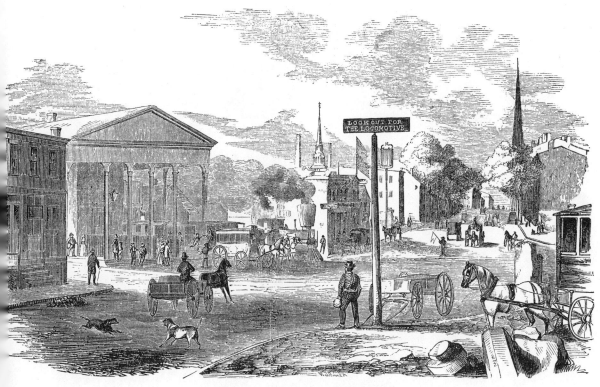

MARKET STREET DEPOT, NEWARK

SHIPPING AT NEWARK

No city in the state could challenge Newark's claim to pre-eminence. Newark made just about everything—corsets, clothing, shoes, harnesses, carriages, machines, jewelry, malt products, paint, trunks, carpetbags, varnish, chemicals, hats, and hundreds of other necessities and luxuries. "Ye town on ye Passaick,"much as it doted on its church spires and colonial greens, faced a future filled with belching smokestacks. Newark showed its might in 1872 in an "industrial Exhibition" that won enthusiastic praise. Joseph Atkinson, Newark historian, called the exhibition "the most remarkable, probably, in the world's history of the mechanical arts." Even given Atkinson's burst of local pride, the show must have been exceptional. Nearly 1000 Newark manufacturers presented their wares when the exhibition opened on August 30. Visitors, potential buyers, and critics flocked to the show, and Horace Greeley and Ulysses S. Grant, rival candidates for the Presidency, stopped by on the likelihood there would be more hands to shake there than anywhere for miles around. Mr. Greeley confessed that he had not been in Newark for more than forty years and expressed astonishment that in the interim the city had grown from 12,000 residents to ten times that number. Greeley had stayed away too long; New Jersey—which had voted against Grant in 1868— went heavily for the General in 1872.

JOHN T. CUNNINGHAM
New Jersey, 1966

Since colonial days, Jersey's main toll roads and turnpikes have crossed the state in a diagonal course, diagramming a true "tale of two cities" . . .

MAIN STREET, RAHWAY

Named after Lady Elizabeth Carteret, the wife of Governor Sir George Carteret, the town of Elizabeth was the first English settlement made in the state. The land was purchased from the Indians for a company called the "Elizabethtown Associates," in 1664, a region pleasantly situated in a level and fertile country. During the Revolution the town suffered much from its contiguity to New York, including the burning of its famed First Presbyterian Church, in January, 1780. A feature that distinguishes the town, the uncommonly wide streets, had been attributed to Governor Philip Carteret, who was the original incorporator of Elizabeth, prior to 1680. The College of New Jersey, now located in Princeton, received its first charter in 1747, and was opened here with eight pupils, under President Dickinson. About five miles away is the town of Rahway, on the Rahway River, a town possessed of varied manufacturing interests that include carriages, hats, felt cloth, and stoneware.

WILLIAM B. SIPES
The Pennsylvania Railroad, 1875

STREET SCENE, ELIZABETH

. . . between New York and Philadelphia, carrying an extraordinary burden of traffic, making the Garden State a corridor for north-south travel

COURT HOUSE, ELIZABETH

NEW BRUNSWICK

Upriver people, particularly at Raritan Landing, two miles above New Brunswick, where sloops might sail when tides were high, envied New Brunswick's growing wealth; they built a bridge across the Raritan to divert traffic from the Inian ferry. This, however, meant a detour of two miles on each side of the river in order to regain the highroad to the Delaware, and not many seasoned travelers were willing to ride the extra distance, if, in addition, they would miss the joys of Inian's inn. A dam built at the Landing stopped flatboats from the interior and gave water power for several gristmills, but at the same time it decreased the depth of water and guaranteed New Brunswick's shipping business.

HARRY EMERSON WILDES

Twin Rivers, 1943

The Great Falls of the Passaic—New Jersey's own Niagara—was ranked, in colonial times, as one of the wonders of the world whose potential for power . . .

Alexander Hamilton built Paterson and to this day he remains its guardian. He saw the Great Falls of Passaic while he was aide-de-camp to Washington and, alone among seventeenth and eighteenth century observers, was impressed by something other than its wild, romantic beauty. Others saw the fearsome cataract falling seventy feet into a swirling maelstrom and praised its charm; Hamilton looked upon the waterfall as a source of power. The proud little genius, who divined the future with lightning speed and by intense concentration and never-ending work carried projects into execution, recognized the Great Falls of the Passaic as a site where would someday arise the world's most fruitful workshop. The tumbling stream, dashing with such force and rushing onward with such vehemence, would, he thought, provide sufficient power to turn the wheels of every factory that the nation could ever build; the splendid river that flowed forward in more placid serenity to the sea could dock the ships to carry the country's entire industrial output to markets in every quarter of the globe. His vision was unbounded; on the high ground within the hairpin bend of the Passaic, sheltered by the rocky slope of Garret Mountain, he foresaw mills and factories thickly clustered, monopolizing manufactures and holding the rest of the United States as its agricultural and mining fief.

HARRY EMERSON WILDES

Twin Rivers, 1943

PASSAIC FALLS

. . . was first recognized by Alexander Hamilton, who foresaw the area's development as an industrial complex near the larger metropolitan centers

THE PASSAIC, BELOW LITTLE FALLS

RAMAPO RIVER

The Passaic is the despair of geographers, for it flows at one time or another toward every point of the compass, but its real triumph comes at Little Falls, where it drops forty feet over a series of cascades into rifts and rapids, and again at Paterson, after making a hairpin curve, it falls vertically seventy feet into a rockwalled gorge that, in colonial times, ranked among the wonders of America. "Passaic Falls, called by some Totowa Falls, is a great curiosity," wrote one awed traveler. "The river runs over large rocky mountains covered with fir trees. An immense body of rock would totally interrupt its passage, had it not been rent into huge clefts, some twenty to thirty feet wide, others only two to three feet, and fifty to seventy feet deep. The whole torrent falls down perpendicularly, with amazing violence and rapidity down a rocky precipice of seventy feet with a tremendous roar and foaming. Interrupted in its course by craggy rocks, it turns abruptly to the right and again to the left, and, falling into huge cavities below, the whole torrent vanishes from sight, but, stepping to another precipice a few yards distant, we behold the same torrent emerging and rushing into a large, rocky basin, filled with forty fathoms of water. Rock walls ascend on all sides sixty feet above the surface of the river. From this the Passaic emerges and, in majestic silence, flows to the sea."

HARRY EMERSON WILDES
Twin Rivers, 1943

It was in Trenton—New Jersey's capital—that George Washington and his men, after crossing the Delaware, defeated the carousing Hessians on Christmas Night, 1776

Railroads were little short of magical to iron men. They carried New Jersey iron products everywhere—and they also became the best customers. Trenton and Paterson showed what the combination of iron and railroads meant to New Jersey. Trenton's industrial rise began in 1845, when Peter Cooper and Abram S. Hewitt opened their Trenton Iron Company to fill a Camden & Amboy Railroad order for $180,000 worth of rails. Within three years Cooper & Hewitt owned mines at Andover and Ringwood and had built the nation's largest blast furnaces at Phillipsburg. They poured out such massive amounts of iron from their fifty-eight furnaces and six rolling mills that the Trenton Iron Company became the nation's foremost iron establishment only five years after its founding. Cooper and Hewitt became the first Americans to try the noted Bessemer steel process, using it at Phillipsburg in 1856. Trenton Iron Company also made the nation's first structural iron beams (I-beams) in 1854—for such varied building as Princeton's rebuilt Nassau Hall, the new Harper & Brothers' building in New York, and more than 100 federal buildings including the Capitol at Washington and Fort Sumter in Charleston Harbor. Trenton Iron Company's success enticed others to the booming city. Makers of anvils and iron grillwork settled in several shops, but the biggest catch was John Roebling, who moved his wire-rope factory from western Pennsylvania to Trenton capital in 1859.

JOHN T. CUNNINGHAM

New Jersey, 1966

STREET SCENE, TRENTON

COUNTY BUILDINGS, TRENTON

STREET SCENE, TRENTON

STATE HOUSE, TRENTON

The city's early industrial growth—aided by its strategic location on the river—centered around iron and steel, pottery, china, and paper goods

BRIDGE OVER THE DELAWARE, TRENTON

"Elaborate exercises" opened the Trenton bridge to traffic on January 30, 1806. The structure stretched 1008 feet from end to end, its five massive wooden arches resting on four tall stone pillars. Builders meant that bridge to stay—and it did. Five other Delaware River bridges washed away in a freshet in 1841, but the Trenton span stood firm. In the 1840s, railroad tracks were laid on the wooden floor and the bridge defied the elements for another thirty-five years before it was replaced in 1876. By 1806, a traveler could proceed on land or over bridges from Philadelphia to Paulus Hook. He could also use the same facilities to reach Hoboken.

JOHN T. CUNNINGHAM
New Jersey, 1966

NEW JERSEY COLLEGE, PRINCETON

*The Jersey strand, 120 miles of gleaming white beaches—
extending from Sandy Hook, at New York's Lower Bay, south
to the tip of Cape May—is a vast stretch of lowlands . . .*

Once in a while a lucky visitor meets a rawhide-tough old-timer whose life typifies its undefiled saltwater habitat. Not too many years ago the little creeks and the tiny coves held many of them. They lived in snuggish shanty boats at peace with a chunk stove that was winter-red with driftwood. They blessed their walls with cardboard calendars which did double duty as wall caulking, and waited out the time they shared with the sea. Now and again, for tobacco money, they'd remember a minor fish hole for a summer visitor, or confide a favored duck slough to a high-school kid bright with a new shotgun and the memory of a hasty summer promise.

CARL L. BIEMILLER

New Jersey, 1947

BEACON HILL, NEVERSINK HIGHLANDS

BEACH AT RED BANK

. . . interrupted only by the Neversink Highlands—
a mecca for millions who fish or enjoy fun in the sun,
at a chain of glamorous or simple seashore resorts

BOAT LANDING, JERSEY SHORE

The most concentrated playtime strand in the United States is a more or less continuous slash of white beach which extends from Sandy Hook, an Army post which rams a fortified finger into New York's Lower Bay, to Cape May. For 125 miles the waters of the Atlantic Ocean are merely a form of liquid money during the months of high summer, and as such are appreciated by the hospitable residents of New Jersey washed by its tides. Along this coast, dominated by the famous resort towns of Long Branch, Asbury Park, Atlantic City, Wildwood and Cape May, the summer seashore vacation in the United States originated and flowered. Along this coast, each summer, the greatest number of hot-weather holiday rovers in the United States happily congregates. Cape May is probably the oldest seaside resort in the United States. The Lenni-Lenape Indians were using the cape as a recreation spot before Henry Hudson sailed by the point in 1609 en route to Sandy Hook. Aristocratic Philadelphians, bored with the war years of the Revolution, sailed Delaware Bay and found recreational pleasure at a fishing village on the same cape before President George Washington took his oath of office. As early as 1788 a boardinghouse at Long Branch on the northern sector of the coast hung out its shingle to attract visitors. The wild and comparatively isolated coast of Jersey has always been a haven for fishermen, nature lovers, people seeking rest cures, fugitives, and for adventurers who couldn't abide the disciplines of city life. It still is.

CARL L. BIEMILLER
New Jersey, 1947

FAIRHAVEN

In the northwest corner of New Jersey—where the winding Delaware marks the boundary with Pennsylvania— are the verdant peaks of the Kittatinny range . . .

The character of North Jersey is shaped by factors other than its people and its institutions. Some of the area, for instance, is made lovely by a simple geologic formation known as the Highlands, which is part of the Appalachian foothills. The extreme northwest corner of the state in Warren and Sussex Counties is Appalachian Valley country, with the flat crested ridge of Kittatinny Mountain overlooking it for more than thirty miles. This reach of ground stretches from the most northerly tip of the state, south to the Delaware Water Gap, where the Delaware River has sliced through rock to form a tourist attraction that annually lures thousands of visitors.

CARL L. BIEMILLER, *New Jersey, 1947*

THE UPPER DELAWARE

DELAWARE WATER GAP

. . . facing the Blue Ridge Mountains—a procession of magnificent scenes that increases in grandeur, as the river turns abruptly to form the Delaware Water Gap

DELAWARE WATER GAP, SOUTH FROM SHAWNEE

The two grand mountains which form the mighty chasm of the Gap have been fittingly named. The one on the Pennsylvania side is Minsi, in memory of the Indians who made the Minisink their hunting ground. The opposing more rugged and rocky cliff in New Jersey bears the name of Tammany, the chief of chiefs, who clasped hands in solemn covenant with William Penn under the elm-tree of Schackamaxon. The ruggedness of the narrow defile is seen in the sketch of the entrance. The bold face of Tammany exhibits vast, frowning masses of naked rock, while the densely wooded Minsi displays a thicket of evergreen, with the railway-track skirting it down by the water's edge. Mount Tammany defies ascent except by a vigorous climber, but the bold and distinct stratification shown in the great rocky mass called the Indian Ladder adds to the grand abruptness of the outlines, and from the narrow mountain top is best beheld the wide, extended view of the magnificent scenery above the Gap.

J. E. RINGWALT

Picturesque America, 1872

MOSS CATARACT

BUSHKILL FALLS

DIANA'S BATH

The environs of the upper Delaware, where it divides New York from Pennsylvania above Port Jervis, abounds in picturesque valleys marked by waterfalls and cascades

The view from High Point is an unbroken one, scanning adjacent Pennsylvania and New York. Enthusiasts claim that from its summit it is possible to see some twenty or more villages, as well as the Alleghenies of Pennsylvania and the Catskills of New York. It is in the hill country of Northwest Jersey that much of metropolitan and suburban New Jersey plays. Some eighty lakes shimmer in Sussex County. There are forty-one more in Passaic County, including the Pompton Lakes area, ten miles northwest of Paterson. Largest of all the cabin- and resort-lined lakes of the North is Hopatcong, whose forty miles of shoreline ramble from Morris County into Sussex. The coves formed by its indentations make more shoreline than one might expect in a lake that is only nine miles long, but this is a condition that pleases the hundreds of cabin owners. The tiny coves provide green privacy, Hopatcong in the summer is a recreational mural in tree green and lake blue, a panorama of rafts, floats, canoes and swimmers. It is a giant fresco of small sails, power boats, and grubby boys picking fishing worms out of cans; of moonlight and dance music; of rocking chairs, lighted cigars and cold beer. There are smaller, more exclusive lake colonies in the North, but the recreational pattern, give or take a few tonier facilities, is about the same. Approximately 250,000 vacationists pour into the region annually, many of them "lake families" who have been coming into these playlands since the turn of the century.

CARL L. BIEMILLER
New Jersey, 1947

SCENES ALONG THE UPPER DELAWARE

Philadelphia . . .
Birthplace of the Nation

NAVY YARD . . . THE SCHUYLKILL . . .

RICHMOND COAL DEPOT . . . FAIRMOUNT

. . . INDEPENDENCE HALL . . . LIBERTY

BELL . . . CARPENTERS' HALL . . . BEN

FRANKLIN'S GRAVE . . . PHILADELPHIA

SCENES . . . UNITED STATES MINT . . .

THE EXCHANGE . . . LEDGER BUILDING

. . . MASONIC HALL . . . ASSEMBLY

BUILDING . . . LA PIERRE HOUSE . . .

SKATING ON THE SCHUYLKILL . . .

FAIRMOUNT WATER-WORKS . . .

EXPOSITION GROUNDS . . .

Philadelphia . . . Birthplace of the Nation

Philadelphia

THE "CITY OF BROTHERLY LOVE"— the largest of all American cities in 1800—Philadelphia for ten years was the capital of the Thirteen Colonies, and the nucleus of culture, gaiety, and fashion. Most of the greatest men from all the Colonies had gathered there— every living public man had some connection with the city. On almost any day Washington, John and Samuel Adams, Madison, Monroe, or Patrick Henry could be seen on the streets. There Benjamin Franklin had won world fame, had founded the American Philosophical Society, and attracted the leading minds of his time. Benjamin Rush, the great physician and teacher of medicine—in the first of American medical schools— drew students from Maine to Georgia. John Bar-

tram, the botanist; David Rittenhouse, the clockmaker; Thomas Godfrey, who invented the double-reflecting sea quadrant—all came together here.

English and French visitors were amazed by the luxury displayed in the city: President Washington's splendid coach and four, his liveried footmen; staid Quakers carrying gold canes and gold snuffboxes, and wearing great silver buttons and buckles; ladies with sky-high coiffures, in costumes of the most costly brocades and velvets, silks, and satins; the grand wigs and queues, knee buckles and silk stockings, worn by the men. "Ladies paid their French maids no less than two hundred pounds a year; and there were statesmen like Gouverneur Morris who had his two French valets and a man to buckle his hair in paillotes." So long as the capital was in Philadelphia, and the Federalists were in power, social life was luxurious and stately.

The city had long been a center for portrait painters—thirty-six were there in the period before the Revolution, and Gilbert Stuart settled there in 1793. Joseph Priestly, English Unitarian, and the discoverer of oxygen, was shocked by the frivolity and luxury of the city, which also amazed John Adams. Founded as a Quaker colony by William Penn, Philadelphia's commercial, industrial, and cultural growth had been rapid. Much of the city's fame was due to Benjamin Franklin, scientist and statesman, who, through his own efforts, had become one of the world's most learned men. Honorary degrees had been granted him by Harvard, Yale, St. Andrews, and Oxford. He was a Fellow of the Royal Society of London, and in America, only Washington commanded equal respect and confidence. Britain continued to impose measures that the colonists regarded as infringements of their rights, and—after the battles of Lexington and Concord, in April 1775—discontent flared and the Revolution developed. At Philadelphia, the Second Continental Congress, led by John Hancock, John Adams, and Samuel Adams, demanded independence from England. A resolution was called for on June 7, 1776, and four days later John Adams, Benjamin Franklin, Thomas Jefferson, Robert N. Livingston, and Roger Sherman were instructed to draft a declaration, the actual writing being left to Jefferson, Franklin, and John Adams. Jefferson revised the first draft before it was sent to Congress, where it was revised again. The final draft was adopted July 4, 1776, a day ever since regarded as America's chief holiday. Considered the most important of all the country's documents, the Declaration of Independence presented to the world a justification of the American Revolution. The first signer was John Hancock, the President of the Continental Congress. America's flag was officially adopted by Congress, June 14, 1777.

"Most visitors to Philadelphia were taken by the charm of its broad, flagged streets" and, in the words of Philippe Suchard, the young Swiss chocolate-maker from Neuchatel, "It is most bountifully provided with fresh water, which is showered and jerked about, and turned on and poured off, everywhere. The Waterworks, which are on a height near the city, are no less ornamental than useful, being tastefully laid out as a public garden, and kept in the best and neatest order. The river is dammed at this point and forced by its own power into certain high tanks or reservoirs, whence the whole city, to the top stories of the houses, is supplied at a very trifling expense." George Bickham, the great calligrapher of the eighteenth century, said of Philadelphia: "Though most of the people are Quakers, yet toleration here is general for all who behave themselves decently. . . . One of the best laid-out cities in the world, the streets cross one another at right angles and, although the space is not all built, it is already a large and populous town, having about 2,000 better houses than are common in most cities in England."

A center of American culture in colonial times, Philadelphia is still the seat of many philosophical, artistic, dramatic, musical, and scientific societies. In Fairmount Park, largest of the city parks and one of the largest in the world, are the Museum of Art, Zoological Gardens, and many historical monuments and shrines. The National History Park—one of the fine examples of the city's urban development projects—encloses Independence Hall, with the Liberty Bell, and the Declaration of Independence; the nearby Congress Hall—occupied by the Congress from 1790 to 1800, where Washington gave his farewell address; and Carpenters' Hall—meeting place of the First Continental Congress. Sightseers also usually seek out the Rodin Museum, the Gloria Dei (Old Swedes') Church, and the Christ Church, representative of Colonial architecture, begun in 1727. Elfreth's Alley—a narrow street of artists' studios—retains its colonial atmosphere, and is near the Betsy Ross house, where, tradition tells us, the first American flag was sewn. Edgar Allen Poe's house has also been preserved. A statue of William Penn surmounts the large city hall. An important trading and manufacturing center, even before the Revolution, Philadelphia now ranks high in the production of textiles, clothing, chemicals, machinery, and a diversity of other products. It also holds an important place in printing and publishing. There is a United States mint in the city, and several naval installations. Germantown is probably the oldest suburb—scene of the Battle of Germantown, and occupied by British troops during the revolutionary war. The magnificent Wissahickon—closed to motorists, beloved of hikers and horse riders—is part of the spacious and beautiful Fairmount Park.

In 1682, William Penn set forth ashore, and founded the "City of Brotherly Love—laid out an orderly, checkerboard plan of city streets, interspersed with eight park squares . . .

Hemmed in, as this stately building now is on all sides, by the obtrusive and inharmonious aggregations or brick and mortar devoted to the prosaic purposes of trade, it may be difficult, if not impossible, for the artist to find a point of view from which its picturesque features can be brought into full relief; but from its belfry the visitor at least beholds a panorama of land and water which will well repay the fatigue of ascent. The broad expanse of the Delaware, with all its varied aspects of commercial highway and grove-fringed, villa-bordered stream, flows between its level banks for many a mile beneath him. Eastward he looks far across the river to the sandy beaches of New Jersey, with Camden and Gloucester in the foreground, and an infinite vista of sombre pinegroves beyond. To the south his roving eye will first be caught by the old Navy-Yard, with its ark-like shiphouses, its tiers of masts and docks, and the green oases of its officers' quarters; while still farther away, where the Schuylkill and Delaware meet on their way to the sea, low and dark on the horizon lies League Island—the Navy-Yard of the future.

C.D. GARDETTE

Picturesque America, 1872

UNITED STATES NAVY YARD

RICHMOND COAL DEPOT, ON THE DELAWARE

. . . the "urban yet sylvan" settlement on the banks of the Delaware—though a hundred miles inland from the sea— soon became the most important seaport of the Colonies

CHESTNUT STREET BRIDGE, ON THE SCHUYLKILL

If the Delaware River is the source of commercial prosperity in Philadelphia, the Schuylkill offers to its citizens their most delightful out-of-door pleasures. The Delaware, broad, swift, and majestic, is of utilitarian benefit. The Schuylkill, narrow, winding, and picturesque, gratifies the sense of beauty. It is at Fairmont that the charm of the Schuylkill begins. Below this point there is not much in the stream calculated to interest the visitor, though the graceful iron arches of the Chestnut Street bridge will attract attention, as being a work in which engineering skill has effectually availed itself of the curved lines in which it is claimed that beauty dwells. Up to this bridge the largest vessels may approach, their tapering masts and graceful yards presenting a picture which, in a bright, sunny day, might have won the admiration and employed the pencil of Turner. The scene at this point is usually a busy one. Noisy steam-tugs, light sail-boats, scows, canal-boats, and other kinds of craft, crowd the stream, and impart that life and vivacity peculiar to the water-front of a flourishing commercial city.

C. D. GARDETTE
Picturesque America, 1872

PHILADELPHIA, FROM THE NEW SOUTH STREET BRIDGE

The city's strategic site on the estuary of the Delaware, and the hub of important rail lines, attracted the U.S. Navy yard, as well as docks and wharves to berth hundreds of ships . . .

The clippers, the most beautiful of all sailing ships, were to come a little later, their development forced, first by the Napoleonic wars and then by the War of 1812. But Philadelphia was already turning out sturdy merchantmen, somewhat bluff-bowed as yet, but with an increasing sleekness of line in both hull and rig that was a prophecy of the grace and the speed that were not far ahead. This industry had much to do with keeping Philadelphia always aware both of the wilderness behind her and of the great world to which the Delaware River was her broad avenue. From the forests, the farms, the little charcoal furnaces pushing deeper and deeper into the continent came the timber, the pitch, the hemp, the iron-work to make ships fit to battle their way around the Horn or Cape Comorin. And the ships coming back up the river were like the navy of Tarshish, "bringing gold and silver, ivory, and apes, and peacocks," but also bringing cargoes of which Solomon's navy never dreamed, English woolens, French wines and silks, Spanish velvets, Dominican mahogany, East Indian spices, Chinese porcelain, more valuable by far than the luxuries Solomon treasured, although ivory and apes and peacocks, too, have actually been landed at Philadelphia. Naturally, it was not Philadelphia ships only that came up the broad avenue. All the maritime nations of the world were represented. All flags were to be seen along what later became Delaware Avenue.

GERALD W. JOHNSON

Pattern for Liberty, 1952

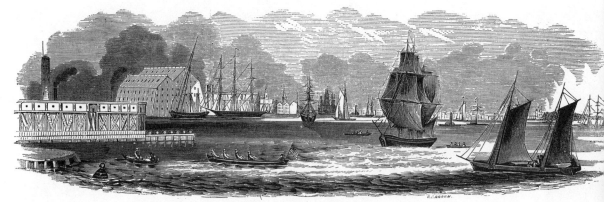

UNITED STATES NAVY YARD

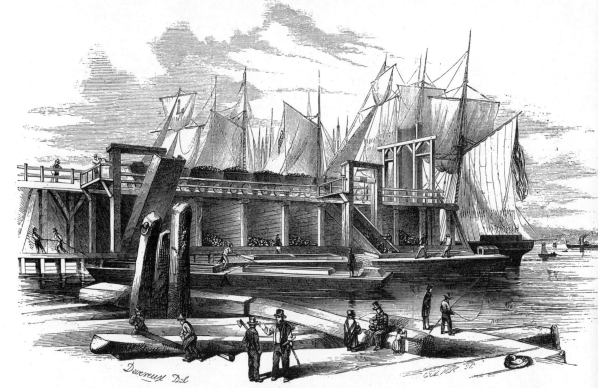

LOADING COAL, PORT RICHMOND

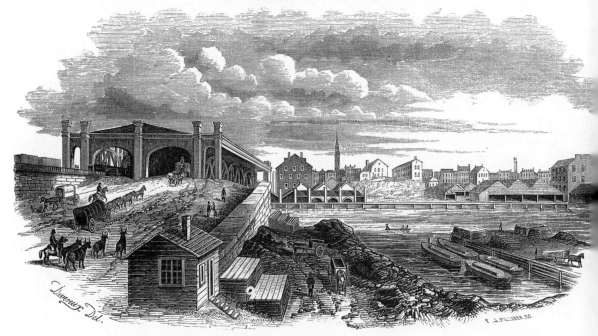

MARKET STREET BRIDGE, PHILADELPHIA

. . . used to transport varied cargoes, especially Pennsylvania's "black gold" from the vast Richmond coal depot, for shipment up and down the Atlantic seaboard

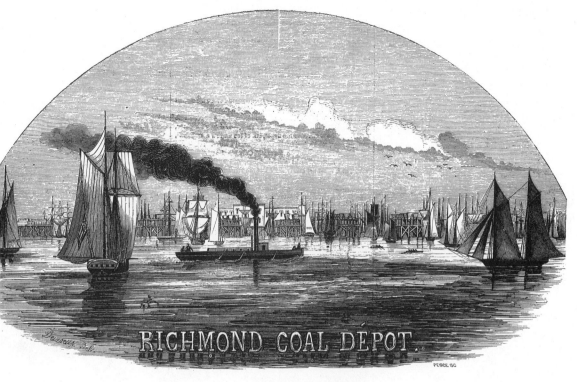

RICHMOND COAL DÉPOT.

Philadelphia seemed destined for prosperity. Its people were intelligent and industrious, its natural advantages outstanding. From the finest agricultural region in the colonies, meat, lumber, coal and crops flowed like a tide. At its wharves commerce and industry increased as shipping moved up and down the Atlantic coast and to the West Indies and Europe. Wholesalers, exporters, importers, often land speculators rather easily grew rich.

NORMAN FOERSTER, ED.
American Poetry and Prose,
1957

SUSPENSION BRIDGE, FAIRMOUNT, NEAR PHILADELPHIA

Independence Hall—where the Continental Congress met and its members wrestled with the shaping of the Constitution—ranks as the nation's most honored historic shrine, the quintessential . . .

I am filled with deep emotion at finding myself standing in this place, where were collected together the wisdom, the patriotism, the devotion to principle, from which sprang the institutions under which we live. You have kindly suggested to me that in my hands is the task of restoring peace to our distracted country. I can say in return, Sir, that all the political sentiments I entertain have been drawn, so far as I have been able to draw them, from the sentiments which originated in and were given to the world from this hall. I have never had a feeling, politically, that did not spring from the sentiments embodied in the Declaration of Independence. I have often pondered over the dangers which were incurred by the men who assembled here and framed and adopted that Declaration. . . .

STATE HOUSE AND INDEPENDENCE HALL

TOWER AND STEEPLE, INDEPENDENCE HALL

. . . I have pondered over the toils that were endured by the officers and soldiers of the army who achieved that independence. I have often inquired by myself what great principle or idea it was that kept this Confederacy so long together. It was not the mere matter of separation from the motherland, but that sentiment in the Declaration of Independence which gave liberty not alone to the people of this country, but hope to all the world, for all future time. It was that which gave promise that in due time the weights would be lifted from the shoulders of all men, and that all should have an equal chance. This is the sentiment embodied in the Declaration of Independence.

ABRAHAM LINCOLN
Philadelphia, 1861

. . . part of our American heritage, where the debates of Franklin, Adams, and Jefferson rang out, giving birth to the immortal words "that all men are created equal . . ."

CARPENTERS' HALL

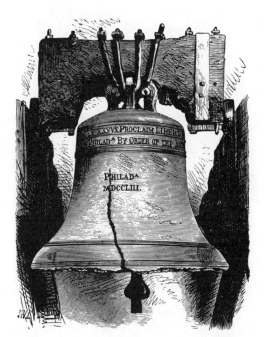

LIBERTY BELL

The greater Philadelphia is the city of Independence Hall and the Liberty Bell, the city where the Declaration of Independence and the Constitution were written, the city where the astonishing Muhlenberg parsons preached for a while and fought for a while, and played politics awhile, where Frederick A. C. Muhlenberg, as first Speaker of the House, started the legislative branch on its long career while Washington was starting the executive branch and John Jay the judiciary. Philadelphia is Franklin, with his books and his kites and his lightning rods and his jokes in the middle of everything. It is Charles Willson Peale, mingling his stuffed animals with painting of presidents and gods and goddesses. It is Abigail Adams and Mrs. Oldmixon, and incomparable Dolley (she insisted on that "e") whom "the great little Madison" snatched away from Philadelphia to a dazzling career in Washington. It is the twenty-eight thousand whose names we do not know but whose courage, cheerfulness, and confidence in the future sustained and encouraged the great men. It is the city where faith and works, because they walked hand in hand, each had life and had it more abundantly.

GERALD W. JOHNSON
Pattern for Liberty, 1952

GRAVE OF BENJAMIN FRANKLIN

SWEDE'S CHURCH

Few cities can boast finer sobriquets than the Quaker city called by John Adams "the happy, the peaceful, the elegant, the hospitable, and the polite city of Philadelphia," often referred to . . .

The clippers, the most beautiful of all sailing ships, were to come a little later, their development forced, first by the Napoleonic wars and then by the War of 1812. But Philadelphia was already turning out sturdy merchantmen, somewhat bluffbowed as yet, but with an increasing sleekness of line in both hull and rig that was a prophecy of the grace and the speed that were not far ahead. This industry had much to do with keeping Philadelphia always aware both of the wilderness behind her and of the great world to which the Delaware River was her broad avenue. From the forests, the farms, the little charcoal furnaces pushing deeper and deeper into the continent came the timber, the pitch, the hemp, the ironwork to make ships fit to battle their way around the Horn or Cape Comorin. And the ships coming back up the river were like the navy of Tarshish, "bringing gold and silver, ivory, and apes, and peacocks," but also bringing cargoes of which Solomon's navy never dreamed, English woolens, French wines and silks, Spanish velvets, Dominican mahogany, East Indian spices, Chinese porcelain, more valuable by far than the luxuries Solomon treasured, although ivory and apes and peacocks, too, have actually been landed at Philadelphia. Naturally, it was not Philadelphia ships only that came up the broad avenue. All the maritime nations of the world were represented. All flags were to be seen along what later became Delaware Avenue.

GERALD W. JOHNSON
Pattern for Liberty, 1952

Market Street, looking down from Sixth Street.

Girard College.

Arch Street, looking up.

Philadelphia, from Independence Hall, looking east.

SCENES IN PHILADELPHIA

. . . by foreigners as "the London of America," whose shores welcomed the distressed and dispossessed, naming it a haven of refuge from Europe's turmoil and discord

WHERE JEFFERSON WROTE THE DECLARATION OF INDEPENDENCE

For this very reason, its first citizen was not permitted to write the Declaration of Independence. In 1776 Benjamin Franklin was by long odds the most celebrated literary man in America and, indeed, the only one whose writings were familiar to any considerable number of Europeans; so it would seem that he was the logical choice for the task of phrasing a document of the utmost importance. But he was passed over in favor of a young, and then relatively unknown, Virginian named Thomas Jefferson. Members of the Congress realized that this called for some explanation, and they were ready with it. Franklin, the incarnation of Philadelphia, was, to be sure, master of a magic pen, but members could not rid themselves of the fear that if he were entrusted with the drafting of the Declaration he would put a joke in the middle of it. It is not unlikely that he would have done just that, and it is highly unlikely that he could have attained the eloquence and power that Thomas Jefferson reached, so the decision was a fortunate one.

GERALD W. JOHNSON
Pattern for Liberty, 1952

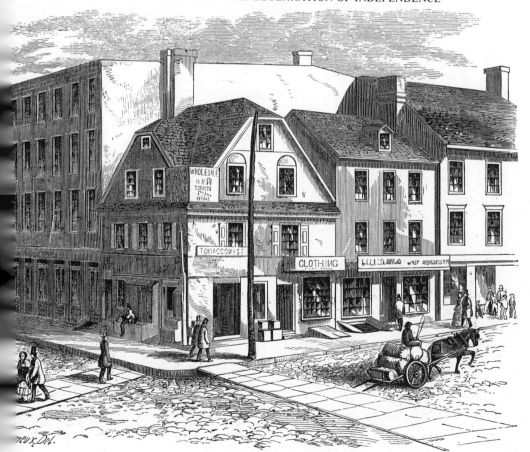

OLD LONDON COFFEE HOUSE, PHILADELPHIA

Then I walked up the street, gazing about till near the market house I met a boy with bread. I had made many a meal on bread, and, inquiring where he got it, I went immediately to the baker's he directed me to, in Second Street, and asked for bisquit, intending such as we had in Boston; but they, it seems, were not made in Philadelphia. . . . Thus I went up Market Street as far as Fourth Street, passing by the door of Mr. Read, my future wife's father; when she, standing at the door, saw me, and thought I made, as I certainly did, a most awkward, ridiculous appearance. Then I turned and went down Chestnut Street, and part of Walnut Street, eating my roll all the way, and, coming round, found myself again at Market Street wharf, near the boat I came in, to which I went for a draught of the river water; and, being filled with one of my rolls, gave the other two to a woman and the child that came down the river in the boat with us, and were waiting to go farther.

*The Autobiography
of Benjamin Franklin, 1868*

City views, especially of street scenes, presented the American illustrator an opportunity to portray pedestrian and traffic situations—with omnibuses and carriages, horsecars and railways

Would it benefit Philadelphians to have an organization for the exchange of ideas? Franklin started one; it thrives today. Were books hard to obtain? Franklin started the country's first circulating library. Were fires too frequent and too costly? Franklin started a fire department and America's first fire-insurance company, besides inventing the Franklin stove. Was it a nuisance to keep changing one's spectacles for near and distant vision? Franklin invented bifocals. Was police service inefficient? Franklin reformed it. Was there need for organized care of the sick or injured? Franklin founded America's oldest hospital. Was higher education in Pennsylvania lagging behind that of other colonies? Franklin founded what became the University of Pennsylvania and was co-founder of Franklin and Marshall College in Lancaster. Was the colonial postal service poor and running in the red? Franklin as postmaster general of the colonies improved it, reduced the rates, and made a profit for the several governments. Did the colonies need protection against the French? Franklin contributed money and supplies and became a colonel of militia. Did the colonies need a representative in London to interpret their views and seek mitigation of oppressive laws? Franklin for many years was that emissary. Was American independence inevitable? Franklin at seventy helped to draft the Declaration and signed it with firm but fine-lined calligraphy. Were the Articles of Confederation inadequate for the needs of the new country? Franklin at eighty-one as a member of the Constitutional convention urged compromises that broke deadlocks, and was one of the six signers of the Constitution who had likewise signed the Declaration of Independence.

CONRAD RICHTER
Pennsylvania, 1947

PHILADELPHIA EXCHANGE AND DOCK STREET

The Custom House, a classic stone structure, on the south side of Chestnut Street between Fourth and Fifth streets, was built for the second United States Bank, authorized by Congress in April, 1816, because of the bad financial condition into which the government had fallen during the War of 1812. The building was designed by William Strickland, in his day the leading American architect, being modeled after the Parthenon of Athens. It was completed in 1824 and was put to its present use in 1845.

FRANK COUSINS AND
PHIL RILEY
*The Colonial Architecture of
Philadelphia, 1920*

CUSTOM HOUSE, AND PARADE OF PHILADELPHIA FIRE DEPARTMENT

In the early days of the republic, Philadelphia—center of art and culture—saw the birth and decay of the Greek revival, the Doric portico, and Corinthian colonnade

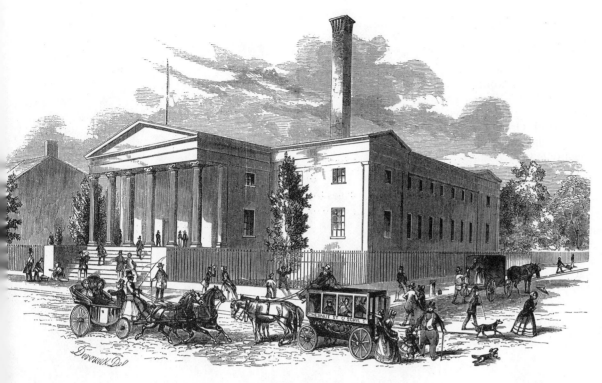

UNITED STATES MINT, PHILADELPHIA

The city increasingly took on an appearance of pillared elegance as new churches and other public, as well as private, buildings brightened its streets. William Strickland and John Haviland, more than any other individuals, were responsible for that elegance. The 1820s saw them at the peak of their architectural activity. The United States Mint at Juniper and Chestnut streets begun the following year, was even more impressively Greek. Another government building by Strickland, the Naval Asylum of 1827-33, also presented a bold pedimented portico. By 1840 the so-called Greek revival had passed its peak of popularity

EDWIN WOLF 2ND

Philadelphia Portrait of an American City, 1975

CORNER, THIRD STREET PHILADELPHIA

Mid-nineteenth-century buildings displayed a great variety of architectural influences—the passing of the Greek Revival manifesting itself in a Victorian lack of taste . . .

The cultural life of the city we may approach through the salons, where celebrities enjoyed the social art of conversation. There were Quaker salons, such as that of Mrs. George Logan, which brought together men like Washington, Jefferson, John Randolph of Roanoke, Gênet, Kosciusko, Dupont de Nemours. In the Anglican set there was, for instance, Elizabeth Graeme, daughter of the leading physician, hostess for Saturday evenings so intelligently animated that Dr. Benjamin Rush called them Athenian. She attracted all the scientific and literary leaders of the city, and men of distinction from all the colonies. Outwardly, Philadelphia was impressive because of its achievements in architecture. It had the finest church building in all the colonies: Christ Church, stately and ornate, with a London organ. An Anglican place of worship, it was attended by persons of wealth, fashion, and position.

NORMAN FOERSTER, ED.

American Poetry and Prose, 1957

LA PIERRE HOUSE, BROAD STREET, PHILADELPHIA

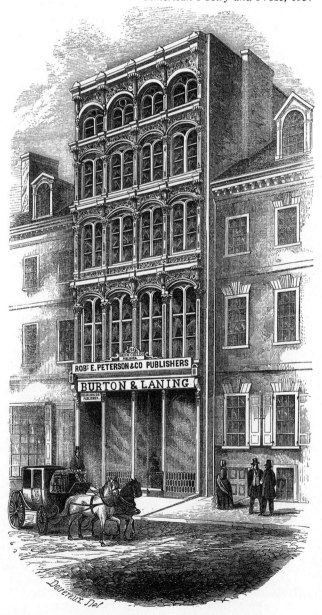

NEW IRON BUILDING, ARCH STREET

ASSEMBLY BUILDING

*. . . chaotic ugliness in commercial buildings and retail
establishments—where overornamented details appear
on Neo-Gothic facades or cast-iron storefronts*

The most famous "natural philosopher" of the
city was of course the ingenious Dr. Franklin
himself. Today most people picture Franklin the
scientist as a bespectacled colonial flying a kite
during a thunderstorm. While the identity of
lightning and electricity was his most celebrated
discovery, he was in fact fruitful in more than a
dozen fields of research, including medicine,
astronomy, oceanography, meteorology. Everything roused his curiosity and study, if only the
most comfortable way to lie in bed. Again and
again he regretted that circumstances kept
pushing him into political life and away from
the investigation of nature. Truly did Tom Paine
say of him: "His mind was ever young; his
temper ever serene; science, that never grows
gray, was always his mistress." Wedded to
public service, he yet served his scientific
mistress so well that his contemporaries were inclined to hail him as a second Newton. Along
with his quiet passion for study, Franklin entertained a deistic outlook on life, but was too
moderate and prudent to display it militantly
like Paine.

NORMAN FOERSTER, ED.

American Poetry and Prose, 1957

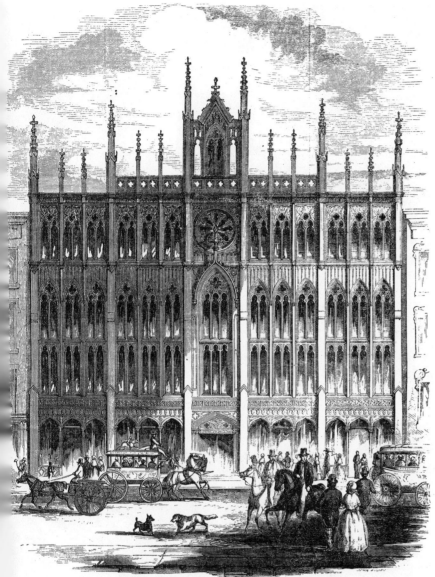

NEW MASONIC HALL, PHILADELPHIA

FARMERS' AND MECHANICS' BANK

STOREFRONT, CHESTNUT STREET

Philadelphia has been the birthplace or home of many outstanding artists: Thomas Sully, Benjamin West, the Peales, Mary Cassatt, Thomas Eakins

SKATING ON THE SCHUYLKILL RIVER

In this intimate and heartwarming picture of the joys of skating on the Schuylkill, native-born Arthur B. Frost—graphic humorist and portrayer of rural life—is at his best

When Josiah White started taming the Falls of the Schuylkill, and when the dam was built there, the effects may have been disastrous for real estate, but they were good for sport. The calm backwater that bred mosquitoes and drove away the owners of country houses encouraged boating in summer and skating in winter. All during the nineteenth century this was Philadelphia's favorite skating ground for all sorts and conditions, as prints of the animated scene testify. It was not particularly safe ground, however. Not only did people drown themselves individually, but there were collective disasters when the whole ice covering broke loose and took everyone over the dam. To mitigate these disasters, a Philadelphia Skating Club and Humane Society was formed in the mid-nineteenth century. The members not only encouraged the art, but went around with ropes tied to their backs to rescue unfortunates. The humane aspect has pretty well worn off, but the Society goes on, and remains as Philadelphia's foremost skating club. A rival Wissahickon Skating Club is of recent date, and teams of ex-college hockey stars play each other, Humane versus Wissahickon.

NATHANIEL BURT
The Perennial Philadelphians,
1961

. . . The wild nature of the Wissahickon Creek, main tributary of the Schuylkill, and its picturesque environs, made it a favorite mecca for picnickers on day-long carriage outings

Fair Mount is a beautiful spot; and standing, as it does, just on the skirt of the town, it serves the additional use of a place of pleasant and healthful public resort. The buildings containing the pump-rooms have considerable pretensions to architecture; and the *façades* and galleries extend along the river, forming a showy object from every point of view, but from the absence of any grand design in the whole, failing of a general fine effect, and presenting what a Londoner would call rather a teagardenish appearance. Steps and terraces conduct to the reservoirs, and thence the view over the ornamented grounds of the country seats opposite, and of a very picturesque and uneven country beyond, is exceedingly attractive. Below, the court of the principal building is laid out with gravel walks, and ornamented with fountains and flowering trees; and within the edifice there is a public drawing-room, of neat design and furniture; while in another wing are elegant refreshment-rooms —and, in short, all the appliances and means of a place of public amusement. It may as well be remarked here, that this last advantage is less improved in America than it would be in any other country. The Water-works of Fair Mount, though within fifteen minutes' walk of every citizen's dwelling in Philadelphia, are unfrequented.

NATHANIEL P. WILLIS

American Scenery, 1840

FAIRMOUNT WATERWORKS

RAILROAD BRIDGE, ON THE SCHUYLKILL, WEST PHILADELPHIA

In Penn's Land ...
Across the Alleghenies
to Lake·Erie

THE SUSQUEHANNA . . . RAILROAD BRIDGE

AT HARRISBURG . . . CANAL AT NANTICOKE

. . . BOLIVAR, ON THE CONEMAUGH . . .

WILLIAMSPORT . . . LOCKHAVEN . . . WEST

PORT . . . EMPORIUM . . . MOUNT PISGAH . . .

MAUCH CHUNK . . . THE JUNIATA . . .

PERRYVILLE . . . DUNCANNON . . . TYRONE

GAP . . . CONEWAGO BRIDGE . . . CONESTOGA

BRIDGE . . . VIADUCT OF THE BALTIMORE

AND WASHINGTON RAILROAD . . . RENOVO

HOTEL . . . THOMSON HOUSE, KANE . . .

CRESSON . . . ALTOONA . . . PITTSBURGH

. . . CUSTOM HOUSE . . . COURT HOUSE . . .

ERIE . . . LIGHT HOUSE, ERIE

In Penn's Land ...
Across the Alleghenies
to Lake Erie

NEAR COLUMBIA, ON THE SUSQUEHANNA

FROM PHILADELPHIA ON THE DELAware, to Pittsburgh on the Allegheny, Pennsylvania is solid substantial, green and fruitful—rich in mountains and rivers, mineral deposits, and agricultural acreage. Appropriately called the Keystone State, literally a keystone—from its northwest border on Lake Erie to the southeast shores on Delaware Bay. Here is an amazing diversity of nationalities and folkways: the elegance of Philadelphia's Main Line communities, the simplicity and charm of the Amish and Mennonite districts, the bleak mining towns, the soot-roofed cities around the steel mills. In between are gracious mountains and lovely rivers, exceptional hunting and fishing areas, somber historical reminders like Valley Forge and Gettysburg. Once Philadelphia was the nation's capital, and once it was the capital of the state. As the hardy settlers fought their way west through forested mountains and gaps etched by the rivers, and settlements were established, the state capital was moved to Lancaster in 1799, and to Harrisburg in 1812.

In 1682, when William Penn arrived in the neighborhood of Philadelphia, it was no wilderness. Swedes and Finns were already there, survivors of the short-lived colony of New Sweden. Although Penn's father—an admiral, a man of title and wealth—was a friend of Charles II and the king's brother, the Duke of York, Penn himself was a staunch Quaker. And Quakers, like Puritans, were persecuted in

England. Even in the American colonies, excepting only Rhode Island, Quakers encountered severe penalties: hangings in Boston, tortures in New York. Like the Puritans, English Quakers had migrated to Holland and Germany.

In 1676, while he was traveling in northern Europe, Penn learned of thousands of Quakers and other persecuted sects eager to emigrate to America. Obtaining the King's grant to what is now the vast province of Pennsylvania, in 1681, as payment for a debt owed his father, Penn promptly wrote an account of the province. He gave directions for the journey, the outfit needed, and the type of immigrant who would be welcome, offering easy terms on land, and complete religious liberty. "Everything went well . . . when Penn was in Philadelphia, as his own governor in 1682-84," Samuel Eliot Morison tells readers in *The Oxford History of the English People*. "He was a man of great charm and persuasiveness, still under forty, tall and athletic, able to impress Indians with his prowess at running and leaping." Penn's promotional account of his province was translated into German, French and Dutch, and widely distributed in Europe. Pennsylvania's population soon became cosmopolitan, though English and Welsh Quakers were in the majority. Mennonites —chiefly linen weavers from Crefeld, Germany—settled Germantown in 1683. They came with Francis Daniel Pastorius, an erudite preacher, whom Penn had encountered in Europe. Eliot tells us that "Penn made a worthy and successful effort to be just to the Indians of his province." But his heirs lacked Penn's ethics and good sense. Many years later, the Indians joined the French in the Ohio valley, and bloody battles occurred in the western part of Pennsylvania.

The Amish had split from the Mennonite church in Bern in 1693, with the preacher, Jacob Ammon. From his name, his followers were called *Amish*. They soon had flourishing settlements in what now are Lancaster, Bucks, Berks, and adjoining counties. A library shelf could be devoted to books on the Amish— their cult and customs, their skill at farming and with livestock, their avoidance of modern inventions like motor cars and mechanized farm implements, and their sturdy independence and scorn of government subsidies and relief. Amish ideals are as admirable as their faces are tranquil and their farms fertile. Sauerkraut, pretzels, shoo-fly pie, and a variety of other delectable foods are legacies from the Pennsylvania Dutch. Although few of the "Plain People" use tobacco, most of them grow it, as well as hay, corn, wheat, barley, potatoes, fruits, and berries.

From the carboniferous period, the state was endowed with enormous deposits of anthracite coal in the east, extensive beds of bituminous ore in the west. These vast resources have been tapped to yield abundantly, through mountain sides slashed with quarries, and mine shafts sunk at strategic spots. Rural centers have sprung up in the valleys. There is much wild country in the upper Alleghenies, the Endless Mountains, and the Black Forest where black bears and deer are plentiful. Its coal enabled Pennsylvania to build huge steel mills, of inestimable value to the nation. With the Bessemer process and coal, mighty forges and furnaces were constructed, to meet the world-wide demand for steel. Its deposits of natural gas, petroleum, cobalt, lead, zinc, feldspar, lime, copper, and nickel also rank Pennsylvania high in the nation in industrial production. In early days, English Quakers—a corporation called the Free Society of Traders—organized whale fishing in Delaware Bay, and set up brick kilns, tanneries, glassworks, and trade with the West Indies. A century later, "Baron" Stiegel established a glassworks at Mannheim, famous for the rare colors and serene shapes of its flasks and bottles—avidly sought today by collectors.

A state of infinite appeal and mighty contrasts: builder of locomotives and stainless steel trains; with a town where chocolate making is the chief industry; famous for coal mining, yet with some of its farmland the richest on earth; a vacation land of mountains and waterfalls, caves and grottoes—primitive wilderness in some areas, in others a cultural haven; with a fine symphony orchestra, music schools, rare collections of paintings, and huge publishing enterprises.

230

The Susquehanna, one of the mightiest rivers in the East, snakes its way down from New York—eventually emptying its waters into Chesapeake Bay—draining massive land areas

We left Baltimore by another railway at half past eight in the morning and reached the town of York, some sixty miles off, by the early dinnertime of the hotel which was the starting place of the four-horse coach wherein we were to proceed to Harrisburg. This conveyance, the box of which I was fortunate enough to secure, had come down to meet us at the railroad station, and was as muddy and cumbersome as usual. As more passengers were waiting for us at the inn door, the coachman observed under his breath, in the usual self-communicative voice, looking the while at his moldy harness as if it were to that he was addressing himself, "I expect we shall want the *big* coach." I could not help wondering within myself what the size of this big coach might be, and how many persons it might be designed to hold, for the vehicle which was too small for our purpose was something larger than two English heavy night coaches, and might have been the twin brother of a French diligence. My speculations were speedily set at rest, however, for as soon as we had dined, there came rumbling up the street, shaking its sides like a corpulent giant, a kind of barge on wheels.

CHARLES DICKENS
American Notes, 1842

BRIDGE AT HARRISBURG

MOONLIGHT ON THE SUSQUEHANNA

*Situated on its right bank—the state capital, Harrisburg,
its factories belching black smoke, while down the river
float busy rafts carrying oak, hemlock, and Pennsylvania pine*

BRIDGE OVER THE SUSQUEHANNA, AT HAVRE DE GRACE

JUNCTION OF WEST AND NORTH BRANCHES OF THE SUSQUEHANNA

Towanda resounded with the noises of celebration when, on May 11, 1826, the people heard the steamboat was coming. "As she appeared round the bend," reported the *Bradford Settler*, "she was hailed by the firing of a *feu de joie*, and the ringing of bells. The banks were at once lined by hundreds." The captain was honored by a public dinner at which local orators made florid speeches. His reply was an appeal for pitch-pine knots to keep his fires blazing.

CARL CARMER
The Susquehanna, 1955

In Paleozoic times the violent erosion—known as the Appalachian Revolution—caused the earth's surface to crease, wrinkle, and erupt into immense parallel ridges . . .

In the mid-1830's, the elegant poet and essayist, Nathaniel Parker Willis, having happily retired from the bustle of New York City to his country villa near Owego, was invited to ride a comparatively new steamboat (again bearing the name *Susquehanna*) on a voyage downriver where her owners hoped to sell her. She had a draft of eighteen inches, and, in addition to her side paddles, boasted a huge stern wheel "which," wrote Willis, "playing on the slack water of the boat would drive her up Niagara if she would but hold together." She had been built, he said, in emulation of salmon and shad which could ascend a fall of twenty feet in the river through "the propulsive energy of their tails."

> *And when I asked the name of the river*
> *from the brakeman, and heard that*
> *it was called the Susquehanna,*
> *the beauty of the name seemed to be part*
> *and parcel of the beauty of the land . . . .*
> *That was the name, as no other could be,*
> *for that shining river and desirable valley.*
>
> ROBERT LOUIS STEVENSON

CARL CARMER
The Susquehanna, 1955

CANAL ALONG THE SUSQUEHANNA, AT NANTICOKE

NEAR BOLIVAR, ON THE CONEMAUGH

. . . whose valleys channeled countless streams and rivulets, forming a drainage pattern where three main river systems emerge—almost devoid of lakes

WYOMING VALLEY

Never abandoning their dream that the Susquehanna would prove a navigable waterway from source to mouth, the river populance excitedly advocated canals which would bypass stretches where rapids and shallows prohibited the passage of ships of shallow draft. The success of commercial steamboats on the Hudson, following hard upon the initial voyage of Robert Fulton's *Clermont* which had been sponsored by the influential Livingston family, stirred the Pennsylvanians to emulation. While they were making plans, a group of Baltimoreans built a steamboat of twenty-two-inch draft which they dubbed *The Susquehanna* and had her towed up the rocky, shoal-obstructed steam to Port Deposit. From there she was transferred to the Maryland Canal which provided smooth passage for ten miles above the town. A band of sweating laborers tugged her by hand the next ten miles against a swift current that sped through such tortuous curves that the men on the ropes were exhausted. She never reached Columbia and the scheme was abandoned.

CARL CARMER

The Susquehanna, 1955

PILLSBURY KNOB

In the north central portion of the Keystone State, the Susquehanna branches out into two main forks, which zigzag their way through vast land masses

Pennsylvania, bulging down the middle with its mountains, is a sharply divided state; Philadelphia in the seaboard orbit, is at one extreme end as everybody knows, and Pittsburgh, close to the Middle West, is at the other, with Harrisburg in between. I asked Senator Edward Martin, when he was governor, how Harrisburg happened to become the capital; he answered amiably, "Darned if I know," and then suggested that, in prerailway days, canals usually determined the sites of cities. Soft coal is at one end of the state, anthracite at the other; steel is in the Pittsburgh area, and textiles in Philadelphia, though Philadelphia has plenty of heavy industry too, for instance the Baldwin locomotive works and the Budd Company that makes stainless steel trains. One geographical curiosity is the abutment to Lake Erie, Pennsylvania is not a Switzerland; it has its own outlet to an inland sea. However markedly divided the Keystone State may be geographically, the ideological divisions are not less acute. The gap between conversation at a Main Line dinner party and what you will hear in a bar at Altoona, to say nothing of talk in a miner's yard near Shenandoah, is as broad as the Rubicon.

JOHN GUNTHER
Inside U.S.A., 1946

SCENES ON THE SUSQUEHANNA

The west branch, from Sunbury northwest, serves Williamsport, Lock Haven, and Emporium; the main river, winding northeast, passes Berwick, Nanticoke, Wilkes-Barre, and Pittston

235

ALONG THE NORTH BRANCH OF THE SUSQUEHANNA

The Susqehanna, though more than two hundred miles longer than the Hudson, is born among men. A few yards from the lake it is not quite four feet deep, and there children swim, shadowed sometimes by the high bank across from Riverbrink. Canoes drift here and fishermen, hardly expecting a catch, idle with short lines dangling in water so clear that the fish can see them. In spring and summer, lawn and stream and high bank across meld varying shades of green, making a lush and subtly arranged background for the fading hues of the house, like a landscape by the French painter, Courbet. And, somehow, ever consistent, through other back yards and through coal towns, through deep chasms and wide flat bottoms, the Susquehanna always keeps a relationship to the men on its banks. Sometimes dangerous, sometimes friendly, it ever maintains its unique unchanging quality, minding its own business, a "character" among streams.

CARL CARMER

The Susquehanna, 1955

*The unlimited reservoir of coal and iron-ore underlying
most of its mountain regions inevitably made
Pennsylvania a great steel-producing state*

The gory border advanced and receded across
Pennsylvania's mountains through the long
French and Indian wars. Today you can cross
these bloodstained mountains with no danger to
your hair. Beyond Philadelphia, traveling north-
westward along the path of the early white men,
you see at first the low Welsh Mountains, little
more than hills. Then, across the garden spots
of Lancaster County, you reach the long broken
line of South Mountain, where the fabulous
Cornwall iron is mined. Beyond lies the fertile
Kittatinny Valley, and north of that, from
almost any point on a clear day, you can see a
wall of mountain hundreds of miles long. This is
the Blue Ridge, called hereabouts the Blue
Mountain. From the south it looks like a

RAILWAY UP MOUNT PISGAH

solitary ridge, but once you cross it you find
yourself in a prodigality of mountains, long
slender with narrow valleys between. The cre
seem to rise higher as you go on, some of th
jumping rivers and changing their names, so
stopping short while new ones of great lengt
start farther on. Finally you reach the still-
higher Alleghenies, in the north-central area
the state, and see the orderly northeast-to-
southwest pattern break up in violent confus
the ridges running in any direction they choo
When you are no longer in the mountains, y
are probably no longer in Pennsylvania.

CONRAD RICHTER
Pennsylvania, 1947

MAUCH CHUNK, FROM FOOT OF MOUNT PISGAH

A typical mining region was Mauch Chunk—its Gravity Road atop Mount Pisgah bringing "black diamonds" from the mines beyond, down to waiting cars and canal barges

But what moved me most deeply about Pennsylvania as a boy, and still does today, is her ancient symbol of freedom, the mountains; not a few isolated ranges, as in some states, but a whole province swarming with them, often one against the other with only narrow valleys between. The sight of their backs raised to the sky, sometimes humped or flared, green and lush in summer, brown, hairy and wild in winter, seldom failed to stir me. I liked to study them and learn the lay of their land, how some ran parallel for twenty or even fifty miles and then turned or joined or threw out spurs to form coves and pinnacles or plateaus; how their aspect changed when seen from different angles; how the benches lay like smaller ridges, often with intervening forest swamps or wild hemlock hollows that the old mountain trails and early roads invariably followed; and how water from one mountain tasted sweeter and purer than that from another.

CONRAD RICHTER

MAUCH CHUNK STAIRWAY

MAUCH CHUNK AND MOUNT PISGAH

Following the tortuous course of the Juniata, running alongside its banks, is the canal serving the state's central districts . . .

Massiveness, softness of outline, and variety are the distinguishing peculiarities of the Juniata scenery. The miniature river, in its course of a hundred miles, through the numerous outlying mountains, has apparently overcome the obstacles in its way by strategy as well as by power. At many places it has dashed boldly against the wall before it and torn it asunder; at others it winds tortuously around the obstruction—creeping stealthily through secret valleys and secluded glens. At some points the mountains appear to have retired from the attacking current, leaving numerous isolated hills standing, as sentinels, to watch its progress.

WILLIAM B. SIPES

The Pennsylvania Railroad, 1875

ON THE BANKS OF THE JUNIATA

THE JUNIATA, NEAR PERRYVILLE

Three great rivers now contend for first place in the scouring of Pennsylvania's land surface: the Susquehanna, which runs a course of 444 miles from Otsego Lake in New York to Chesapeake Bay, draining 46.4 per cent of the state; the Alleghany, which runs some 300 miles from Potter County to Pittsburgh and, with the Monongahela and Ohio, drains some 34.5 per cent; and the Delaware, which rises in the New York Catskills and runs 375 miles to the sea, but captures only 14.3 per cent of Pennsylvania's drainage. The Potomac gets most of the remainder with its 3.5 per cent. A little goes into Lake Erie. But it is the three big rivers—the Delaware, Susquehanna, and the Alleghany-Ohio (the Indians quite properly regarded these last two as but one stream, the Great or Beautiful River, the Delaware word for which *Alleghany* while the Iroquois word was *Ohio*)—that have emerged victors in the age-long struggle for supremacy.

PAUL A. W. WALLACE

Pennsylvania,
Seed of a Nation, 1962

. . . weaving its way past the ridges of Mahoney and Buffalo Mountain, Tuscarora, Jacks and Shade Mountains, Bald Eagle Ridge—all part of the vast Allegheny Mountain chain

DUNCANNON, MOUTH OF THE JUNIATA

Gay was the mountain song
   Of bright Alfarata
Where sweep the waters
   Of the blue Juniata.
"Strong and true my arrows are
   In my painted quiver;
Swift goes my light canoe
   Adown the rapid river.

Bold is my warrior true—
   The love of Alfarata,
Proud waves his snowy plume
   Along the Juniata.
Soft and low he speaks to me,
   And then, his war-cry sounding,
Rings his voice in thunder loud,
   From height to height resounding."

So sang the India girl,
   Bright Alfarata,
Where sweep the waters
   Of the blue Juniata.
Fleeting years have borne away
   The voice of Alfarata,
Still sweeps the river on,
   The blue Juniata.

MARIAN DIX SULLIVAN
The Blue Juniata

TYRONE GAP, FROM THE BRIDGE

The expansion of railways across Pennsylvania, vigorously pushed forward during the late sixties and seventies, involved spanning of numerous rivers . . .

CONEMAUGH VIADUCT

The Conemaugh Viaduct, built in 1855, is a beautiful arch with a span of 80 feet, and is 70 feet high. A description written in 1855 said, "While it can scarcely be surpassed in the neatness and symmetrical proportions of the design, it is as durable as the eternal foundation upon which it rests." Nevertheless, it was destroyed in 1889 by the Johnstown Flood.

EDWIN P. ALEXANDER

The Pennsylvania Railroad, 1947

CONEWAGO BRIDGE

George Washington and many other dreamers about the future of America had seen the need of a waterway to connect the eastern seaboard with the country beyond the Alleghenies. To meet this need, New York State utilized the Mohawk Gateway in building the Erie Canal, which was opened in 1825—a date that heralded the downfall of Philadelphia as the nation's first port. Meanwhile Pennsylvania had set a number of canal projects in motion. The first, the Conewago Canal, was opened below York Haven in 1797 in order to carry boats round the rocky rapids known as the Conewago Falls of the Susquehanna River. The Schuylkill Navigation Company, spurred by the discovery of anthracite coal, was opened from Philadelphia as far as Pottstown in 1824, and all the way to Port Carbon (108 miles) in 1825. When the Union Canal was opened in 1827, connecting Delaware and Susquehanna navigation by way of the Schuylkill River, Tulpehocken Creek, and Swatara Creek, much of the Susquehanna Valley trade was drawn away from Baltimore.

CARL CARMER

The Susquehanna, 1955

. . . . difficult engineering challenges that were solved in a variety of ways—wooden-trussed bridges and fine masonry structures—eventually replaced with iron and steel spans

CONESTOGA BRIDGE

The Conestoga Road was expected to bring the products of the Susquehanna Valley to the port of Philadelphia. But these expectations were not fulfilled. The huge oakframed Conestoga wagons—deep bedded to keep their loads from shifting on the hills—tore the road to pieces. A little rain reduced it to a quagmire. Six horses (the normal complement for a Conestoga wagon, though eight were sometimes used) could drag only a little over two thousand pounds from Lancaster to Philadelphia. As the hinterland developed, this road, the main channel by which inland products reached their chief market, became choked. Baltimore, Philadelphia's perpetual rival, reaped the benefit. It was fear of Baltimore that inspired Philadelphia, through a private company, to build the Lancaster Turnpike (chartered in 1792, completed in 1795) and so to initiate the era of the American "pike." Philadelphia was resolved not to lose the trade of the Susquehanna Valley, especially at a time when the great surge of population into the West had begun. The first macadam road in the United States was built from Philadelphia to Lancaster and soon extended to Columbia. On this new and astoundingly successful road the Conestoga wagons were able to carry double their previous load.

CARL CARMER

The Susquehanna, 1955

VIADUCT OF BALTIMORE AND WASHINGTON RAILROAD

As the "Pennsy" pushed its rail lines into lush countryside along the fertile river valleys—into isolated mountain regions unknown to urban dwellers . . .

At Renovo, the business of man interrupts the lonely beauty of the stream. Renovo has had an exciting history in the past decade. It used to be a small town dependent on the Pennsylvania Railroad shops and a tannery for its economic security. That was before Dorcie Calhoun who lived in Leidy Township, twelve miles northwest, persuaded himself and some neighbors that there was natural gas under his mother's farm. They were not surprised when the hole they hired dug became a roaring oil fountain but the nation's oilmen were dumbfounded—and envious. The town doubled in population. The tannery went into the oil business. New hotels, motels, trailer camps sprang up.

CARL CARMER

The Susquehanna, 1955

RENOVO HOTEL

The country surrounding Kane on all sides is covered with a luxuriant growth of hemlock timber, and abounds in limpid streams and springs. These wide-extending forests are the homes of deer and all varieties of forest game found in northern Pennsylvania, while the waters are stocked with mountain trout, rendering the region highly attractive to sportsmen. To meet the requirements of these, and to entertain the many visitors seeking here a pleasant and salubrious resort in summer, an elegant hotel, named the "Thompson House," has been erected, capable of accommodating four hundred guests. It enjoys an elevation of more than two thousand feet above sea level, and in consequence its atmosphere is of unrivaled purity.

WILLIAM B. SIPES

The Pennsylvania Railroad, 1875

THOMSON HOUSE, KANE

. . . like a magical Pandora's box, it signaled the opening of new communities and the building of spacious resort hotels featuring "all modern conveniences"

ALTOONA DEPOT

BRYN MAWR STATION

CRESSON HOTEL

The crowd and bustle attendant upon the arrival of every train—the change to the cars which stood ready for the mountain passage—the immense locomotives provided by the State to draw the trains to the foot of "Plane 10"—the anxious pause there while the clanking of chains indicated to the passengers that their car was being attached to the wire rope which was to draw it up the steep ascent—the halt at the top of the plane while this attachment was severed, and horses or a locomotive hitched on to draw it to the next summit, was continued until the train was made up again and went on its way to Pittsburgh—can never be forgotten by those who participated in the passage. This means of crossing the mountain was used until 1854, when the great tunnel was finished, and the trains then continued on from Altoona, without interruption.

WILLIAM B. SIPES

The Pennsylvania Railroad,
1875

At Pittsburgh's Golden Triangle—Allegheny and Monongahela join to become the Ohio—where Indian trails merged into Conestoga turnpikes, and rail lines into a mighty hub . . .

And over the whole bosom of the river is enacted a pageant of echoed light more wonderful than the radiance of any noon that ever burned down upon the city of beautiful smoke. The true pilgrim, however, must take the bitter with the sweet. To offset an exalted hour on such a bridge he is made to feel the squalor of many a slum; for a sunset from Mt. Washington he is made to realize the frightful mortality of the mills. One of the most disturbing spectacles is the sight of the dull, or keen, or abstracted faces of the average citizens as they hurry by, the great bulk of them utterly oblivious to the beauty about them. They seem like famished folk racing desperately through a lane of delicious fountains. It is a sorry spectacle. For beauty is one of the things our crude, young nation most needs. And who of us has yet drunk so deep at its source that he can afford to turn his back upon it? Yet it seems as though the larger part of the Pittsburghers were so intent on making smoke, which shall make them money, which, in turn, shall enable them to withdraw to smokeless climes, that they have neither the time nor the creative energy left to enjoy the unheard-of loveliness which their smoke has conjured into being. "The larger part," I say; for I have met with not a few who have discovered and have fallen in love with the charm of their own city. It will not do to accept the word of that amusing volume, "Baedeker's United States" that "Allegheny City or the North Side . . . offers few attractions to the visitor." On the contrary, the visitor would be well advised to explore for himself. Here and there, near the waterside and in the Manchester quarter, he will come upon quaint dwellings of brick with step gables and curiously rounded corners, cousins german to the old tavern across the river at Thirty-fifth Street and Penn Avenue. The city is piled helter-skelter on a hundred hills, with industry busily reeking in every valley.

ROBERT HAVEN SCHAUFFLER
Romantic America, 1913

MONONGAHELA BRIDGE, PITTSBURGH

COURT HOUSE, PITTSBURGH

CUSTOM HOUSE, PITTSBURGH

. . . here Vulcan's blast furnaces and forges spew out tons of steel, coke, aluminum, cork, glass, and a variety of products shipped round the world

FIFTH AVENUE AND SIXTH STREET, PITTSBURGH

UNION DEPOT, PITTSBURGH

PITTSBURGH, FROM COAL HILL

Pittsburgh . . . a smoky beauty, whose hair by day drifts gray over the darkening streets, and by night is husts of fire flaring a lightning along the rivers . . . There she stands, a skyscraper city set among a Y of rivers, and all circled with workshops and mills and mines . . . And here gift to the world is the bone-work of civilization, Steel.

JAMES OPPENHEIM
Romantic America, 1913

It was here—on the shores of Lake Erie—that Commodore Oliver Perry built the fleet that defeated the British, in 1813, as the battle cry rang out "Don't Give Up the Ship"

ERIE, FROM THE LAKE

The present town of Erie was incorporated as a borough in 1805. In its bay Commodore Perry built most of the vessels of his famous little fleet, having for material only the trees of the forest, and for plans only his iron determination. A modern ship-builder would stand aghast before such a problem: given, a forest and a bay; wanted, a fleet. But in seventy days the vessels were completed, and, whether well-modelled or not, they sailed away bravely from the Presque Isle harbor, fought the battle of Lake Erie, and returned in triumph with a line of British ships in tow. The remains of Perry's flagship, the Lawrence, lie in the Erie harbor, and on the bank above the enbankments of the old French Fort Presque Isle can be traced. Erie is a thriving town—the outlet of the iron and coal district of Western Pennsylvania; it is the principal market for bituminous coal on the lakes.

CONSTANCE F. WOOLSON

Picturesque America, 1872

MAIN LIGHT, AT ERIE

The Nation's Capital & Its Environs

THE CAPITOL . . . THE POTOMAC . . .

THE JAMES . . . THE PATAPSCO . . .

MARYLAND HEIGHTS . . . GOVERNMENT

BUILDINGS . . . THE SMITHSONIAN . . .

WAR DEPARTMENT . . . TREASURY . . .

POST OFFICE . . . WHITE HOUSE . . .

PATENT OFFICE . . . PENNSYLVANIA

AVENUE . . . MOUNT VERNON . . .

GEORGETOWN . . . GREAT FALLS OF

THE POTOMAC . . . FORT WASHINGTON

. . . BALTIMORE . . . FORT MC HENRY . . .

DRUID HILL PARK . . . LAKE ROLAND

. . . HAMPDEN FALLS . . . ILCHESTER

THE CAPITOL, FROM THE BOTANIC GARDENS

The Nation's Capital
& Its Environs

SEEKING A PERMANENT SITE FOR THE national capital, delegates to the Continental Congress in Philadelphia encountered a sharp division between the North and South—each side was eager for the honor. When, in 1790, Thomas Jefferson's followers supported the plan of Hamilton—that the federal government assume state debts—Hamilton's followers, to return the courtesy,—voted to support Jefferson's plan: to establish the capital on the Potomac. The precise spot for the "federal city" was chosen by George Washington, who entrusted the city's planning to Pierre L'Enfant. Born in Paris, this young man had enlisted as a private to fight for liberty in the American Revolution. He rose to the rank of major and, as an engineer and architect, had come to General Washington's notice. His plans, submitted in 1791, were opposed by Jefferson and the Congress, and set aside. Dismissed, L'Enfant was offered a plot of land in Washington and five hundred guineas in payment, which he declined. Construction on the White House was begun in 1792, and on the Capitol the next year. The Congress moved from Philadelphia and held its first session in Washington in 1800. The first presidential inauguration held in the new capital, was that of Thomas Jefferson. But tranquility was short lived. In the War of 1812, the British captured the city and sacked it, burning the White House, the Capitol, and many other public buildings.

Growth was slow. Washington was called "a sea of mud" . . . "rural" . . . "unkempt," as late as 1860. In 1889—a century after L'Enfant had been asked to plan the city, and sixty-four years after his death—his plans were unearthed from the national archives and, in 1901, the capital was developed after his design. L'Enfant's ashes were transferred to Arlington National Cemetery.

Occupying sixty-nine square miles of land, eight square miles of water area, with broad, tree-shaded streets, government buildings of gray or white stone, many fine residences, foreign embassies, and legations along "embassy row" on Massachusetts Avenue, Washington developed into a gracious and urbane city. Its many fine parks include West Potomac, extending south from the Lincoln Memorial, with the famous Japanese cherry trees nearby; East Potomac, on reclaimed land, which projects south from the Jefferson Memorial; and Rock Creek Park, with acres of glorious natural woodlands. Among many majestic monuments and statues are: Washington Monument at the end of the narrow mall; Lincoln Memorial—its pool reflecting the marble shaft of Washington Monument; and overlooking the tidal basin, Jefferson Memorial. Arlington National Cemetery, across the Potomac, is connected with the city by the Arlington Memorial Bridge. Arlington has many residential communities within its borders, as well as the National Cemetery, the Custis-Lee Mansion, and the Pentagon. Alexandria, a port of entry on the Potomac, was patented in 1657, and permanently settled in the early 1700s. A residential suburb of Washington, many of its historic buildings have been restored. Mount Vernon, near Alexandria, was built by Lawrence—George Washington's half brother—in 1743, and was the home of George Washington from 1747 to his death in 1799. The old Georgian mansion contains many fine examples of family antiques and furniture. The federal city, on its other three sides, is bordered by Maryland, with scores of lively suburban towns, homes of the capital's vast army of workers.

Upper Chesapeake Bay is a gracious stretch of country, with deep rivers or arms of the sea reaching far into the land, on both the western and eastern shores. Oysters, crabs, and fish are plentiful. Sailing up the James, the York, or another tidal tributary of Chesapeake Bay, a traveler in the eighteenth century would find, every few miles, a clearing with a wharf, a modest mansion, cottages for servants, a kitchen garden, an orchard, corn patch, and fields green with tobacco plants. Because travel was mostly by boat, every plantation had a place on the "tobacco pipeline" to England. An "inconveniency"—this forced ships to stop at every settlement; it was also a hindrance to the growth of towns, but it spared the planters having to ship their produce to a marketing center.

When Charles I, in 1632, sliced a huge area from Virginia, to give to his friend, Sir George Calvert, a three-century long conflict was precipitated with Virginia's crab and oyster fishermen. For the king's grant included the entire Potomac River, to its outlet on Chesapeake Bay. Great wisdom accompanied the Calverts' use of their grant. Although Catholic, they took care not to interfere with the Protestant faith of the early settlers. The first Lord Baltimore died; the second never visited America. But he sent his brother, who governed admirably, enabling the family to live in great elegance in England—on Maryland's tobacco and other produce. Maryland was prosperous from the start, and had no "starving time," as Jamestown did. Food could be supplied from settlements only a short sail away. Leonard Calvert—who sailed with the first two shiploads of immigrants—chose an ideal location on the Patapsco River for Maryland's first settlement, eventually named Baltimore. Early on, it became an important seaport and commercial center, and in 1776, when the British occupied Philadelphia, the Continental Congress met in Baltimore. Near Fort McHenry, close to Baltimore, Francis Scott Key—an American prisoner on a British man-of-war—wrote the words for the *Star Spangled Banner*. The printer-boy who set the words in type, and the paper used to print them, still survived in 1873. Baltimore competed with New York as a port of entry and re-shipment point across the Alleghenies. Bremen steamers landed freight and passengers at the docks, where cars were waiting and immigrants were taken aboard for the West.

With his beloved Paris boulevards in mind, Major Pierre L'Enfant planned Washington's wide streets and diagonal avenues to intersect, forming little parks and "circles"

When the District of Columbia was set apart in 1791, the only towns within its limits—both small but growing and ambitious—were Georgetown north of the Potomac on the Fall Line and Alexandria on the right bank of the Potomac in the southeast corner. Both banks of the river were lined with plantations where flourished a polished and horsy manorial aristocracy based on rich soil, slave labor, and water transportation that made them largely independent of nearby towns. Wedged in between the larger land grants of a square mile or more and reaching out into the hinterland were irregular blocks and slivers of poorer, even marginal land where humbler farmers eked out a drab subsistence. North of the outlying farms the land resembled what the area between Washington and Baltimore would look like today if divested of its super-highways and if its original forests had not been replaced by second or third growth. To rise just east of, and eventually to include, Georgetown a French engineer planned a city that in its streets and boulevards would rival Paris. Except for throughways built as afterthoughts at the cost of extensive demolition, Salt Lake City is perhaps the only American city that invites plat-with-plat comparison—and even Brigham Young neglected to provide for his city west of the Wasatch the broad and sweeping diagonal avenues so prophetically laid out for Washington by L'Enfant.

PHILIP A. KNOWLTON
The Romance of North America, 1958

SMITHSONIAN INSTITUTE

OBSERVATORY

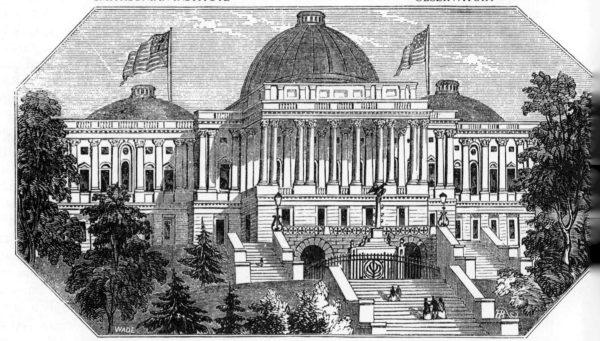
THE CAPITOL

WAR DEPARTMENT

ARSENAL

The pronounced classical influence of ancient Greece and Rome, used by architect Latrobe and his distinguished pupil, Robert Mills, is evident in long Ionic colonnades and Doric facades

POST OFFICE

TREASURY

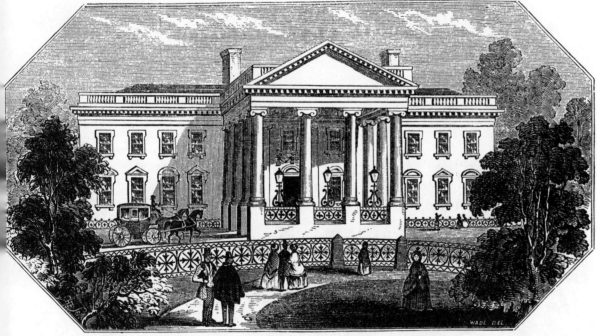

THE PRESIDENT'S HOUSE

PATENT OFFICE

PENSION OFFICE

As the city of Washington spreads out from its historic "ten mile square" it comes into collision with the older life of the Potomac. Absolute federal power and authority do not carry beyond the Federal District. The most desirable land for the future city is not the valueless, looted soil of the old tobacco plantations in the immediate suburbs (although the Quakers at Sandy Spring, and the Amish at Charlotte Hall, show what can be done with it). It lies to the west. There is no longer enough water in the river, or land in the valley, as they are now being used—or abused—for the region and the metropolis at Washington too. The Potomac country into which metropolitan Washington is growing is more able to support by taxation a high standard of municipal services than was the city of Washington in 1860. The city and the region are finding themselves increasingly at odds with each other; and the conflict must grow. Both must come to terms with the natural facts of the region. Its resources are not inexhaustible. Many of them are depleted. Others have substantially reached their limits of present use. Yet resources can be cultivated and developed. The valley is still rich, and it is full of promise for those who will trouble to understand it, discover it and work with it. For those who will not, it is a fickle mistress.

FREDERICK GUTHEIM
The Potomac, 1949

The combined vision of Washington and Jefferson—insisting upon classicism and monumentality—set the course for buildings of the new republic along classic rather than English Renaissance lines

The cornerstone of the Capitol building was laid in the autumn of 1793 and Congress first sat in the building in 1800. But only in 1824, after a succession of architects had modified the original plan of Dr. William Thornton, and after the building had been reconstructed following its burning at the hands of the British in 1814, was it considered complete. Its present appearance was not approximated until the new dome and far-spreading wings were added during the Civil War. Mrs. Trollope and her party, however, were "struck with admiration and surprise" to find such a structure rising out of the landscape of the raw young city. For long years the Federal City continued to seem a "'City of Magnificent Intentions'"—"a little village in the midst of the woods"—"a capital without a city." Unpretentious private and boarding houses and shops, some no more than shanties, offered "an awful contrast" to the few public buildings. Even in 1842 Dickens compared it to a London slum suburb—"put green blinds outside all the private houses . . . plough up all the roads. . . erect three handsome buildings in stone and marble, anywhere, but the more entirely out of everybody's way the better . . . make it scorching hot in the morning and freezing cold in the afternoon, with an occasional tornado of wind and dust; leave a brickfield without the bricks, in all central places where a street may naturally be expected: and that's Washington."

MARSHALL B. DAVIDSON

Life in America, 1951

CAPITOL BUILDING

The design competition for a capitol, won by Dr. William Thornton, and executed by Latrobe, appointed as supervisor in 1803, confirmed victory for those favoring the classic ideal

CAPITOL.

I went to the Capitol prepared to think about politics and history, and found myself instead thinking about art. For the "official art" in the Capitol is absolutely overpowering, and most of it is overpoweringly bad. Not all of it; I admire the Senate Chamber and the old Supreme Court Chamber; and the President's Room, with its deep colors, its frescoes, its too-big chandelier, and its black leather chairs, is a florid, rococo delight. But the rest—the crawling Brumidi frescoes, the overblown pageants in oil, the Italianate corridors, the stone statesmen in double-breasted suits—must be seen to be disbelieved. Oddly enough, they did not upset me in the least. I had the same feeling about the building itself. The Capitol is all wrong: there are too many banks of stairs, too many wedding-cake tiers of columns; the dome is much too heavy, and the building's best profile, the East Front, faces in the wrong direction. But I could not, for all that, find the Capitol anything but beautiful. I was touched by the rather pathetic bravery of our Government in having set out so confidently to surround itself with nobility and Great Art, and impressed by the dimensions of its effort and the gallantry of its failure.

ROGER ANGELL

American Panorama, 1947

The Executive mansion had been burned when the British sacked the capital in 1814, only to be rebuilt and painted white to hide its charred timbers—hence the name "White House"

Perhaps it is still too easy to think of Washington as a country gentleman at Mount Vernon, sitting on the terrace of that famous mansion, looking across his well-manicured lawns with their deer parks and ha-has to the broad Potomac. This was not the environment that produced Washington the military genius, the political leader, the revolutionist. For the roots of that Washington we must look to the west. To know this Washington we must picture him not at Mount Vernon but at his Bullskin plantation at the foothills of the Blue Ridge in Frederick County, Virginia. We must think of him not as the central figure of some stiffly posed lithograph, surrounded by the tobacco panjandrums and adoring Negro slaves, but in a lively scene crowded by traders and land speculators, wheat farmers and men of the cowpens, backwoodsmen and the proprietors of sawmills, flour mills, and other frontier enterprises. Most of all we must steadily recall that his private fortune was not sunk in Tidewater tobacco land but carefully invested in vast tracts of wilderness acreage and held against rising values.

FREDERICK GUTHEIM
The Potomac, 1949

INAUGURATION DAY PARADE, 1853, WASHINGTON

THE WHITE HOUSE AND PUBLIC GROUNDS

Finally retiring, in 1797, after many years of public service, George Washington returned to his beloved plantation on the banks of the Potomac—but died after two years as "first farmer"

SMITHSONIAN INSTITUTE

Along this path he walked,
  great Washington,
Who built a nation
  out of selfish men;
These trees he planted,
  here he stood and mused
On spring's first blossoms,
  or on autumn's gain.
By this loved river,
  flowing wide and free,
He sighed for rest from
  all the cares of state.
How dear his home! And yet
  he could not pause
While traitors tore his land
  with greed and hate;
He could not free himself,
  whose character
Was part and parcel of
  his country's name.
He found no lasting rest,
  though worn and spent,
Till death relieved him
  from the bonds of fame.
Through all the years, till
  freedom's day is run,
One name shall shine with
  splendor—
    WASHINGTON.
      THOMAS CURTIS CLARK
      At Mount Vernon

BIRTHPLACE AND RESIDENCE OF GEORGE WASHINGTON, MOUNT VERNON

*Below the District of Columbia, the Potomac widens into
an arm of Chesapeake Bay—its tidewater regions break
into intermediate rolling valleys and fertile acres . . .*

To the falls of the Potomac above Georgetown, the river formed a broad highway; but
there it was equally a barrier to travelers who
wished to cross. Above the falls the river
became shallower, islands appeared, and here
and there were places where a man on horseback, or a pack train, could ford the stream.
At one place, above the juncture of the
Shenandoah and the Potomac, the immigrant
Robert Harper established a ferry in 1734.
Here the natural lines of travel through the
upper river basin lay north and south in the
great folds of the land, wide limestone valleys
running from the rich agricultural counties of
Pennsylvania deep into the Carolinas, and
leading to the virgin headwaters of those
southern streams which penetrated the mountain barrier and flowed to the Mississippi.

FREDERICK GUTHEIM
The Potomac, 1949

GREAT FALLS OF THE POTOMAC

FROM RED HILL, BACK OF GEORGETOWN

. . . to the northwest, as the Piedmont approaches the Appalachians, and the river is broken by falls, Great and Little, affording magnificent stretches of beauty

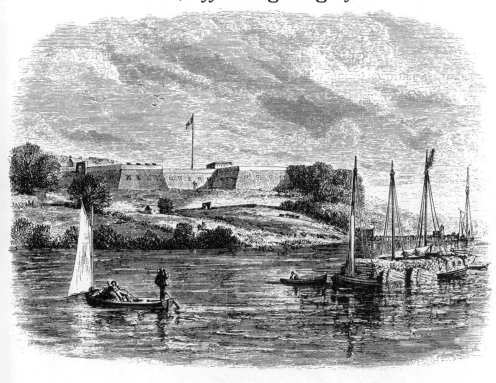

FORT WASHINGTON

By broad Potomac's shore, again old tongue,
(Still uttering, still ejaculating, canst never
    cease this babble?)
Again old heart so gay, again to you, your
    sense, the full flush spring returning,
Again the freshness and the odors, again
    Virginia's summer sky, pellucid blue and
    silver,
Again the forenoon purple of the hills,
Again the deathless grass, so noiseless soft
    and green,
Again the blood-red roses blooming.

Perfume this book of mine O blood-red
    roses!
Lave subtly with your waters every line
    Potomac!
Give me of you O spring, before I close, to
    put between its pages!
O forenoon purple of the hills, before I close,
    of you!
O deathless grass, of you!

WALT WHITMAN

By Broad Potomac's Shore

LOOKING DOWN THE POTOMAC, FROM CHAIN BRIDGE

Located on the north shore of the Patapsco's tidewater head, Baltimore boasts deepwater shipping facilities, on four estuary branches, afforded by over a hundred miles of waterfront

On the morning of September 14, 1814, two fleets of British warships convoying seven thousand troops attempted to land their forces near Fort McHenry, in Baltimore harbor. Firing continued all day, and into the night when the fort's thousand man garrison swamped landing boats with their heavy fire. On the British sloop "Minden," Francis Scott Key, who had boarded to negotiate the release of an American hostage, Doctor William Beanes, was overjoyed when dawn came to see the United States flag flying over the fort. His key phrase "by the dawn's early light" as the colors still were visible over the ramparts of the McHenry defenses developed into "The Star Spangled Banner," a poem of singular beauty known to every American for over a century and a half since the tribute was composed.

The American Guide, 1949

BALTIMORE, FROM FEDERAL HILL

DRUID HILL PARK

It was this very ideal setting of the seaport that invited the British bombardment, during the War of 1812—inspiring the birth of the "Star Spangled Banner," our national anthem

FORT MC HENRY, BALTIMORE HARBOR

Oh, say, can you see, by the dawn's early light,
What so proudly we hailed at the twilight's
last gleaming,
Whose broad stripes and bright stars through the
perilous fight,
O'er the ramparts we watched were so gallantly
streaming?
And the rockets' red glare, the bombs bursting in air,
Gave proof thro' the night that our flag was still
there.
Oh, say, does that star-spangled banner yet wave
O'er the land of the free, and the home of the brave!

FRANCIS SCOTT KEY
The Star-Spangled Banner

LOCUST POINT.

CALVERT STREET.

PUNGIES COMING UP THE CHESAPEAKE.

NIGHT SCENE IN PATTERSON PARK.

FORT McHENRY.

SPEAR'S WHARF.

EXCHANGE PLACE.

SCENES IN BALTIMORE

Within Baltimore's city limits and its immediate vicinity, nature has providentially supplied many picturesque spots on lakes, ponds, and rivers

The chain of lakes and reservoirs, in which Druid Lake is but a link, and which supplies the city with pure water, extends through one of the most beautiful portions of this country. Druid Lake itself is but a storage-lake, with the capacity to afford the city, if needed, sixty days consumption. Near the city lies Mount-Royal Reservoir, and above, Hampden Reservoir. We now follow Jones Falls, which presents us with some water-views—Hampden Falls, and the Cotton Mills of Mount Vernon; and then we come to Lake Roland, clasped in the embrace of bold hills, and winding, river-like, around jutting peninsulas. It is a charming scene. In the fresh, dewy sparkle of early morning, or in the soft closing-in of the evening shadows, it is beautiful in varying moods as the ever-changing, ever-new face of the waters answers to the drifting clouds, the heavy hill shadows, the trees that sentinel its margin, or come down a disorderly, irregular troop to mirror themselves in its bosom; or to the fitful caprices of Nature around, now bright with glint and gleam of sun or stars; now sombre and murky under driving winds and masses of slow, drifting clouds, pelting with the rain, as with falling shot, the gray surface.

J. C. CARPENTER
Picturesque America, 1872

LAKE ROLAND

HAMPDEN FALLS

Lake Roland, Sherwood Gardens, and Hampden and Jones Falls in Druid Hill Park are noted as sylvan recreation areas within reach of all Baltimoreans

SCENE ON LAKE ROLAND

THE PATAPSCO AT ILCHESTER

All the streams around Baltimore afford scenes of much quiet beauty. Herring Run to the east has been honored by the brush of more than one artist; and Gwynn's Falls, a rapid stream to the west, presents many quaint old mills on its banks, which seem to have fallen asleep listening to the ceaseless monotone of the waters flowing past. Reminiscences these, gabled, steeproofed, weather-worn, of the time not long after the Revolution, when Baltimore was the largest flour-market in the United States. The Patapsco, in what is known as the North Branch, is also a favorite sketching-ground. With all their beauty these streams are at times terrible agencies of destruction. Down they come, bearing everything before their restless force, those freshets and floods of which the history of the city records many.

J.C. CARPENTER

Picturesque America, 1872

As the Potomac meanders in a northwest direction toward Pennsylvania, the rolling countryside contrasts sharply with the portion of Maryland bordering on the Chesapeake and the Atlantic

The passage of the Potomac through the Blue Ridge is perhaps one of the most stupendous scenes in nature. You stand on a very high point of land. On your right comes up the Shenandoah, having ranged along the foot of the mountain a hundred miles to seek a vent. On your left approaches the Potomac, in quest of a passage also. In the moment of their junction they rush together against the mountain, rend it asunder, and pass off to the sea. The first glance of this scene hurries our senses into the opinion, that this earth had been created in time, that the mountains were formed first, that the rivers began to flow afterwards, that in this place particularly they had been dammed up by the Blue Ridge of mountains, and have formed an ocean which filled the whole valley; that continuing to rise they have at length broken over at this spot, and have torn the mountain down from its summit to its base. You cross the Potomac above the junction, pass along its side through the base of the mountain for three miles, its terrible precipices hanging in fragments over you, and within about twenty miles reach Fredericktown, and the fine country around that. This scene is worth a voyage across the Atlantic.

THOMAS JEFFERSON

Notes on the State of Virginia, 1785

THE POTOMAC FROM MARYLAND HEIGHTS

The Old Dominion & the Carolinas

THE JAMES, ABOVE RICHMOND . . .

RAPIDS ON THE JAMES . . .CANAL

SCENE . . .PANORAMIC VIEW OF

RICHMOND . . .NATURAL BRIDGE

. . . HARPERS FERRY PETERSBURG

GAP . . . THE FRENCH BROAD . . .

MOUNTAIN ISLAND . . . WILMINGTON

. . . STATE HOUSE, RALEIGH . . .

. . . PICKING COTTON . . .CHARLESTON

. . . DOCK SCENES . . . BATTERY

PROMENADE . . . CHARLESTON HOTEL . . .

MAGNOLIA GARDENS . . . CUSTOMS HOUSE

. . . MILLS HOUSE

The Old Dominion & the Carolinas

THE JAMES, ABOVE RICHMOND

"I have been planing what I would shew you: a flower here, a tree there ... on this side a hill, on that a river. Indeed, madam, I know nothing so charming as our own country"—

Thomas Jefferson

HE "OLD DOMINION" HAS PROfoundly touched us in a way quite unlike any other region. Like its western ridges, the spine of the Appalachian range that divides the coast from the prairie, Virginia and the Carolinas contains an enigma that fires the imagination and that changed the nation's history.

Coastal settlement began early, at Jamestown in 1607. Extending throughout Virginia and the Carolinas, the coastal plain rises gently from the Tidewater Basin in Virginia to the rolling foothills at the base of the Appalachians. These foothills, known as the Piedmont plateau, run down through the Carolinas. Under British rule the area developed quickly. Tobacco and indigo were the main crops and enjoyed a bounty. By the time of the Revolution the area was thickly settled. The increasing scarcity of land gradually pushed settlers westward. As they reached the Blue Ridge, Allegheny, and Great Smoky mountains a distinct difference arose. The mountainous terrain made larger plantations impractical. The land necessitated smaller, more self-sufficient farms on tracts of about a hundred acres. The rugged character of the land gave rise to a political division that would forever separate the mountain people from the Piedmont and its political control.

The mountain people lived in a situation that was far removed from the "genteel" elegance of Richmond or Charleston. They developed their own culture, techniques of curing meat, and handicrafts to fit the unique conditions of their lives. Like the sounds they teased out of a dulcimer or fiddle, the mountain people created a pleasing though primitive world whose basis was simplicity itself.

In contrast, the bustling seaports of Wilmington in North Carolina, and Charleston in South Carolina, were vital in a Southern economy that was buoyant on the cotton trade. During the "war for secession" both ports became havens for rakish blockade runners who traded cotton for munitions. The center of rebellious spirit, Charleston did not surrender Fort Sumter in its harbor until February of 1865. Four years earlier the Civil War began when General Beauregard opened fire on federal forces stationed there.

Mansions like Shirley and Westover on the James River and other proud old buildings cast shadows that hold riddles and secrets. The Tredegar Iron Works in Richmond and houses that stood witness to battles like Chancellorsville and Manassas—all have tales to tell. Deep within Monticello and Mount Vernon or the painstaking restoration of colonial Williamsburg, both questions and answers await. These shadows have seen all the dreams come and pass by: the Confederate States of America, a crumbling dream that hung on like a wildflower clinging to the jagged ridgeline of Old Rag mountain; the bittersweet dream of the Cherokee nation that died on the "Trail of Tears"; liberty, the burning dream in the eyes of Patrick Henry, Thomas Jefferson, and George Washington. These hammer relentlessly like the surf pounding the shore at Cape Hatteras. While the muddy James River turns the Atlantic brown at Hampton Roads and John Brown's ghost stalks Harpers Ferry, the enigmatic fire that springs from this pastoral land remains.

How is it that rebellion is spawned in a place such as this? The iron fences of Charleston and the sun-bleached tobacco drying barns of the Piedmont attest to a paradox. Mountains ripping four thousand feet out of soft hills. Dunes of fine sand drifting in ocean breezes on the Outer Banks. Rivers like the James, Potomac, and Rappahannack that flow serenely through green hills. Virginia and the Carolinas embody thousands of striking contrasts. The Blue Ridge and Allegheny mountains as they rise creating the Shenandoah valley. The defiant battery at Charleston jutting out toward the Atlantic. The squalor of the tenant farmer. The aristocratic elegance of the plantation houses.

One of the greatest riddles that remains unsolved concerns the "lost colony" on Roanoke Island—located in the region safely protected from Carolina's Outer Banks and the seventy-mile strip of reef above Cape Hatteras—where an English colony vanished. In 1585 Raleigh sent out his first group to the domain he called "Virginia." This colony left for England after enduring many hardships, on Sir Francis Drake's fleet. Only a few days after their departure Sir Richard Grenville arrived with fresh provisions and more colonists. Of the original colony none was found alive, and the only trace of its existence was the word "Croatan" carved on a tree. Virginia Dare, the first white child born in America, was the granddaughter of John White, the leader of this new group of colonists.

There are further mysteries that defy solution, like the "bald spots" in the Blue Ridge Mountains. These are all elements comprising the enigmatic character of the "Old Dominion" and the Carolinas. The striking beauty of these contrasts has inspired and drawn the respect of many who built this nation. A middle-aged major, speaking to a class of cadets at Virginia Military Institute before the outbreak of the Civil War put it this way: "The time may be near when your state needs your services, but it has not yet come. If that time comes then draw your swords and throw away the scabbards." History would know Major Thomas Jackson better as "Stonewall." He, and others like him, born in this land of striking beauty, would forever change the face of our nation.

Because of its importance, Richmond—Virginia's proud capital, and capital of the Confederacy—suffered the ravages of war as did few other cities

Very few cities in America can compare with Richmond, a stately rectilinear town, for concentration of historical allusion. It has celebrated monuments to Lee, Jefferson Davis (for Richmond was the second capital of the Confederacy), and Stonewall Jackson; General Lee's home, now the headquarters of the Virginia Historical Society, is here, and so is that of Edgar Allan Poe. But what I liked best, next to the incomparable executive mansion, is the heroic (and heroically ugly) equestrian statue of George Washington, which was cast in Munich of all places, and which now stands in Capitol Square. The general's eyes look sternly at the state house and his finger, like a flail, points to the penitentiary! Richmond is not a very large city, but it has great wealth; most of the modern fortunes come from tobacco. It is heavily industrialized, and is the biggest cigarette manufacturing center in the world. Tobacco is a small man's crop; the average holding in the American South is about three acres. In Virginia and western North Carolina most growers are owners; in Georgia they are mostly tenants. There are no great tobacco "plantations" like cotton plantations.

JOHN GUNTHER
Inside U.S.A., 1947

SCENE ON THE CANAL

RICHMOND, FROM THE DRIVE OVERLOOKING THE CITY

Richmond's broad streets and drives are starred with buildings and monuments of historic note: the fine executive mansion, state capitol and monuments to Washington, Lee, and Davis

RICHMOND FROM HOLLYWOOD

The point from which the most commanding and comprehensive view of Richmond is visible, bears the name of Hollywood Cemetery, a picturesque elevation in the northwestern suburbs, where rest the remains of many illustrious men, and of thousands who in the recent struggle "Went down to their graves in bloody shrouds." The scene from President's Hill, in Hollywood, is one that never tires the eye, because it embraces a picture which somewhere among its lights and shadows presents features that constantly appeal to imagination and refined taste. In the great perspective which bounds the horizon the distant hills and forests take new color from the changing clouds; while nearer—almost at your feet—the James River, brawling over the rocks, and chanting its perpetual requiem to the dead who lie around, catches from the sunshine playing on its ruffled breast kaleidoscopic hues. Intermediate in elevation between the river and the summit of President's Hill winds, in a graceful curve, the canal, seeking its basin at the town; and not far away are the forges of the Tredegar Iron-works, the fiery chimneys of which at night belch forth flames that send their sparkle into a thousand windows, and make pictures in the rippling waters.

J. R. THOMPSON
Picturesque America, 1872

Towering 215 feet above Cedar Creek, the limestone arch—
called the Natural Bridge—is one of Virginia's unique
wonders, characterized by many as a "freak of nature" . . .

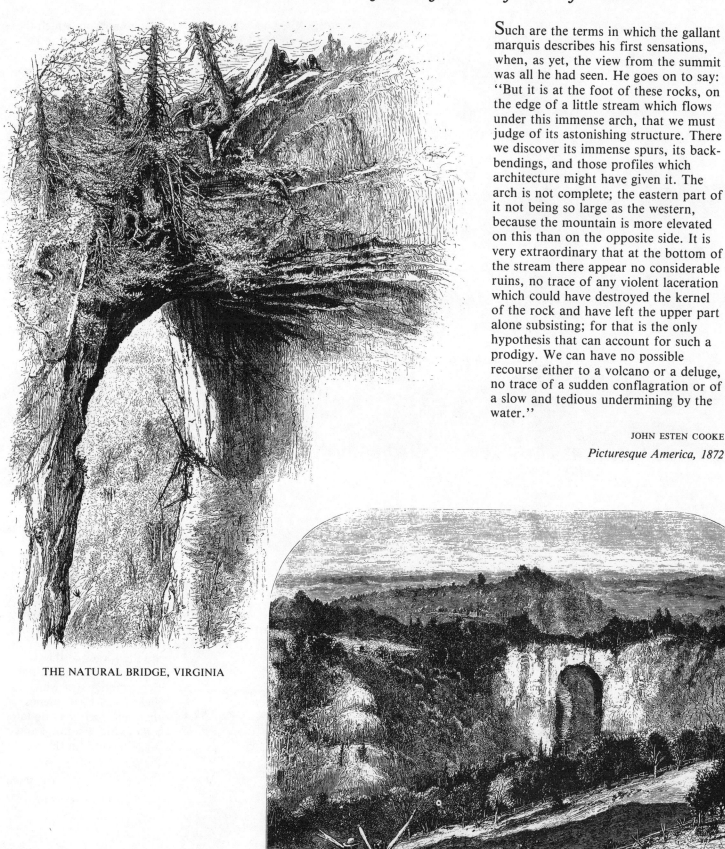

Such are the terms in which the gallant marquis describes his first sensations, when, as yet, the view from the summit was all he had seen. He goes on to say: "But it is at the foot of these rocks, on the edge of a little stream which flows under this immense arch, that we must judge of its astonishing structure. There we discover its immense spurs, its back-bendings, and those profiles which architecture might have given it. The arch is not complete; the eastern part of it not being so large as the western, because the mountain is more elevated on this than on the opposite side. It is very extraordinary that at the bottom of the stream there appear no considerable ruins, no trace of any violent laceration which could have destroyed the kernel of the rock and have left the upper part alone subsisting; for that is the only hypothesis that can account for such a prodigy. We can have no possible recourse either to a volcano or a deluge, no trace of a sudden conflagration or of a slow and tedious undermining by the water."

JOHN ESTEN COOKE
Picturesque America, 1872

THE NATURAL BRIDGE, VIRGINIA

THE NATURAL BRIDGE AND ITS SURROUNDINGS

. . . shaped and eroded by the stream below—a sublime and rugged formation—visited by Washington and Jefferson, whose accounts spurred thousands to view the spectacle

UNDER THE NATURAL BRIDGE

The whole arch seems to be formed of one and the same stone; for the joints which one remarks are the effect of lightning, which struck this part in 1779. The other head has not the smallest vein, and the intrados is so smooth that the martins, which fly around it in great numbers, cannot fasten on it. The abutments, which have a gentle slope, are entire, and, without being absolute planes, have all the polish which a current of water would give to unhewn stone in a certain time. The four rocks adjacent to the abutments seem to be perfectly homogeneous, and to have a very trifling slope. The two rocks on the right bank of the rivulet are two hundred feet high above the surface of the water, the intrados of the arch a hundred and fifty, and the two rocks on the left bank a hundred and eighty. If we consider this bridge simply as a picturesque object, we are struck with the majesty with which it towers in the valley. The white-oaks which grow upon it seem to rear their lofty summits to the clouds, while the same trees which border on the rivulet appear like shrubs.

MARQUIS DE CHASTELLUX, 1781

Picturesque America, 1872

Where the Shenandoah flows into the Potomac—and three states meet—on the extreme edge of West Virginia's eastern border, is Harpers Ferry, famed in pre-Civil War days

After Brown made his historic raid on Harpers Ferry, he was captured by Colonel Robert E. Lee and Lieutenant "Jeb" Stuart of the United States Army. He was tried, convicted, and hanged for murder, for inciting slaves to revolt, and for treason. Before being put to death, he told his inquisitors, " . . . I pity the poor in bondage that have none to help them; that is why I am here; not to gratify any personal animosity, revenge or vindictive spirit. It is my sympathy with the oppressed and the wronged, that are as good as you and as precious in the sight of God . . . I wish to say, furthermore, that you had better—all you people at the South—prepare yourselves for a settlement of that question that must come up for settlement sooner than you are prepared for it. You may dispose of me very easily. I am nearly disposed of now; but this question is still to be settled—this negro question I mean; the end of that is not yet . . . "

JOHN BROWN
Before his death
December 2, 1859

HARPERS FERRY

PETERSBURG GAP

Here, the abolitionist John Brown and his followers
captured the federal arsenal for which Brown was hanged,
though many sympathized, regarding him as a martyr

A hundred miles away in an arrow-line

Lies the other defended king of the giant

    chess,

Broad streeted Richmond...

The trees in the streets are old trees used

    to living with people,

Family-trees that remember your grand-

    father's name.

It is still a clan-city, a family-city, a city

That thinks of the war, on the whole, as

    a family matter...

STEPHEN VINCENT BENET
John Brown's Body, 1927

MARYLAND ROAD

This spot, so celebrated for its wild and
majestic scenery, is in Jefferson County,
at the confluence of Shenandoah and
Potomac Rivers, where, after the union
of their waters, they find a passage
through the rocky barrier of the Blue
Ridge, twelve hundred feet in height.
Mr. Jefferson, in his *"Notes on Virginia,"* has given a full and graphic account of the scene, which he charac-
terizes as "one of the most stupendous
in nature." "Jefferson's Rock," the
spot where it is said Mr. Jefferson wrote
the description, is a pile of huge, detached rocks, leaning over the precipitous cliffs of the Shenandoah, and
looking into the mountain gorge of the
Potomac... There is also a most enchanting prospect obtained from the
summit of a mountain opposite, about a
mile and a half farther up, on the
Maryland side of the river. The eye here
reaches a very wide extent of country,
fields, woodlands, and plantations;
while the Shenandoah, as it is traceable
upon the magic picture, appears like a
series of beautiful lakes.

MARYLAND HEIGHTS

Gleason's Pictorial
July 29, 1854

Along the western fringes of North Carolina, the French Broad winds its way between ragged escarpments of the Blue Ridge and the Great Smokies . . .

Still another section of the country which seems destined at no distant day to become a place of recreation, and to attract the artist and lover of Nature, is that portion of Western North Carolina through which course the beautiful waters of the French Broad River and other mountain-streams, and which may be described in general terms as the table-land of the Blue Ridge. The fame of the beauty and the sublimity of the scenery is extensive, and the realization does not belie the report. Tall, grim, old rocks lift their bald heads far, far toward the heavens, in all the sublimity of solemn grandeur; while in the vision of the distant lowlands, that may be enjoyed from this summit or that, is a soft, sweet delicacy which breathes almost of the celestial, and makes one feel unconscious of aught save the panorama of loveliness before him. Indeed, it would seem as if Nature had selected this region for the display of her fantastic power in uplifting the earth, and giving to it strange shapes and startling contrasts—in imparting curious physiognomies to the mountains and evoking melody from the water-falls.

F. G. DE FONTAINE
Picturesque America, 1872

FERRY ON THE FRENCH BROAD

MOUNTAIN ISLAND

. . . its course cutting through rugged terrain, giving way to rocky canyons and mountainous ravines of singular beauty

THE FRENCH BROAD

And how fair is this same forest in late autumn...The damp earth is elastic under your feet; the high blades of grass do not stir; long threads lie shining on the blanched turf, white with dew. You breathe tranquilly; but there is a strange tremor in the soul. You walk along the forest's edge, look after your dog, and meanwhile loved forms, loved faces dead and living, come to your mind; long, long, slumbering impressions unexpectedly awaken; the fancy darts off and soars like a bird; and all moves so clearly and stands out before your eyes. The heart at one time throbs and beats, plunging passionately forward; at another it is drowned beyond recall in memories. Your whole life, as it were, unrolls lightly and rapidly before you: a man at such times possesses all his past, all his feelings and his powers—all his soul; and there is nothing around to hinder him—no sun, no wind, no sound...

IVAN TURGENEV

A Sportsman's Sketches, 1852

May I be dead when all the woods are old,
And shaped to patterns of the planners' minds,
When great unnatural rows of trees unfold
Their tender foliage to the April winds,
May I be dead when Sandy is not free,
And transferred to a channel not its own,
Water through years that sang for her and me.
Over the precipice and soft sandstone...
Let wild rose be an epitaph for me
When redbirds go and helpless sike pokes must,
And red beans on the honey-locust tree
Are long-forgotten banners turned to dust...
I weep to think these hills where I awoke.
Saw God's great beauty, wonderful and strange,
Will be destroyed, stem and flower and oak,
And I would rather die than see the change.

JESSE STUART

May I be Dead

"THE LOVERS' LEAP"

When Wilmington—once the state's leading port—on the Cape Fear River, fell to the North, blockade runners were cut off, and the end of the war for the South was in sight

TURPENTINE DISTILLERY, WILMINGTON

MARKET STREET, WILMINGTON

In 1792, Raleigh—the newly chosen capital city—was carved out of the wilderness, its architects accused of building "a city of streets without houses"

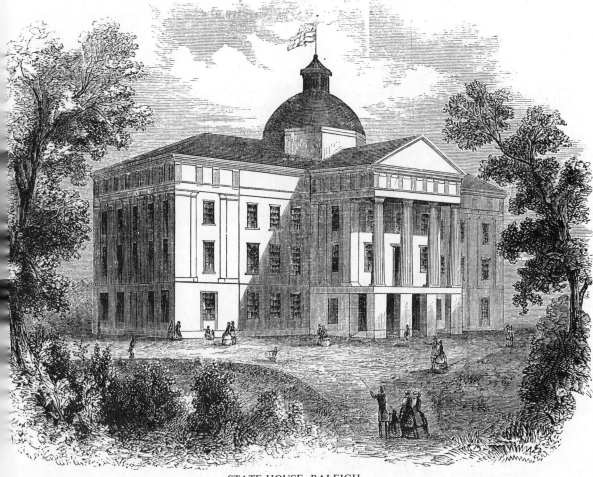

STATE HOUSE, RALEIGH

CAPE FEAR BANK, WILMINGTON

Roanoke Island is the well-known setting, with the smell of red honeysuckle and partridge-berry blossoms filling the air, of Paul Green's *The Lost Colony;* and despite the passage of years, it still has the power to move audiences to wonder at the disappearance of the early colonists into the wilderness. Blackbeard's ghost, romantics say, still haunts Ocrakoke Island, where wild ponies once ran free. From Oregon Inlet to Ocrakoke the sea, sand, and beach grass in their unspoiled state provide a lonely, contemplative setting. The Great Dismal Swamp, at the upper edge of North Carolina's coast plain and spilling over into Virginia, is still largely inaccessible. A spongy quagmire of cypress, black gum, and juniper that filter out the sunlight, it is truly the "region of unearthly darkness lying across sunlit land" that Pierce describes, one of the still secret places of the American terrain. But it is western North Carolina—across the Piedmont and in the powerful presence of the ragged escarpment of the Blue Ridge—that really captures one.

ARNOLD EHRLICH, ED.
The Beautiful Country

Decades before the Civil War the production, shipping, and marketing of cotton dominated every aspect of Southern life, its culture and economy . . .

The plantation system throughout most of the southern states was almost equally divided between the larger estates, held by those descended from the colonial aristocracy— Washington's type as well as his kinsmen, the Lees; the old Hugenot families of South Carolina; wealthy planters of French creoles of Louisiana—and smaller planters who owned no more than one or a dozen slaves. Of this group, poorly equipped with clumsy hoes and mule-drawn plows, slaves were often beaten by "drivers," assigned to discipline the laggards by flogging at night, after the day's labors ended. These little "one horse plantations" were described by Mark Twain: "A rail fence around a two-acre yard . . .big double log house for the white folks— hewed logs, with the chinks stopped up with mud or mortar, and these mud-stripes had been white-washed some time or another; round-log kitchen, with a big, broad, open but roofed passage joining it to the house; log smoke-house back of the kitchen; three little log nigger-cabins in a rot t'other side the smoke-house . . . outside of the fence a garden and a water-melon patch; then the cotton fields begin; and after the fields, the woods."

MARK TWAIN

Huckleberry Finn, 1884

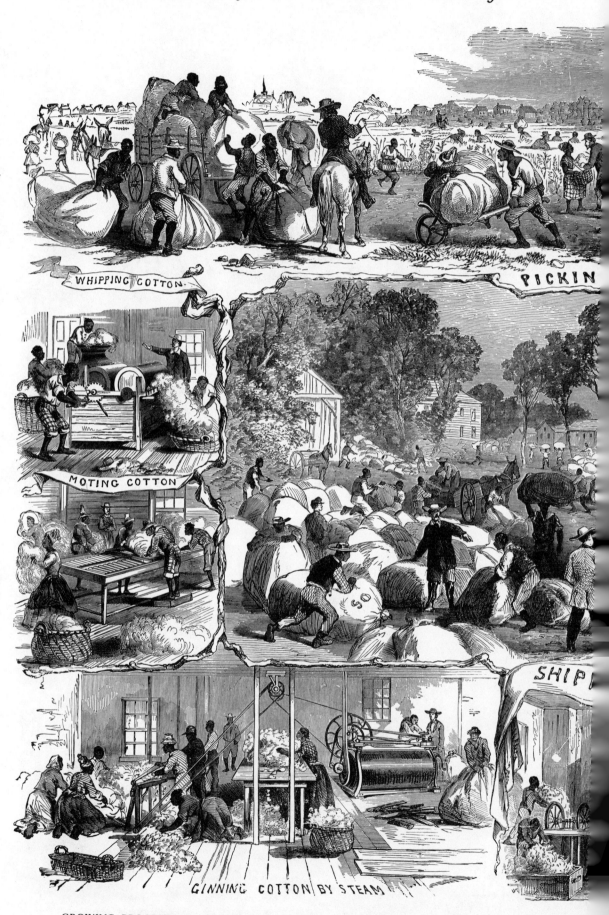

WHIPPING COTTON.   PICKIN

MOTING COTTON

SHIPP

GINNING COTTON BY STEAM

GROWING, PROCESSING AND SHIPPING   THE COTTON CROP, SEA ISLANDS, PORT ROYAL, S.C.

. . . as the demand from abroad, for cash crops, encouraged the development of the plantation system, where land was rich and productive, manned by the cheapest human labor

PLANTING COTTON.

HOEING COTTON.

PACKING COTTON.

Planters, particularly native planters, have a kind of affection for their Negroes, incredible to those who have not observed its effects. If rebellious they punish them—if well behaved, they not infrequently reward them. In health they treat them with uniform kindness, in sickness with attention and sympathy. I once called on a native planter—a young bachelor, like many of his class, who had graduated at Cambridge and traveled in Europe—yet Northern education and foreign habits did not destroy the Mississippian. I found him by the bedside of a dying slave, nursing him with a kindness of voice and manner, and displaying a manly sympathy with his sufferings, honorable to himself and to humanity. On large plantations hospitals are erected for the reception of the sick, and the best medical attendance is provided for them. The physicians of Natchez derive a large proportion of their incomes from attending plantations. On some estates a physician permanently resides, whose time may be supposed sufficiently taken up in attending to the health of from one to two hundred persons. Often several plantations, if the force on each is small, unite and employ one physician for the whole.

JOSEPH HOLT INGRAHAM

South-West, 1835

During the flush days when "king cotton" fetched top prices, the exports meant busy times and full employment at the Charleston wharves . . .

The first impression the streets of Charleston give is that of retiring respectability. There are no splendid avenues, no imposing public structures; but a few fine old churches and many noble private mansions standing in a sort of dingy stateliness amid their embowering magnolias, command our attention. Our New York custom, derived from our Dutch ancestors, of painting our brick fronts, is not in vogue here, where the houses have the sombre but rich toning that age alone can give when its slow pencillings are never disturbed by the rude intrusion of the painter's brush. The Charleston mansions are nearly always built with the gable-end to the street. At one side rises a tier of open verandas, into the lower of which the main entrance to the building is placed. Usually, after the English fashion, a high brick wall encloses the grounds of the house, and it is only through an open gate-way that one catches a glimpse of flowers, and shrubs, and vines, that bloom and expand within the enclosure. But the rich dark green of the magnolia half screens the unsmoothed brick walls far above, and seems to hold the ancient structure in the hush of venerable repose.

O.B. BUNCE

Picturesque America, 1872

LOADING COTTON, CHARLESTON

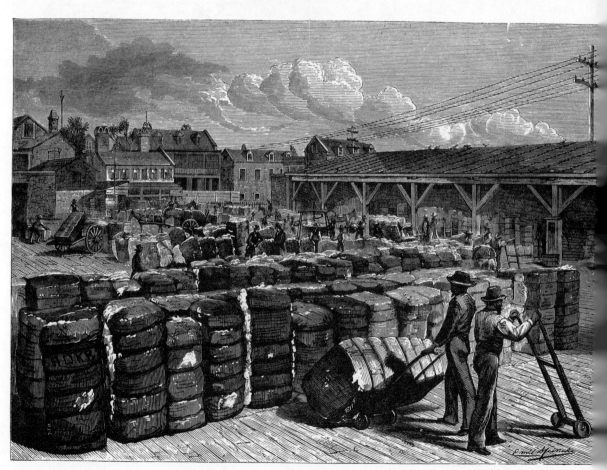

A COTTON WHARF, CHARLESTON

. . . yet on quiet city streets and squares of this "American Venice," the languid serenity of the Southern tempo was in sharp contrast with dockside activity

CHARLESTON AND BAY, FROM ST. MICHAEL'S CHURCH

So much has been written of Charleston, and Charlestonians are so touchy, that you sometimes wonder what to say. Still, there is one very evident thing about Charleston: it is the most glamorous city in America, a city with an antique grace so discreetly guarded it makes one think of heirlooms in daily use, a city that has blessedly escaped both the bulldozers and the ministrations of antiquarian wealth. Its colonial aspect seems less glamorous, however, than its fame for Castilian pride of birth. Old Charlestonians are admittedly complacent, but less remote often than the families of softdrink barons with villas at Myrtle Beach. Content with their own company, they can and do receive cordially; and sometimes they even mix their blue blood in marriage with outlander red. But the myth seduces. Most Americans are homesick for lords and ladies; they like to think that somewhere lofty beings fit their ideal of nobility. So what is Charleston more famous for than the St. Celia Society, the ball-giving social fortress which legend erects to Trojan heights of impregnability? The myth is implicit in these doggerel lines:

> In Boston the Lodges
>   speak to the Cabots
> And the Cabots speak only
>   to God;
> In Charleston the Pinck-
>   neys speak to the Rhetts
> And the Rhetts don't
>   bother about God.

WILLIAM FRANCIS GUESS

South Carolina, 1947

Visitors from the North came to enjoy the cool delights of Charleston's balmy climate—to promenade on the Battery—to partake of its "different" atmosphere

CHARLESTON, FROM THE BAY

Charleston is in fact a gem; it is also a kind of mummy, like Savannah. I heard one unkind friend nickname it "Death on the Atlantic," and call it "a perfect example of what the South must never be again." Be this as it may, it belongs in that strange eclectic category of American "sights" not to be missed, practically like the Taos Pueblo and Niagara Falls. Once it was the fourth biggest city in America, and probably the most brilliantly sophisticated; today much of its polish has worn off, though it still retains a cardinal quality of grace. Also, a city on a narrow island between two small rivers, it has great local pride. "Charleston, sir," one of the local worthies once told a Yankee interloper, "is that untarnished jewel shining regally at that sacred spot where the Ashley and the Cooper join their majestic waters to form the Atlantic Ocean." Once Charleston was known as "Capital of the Plantation;" but it is a seaport, and so has been vulnerable to the incursions of the foreign-born. The leading commercial family today derives from a group of six Sicilian brothers, who own theaters, hotels, automobile agencies, and the like; there are also Chinese, Greek, Portuguese, and Sephardic Jewish communities. Many of the great old houses are, one by one, being sold or boarded up. Some were used during the war by the Army and Navy (Charleston played an active and honorable role in war activities); some, leased by northern owners, are empty most of the year; in some the last entrenched survivors of the old society—in the main wealthy widows who inherited fortunes made on rice—still hold out.

JOHN GUNTHER

Inside U.S.A., 1947

EAST BATTERY, PROMENADE

"In no part of America," noted Morse in his American
Geography, *"are the social blessings enjoyed more
rationally and liberally than in Charleston"*

CHARLESTON HOTEL

A CHARLESTON GARDEN

AY STREET, CHARLESTON

MAGNOLIAS

Shipments are no longer raw cotton by the bale, but finished cotton by the bolt, woven in the large number of textile plants in the Charleston area

The town was Charleston and on their city homes the rice aristocracy lavished wealth from their swamps. In urban retreat they lived out the summer season, giving themselves "every pleasure and convenience to which their warmer climate and better circumstances invite them." The city itself seemed unpleasantly exotic to some visitors. Picturesque houses built to suit the climate and the polyglot background of the people broke too many rules of proportion and academic form. "In Charleston persons vie with one another, not who shall have the finest, but who the coolest house," wrote La Rochefoucauld-Liancourt. The aristocratic nature of the city's social life was maintained long after wealth had shifted to new sections, and in a region of few cities its preeminence was indisputable.

MARSHALL B. DAVIDSON

Life in America, 1951

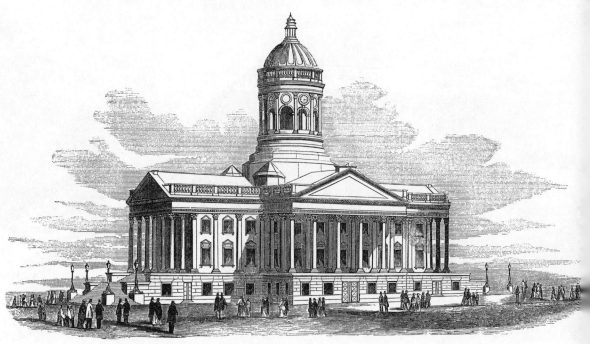

NEW CUSTOM HOUSE, CHARLESTON

MILLS HOUSE, CHARLESTON

From the Savannah...
to the Suwannee River

THE SAVANNAH . . . AUGUSTA . . .

TEXTILE MILL . . . COTTON BOATS . . .

FORSYTH PARK, SAVANNAH . . . VIEW

OF THE HARBOR . . . BULL STREET . . .

GEORGIA VILLAGE MARKETPLACE . . .

ATHENS . . . ROME . . . ATLANTA . . .

THE CAPITOL . . . ATLANTA BUILDINGS

. . .RESIDENCES . . . ST. JOHN'S RIVER

. . . GREEN COVE SPRINGS . . .

THE OCKLAWAHA . . . ST. AUGUSTINE

. . .ST. MARK'S CASTLE . . . CITY GATE

. . . THE EVERGLADES . . . LAKE

OKEECHOBEE . . . PENSACOLA

THE SAVANNAH

From the Savannah...
to the Suwannee River

AJOURNEY BEYOND THE BANKS OF THE Savannah River into Georgia and the heart of the Old South begins where the river meets the sea, at Georgia's oldest city and first capital, Savannah. Here, in an area of magnolia, pine, and live oak, settlers led by James Oglethorpe landed in 1733. From this point, settlement began to move slowly west and south into Georgia's southern coastal and Piedmont areas and into Florida.

The Savannah River was already carrying traffic at the time Oglethorpe and his party reached the coast. Augusta, up the river from Savananah, had been a trading post since 1717. After the American Revolution it boomed, and by 1820 it had become an important terminus for riverboats, wagon trains, and traders, moving produce from the interior to the sea.

Augusta and Savannah are among Georgia's oldest cities, and as settlers moved west into the interior to establish plantations in the fertile red-dirt valleys, these towns became the political, cultural, and commercial centers of Georgia's rich agricultural empire. Tobacco and cotton moved through these cities on their way to other American and European ports, and the secession issue, first from the Crown and then from the Union, was debated there by Georgia's statesmen and journalists.

Atlanta, Georgia's capital since 1868, and now the busy industrial and commercial center of the New South, is a relatively new town compared to Augusta and Savannah. Hardy Ivy, Atlanta's first settler, built his cabin there near the Appalachian foothills only in 1833. In 1837, Terminus, an end-of-the-line railroad town, was founded there. Incorporated in 1843 as Marthasville, it was renamed Atlanta in 1845. By then it was a major railroad and marketing hub, and it became a vital commercial and supply center for the Confederacy during the Civil War.

Beyond the cities, where the merchants built magnificent homes and laid out manicured gardens, stretched the real heart of Georgia—the hills, woods, marshes, and flatlands in which the great majority of its citizens lived well into the present century. Here lumber was cut from the great pine forests; marble, clay, and iron were dug from the earth; and tobacco and cotton were planted and harvested in mile after mile of fertile field.

Georgia's wealth came from the land, and especially from cotton. Aided by the cotton gin, and by an abundance of slaves, the wealth of Georgia's planter class was prodigious. The legendary and languid life of the Old South flourished here for almost three-quarters of a century, until bitter disputes with the industrial North led to secession and war. Georgia became first a supply center and then a battleground: in 1864 Union troops under W. T. Sherman entered Atlanta, burned it to the ground, and began a march to the sea, during which they plundered and burned everything for fifty miles along their path.

In the southeastern tip of Georgia lies the great Okefenokee Swamp, where the Suwannee River has its source. The Suwannee—immortalized by Stephen Foster, who never saw it, and could not spell its name—flows along moss-lined banks, through pine and oak forests, in a land that closely resembles much of Georgia. Towns in this region were always small, and though a plantation economy developed here based on cotton and sugar, it never grew to a scale to match Georgia's.

A Spanish possession until 1819, Florida was settled chiefly by missionaries, explorers, traders—not farmers. In a hilly agricultural area in the middle of Florida's northern section stands Tallahassee, Florida's capital. Situated among lakes, springs, forests, and lush, tropical gardens, Tallahassee successfully repulsed Union attacks in the last months of the war, and retains many antebellum homes.

To the south, along Florida's Atlantic coast, is St. Augustine, the oldest city in America, founded by Europeans. It was established in 1565 on a peninsula between the Matanzas and San Sebastian rivers, near the site where Ponce de Leon landed in 1513 in his search for the fountain of youth. South and west of St. Augustine is Florida's agricultural region, now growing one of America's largest citrus crops, the first seeds of which were brought to Florida from Spain by de Leon. Farther south is the area dominated by Lake Okeechobee, the second largest lake wholly within the United States.

Below Lake Okeechobee lie the Everglades, one of the few sections of the United States that has never been fully explored. It is inhabited largely by the Seminole Indians, who call it Pa-hay-okee, or "grassy water." The Seminoles retreated to the Everglades after they engaged with the United States in the most costly of its Indian wars.

The Everglades is really a giant tray of water, which acts as a river draining Lake Okeechobee. It is filled with saw grass, clumps of mangrove trees, and islands lush with vegetation. Monotonously flat, the land never rises more than about ten feet above sea level.

Below the Everglades is a string of twenty-five major islands called the Florida Keys, which form an arc, one hundred fifty miles long, southwest of the mainland. While Florida was still controlled by the Spanish, the Keys were inhabited largely by pirates, smugglers, and adventurers. After 1819, when Florida was ceded to the United States, salvaging became the principal trade of the islands, since there were no lighthouses to guide boats through the often dangerous waters. After the 1830s, however, warning systems were installed by the navy, and the islanders turned to cigar making and fishing.

Although the Spanish were exploring and settling Florida long before Europeans entered Georgia, Florida's growth was much slower. Except for the northernmost part of the state, it did not share in pre-Civil War wealth; nor did it share so deeply in the South's defeat. But by the turn of the century, Florida, like Georgia, its neighbor to the north, was becoming a leader of the New South—developing new sources of wealth that would rival in their potential anything the Spanish had dreamed of, or the planters had reaped.

*For over a century, Augusta—cotton and textile
manufacturing center, situated on the Savannah—
has been famous for friendly old-time charm*

A few days after our arrival at Augusta, the chiefs and warriors of the Creeks and Cherokees being arrived, the Congress and the business of the treaty came on, and the negociations continued undetermined many days; the merchants of Georgia demanding at least two millions of acres of land from the Indians, as a discharge of their debts, due, and of long standing: the Creeks, on the other hand, being a powerful and proud spirited people, their young warriors were unwilling to submit to so large a demand, and their conduct evidently betrayed a disposition to dispute the ground by force of arms, and they could not at first be brought to listen to reason and amicable terms; however, at length, the cool and deliberate counsels of the ancient venerable chiefs, enforced by liberal presents of suitable goods, were too powerful inducements for them any longer to resist, and finally prevailed. The treaty concluded in unanimity, peace, and good order; and the honourable superintendent, not forgetting his promise to me, at the conclusion, mentioned my business, and recommended me to the protection of the Indian chiefs and warriors. The presents being distributed among the Indians, they departed, returning home to their towns. A company of surveyors were appointed by the governor and council, to ascertain the boundaries of the new purchase; they were to be attended by chiefs of the Indians, selected and delegated by their countrymen, to assist, and be witnesses that the articles of the treaty were fulfilled, as agreed to by both parties in Congress.

WILLIAM BARTRAM
Travels of William Bartram,
1791

Georgia Landscape

A Cotton Boat

The Old Bell Tower

A Model Mill

SCENES AROUND AUGUSTA

Its wharves and warehouses on a long waterfront,
its dockside activity, its more than a hundred mills
and plants rank it a city of industrial importance

Soldier's Monument

Cotton Boats Shooting Rapids

"It was an article of faith in the Confederacy that Northern industry would collapse when cut off from its Southern markets and its supply of cotton. For a while, there was unemployment in cotton mills, but American factory operatives, more mobile and less dependent than their English fellows, returned to the farms whence many of them had come, or shifted into woolen and other industries; and after mid-1862 enough cotton was obtained from occupied parts of the South to reopen many closed mills." The slow normalization that followed during the Reconstruction saw the development of many mills and their communities, as they grew into prosperous manufacturing centers.

SAMUEL ELIOT MORISON

The Oxford History of
the American People, 1965

A Characteristic Home.

Georgia's oldest city and busiest seaport, Savannah, typifies the Southern city of grace—stately mansions, cobblestone streets, impeccably kept gardens

Savannah is one of the most attractive cities in the South for a number of reasons, one being the large number of separate, small parks scattered through the downtown area. Besides, one of the greatest trees in America grows well there, and Savannah has taken inspired advantage of it: *Quercus virginiana,* the great live oak. The city is graced with several major park boulevards of four lanes separated by double rows of spreading oaks. The majesty and charm and beauty of these trees defies description. They make Savannah one of the most pleasant places to live in the entire United States. The city is "picturesque," too, and like other seacoast cities, has almost an Old World atmosphere. Much that can be said about New Orleans or Charleston can also be said about Savannah: quiet, "gracious" living, a highly refined society of old families, excellent restaurants, a dash of night life. Today, however, Savannah is in commercial turmoil. An old friend, whose insurance offices are located in truly Old World surroundings, expressed the thought that perhaps he should modernize; and when a man of his traditionalism, talks of modernizing, Savannah *is* in turmoil.

CALDER WILLINGHAM

American Panorama, 1947

AUGUSTA, FROM SUMMERVILLE

Along Bull Street and in other sections of the city, many spacious squares are planted with magnificent gardens of magnolias, azaleas, oleanders and evergreens

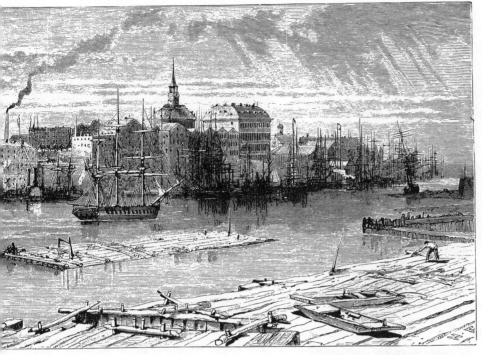

SAVANNAH, FROM THE RIVER

BULL STREET, SAVANNAH

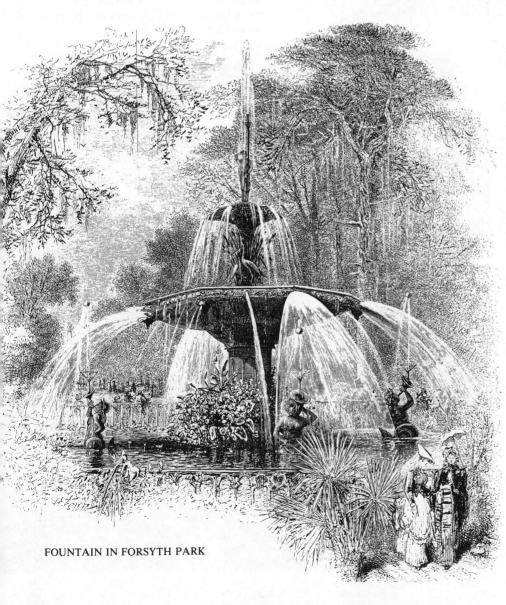

FOUNTAIN IN FORSYTH PARK

Although the gentry gave the tone to Southern white society, there were relatively few of them, probably not more than 15,000 families. The typical Southerner was a farmer who owned his land and buildings, and with his own labor and that of half a dozen slaves cultivated the cash crop—sugar, tobacco, or cotton—which seemed most profitable. He also raised cattle, swine, and a large part of his own food; and there were several hundred thousand Southern families who owned no slaves. These were the backbone of the country, who proved so difficult for Union armies to defeat. Small slave-owners and non-slaveholding yeomen lived in a double log cabin or bare frame house without conveniences, on a diet largely of "hog and hominy," read no literature but the Bible and a weekly paper, enjoyed no diversions but hunting, fishing, and visits to the county seat.

SAMUEL ELIOT MORISON

The Oxford History of the American People, 1965

Every phase of the Southern economy focused on the growing of cotton—every river saw cotton boats and barges— every marketplace teemed with bales by the wagonload

THE SAVANNAH, NEAR AUGUSTA

Cotton planting advanced from South Carolina and Georgia across the "black belts" (so called from the color of the soil) and Indian cessions of the Gulf states, occupied the Mississippi valley up to Memphis, pushed up the Red river of Louisiana to Indian Territory, and passed the boundary of Mexico into Texas. On the march King Cotton acquired new subjects: monied immigrants from the North, or ambitious dirt farmers who purchased a slave or two on credit, and with good luck became magnates. In every region fit for cotton, the richest lands were absorbed by plantations during the first generation of settlement. Hunter folk moved westward and poor whites closed in on the gullied hillsides and abandoned fields. Some of the best minds of the South endeavored to arrest this process by scientific methods of agriculture; but as long as good land remained plentiful and cheap, whether within the United States or adjacent under the feeble sovereignty of Mexico, the cotton growers preferred their old ways.

On a first-class plantation, with improved implements, healthy Negroes, strong mules, and a competent overseer, ten acres of cotton or corn could be cultivated per able-bodied field hand. On rich soil, with a proper division of labor, five bales (2,000 pounds) or more of cotton per field hand could be produced; but a more nearly average figure, in the Carolina and Georgia piedmont, would be 1,200 pounds.

SAMUEL ELIOT MORISON

The Oxford History of the American People, 1965

SPANISH MOSS, BONAVENTURE CEMETERY

Throughout Georgia, from Albany to Athens, Waco to Waycross —cotton was king—the ubiquitous mule team hauling crops over rutty dirt roads for shipment to mill centers

MARKETPLACE IN A SMALL GEORGIA VILLAGE

Across the Georgia Piedmont, stretching in an undulating plain through the center of the state, is the broad band of regions most vital to the Peach State's economy

FRANKLIN COLLEGE, ATHENS

Rome, in north Georgia, is the capital of the valley-and-hill region, a town built among the hills at the junction of the Oostanaula and Etowah rivers, which form the Coosa. The town is known, among other things, for the nearby Berry Schools and College, a fabulous educational empire created out of nothing, except an iron will and vision, by Miss Martha Berry. The students are chosen almost entirely from the rural South and do not pay to attend; but they all contribute by working (in the field of agriculture, mostly), and thus gain experience along with book learning—an educational system widely admired for many reasons. The campus of the Berry Schools has been called, with justice, the most beautiful in America. It is certainly one of the largest. Miss Martha, by the time of her death, had accumulated more than thirty thousand acres for the "grounds" of her schools.

CALDER WILLINGHAM

American Panorama, 1947

VIEW OF ROME

Here, with the exception of coastal Savannah, are located the largest cities—Atlanta, Augusta, Athens, Columbus, La Grange, Macon, Milledgeville

RAILROAD YARDS, ATLANTA

General Sherman's efficient army demolition squads destroyed ninety per cent of Atlanta in 1864, just before he began his historic march to the sea. The city rose from its ashes to become the state's great capital city—the South's largest industrial, financial, and educational center. The visitor in the capital city of the Peach State finds that today it is less the nostalgic city of "Gone with the Wind" than the cultural and economic heart of the Southeast. Peachtree Street is still counted among the South's most famous avenues, but today it is more exciting than it is romantic, for huge new office buildings, apartments, excellent museums, and lavish shops have sprung up along it. Little of Georgia is drowsing beneath the magnolias these days.

Texaco Touring Atlas,
1965

COMMERCIAL CENTRE, ATLANTA

Atlanta—mercilessly battered and burned during the Civil War, when eighty thousand Northern troops destroyed stores, factories, and public buildings . . .

What is the South? It is not what people say it is—and never has been. From the time of the landing of Amadas and Barlowe on Roanoke Island "in Virginia" to the time of Thomas Nelson Page, say from 1584 to 1884, the region was, by its own admission, "the goodliest land under the cope of heaven," peopled by angels in human form, with a few foreign devils from "up North" thrown in by way of contrast. From the time of Page to that of Erskine Caldwell, William Faulkner and Lillian Smith, the South has somehow become transformed into a never-never, Krafft-Ebing land of psychopathia sexualis, peopled by sadists, masochists, rapists, satyrs, nymphomaniacs, and necrophiles, to mention a few of the better known types, together with assorted murderers, arsonists and lynchers, although it seems to draw the line at cannibalism, even during a failure of the turnip crop. The notion that the South is a geographical region of the United States of America, populated by rather easy-going people of various shades of complexion, who live rather ordinary lives... is too fantastic a thought to be entertained seriously by writers or readers of modern South literature.... The South has become a cross between a Gothic romance and a Greek tragedy rewritten by Freud....

WILLIAM T. POLK
Southern Accent, 1953

On Capitol Avenue.

A Modern Residence

A Peachtree St. Cottage.

A Villa.

A Doctor's residence.

Cor. Whitehall and Hunter Sts.

On Washington St.

Home of a Merchant.

A Suburban Home.

A Peachtree St. residence.

RESIDENCES, ATLANTA

. . . turned immediately, on departure of the enemy, to the task of reconstruction, and within a decade of hectic building activity the "New South" was born

The architects of the time saw to it that their work was well done. It was an age of commercialism rampant, the beginning of the present age of salesmanship and advertising. The architects, with, of course, a few honorable exceptions, were quite up to the times; books of plans and details were broadcast, and their "villas" and residences and commercial buildings are all mixed without rhyme or reason.

TALBOT HAMLIN

The New South is enamored of her new work. Her soul is stirred with the breath of a new life. The light of a grander day is falling fair on her face. She is thrilling with the consciousness of growing power and prosperity. As she stands upright, full-statured and equal among the people of the earth, breathing the keen air and looking out upon the expanding horizon, she understands that her emancipation came because in the inscrutable wisdom of God her honest purpose was crossed and her brave armies beaten.

HENRY W. GRADY
The New South, 1886

In her streets and in her buildings Atlanta shows the influence that Georgia granite and marble has on her architecture. The new State Capitol, in a general way, resembles the Capitol at Washington, and is the work of Edbrook & Burnham, of Chicago.

THE CAPITOL, ATLANTA AND RECENT BUILDINGS

Although Florida was the site of the earliest European settlement —preceding Jamestown and Plymouth by more than a half-century —only its northern coastal tip was touched by the Spaniards . . .

Florida is a strange land, both in its traditions and its natural features. It was the first settled of the States, and has the most genial climate of all of them; and yet the greater part of it is still a wilderness. Its early history was one long romance of battle and massacre, and its later annals are almost equally interesting. The Spaniards, who were the first Christian people to visit it, were much impressed with its mystery and its scenery, and, as they discovered it on Easter Sunday, which in their language is called "Pascua Florida," they commemorated the event by giving the new territory its present appellation. The time was when Florida was an immense sand-bar, stretching into the Gulf of Mexico, and probably as barren as can be conceived. But in the semi-tropical climate under which it exists, in the course of ages the seeds carried to its shores by the sea and the winds and the myriads of birds which find it a resting-place, have clothed it with luxuriant vegetation, interspersed with tracts of apparently barren sands. It is a land of peculiar scenery, which the pencil of the artist has heretofore scarcely touched. Its main features illustrate the absurdity of the common notion that the landscapes of tropical and semi-tropical latitudes are superior in luxuriance of vegetable production to those of the temperate zones.

J. B. THORPE

Picturesque America, 1872

LIGHTHOUSE, MOUTH OF ST. JOHN'S RIVER

. . . leaving the wild interior of dense swamps, "grassy water" and crocodile-infested rivers to be penetrated and settled at a much later date

MAKING CYPRESS SHINGLES

In this heat and wetness life breeds and spawns as it has for millions of years. Mostly, it is shy, night-feeding, night-hunting, but you sense its presence and feel that eyes are watching you: the green-glowing eyes of panthers, the liquid eyes of deer, the cold eyes of rattlesnakes and cotton-mouths, the black-masked eyes of raccoons. These last you will probably see as they move across the road with their high-shouldered, flat-footed shuffle, or as with their deft little hands they wash their food in a patch of clear water among the mangroves. A slow swirl in one of the coastal rivers may show where a manatee—fat, wrinkled, childishly blue-eyed—is feeding on water weeds.

BENEDICT THIELEN

GREEN COVE SPRINGS

POST OFFICE ON THE OCKLAWAHA

Burned and sacked by the English buccaneer Sir Francis Drake, in 1586—St. Augustine survived slaughter and pillage through three centuries of occupation by Spanish, French, and English

The quaint little city of St. Augustine, Florida, the oldest European settlement in the United States, is situated on the Atlantic coast, in a narrow peninsula formed by the Sebastian and Matanzas Rivers, on the west side of a harbor which is separated from the ocean by the low and narrow island of Anastasia. It lies about forty miles south of the great river St. John's, and about one hundred and sixty miles south from Savannah, in Georgia.

J. B. THORPE
Picturesque America, 1872

ST. MARK'S CASTLE, ST. AUGUSTINE

STREET IN ST. AUGUSTINE

ST. AUGUSTINE CATHEDRAL

Oldest city in the United States, founded in 1565— resort of Tories during the Revolutionary War—rich in Hispanic culture, impregnable forts, fine cathedrals

At St. Augustine as at other points, the Spanish arrivals remained largely soldiers at a far outpost. Twenty years after Menéndez' exploit, Sir Francis Drake made a raid on St. Augustine and burned it to the ground. In 1665 another English freebooter looted it. This time the court ordered a stronger fort, and for decades men worked to erect thirty foot walls, twelve feet across at the base, of coquina or shellstone. Examining the costs, the king said wryly that its bastions must have been made of silver. Still, the Castillo de San Marco was an impressive example of power and grace. Several times the people fled to it, to survive while their community was razed. Today the fort still remains, and so does something of older St. Augustine. The city gates, several times rebuilt, stand where they did when they bordered the early moat, as tall rectangles topped with Moorish designs. A part of St. Augustine lingers as the Southeast's most tangible relic of the Spaniards' bid for power.

HARNETT T. KANE
Gone Are the Days, 1960

WATCHTOWER,
ST. MARK'S CASTLE

THE CITY GATE, ST. AUGUSTINE

INTERIOR, ST. MARK'S CASTLE

CONVENT GATE

Florida's rivers twist and turn through low, trackless sawgrass prairies—the Suwannee, the St. Johns and the Oklawaha—their banks lined with royal palms, gumbo-limbo, mahogany and the strangler fig

But even around the Everglades, intrusions of commerce are causing profound concern for its future as a place for human enjoyment. Yet what survives in this steaming world where life has spawned for millions of years is indeed wondrous. *Pa-hay-okee* in Indian language means "grassy water," which is what the Everglades are: a river of grass. "But their grass is not grass as we know it," writes Benedict Thielen, whose appreciation of the Everglades is that of a lyrical naturalist. "It does not bend and ripple under the wind. It stands stiff, straight, and unyielding. It is really not grass at all but a flowering sedge, one of the oldest forms of green life on earth. It grows with fierce luxuriance, eight, ten, and in some places, fifteen feet high. It is set with tiny, sharp teeth of silica, and this is why they call it saw grass. The blades of this grass are truly blades— they can tear off a man's clothes and rip open his flesh. Like an impenetrable stockade they stand here, upthrust in their countless millions, a wilderness of sharpened swords. Spreading over thirty-five hundred square miles, the saw grass grows in the shallow water, fed by the sun and the deep rich rot of forty centuries of alternating life and death.... The grass does not move. But below it, invisibly, the water moves...from Lake Okeechobee southward, it flows slowly to the sea."

BENEDICT THIELEN

ON THE OCKLAWAHA

The Everglades, in the lower third of the Florida peninsula—covering a vast stretch of grasslands, sloughs and tropical vegetation—sanctuary for the pink ibis, snowy egret, vicious 'gators and wildcats

This is one of the most remote and primitive areas in the United States. Here the resourceful Seminoles finally found sanctuary in the "grass water" prairies out of which rise fertile hammocks, or islands, heavily grown with royal palms, mahogany, tamarind, the redbarked gumbo-limbo, and the cruelly beautiful strangler fig. Here the Indians who refused the indignity of being removed en masse to Oklahoma built their villages and planted their squash and bananas, confident that this insidious marsh country of the redbug and the moccasin would be theirs by default because it was the one section of Florida the white man could not endure. The only other inhabitants of these impenetrable mangrove swamps were squatters, outcasts, moonshiners who lived in shacks raised on stilts over the shallow Florida Bay flats at a now vanished community well-named Snake Bite, or in lawless little bands on the islands of Whitewater Bay.

BUDD SCHULBERG

Florida, in American Panorama, 1947

SCENES IN THE FLORIDA EVERGLADES

Pensacola, at the extreme northwestern tip of the Sunshine State—in atmosphere and character more like an old Spanish town—still abia by the proverb: "The night is made for sleep, and the day for res

The years immediately following the Civil War found Pensacola a drowsy old town, 4 squares wide and 8 long, its streets deep in sand. Upon recovery from the Reconstruction period, Pensacola enjoyed a second era of prosperity, due largely to railroad development of the territory and exports of timber and naval stores. In the early 1870's began the development of the waterfront. The harbor was filled with steamboats and square-riggers from the ports of the world. Vessels, before loading with cargo, discharged their ballast, which was hauled and dumped along the shore, and 60 acres of land were created in a few years. Thus Pensacola's reclaimed shoreline is made up of red granite from Sweden, blue stone from Italy, broken tile from France, and dredgings from the River Themes and the Scheldes of The Netherlands.

FLORIDA
American Guide Series, 1939

SCENES IN PENSACOLA

Down the Ohio...from Pittsburgh to Paducah

ON THE OHIO, BELOW PITTSBURGH

... SOUTH PITTSBURGH ... VIEW OF

THE CITY OF PITTSBURGH ...

COLUMBUS ... ASHTABULA ...

BIG DARBY ... CINCINNATI ... PUBLIC

LANDING ... COURT HOUSE ... CUSTOM

HOUSE ... "THE RHINE" ... NEWPORT

... COVINGTON ... LOUISVILLE ...

PARKERSBURG ... JEFFERSONVILLE ...

NEW ALBANY ... INDIANAPOLIS ...

MADISON ... CAIRO, JUNCTION OF THE

OHIO AND MISSISSIPPI RIVERS

THE OHIO BELOW PITTSBURGH

Down the Ohio... from Pittsburgh to Paducah

IT WAS CALLED "OHIO FEVER"—THE FIRST great push westward after the American Revolution. In 1787 the new congress established the Northwest Territory and opened for settlement the vast region beyond the thirteen original states. By 1811 a manual for river pilots could already tell travelers of the changing face of the newly settled Ohio River valley: "Now the immense forests recede, cultivation smiles along its banks, towns every here and there decorate its shores, and it is not extravagant to suppose, that the

day is not very far distant when its whole margin will form one continued village." The prediction was not extravagant. Today the Ohio River basin is one of the most populated and industrialized regions in the United States.

Settlers flocked west in the thirty years following the opening of the territory. Some came down the Ohio River by flatboat and canoe; others drove Conestoga wagons along the Genesee, Forbe's, Cumberland, and Wilderness roads. By boat or by wagon, they responded to people such as Manasseh Cutler, who told them of "the most agreeable, the most advantageous, the most fertile land which is known to any people of Europe, whatsoever." Some years later, a less enchanted Charles Dickens could observe nothing there but "sky, wood, and water, all the livelong day; and heat that blistered everything it touched." But most settlers, hungry for land and yearning for the freedom of limitless prairies, forest, and mountains, ignored such fastidious objections. In 1811, the *New Orleans* became the first steamboat to sail the Ohio, and by 1837 over three hundred steamboats were churning the river.

At the Ohio's point of origin, where the Allegheny and Monongahela rivers meet, lies Pittsburgh, the first of many cities to flourish as the result of the busy river traffic. Because of its strategic position at the junction of the two rivers, Pittsburgh was an early outpost. Fortified first by the French—who called it Fort Duquesne—and then by the English—who renamed it Fort Pitt—it was already settled as a town in the 1760s. By the end of the eighteenth century, it had become an important shipbuilding center and port of departure for people and goods moving west.

From Pittsburgh, the Ohio flows southwest, through the nation's richest coal country. Wheeling, on the river's eastern bank, is West Virginia's chief river port. East of Wheeling stretch the green hills, ridges, and mountains created millennia ago by great geological upheavals, which also deposited the mineral riches of the region. Upheavals of a more recent nature bitterly rent West Virginia and its people. In 1859 John Brown attempted his abolitionist insurrection at Harpers Ferry, in the easternmost tip of the state. In the years that followed, loyalties to the North and the South split families and friends throughout the state. In the west, miners struggled against the stubborn earth and the equally stubborn mine owners, and along the Kentucky border the Hatfields and McCoys feuded for twenty years.

On the Ohio's western bank lies the state to which the river has given its name. Although it is really the Middle West, Ohio is the place where the Middle West begins, and where, for pioneers heading west, civilization once offered its last outposts. The Cumberland Road—renamed the National Road in the 1830s—crossed the center of the state; and at Springfield a statue, the *Madonna of the Trail*, stands to commemorate the women who crossed the Ohio to face the harsh frontier. For many, however, the journey would end in this region. Those who did stop founded towns that prospered from fertile land and a century of westward migration.

Columbus, Ohio's capital and second largest city, stands in the center of the state, near the route of the old National Road. South of Columbus lie the Pickaway Plains, where the Shawnees' fierce resistance to European encroachment once bloodied the land. Cincinnati, situated on the river, already had a population of over twenty thousand by the 1830s, and it continued to grow as traffic along the Ohio increased. Although Mrs. Trollope, who established an exotic but unsuccessful "bazaar" there in 1827, found the city's large commerce in hogs distasteful, she recognized that it was 'a city of extraordinary size and importance . . . and every month appears to extend its limits and its wealth."

Southern Illinois is a hilly, wooded land, where the sycamores dominate the forests along the river. North, just above what is today Terre Haute, the Battle of Tippecanoe was fought in 1811 against the great Tecumseh. Farther south, a town of more peaceful memory, New Harmony, was founded in 1814, by George Rapp and his austere society.

On the southern bank of the Ohio, on a low plain where the river breaks over falls, lies Louisville, Kentucky's biggest and economically most important city. A canal was built around the falls in 1830, and the city's fortunes have continued to be largely dependent on the river traffic.

Kentucky, like West Virginia, knew both the bitter divisions of the Civil War and the equally bitter struggles of the miners.

At the very western end of the state the Ohio flows past Paducah, now a prosperous industrial center. Here the river, which in its thousand-mile course has received the waters of the Cumberland, the Wabash, the Kentucky, the Muskingum, and a score of other rivers, is joined by the Tennessee. Then, swollen to its full, it flows into Illinois and ends its own course in a majestic junction with the Mississippi.

O-He-Yo, the Wyandot word for "fair to look upon"
—la Belle Riviere to the French settlers—became
the Ohio when the name was Anglicized . . .

Pittsburgh is situated at the conflux of the rivers Monongahela and Alleghany, the uniting of which forms the Ohio. The even soil upon which it is built is not more than forty or fifty acres in extent. It is in the form of an angle, the three sides of which are enclosed either by the bed of the two rivers or by stupendous mountains. The houses are principally brick, they are computed to be about four hundred, most of which are built upon the Monongahela; that side is considered the most commercial part of the town.

F. A. MICHAUX
Travels, 1805

CITY OF PITTSBURGH

These ships were to go, in the spring following, to New Orleans, loaded with the produce of the country, after having made a passage of two thousand two hundred miles before they got into the ocean. There is no doubt but they can, by the same rule, build ships two hundred leagues beyond the mouth of the Missouri, fifty from that of the river Illinois, and even in the Mississippi, two hundred beyond the place whence these rivers flow; that is to say, six hundred and fifty leagues from the sea; as their bed in the appointed space is as deep as that of the Ohio at Pittsburgh; in consequence of which it must be a wrong conjecture to suppose that the immense tract of country watered by these rivers cannot be populous enough to execute such undertakings. The rapid population of the three new western states, under less favourable circumstances, proves this assertion to be true. Those states, where thirty years ago there was scarcely three hundred inhabitants, are now computed to contain upwards of a hundred thousand; and although the plantations on the roads are scarcely four miles distant from each other, it is very rare to find one, even among the most flourishing, where one cannot with confidence ask the owner, whence he has emigrated; or, according to the trivial manner of the Americans, "What part of the world do you come from?"

F. A. MICHAUX
Travels, 1805

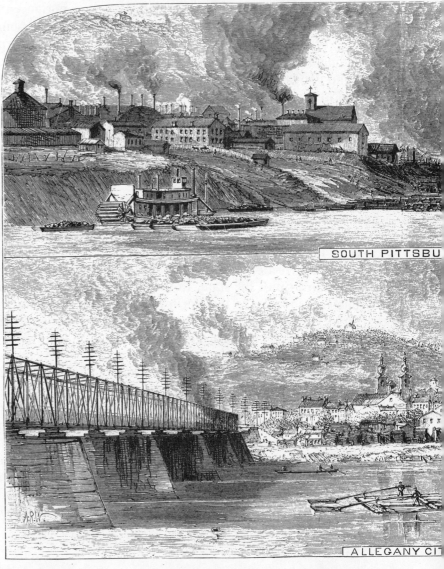

SOUTH PITTSBURGH AND ALLEGHENY CITY

*. . . the only major American river flowing westerly—
from the confluence of the Monongahela and the Allegheny
—a strategic junction where Pittsburgh was built*

PITTSBURGH, FROM SOLDIERS' MONUMENT

Pittsburgh smoke and fog make strange companions. I remember one murky morning when from the tower of the Allegheny Library the city resolved itself into a steaming caldron, with the sky-scrapers emerging as though a race of giants had been condemned to have their feet parboiled. About this one feature of the local pageant one might run on without end. But any such account as this of the picturesque side of the city of beautiful smoke perforce must rigorously select a mere handful of effects out of as many as would fill fat volumes. On arriving in Pittsburgh the first thought of the wise beauty-lover is to visit Mt. Washington, a height on the further bank of the Monongahela River which offers the best view of the Y shaped city. The Monongahela forms the right prong of the Y, the Allegheny the left. And they flow together into the stem, which is the Ohio. The two prongs are laced with bridges. The apex of the peninsula between them is flat like the toe of a boot. This rises, as the rivers diverge, into a high instep known as "The Hill." So much for geography. The pilgrim crosses the Smithfield Street Bridge, enters the small, misshapen car of one of those startlingly European "inclines" that hale him up the crag at an angle of forty-five degrees, or so, and stands straightway upon an eminence. "Above the smoke and stir of this dim spot which men call Pittsburgh."

ROBERT HAVEN SCHAUFFLER
Romantic America, 1913

"Ohio fever"—the great migration to the West—infected thousands who journeyed by Conestoga wagon across the Alleghenies and down the Ohio—the "shining road"...

In 1838 Caleb Atwater of Circleville published *A History of Ohio,* the first and most buoyant outline of the state. This Massachusetts Yankee, a failed businessman and lawyer with nine children to support, had soon caught the Ohio excitement. Remarking on Columbus as a seat of government, he stated: Its buildings are, many of them, large, commodious and handsome. The state house is not such a one as Ohio ought to have this day . . . . The penitentiary is a large, handsome building of stone, built mostly by the convicts who are confined in it. . . . That we have prospered [despite hardships and dangers and sufferings] more than any other people did in the world, is most certain; but our exertions to improve our conditions are by no means to be relaxed—to make Ohio what it ought to be, the first state in the Union in numbers, knowledge, wealth, and political power. . . . Our position in the nation is peculiarly felicitous as to soil, climate, and productions, and it will be our own fault if we are not the happiest people in the Union.

CALEB ATWATER

A History of Ohio, 1838

BRIDGE OVER THE BIG DARBY

HOWE TRUSS BRIDGE, ASHTABULA

. . . inspiring the hectic settlement of the Buckeye State
—the spread of rail lines—the spanning of rivers
by bridges of wood, iron, and suspension cable

COVERED RAILROAD BRIDGE, COLUMBUS

I embarked a few years since, at Pittsburg, for Cincinnati, on board of a steam boat—more with a view of realising the possibility of a speedy return against the current, than in obedience to the call of either business or pleasure. It was a voyage of speculation. I was born on the banks of the Ohio, and the only vessels associated with my early recollections were the canoes of the Indians, which brought to Fort Pitt their annual cargoes of skins and bear's oil. The Flat boat of Kentucky, destined only to float with the current, next appeared; and after many years of interval, the Keel boat of the Ohio.

MORGAN NEVILLE
The Western Souvenir, 1829

NEW SUSPENSION BRIDGE OVER THE OHIO, CINCINNATI

310

Tocqueville, ever the keen observer, described Ohioans as a "people without precedence, without traditions, without habits, without dominating ideas even . . .

Cincinnati, midway along the great artery, gateway to the rich Miami country, took the lead. In 1832 in the *Edinburgh Review* a traveler from Scotland reported: Cincinnati on the Ohio: thirty years ago a forest crossed only by the red man; now a rising town, with 20,000 inhabitants, and increasing at the rate of 1400 houses a year. . . . Our astonishment has been speechless in finding that such a spot possessed in 1815 a Lancastrian school, a public library of 1400 volumes, four printing-offices, and three weekly papers. During Mrs. Trollope's stay, Mr. [Timothy] Flint printed there his 'Western States' in two volumes 8vo; a work that would do honour to a London publisher. She speaks of two museums of natural history, a picture gallery, and an attempt by two artists at an academy of design. After this, what town in England, Scotland, or even Ireland, will turn up its nose at Cincinnati? The men can have little or no leisure. But what must be said of the spirit of the place!

WALTER HAVIGHURST

Ohio, 1976

VIEW OF CINCINNATI, FROM NEWPORT BARRACKS

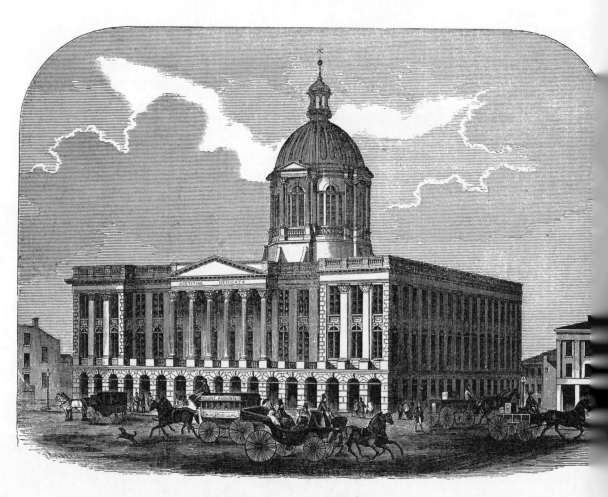

NEW COURT HOUSE, CINCINNATI

. . . cutting out its institutions, like its roads,
in the midst of the forests . . . sure to encounter
neither limits nor obstacles''

PUBLIC LANDING, CINCINNATI

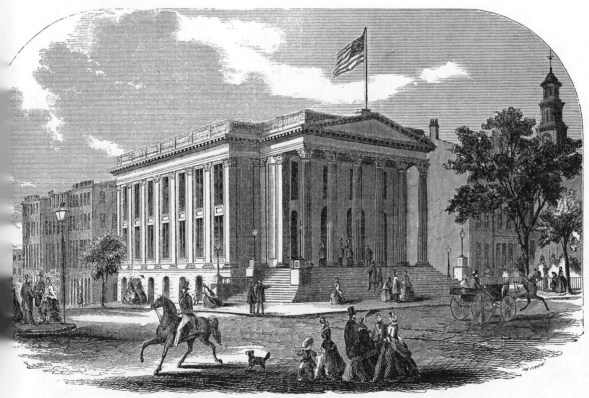

CUSTOM HOUSE AND POST OFFICE, CINCINNATI

MARSHALL DAVIDSON
Life in America, 1951

In the rivalry between the Atlantic ports and New Orleans for the western trade, Cincinnati occupied a strategic place with convenient outlet in either direction, down the Ohio or by way of the Erie Canal. The downriver route was long favored for bulkier products destined for the east coast. At one time eighty per cent of the pork and grain from Cincinnati went down the Ohio. The long line of steamboats and the masses of merchandise piled on the levee were a sign of the "Queen City's" flourishing prosperity. Dickens remarked that it had risen out of the forests like an Arabian Nights city. Even Mrs. Trollope was impressed by the activity along its waterfont. "Its landing is a notable place," she wrote, "extending for more than a quarter of a mile. . . . I have seen fifteen steamboats lying there at once and still half the wharf was unoccupied."

Longfellow called Cincinnati the "Queen City of the West," recognizing its rich cultural heritage—a city founded at the close of the Revolution . . .

"THE RHINE"

During nearly two years that I resided in Cincinnati, or its neighbourhood, I neither saw a beggar, nor a man of sufficient fortune to permit his ceasing his efforts to increase it; thus every bee in the hive is actively employed in search of that honey of Hybla, vulgarly called money; neither art, science, learning, nor pleasure can seduce them from its pursuit. This unity of purpose, backed by the spirit of enterprise, and joined with an acuteness and total absence of probity, where interest is concerned, which might set canny Yorkshire at defiance, may well go far towards obtaining its purpose . . .

CINCINNATI, VIEW FROM THE CARLISLE HOTEL

. . . on the banks of the Ohio—in the southwest corner of the Buckeye State—where Kentuckians, Virginians, and New Englanders welcomed the influx of Germans and Irish, in the forties and fifties

FOURTH STREET, CINCINNATI

. . . Perhaps the most advantageous feature in Cincinnati is its market, which, for excellence, abundance, and cheapness can hardly, I should think, be surpassed in any part of the world, if I except the luxury of fruits, which are very inferior to any I have seen in Europe. There are no butchers, fishmongers, or indeed any shops for eatables, except bakeries, as they are called, in the town; every thing must be purchased at market; and to accomplish this, the busy housewife must be stirring betimes, or, 'spite of the abundant supply, she will find her hopes of breakfast, dinner, and supper for the day defeated, the market being pretty well over by eight o'clock. The beef is excellent, and the highest price when we were there, four cents (about two-pence) the pound. The mutton was inferior, and so was veal to the eye, but it ate well, though not very fat; the price was about the same. The poultry was excellent; fowls or full-sized chickens, ready for the table, twelve cents, but much less if bought alive.

FRANCES TROLLOPE
Domestic Manners of the Americans, 1832

On the Cincinnati riverfront in the spring of 1848 a new bookkeeper began work in a shipping office. His name was Stephen Collins Foster. In his big ledger each page was a packet: *Fairmont, Messenger, Oswego, Bolivar, Ohio Belle, Gladiator, Hibernia.* Outside his window, carts rumbled on the pavement, passengers thronged the wharf boat, and a parade of big white steamers lined the levee. In the chill wind, tatters of smoke blew from the tall chimneys. But the river led to the languid, fragrant Southland. Stephen Foster had melodies in his mind. Forgetting bills of lading, he began to write:

> I come from Alabama
> Wid my banjo on my knee.
> I'm gwan to Louisiana
> My true love for to see.
> Oh! Susanna, do not cry for me.
> I come from Alabama,
> Wid my banjo on my knee.

WALTER HAVIGHURST
Ohio, 1975

"THE RHINE"

*Across the Ohio, from Cincinnati, are Newport and Covington
—satellite towns in neighboring Kentucky, the Bluegrass
State, famous for its breeding of horses and the Derby*

Steamboat travel was both glamorous and squalid. The stately four-deckers, white as a wedding cake, had floral carpets, inlaid woodwork, and oil paintings on the stateroom doors. They provided a nursery, a barbershop, gaming rooms, and a gleaming bar. Their cabin passengers sat down to five-course dinners with orchestra music. But most of the travelers never saw the splendors of the grand saloon. Immigrants, woodsmen, and frontier farmers were crowded among cargo and livestock on the lower deck, cooking porridge on the boiler flues and drinking river water. They slept on bales and boxes. Living close to the engines and the waterline, they were the first victims of collision and explosion. The one inducement to deck passage was economy. For a dollar a decker could travel five hundred miles—one-fifth the fare for cabin passengers.

WALTER HAVIGHURST
Ohio, 1975

MARKET AND SQUARE, COVINGTON, KENTUCKY

NEWPORT BARRACKS ON THE OHIO

On the falls of the Ohio—downriver about 130 miles from Cincinnati—lies Louisville, where many an early traveler broke his journey and settled down

SPEED MARKET, LOUISVILLE

Because Lexington is known as the center of Thoroughbred breeding, many of the uninitiated think the Kentucky Derby is run there. It isn't. It's run at Louisville's Churchill Downs. Louisville is Kentucky's biggest city and, businesswise at least, its most important. Its residents estimate a metropolitan district that counts more than half a million. It lies on a low plain where the Ohio River broke over falls as lucrative to early-day pilots, porters and towline hands as they were vexing to vessels and crews. The falls aren't impressive any more. The Government system of locks and dams has reduced them substantially. Until about 1870 the city's prosperity rose and fell with river traffic, in which the steamboat made its first entrance in 1811. A good many northerners terminated their river journeys at Louisville— which accounts for the fact that the town still casts a lusty if not majority Republican vote. "Louisville," says the Kentucky WPA guidebook of 1939, "is a border metropolis that blends the commerce and industry of a Northern city with the Southern city's enjoyment of living." It might have said that Louisville is a big, friendly, country town, notable by outward reputation as the home of the *Courier-Journal*, the Louisville Slugger and the Derby.

A. B. GUTHRIE, JR.
Kentucky, 1947

GREEN AND SIXTH STREETS, LOUISVILLE

River traffic comprised every type of craft—from simple raft or flat-bottomed keelboat, called "broadhorn"—steered by long oars . . .

To Pittsburgh in the early years came families worn and weary from a punishing journey across the mountains. Some had jolted over the rocky road in cart or wagon. Some had left the wagon broken at a fording place and come on, trundling a few goods in a wheelbarrow. Many had measured, step by step, the Allegheny ridges; years, later a Marietta woman remembered her mother leading a reluctant cow, leaning on the creature during the long way up and over Laurel Mountain. For all, it was the dream of a river flowing west that kept them going. At Pittsburgh, at last, they saw the Monongahela and the Allegheny join to form the dreamed Ohio. After the looming barrier ridges, after the dark trace hemmed in forest, after mud and mire, rocks, roots, and tree stumps, there lay the river, the beckoning, sunlit river winding westward between the wild green shores. This was the main channel of the westward rush, the current that carried the greatest tide of settlement and expansion the world has known. All their lives the immigrants would remember that shining road, like a gift, like a promise, like God's providence in an unfeeling world . . .

SCENES ON THE OHIO

. . . to the ornate, romantic, stern-wheeled packets—the "river queens"—carrying hundreds of passengers on triple decks, with all the amenities of an exclusive hotel

RAILROAD BRIDGE, PARKERSBURG, WEST VA.

At the Pittsburgh boatyards thirty-five dollars would buy an oblong flat-bottomed craft with a shedlike shelter for its people and a railed deck for horses and cattle. Commonly called a "broadhorn," it had a pair of long steering oars set in timber crotches on the shed roof. Like a floating barnyard it moved down the shining road, horses munching at a pile of hay and chickens scratching at their feet. On the roof a woman rocked a cradle and a man leaned on the steering oar while the tireless river carried them toward the future. By a great gift of geography the promised land of Ohio had a moving, gleaming highway to bring its people home. At Wheeling a flatboat family could put in for stores—salt pork, hominy, dried apples, cornmeal, and molasses. Then on the way again, past great headlands, little creek mouths, long, curved willow islands, and shelves of green bottomland under the lifting hills. While the changing shores slid past, emigrant families talked of lands they would claim, houses they would build, harvests they would gather. The flatboat was a one-way craft. At journey's end it was broken up and put together again as a one room dwelling.

WALTER HAVIGHURST

Ohio, 1975

NEW ALBANY, INDIANA

JEFFERSONVILLE, INDIANA

Indianapolis, centered in the Hoosier State, the largest state capital after Boston—chosen in 1821 in newly acquired Indian Territory . . .

In 1818 at St. Mary's, Ohio, three Indiana commissioners met a group of Indian chiefs and bought from them the entire central section of Indiana. Surveyors soon divided this "New Purchase" into townships, and settlement began. In this district a site was chosen for the new Hoosier capital; the town was laid out by a young English engineer, Elias Pym Fordham, who had come to America with Morris Birkbeck. In 1824 four farm wagons moved the seat of government from the old State House at Corydon to the new, centrally located capital.

WALTER HAVIGHURST

Land of the Long Horizons, 1960

VIEW OF MADISON, INDIANA

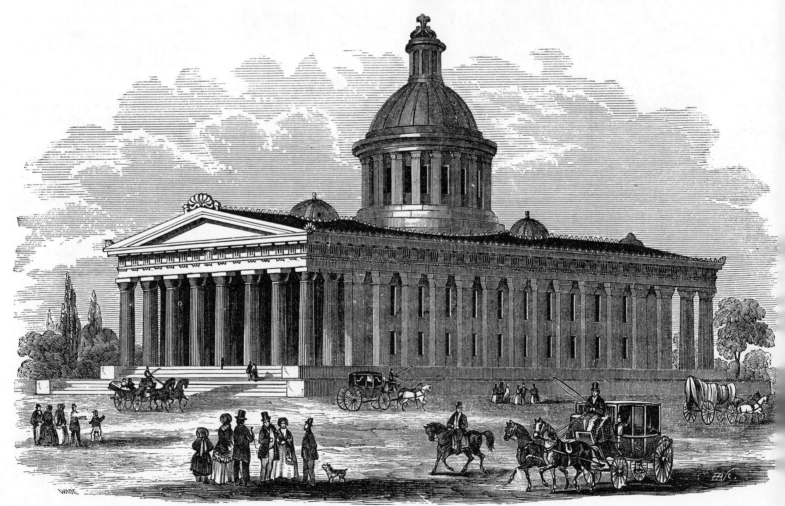

STATE HOUSE, INDIANAPOLIS

. . . built sturdily in classical style—the seat of government and its institutions expressing a solidity unmatched in other young Midwest communities

STATE HOSPITAL, INDIANAPOLIS

The principal reason for transferring the seat of government from Corydon to Indianapolis was that Corydon was inaccessible to settlers moving into the north and central areas of the state. In 1825 only two stage lines led to the town, one from Centerville and one from Madison. The only other main routes in the state were the Vincennes-New Albany trail, and another from New Albany by way of Salem, Bedford, and Bloomington to Lafayette. Neither of these directly served the new capital.

WILLIAM E. WILSON

Indiana, 1966

INSTITUTE FOR THE BLIND, INDIANAPOLIS

Downstream, the Ohio flows past Paducah and reaches Cairo, where it meets the Mississippi—forming the junction of three states: Illinois, Kentucky, and Missouri

On they toiled through great solitudes, where the trees upon the banks grew thick and close; and floated in the stream; and held up shrivelled arms from out the river's depths; and slid down from the margin of the land, half growing, half decaying, in the miry water. On through the weary day and melancholy night: beneath the burning sun, and in the mist and vapour of the evening: on, until return appeared impossible, and restoration to their home a miserable dream. They had now but few people on board, and these were as flat, as dull, and stagnant, as the vegetation that oppressed their eyes. No sound of cheerfulness or hope was heard; no pleasant talk beguiled the tardy time; no little group made common cause against the dull depression of the scene. But that, at certain periods, they swallowed food together from a common trough, it must have been old Charon's boat, conveying melancholy shades to judgment. At length they drew near New Thermopolae; where, that same evening, Mrs. Hominy would disembark. A gleam of comfort sunk into Martin's bosom when she told him this. Mark needed none; but he was not displeased. It was almost night when they came alongside the landing-place. A steep bank with an hotel, like a barn, on the top of it; a wooden store or two, and a few scattered sheds.

CHARLES DICKENS

Martin Chuzzlewit, 1844

CAIRO, AT THE JUNCTION OF OHIO AND MISSISSIPPI RIVERS

CANAL LOCKS, MUSKINGUM, OHIO

West of the Appalachians...
& South to the Gulf

THE TENNESSEE RIVER . . .

CUMBERLAND GAP . . . EAGLE CLIFF

. . . KNOXVILLE . . . CHATTANOOGA . . .

LOOKOUT MOUNTAIN . . . FERRY AT

CHATTANOOGA . . . MOBILE BAY . . .

GRANT'S PASS . . . FORT MORGAN . . .

CITY HALL AND NEW MARKET . . .

MONTGOMERY . . . THE CAPITOL . . .

ALABAMA RIVER . . . LOADING COTTON

. . . PLANTER'S HOME . . . FLOODS IN

ALABAMA

THE TENNESSEE

West of the Appalachians...
& South to the Gulf

AT THE TIME OF THE AMERICAN REVO-
lution, the land west of the Appalachian Mountains was still largely unexplored. Cities and towns
lined the Atlantic coast and settlers had pushed
inland. But the rugged mountain range that
cuts across the United States from Canada
almost to the Gulf of Mexico stopped all but
the most intrepid explorers. By the last decades

of the eighteenth century, however, buckskin-
clad frontiersmen were crossing the mountains,
scouting trails and hearing the Indians' tales of
the land farther to the west. Soon the "long
hunters" in the lowlands of Virginia and the
Carolinas were making regular forays into the
mountains, stalking elk, buffalo, deer, and
bear; they often spent months in the uncharted
wilderness. These hunters brought back reports

that excited the imaginations of men who were already growing tired of the "crowded" East.

The most famous of these men, Daniel Boone, crossed the mountains in 1769 and "saw with pleasure the beautiful level of Kentucky." He described it as a second paradise. Later, he moved his family and a large party of settlers through the Cumberland Gap and into central Kentucky. As they made their way across the Appalachians they carved the Wilderness Road, and thereby opened the West to settlement. Following men like Daniel Boone, thousands of settlers were soon traveling the Wilderness Road or taking the longer journey by river. By the turn of the century, settlement had reached such proportions that both Kentucky and Tennessee were admitted to the Union.

To men first seeing these new lands, they must indeed have seemed a second paradise. Where the Cumberland and Pine mountains begin to slope down into eastern Kentucky, they form steep valleys and sharp ridges, canyons and natural rock arches. Laurel azalea and tulip trees bloom on the slopes, and beyond the hills stretch the bluegrass plains.

After selling some Kentucky land to white settlers, a Cherokee Chief, Dragging Canoe, warned that although the land was indeed beautiful, it was "under a cloud and a dark and bloody ground." His warning proved true. In frontier days, settlers were prey both to Indian attacks and to the lawlessness that reigned in those loosely organized lands. In the middle of the nineteenth century bitter divisions over secession pulled families and friends apart, and some of the bloodiest battles of the war itself were fought in Tennessee: Shiloh, Chattanooga, and Knoxville. After the war the Ku Klux Klan was born in Tennessee, and, in more recent times, Harlan County, Kentucky became the scene of bloody industrial strife.

Although Kentucky and Tennessee have given the nation some of its most violent moments, they have also provided some of its most pleasurable ones. Kentucky's bluegrass country is famed both for the music to which it has given its name, and for one of the finest breeds of race horse, the thoroughbred. In Louisville the Derby has been run on the first Saturday of every May, since 1875. The blues

were born on Memphis's Beale Street, and in Nashville, the "Athens of the South," country music has coexisted with some of the South's oldest academies.

Alabama had its earliest European settlement as early as 1710, when Sieur de Bienville established Mobile as the capital of French Louisiana. Although Mobile itself remained a fairly busy port, settlers came to Alabama in large numbers only after the end of the eighteenth century. Except for the mountainous northeast, where the Cumberland plateau ends, Alabama is a rolling plain, once inhabited by the Creek, Cherokee, Choctaw, and Chicksaw Indians. Defeated by Andrew Jackson at Horseshoe Bend in 1814, they retreated west and left the state free for European settlement.

Farmers moved south from Tennessee, west from Georgia, and north through the port of Mobile. They were all seeking more land on which to raise the cotton that was enriching the South. They found it in Alabama's rich black belt, so named for the color of its fertile soil. Farms were first established in the center of the state, in the area drained by the Alabama and Tombigbee rivers; but by 1850 most of Alabama was covered both by the fabled great plantations of the Old South and by countless smaller farms.

Most of Alabama's early wealth was agricultural, largely derived from cotton. After the Civil War, when the cotton market crashed, most of Alabama's wealth disappeared. Railroads were built there only during Reconstruction, when coal mining also began. Birmingham was founded in 1870 and quickly became the South's leading iron and steel producer; its roaring blast furnaces form a striking contrast to the largely rural character of the state.

Mobile was the haven for Confederate ships running the Union blockade, and it was the scene of the Civil War's greatest naval battle, finally won by the Union's Admiral D. G. Farragut. Mobile is still a city of stately pre-Civil War homes and lush, carefully tended gardens. Montgomery, in the center of the state, at the head of Alabama River navigation, became the state's capital in 1847, and the capital of the Confederacy in 1861. Jefferson Davis was inaugurated as President of the Confederacy on the steps of the capitol building.

Intrepid frontiersman Daniel Boone blazed the Wilderness Road through Cumberland Gap—a natural pass in the mountains where Virginia, Kentucky, and Tennessee meet

The approach to the range from the northeast side, after leaving Abingdon, Virginia, is over a rough, broken country; and the only compensation to the traveller, as he saunters along on horseback, is in the enjoyment of bits of scenery wherein rocks and running streams, mountain-ferries, quaint old-fashioned mills, farm-houses and cabins perched like birds among the clefts of hills, lovely perspectives, wild-flowers and waving grain, and a homely but hospitable people, combine in charming confusion to keep the attention ever on the alert. The road through the gap, winding like a huge ribbon, to take advantage of every foot of rugged soil, up, down, and around the mountains, is but the enlarged war-trail of the ancient Cherokees and other tribes, who made incursions from one State to the other. You are following the path pursued by Boone and the early settlers of the West. Passing through the scenes of bloody ambuscades, legends, and traditions, it would seem almost a part of the romance of the place if now an Indian should suddenly break the reigning silence with a war-whoop, and its dying echoes be answered by the rifle-shot of a pioneer. In short, it is an old, old region, covered with the rime of centuries, and but slightly changed by the progress of events.

F. G. DE FONTAINE

Picturesque America, 1872

CUMBERLAND GAP, FROM EAGLE CLIFF

Thousands of settlers followed Boone's trail—an endless chain of hopeful pioneers blazing a path of empire, either by wagon or trudging along by shank's mare

CUMBERLAND GAP, FROM THE EAST

The "ridges" referred to are among the curiosities of the Cumberland region. Aside from the fact that they observe a species of parallelism to each other, they contain numerous "breaks," or depressions, which, in the peculiar configuration of the country, appear to the traveller who is at the foot of the mountain to be distant only a few hundred rods; yet he must frequently ride for miles through a labyrinth of hills, blind roads, and winding paths, before he can reach the entrance and pursue his journey. The chief and most celebrated of these great fissures, or hall-ways, through the range, is known as "Cumberland Gap." This gap is situated in East Tennessee, near the Kentucky border, about one hundred and fifty miles southeast from Lexington, and may be regarded as the only practical opening, for a distance of eighty miles, that deserves the name of a "gap." There are other places which are so called, but it is only for the reason that they are more easy of access than because of any actual depression in the mountain. At a place called "Rogers's Gap," for example, which is eighteen miles distant from Cumberland Gap, there is no gap whatever; but the road, taking advantage of a series of ridges on the northern side, and running diagonally on the southern side, is rendered, with great exertion, passable by man and beast.

F. G. DE FONTAINE
Picturesque America, 1872

Originally known as the state of Franklin—Tennessee has three regions that differ vastly from one another: scenic mountains in the east, with Knoxville its leading city . . .

In 1786, twenty-five years after the first white man traveled through the region, Captain James White built a log cabin near the present Farragut Hotel, and became Knoxville's first settler. During the Civil War, because the majority of East Tennesseans were loyal to the union, a Confederate army of occupation was sent into the area in 1861; two years later, in preparation for battles around Chattanooga these troops were withdrawn, to be followed by a Federal force under the command of Major General A. E. Burnside. Confederate troops under Longstreet tried to capture the city by direct assault, and after heavy losses by both sides his army retired to winter quarters near Morristown. When peace came, the city's restoration was rapid. Industries that have sprung up, mainly in cotton textiles, marble, and hardwood furniture. Knoxville is the uppermost terminal of the navigable portion of the Tennessee River.

The American Guide, 1949

Lyon's View.

An Old-Time Hut.

Private Residence.

KNOXVILLE AND VICINITY

. . . the vast Bluegrass area in the center, with Nashville its classic capital; and, on the banks of the Mississippi, Memphis—"heartbeat of the West"

Nevertheless, certain differences persist. Nashville, the second largest city and capital of the state and of Middle Tennessee, has a serene, Athenian quality, as if it were more attuned to its eight universities and colleges than to its industrial plants. A Nashvillian speaks more readily of his city's book houses and writers, its symphony and its statelier past, than of its more material promise. Memphis lacks this quiet assurance, for it grew from a brawling boom town on the river to the state's largest city so hurriedly that it has hardly had time to assess itself. Energetic, clean and preoccupied with its almost incredible industrial expansion. Memphis seems—despite its Beale Street, its heavy Negro population, its Cotton Carnival, and a commanding position as the deep South's cotton-trade center—more like a bustling Midwestern city than the mecca of Mississippi planters.

HODDING CARTER
American Panorama, 1947

Knoxville University

KVILLE
from across the River.

Marble Barges.

Lookout Mountain, on the fringe of the city of Chattanooga, is famed as both a scenic and historic site, where Civil War legions fought the dramatic "Battle of the Clouds"...

East Tennessee, Middle Tennessee, West Tennessee. So much in each of which a man might boast. The refashioned river itself; Fall Creek Falls, with a water drop of 265 feet, the highest east of the Rockies. And Lookout Mountain dominating Moccasin Bend, a lofty rock-faced promontory carved through thousands of years by the downrushing Tennessee. From Lookout Mountain, a man can see seven states on a clear day. If he is a good Tennessean, he will prefer the nearest. And within the state, he will prefer his section and the city which dominates it. Time was when the four principal cities of Tennessee could be defined by characteristics as well as by location. This is less true now, for a common industrialization tends to level their differences. They share a determination to grow, to industrialize.

HODDING CARTER

American Panorama, 1947

CHATTANOOGA AND THE TENNESSEE, FROM LOOKOUT MOUNTAIN

*. . . on the summit and in the nearby regions of
Missionary Ridge and Chickamauga—where huge armies of
the North and South maneuvered, battled, and retrenched*

LOOKOUT MOUNTAIN, FROM THE "POINT"

On the summit of Lookout Mountain the northwest corner of Georgia and the northeast extremity of Alabama meet on the southern boundary of Tennessee. The mountain lifts abruptly from the valley to a height of fifteen hundred feet. It is the summit overhanging the plain of Chattanooga that is usually connected in the popular imagination with the title of Lookout, but the mountain really extends for fifty miles in a southwesterly direction into Alabama. The surface of the mountain is well wooded, it has numerous springs, and is susceptible of cultivation. In time, no doubt, extensive farms will occupy the space now filled by the wilderness. There is a small settlement on the crest of the mountain, consisting of two summer hotels, several cottages and cabins, and a college. It is a grand place for study, and the young people of this sky-aspiring academy have certainly superb stimulants in the exhilarating air and glorious scenes of their mountain *alma mater*.

O. B. BUNCE
Picturesque America, 1872

Rising amid lakes and lofty peaks of the Cumberlands, to the east—the great Tennessee River twists its tortuous course, turning first south into Alabama, and then north

Under the intelligent direction of Lieut. Adams of the United States Army, the Government is now endeavoring to remove the obstructions and widen the channel, which at this point is narrowed from the average of six hundred feet to two hundred and fifty; and hence the novel and picturesque sight of a steamer struggling up against an adverse current by means of a windlass on the bank, with the songs and shouts of the laboring deck-hands, will soon be, if it is not now, a thing of the past. To visit this famous "Suck," and get a sketch or two of the shore, was the purpose of our journey along the Tennessee. The three days of wintry airs on Lookout Mountain had made out-of-door sketching chilling work, but now a soft and balmy April day invited us upon the jaunt; so Mr. Fenn packed his sketching-traps; a vehicle stout in spring, and equal to the vicissitudes of a rough and rocky road, was procured, and we sallied forth.

O. B. BUNCE
Picturesque America, 1872

STEAMER ON THE TENNESSEE, WARPED THROUGH THE "SUCK"

THE TENNESSEE AT CHATTANOOGA

A small town before the Civil War, Chattanooga, on the banks near the Georgia border, became an important military center after its capture by the Federalists

FERRY POINT AT CHATTANOOGA

The method adopted at this ferry is occasionally found in the South, but, ordinarily, ferry-boats are carried from one side of the stream to the other by means of a suspended rope from shore to shore. The Chattanooga ferry is very picturesque, apart from the method of progression. In busy times a sort of tender accompanies the larger boat, and upon this our carriage, with some difficulty, was driven. Boat and tender were crude in construction, old, and dilapidated. The main vessel had a small enclosure, of a hen-coop suggestiveness, which was called a cabin, and which, at a pinch, might give shelter to three or four people. The groups upon its decks were striking. There were sportsmen with their Texan saddles and wide *sombreros*, vehicles, and groups of cattle, all mingled with the most happy contrast of color and form. On the opposite shore, as we drew near, were visible great numbers of waiting horsemen and cattle, giving evidence of the active business of the ferry, and emphasizing the wonder that the bridge has not been restored.

O.B. BUNCE

*Picturesque
America, 1872*

A KENTUCKY ROAD, FROM CUMBERLAND GAP

In Montgomery—Alabama's capital, and first capital of the Confederacy—hundreds of thousands of cotton bales were shipped each year, though now superseded by cattle and hogs

THE CAPITOL, MONTGOMERY

Northern Alabama when I first knew it was a mountain country with a river running through it. Hill cabins perched dangerously on steep acres high above the Tennessee ("Fire your shotgun up the chimley and your punkin crop'll drop into the fireplace"). It was a land of fiddlers' conventions and all-day sings and square dances and court weeks. Few Negroes lived here—their homes were in the Black Belt towns where their slave ancestors had worked for rich white folks. The mountain people plowed their acres six days a week and on the seventh attended little unpainted churches where the wrath of a jealous God was expounded with emphasis. Now this area, because of the damming of the Tennessee River, is a lake country. The rutted roads that once ran near the river are gone, and blacktops run smooth along the ridges from which motorists look down on families picnicking beside clear water.

CARL CARMER

American Panorama, 1947

WATCH AND BELL TOWER, MOBILE

Reminiscent of its past: its Spanish and French heritage, Mobile—at the head of Mobile Bay, on the Gulf of Mexico— is an important seaport serving diversified interests

CITY HALL AND NEW MARKET, MOBILE

LIGHTHOUSE, CHOCTAW POINT, MOBILE

GRANT'S PASS, NEAR MOBILE

Mobile stays in the heart, loveliest of cities. I have made many journeys down the Black Warrior and I have always found happiness at its mouth. And so I summarize my impressions rather than tell the story of a visit. Few travelers "pass through" Mobile. The old city rests apart, remembering the five flags that have flown over her. Spain and France and England and the Old South, grown harmonious through the mellowing of time, are echoes in the streets. But since only people who "are going to Mobile" are her visitors, her charms have been less exploited than those of any of the other sea cities of the South. Whether you come by train or by boat, you arrive in the same part of town. There is a smell of hemp and tar about it. Long low two-story buildings, their intricate iron balconies interrupted here and there by signs—"Sailors' Supplies," "The Army and Navy Store," line the narrow streets. Sometimes the balcony overhangs the sidewalk and makes a roofed passage for pedestrians, ornate iron pillars supporting it at the street's edge. These buildings once housed a roistering assembly. The crews of ocean windjammers found liquor here in gilded saloons. They lined up at the mirrored bar with the bully-boys of North Alabama—keel-boatmen on the Black Warrior, planters' sons arrived by side-wheel steam packet from the wide estates on the Tombigbee, badman gamblers in extravagant apparel. The waterfront itself is no longer as picturesque as it was in the days of the clipper ships or the river packets. The gay welter of colorful types has disappeared.

CARL CARMER

Stars Fell on Alabama, 1934

Once an Indian settlement, Mobile became a French colonial capital when Jean Baptiste Le Moyne came ashore in 1702, followed by the British in 1763—an occupation of short duration . . .

The air is soft in Mobile—filled with sea moisture. The tropics reach toward the town from the south. Palms raise straight trunks to the greening tufts that cap them. Fig trees and oleanders, magnolias and Cape Jasmine, Cherokee roses and azaleas make the breezes heavy with sweet odor through the long warm season. It is a gentle air. Like the atmosphere that the people of Mobile create among themselves, it is friendly and easygoing. It folds with equal warmth about the white pillars lifted by a retired Black Belt planter and the wrought-iron patterns of a façade conceived by a French immigrant. Unlike the New Orleans Creoles, with their enclosed patios, Mobile's Latin colonists chose to build homes that looked out on the world. The lawns on which the French and Spanish houses rest have been green for almost two centuries. Outside the commercial streets down by the waterfront, Mobile is a city of leisured space. The old part of the town is a honeycomb of exquisite design. Fleurs-de-lis in formal grace adorn a balcony that faces a wild profusion of grape clusters across the street. The bees of Napoleon, were they to take flight from their iron frame, might light upon the roses of Provence that clamber over the railing of both upper and lower galleries next door. At the city market, once the Spanish government buildings, the iron curves have a cleaner, freer sweep and they turn more delicately against the white stone.

OUR FLEE

VIEW OF

Grant's Pass.

SCENES AROUND MOBILE

. . . for in 1780 the Spanish superseded the British. An American force under General James Wilkinson seized the city in 1813—site of the famous Battle of Mobile Bay

MOBILE.

OBILE ALA.

Fort Morgan.

Mobile has not always been a city on a byway. In the days of her glory the big-hatted, bright-waistcoated planter brought his wife and daughters down the Black Warrior for the theater, the horse racing, the shopping. Perhaps they embarked at Wetumpka on the famous *St. Nicholas*, its calliope tooting out *Life on the Ocean Wave* to the panic of negroes along the shore. Or they may have come from Gainesville down the Tombigbee on that gorgeous packet *Eliza Battle*, fated to be consumed in flame with a loss of forty lives. In a bayou up the Warrior, a few miles from Mobile, lie many of the sisters of these ships. In that grave-yard of the steamboats few names are discernible now. Perhaps the *Southern Belle* rests there, and the *Orline St. John*, the *Ben Lee*, stern-wheeler, the *Allen Glover* (named for her planter owner) . . . . Though these days are memories now, the city has not forgotten. With all its outward semblance of calm, Mobile is gayest of American cities. Its free spirit, less commercialized than that of New Orleans, has kept its Gallic love of the fantastic and amusing. Behind the ornate balconies and long French windows that sedately face the streets, live a people to whom carnival is a natural heritage.

CARL CARMER

Stars Fell on Alabama, 1934

Picking, harvesting, and baling the cotton crop—for shipment to market—presented the planter with problems for which he managed to find various and often ingenious solutions

LOADING COTTON ON THE ALABAMA RIVER

Only a small percentage of the Southern whites had owned slaves, but cotton had opened new visions of riches. Since the beginning of the century there had been much to turn our heads from the older and slower ways of building up a property. The breathless speed at which certain manufacturers had grown, the easy money to be made in starting banks, the speculation in Western lands, the risks of commerce in the war, the rapid rise in city real estate as population concentrated, and the effect of the cotton gin, had all been breeding a spirit which demanded riches overnight instead of by efforts of a lifetime of toil. In the South everyone turned to cotton. "The lawyer, and the doctor, and the schoolmaster, as soon as they earned any money, bought land and negroes, and became planters . . .

PLANTER'S HOME IN ALABAMA

Throughout the South, many rivers became broad highways of commerce, offering a changing spectacle that touched not only the life of travelers, but that of the people on shore

COTTON CHUTE

LOADING COTTON

. . . The preacher who married a rich heiress or rich widow, became owner of a plantation. The merchant who wished to retire from the perplexities of business . . . passed his old age in watching the cotton plant spring up from the fresh-plowed ground.'' But as the slave trade had been prohibited, the price of slaves advanced rapidly. It was estimated in 1839 that a planter could get a thousand acres of good cleared cotton land for $10,000.

JAMES TRUSLOW ADAMS
The Epic of America, 1933

The rivers of Alabama served to speed the flow of goods—but they were also frequently the cause of much havoc and destruction by flooding of their low-lying banks

Fortunately, a flooding river sometimes overflows its banks or bursts its levees slowly enough to allow evacuation of endangered populations. But not always. Sometimes, a flood wave, or waves, can make a river, or convergence of rivers, crest so much more quickly and higher than expected that the results are as sudden and as deadly as those produced by the burst dam or flash flood. More often, the river flood kills by inches, destroying all a community has worked for in the past, and sometimes all possibility of future subsistence. In terms of regularity and damage, river floods are the worst enemy, though much has been done to effect their control. Dams and reservoirs have been built to control river flooding, as well as levees that are most effective. There are places where a river will flood, no matter what.

WOODY GELMAN and
BARBARA JACKSON
Disaster Illustrated, 1976

FLOODS IN ALABAMA

Along the Great Lakes: from Erie to Superior

BUFFALO . . . GRAIN ELEVATORS . . .
SHIP CANAL . . . SANDUSKY . . .
LUMBER BOATS . . . CLEVELAND . . .
SCRANTON'S HILL . . . LIGHT HOUSE
. . . FOUNTAIN AND SQUARE . . . MOUTH
OF THE CUYAHOGA . . . ROCKY RIVER
. . . PUT-IN-BAY . . . KELLY'S ISLAND
. . . TOLEDO . . . DETROIT . . . DETROIT
RIVER . . . FORT WAYNE . . . JEFFERSON
AVENUE . . . WOODWARD AVENUE . . . OLD
STATE HOUSE . . . ARCHED ROCK . . .
ROBINSON'S FOLLY . . . CHIMNEY ROCK
. . . SAULT STE. MARIE . . . FORT BRADY
. . . BEAVER BAY . . . SILVER CASCADE . . .
LA CROSSE HARBOR . . . DULUTH . . . WINTER
SCENES IN MINNESOTA . . . LOGGING . . .
ICE HARVEST . . . WINTER SCENES IN
THE NORTHWEST

WINDMILL, OPPOSITE DETROIT

Along the Great Lakes...
from Erie to Superior

WHILE THE EARLY COLONIAL-
ists were still clinging to the
shores of the Atlantic,
French explorers and traders
had discovered, almost a thousand miles to the
west, bodies of fresh water greater than any
European had ever known, and greater indeed
than the explorers themselves would realize for
many years to come: the Great Lakes. Hidden
by thick pine forests, fed by hundreds of
streams and rivers, closed almost half the year
by ice, and protected by fierce and unyielding
Indian tribes, these lakes would eventually provide the source for the commercial and industrial development of the American Middle West.

By the close of the American Revolution,
the extent of the Great Lakes had been
charted, and the fur, timber, and mineral
wealth of the land surrounding them had
drawn the French, the English, and the
Americans to their shores. The Revolution had
settled the question of who controlled the
eastern seaboard, but not until the conclusion
of the War of 1812 would the fierce contest
for the Great Lakes region be settled in favor
of the United States. Because of this, and
because of the hazards of exploration and settlement, the shores of Lakes Superior,
Michigan, Huron, Erie, and Ontario were only
sparsely settled during the first decade of the

nineteenth century. But as claims to the land were secured and the westward expansion of the United States began in earnest, these great northern lakes and the lands they sheltered heard the crash of the logger's axe and the shrill whistle of the steamboat. Cities lined the shores and, for a while at least, they would rival New York, Boston, and Philadelphia.

Buffalo, Cleveland, Toledo, and Detroit had all been settled by the early 1800s, but served as little more than military outposts or trading centers. Real growth began only in the 1830s. In those years, inland water navigation was vital to the pioneers who were pushing into the newly opened Northwest Territories and the lands acquired in the Louisiana Purchase.

Buffalo, strategically located on Lake Erie, where the Niagara and Buffalo rivers enter the lake, was laid out in 1803. Almost completely destroyed by fire in 1813, during the war with the British, its recovery was so slow that some observers saw no hope for it. But when the Erie canal opened in 1825, its future was secure. Buffalo's thirty-seven miles of water-front made it an important harbor. Steamboats connected it with other cities along the Great Lakes, and a network of canals—the Erie, the Ohio and Erie, and the Illinois and Michigan—permitted continuous navigation all the way from the Hudson to the Mississippi. By 1850 Buffalo's population of over forty thousand exceeded even Chicago's.

With the opening of the Erie Canal and with the laying of plans for other canals, a fever of land speculation began in Buffalo and spread throughout the Great Lakes region. Towns that did not hold more than a few thousand inhabitants suddenly clamored to become cities.

Cleveland and Toledo, Ohio's two largest ports, both owe their birth to the canals and the busy Great Lakes traffic. Cleveland's growth was fueled by the building of the Ohio and Erie Canal, which opened in 1827, and the railroads, which reached it in 1851. Situated on Lake Erie, on the mouth of the Cuyahoga River, it lies midway between the rich coal and oil fields of Pennsylvania and the iron mines of Minnesota.

Toledo's history, perhaps more starkly than most, tells of both the hopes and the cruel disappointments which followed the land speculation that seized the region. In the 1840s two canals connected Toledo, by way of the Maumee River, to the busy Ohio River: the Wabash and Erie, and the Miami and Erie. Between 1840 and 1850, Toledo's population more than doubled, but a growth from two thousand to just around five thousand was insufficient to sustain the hopes of the speculators. The Panic of 1837 and the natural limits to expansion even in those busy years brought building to a halt. An observer described the crash that followed: "In 1844, Toledo was little more than the dead carcass of speculation. Its previous existence had been abnormal, but its condition was worse than negative." Only the great increase in manufacturing following the Civil War and the eventual coal and oil exploitation rescued Toledo and its neighbors.

Among the cities of the Great Lakes, only Detroit can claim a solid lineage dating to long before the Revolution. The French had traded and settled there as far back as 1701, when Antoine de la Mothe Cadillac founded a fort on the strait between Lake St. Clair and Lake Erie. He named it for its situation, Ville d'étroit—"city of the strait." It was captured in 1760 by the British, who ceded it in 1796 to the United States. It burned almost entirely in 1805, but was rebuilt by Pierre L'Enfant, whom Washington had commissioned to plan the new capital. Although well established by the early 1800s, Detroit, like its neighbors in Ohio and New York, did not really grow until the 1830s.

Travelers a century ago, like travelers nowadays, were struck with the lively industry and commerce of the Great Lakes and their bustling ports. But beyond the shores where the cities clustered, lay a region which, but for the half century following the Civil War, has known few travelers and even fewer settlers— the great forests of Michigan. In the 1850s there were still twenty-five thousand miles of them; mostly pine, but also some hardwoods, maple, and beech. The land existed in "an eternal green twilight," as Bruce Catton once described it, sheltering hundreds of cold, blue lakes. The trees of Michigan's Lower Peninsula were exploited savagely, and the lumber industry spawned dozens of towns, like Saginaw and Muskegon. But by the turn of the century, the trees were gone and the loggers were gone; the towns receded, and many disappeared. The Upper Peninsula, however, remained virtually untouched, even by the loggers. There, in an immense finger of land almost three hundred miles long, lakes, forests, and bleak outcroppings of rock still live in the "eternal green twilight" of the American North.

Buffalo, at the crossroads of commerce—the eastern end of Lake Erie and the western terminal of New York's Erie Canal—was transformed from a frontier fortress . . .

Buffalo is one of the wonders of America. It is hardly to be credited that such a beautiful city could have risen up in the wilderness in so short a period. In the year 1814 it was burnt down, being then only a village; only one house was left standing, and now it is a city with twenty-five thousand inhabitants . . . . The city of Buffalo is remarkably well built; all the houses in the principal streets are lofty and substantial, and are either of brick or granite. The main street is wider and the stores handsomer than the majority of those in New York. It has five or six very fine churches, a handsome theatre, a town hall, and market, and three steamboats. It is almost incomprehensible, that all this should have been accomplished since the year 1814. And what has occasioned this springing up of a city in so short a time as to remind you of Alladin's magic palace?—the Erie Canal, which here joins the Hudson river with the lake, passing through the centre of the most populous and fertile states.

FREDERICK MARRYAT

A Diary in America, 1839

MAIN STREET, BUFFALO, FROM ST. PAUL'S CHURCH

. . . when "Clinton's Ditch" opened, in 1825, spiraling land values, the building of wharves, warehouses, and grain elevators—producing a great milling and cereal center

GRAIN ELEVATOR, BUFFALO

An elevator is as ugly a monster as has yet been produced. In uncouthness of form it outdoes those obsolete old brutes who used to roam about the semi-aqueous world and live a most uncomfortable life with their great hungering stomachs and huge, unsatisfied maws. River of corn and wheat run through these monsters night and day. And all this wheat which passes through Buffalo comes loose, in bulk; nothing is known of sacks or bags. To any spectator in Buffalo this becomes immediately a matter of course; but this should be explained, as we, in England, are not accustomed to see wheat travelling in this open, unguarded, and plebian manner. Wheat with us is aristocratic, and travels always in its private carriage.

ANTHONY TROLLOPE
North America, 1862

SHIP CANAL, BUFFALO

Midway between Cleveland and Toledo, Sandusky—gateway to Lake Erie's chain of islands, ferry point for Canada—was an important shipping point for the heartland's vast lumber supply

On Sandusky's lakefront the tang of timber mixed with the smell of fish. By 1880 the harbor was walled for half a mile with pine lumber and for another mile with fish houses. Fish came from the rich waters of western Lake Erie, lumber from the great woods of Michigan. Year by year the commerce grew, schooners beating in past Marblehead, where John Clemens, a kinsman of Mark Twain, was in the limestone business with tugboats and a fleet of barges. Now a new word was being used; men talked about the "biggest." Sandusky had the biggest wagon-wheel works in the world, and the biggest oar factory; it was called the greatest fish market on the globe. In 1880 a Sandusky man contracted to furnish cross-arms for a line of telegraph poles from Kansas to California.

WALTER HAVIGHURST

Ohio, 1976

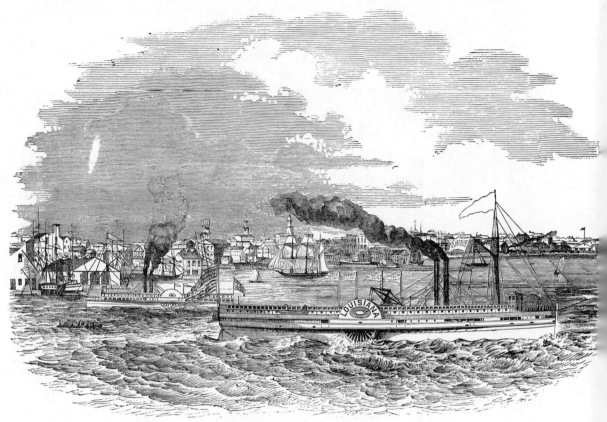

SANDUSKY, ON LAKE ERIE

LUMBER BOATS, SANDUSKY

In 1836, the little community of Cleveland—where the Cuyahoga River meets Lake Erie, a stagecoach stop on the Buffalo-Detroit road—was a city of a few thousand

CLEVELAND, FROM THE LAKE

Until the mid-nineteenth century the Cuyahoga was a clear stream winding through marsh grass and wildflowers, but in 1880 it was lined with sawmills, coal docks, blast furnaces, and overhung with smoke. Oil tanks rose like fortifications; a trestled maze of pipes laced the tanks to loading terminals where boiler-shaped cars crept under a forest of chimneys. At times a viscous oil glaze on the river caught fire and went smoking to the lake. Almost as rapid as development of the oil business was the growth of Cleveland's iron and steel industry. Coal, limestone, and iron ore go into the making of steel. Geography put Lake Erie's cities in the path of these resources. Vast coal beds lay in Ohio's Hocking Valley, limestone quarries whitened the shores of Lake Huron, huge iron ranges ringed Lake Superior; and the lakes made a highway for transport of bulk cargoes.

WALTER HAVIGHURST

Ohio, 1976

CLEVELAND, FROM SCRANTON'S HILL

The mouth of the Cuyahoga—where schooners docked to load lumber and iron ore for shipment to Buffalo and the Erie Canal—was one of the busiest ports along Lake Erie's shores

With 65,000 people in 1865, Cleveland had schooners and steamers crowding the river mouth, elevators, mills, and furnaces spreading in the smoky flats, a big new Union Station at the foot of Water Street, carriages rolling past the mansions on Euclid Avenue. On St. Clair and Water streets were offices of the iron merchants, dealing in Lake Superior ore. War had boomed the iron industry, which grew immensely in the postwar years. Two hundred thousand tons of ore came down the lakes in 1865; ten years later the annual cargoes exceeded half a million. David Tod, who would be governor of Ohio, 1862-1864, grew up on Brier Hill farm, overlooking the village of Youngstown. The land was mostly sheep pasture, but it contained rich coal banks, easily worked, along the Mahoning River. That coal, the best in the valley, proved excellent for engine fuel and, eventually, for blast furnaces. About 1850 David Tod persuaded some Cleveland steamboat captains to try his coal in their boiler rooms. Within a decade coal supplanted wood as steamboat fuel. After the Civil War, Governor Tod turned to iron-making. On the Mahoning grew the Brier Hills Furnaces, with charcoal ovens, mill sheds, skip hoists, and big furnace stacks topped by smoking chimneys.

WALTER HAVIGHURST

Ohio, 1976

MOUTH OF THE CUYAHOGA RIVER, CLEVELAND

COURT HOUSE, CLEVELAND

On the streets of Cleveland—where east and west sides vied for supremacy—exclusive Euclid Avenue chateaux and villas were the homes of the city's nouveau riche

LIGHTHOUSE, CLEVELAND

FOUNTAIN AND SQUARE, CLEVELAND

While industry was darkening the Cuyahoga flats, the pride of Cleveland was Euclid Avenue, a regal street arched by great trees and lined with mansions and gardens of the millionaires. English manor houses, French chateaus, Italian villas and palazzos, graced the avenue. In them was a king's ransom of imported enamels, lacquers, ceramics, sculpture, Persian rugs, Oriental bronzes, and the paintings of European masters. A New York reporter wrote that Euclid Avenue was the finest in the West. Its opulence and ostentation dazzled everyone but Cleveland's tramp journalist Artemus Ward who reported that visitors, after carefully wiping their feet, were allowed to roam the elegant highway free of charge. "All the owners of Euclid Street homes," he explained, "employ hired girls and are patrons of the arts. A musical was held at one of these palatial homes the other day with singing . . . The tenor had as fine a tenor voice as ever brought a bucket of water from a second-story window." Money bathed Euclid Avenue with a golden light, but in the river flats miles of narrow streets and alleys lay under a pall of smoke and cinders.

WALTER HAVIGHURST
Ohio, 1976

The victory of Commodore Perry at Put-in-Bay gave the Americans complete control of Lake Erie, and the numerous settlements east and west along the lake shores

Captain Oliver Perry, with headquarters at Presqu'ile (Erie), Pennsylvania, had been given orders by President Madison to maintain the American supremacy on Lake Erie. During the winter of 1812-13 he managed to construct a fleet of stout little ships, which, though built of green boughs, were able to function as a well-integrated naval unit. On August 4, 1813, he sought out the British squadron, and a month later engaged the enemy fleet at Put-in-Bay, among the islands at the western end of the lake. A strange naval battle followed. Perry's flagship *Lawrence* carrying his flag bearing the motto "Don't Give Up the Ship" led the way into action against Barclay's *Detroit* whose long guns had the advantage over Perry's short-range cannonading. The *Lawrence*, though severely battered, came close enough to

LAKE ERIE, NEAR MOUTH OF ROCKY RIVER

PUT-IN-BAY, LAKE ERIE

At the most westerly point of Lake Erie, Toledo—on the mouth of the Maumee—typified the amazing progress of Midwest cities, the rapid rate of their growth

KELLY'S ISLAND, LAKE ERIE

PERRY'S LOOKOUT, GIBRALTER ISLAND

enable her batteries to make an effective reply, though she was pounded into a helpless wreck. It was the British who quit. Perry's laconic report "We have met the enemy, and they are ours," was literally true and became one of the navy's most memorable mottoes.

CONSTANCE F. WOOLSON
Picturesque America, 1872

TOLEDO, ON THE MAUMEE RIVER

There are actually two Michigans—the Upper and Lower peninsulas —touched by four of the five Great Lakes, and separated by the Straits of Mackinac and the waters of the Sault Ste. Marie

The city of Detroit itself stands upon an elevated piece of table-land, extending probably for some twenty miles back from the river, and being perfectly unbroken for at least two miles along its margin. Beneath the bluff—for the plain is so high as almost to deserve the name—is a narrow bustling street of about half a mile in length, with the wharves just beyond it; and fifty yards inboard runs a spacious street called Jefferson Avenue, parallel with the lower street and the river; the chief part of the town extends for a mile or two along the latter. The dwelling-houses are generally of wood, but there are a great many stores now building, or already erected, of brick, with stone basements. The brick is generally of an indifferent quality; but the stone, which is brought from Cleaveland, Ohio, is a remarkably fine material for building purposes. It is a kind of yellow freestone, which is easily worked when first taken from the quarry, and hardens subsequently upon exposure to the air. There are at this moment many four-story stores erecting, as well as other substantial buildings, which speak for the flourishing condition of the place . . .

LOOKING DOWN FROM CITY HALL, DETROIT

*Released by the British after Perry's victory
on Lake Erie in 1813, Detroit came into its own
as an industrial center following the Civil War*

DETROIT RIVER, ABOVE THE CITY

. . . The want of mechanics is so great, however that it is difficult as yet to carry on these operations upon the scale common in our Atlantic cities, although the demand for houses, in Detroit, it is said, would fully warrant similar outlays of capital. The public buildings are the territorial council-house, situated upon an open piece of ground, designated on an engraved plan of the city as "The Campus Martius," a court-house, academy, and two banks. The population of Detroit is, I believe, between three and four thousand—it increases so rapidly, however, that it is difficult to form an estimate. The historical associations, the safety, and commodiousness of the harbour, with its extensive inland commercial advantages, must ever constitute this one of the most interesting and important points in the Union.

CHARLES FENNO HOFFMAN
A Winter in the West, 1835

DETROIT RIVER, FROM FORT WAYNE

Detroit's ideal location—at the junction of Great Lakes waterways—helped it develop into a transportation hub, as rails fanned out, a network in all directions

Such was Detroit—a place whose defenses could have opposed no resistance to a civilized enemy; and yet, far removed as it was from the hope of speedy succor, it could only rely, in the terrible struggles that awaited it, upon its own slight strength and feeble resources. Standing on the water bastion of Detroit, a pleasant landscape spread before the eye. The river, about half a mile wide, almost washed the foot of the stockade; and either bank was lined with the white Canadian cottages. The joyous sparkling of the bright blue water; the green luxuriance of the woods; the white dwellings, looking out from the foliage; and, in the distance, the Indian wigwams curling their smoke against the sky, —all were mingled in one broad scene of wild and rural beauty. Pontiac, the Satan of this forest paradise, was accustomed to spend the early part of the summer upon a small island at the opening of the Lake St. Clair, hidden from view by the high woods that covered the intervening Isle-au-Cochon. "The king and lord of all this country," as Rogers calls him, lived in no royal state. His cabin was a small, oven-shaped structure of bark and rushes. Here he dwelt, with his squaws and children; and here, doubtless, he might often have been seen, lounging, half-naked, on a rush mat, or a bear-skin, like any ordinary warrior.

FRANCIS PARKMAN

The Conspiracy of Pontiac,
1851

DETROIT, FROM THE CANADIAN SHORE

JEFFERSON AVENUE, DETROIT

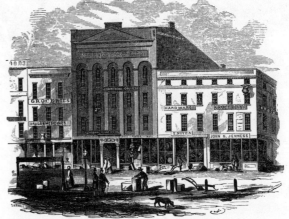

ODD FELLOWS' HALL, DETROIT

Its principal streets, lined with stores and public buildings, converge like the spokes of a wheel—its other half cut off by the Detroit River and its huge industrial plants

OLD STATE HOUSE, DETROIT

POST OFFICE, WOODWARD AVENUE, DETROIT

WATER WORKS, DETROIT

ST. ANN'S CHURCH, DETROIT

The boats came up from Lake Erie ports, Cleveland and Buffalo and Sandusky, and they gave a theatrical touch to the whole business. Lake Erie is beautiful and shallow and treacherous, with a capacity for whipping up unexpected storms that would bother any mariner who ever lived, although mostly it is pleasant enough; and the old side-wheelers came paddling down its length, usually in the middle of the night—it was nice sleeping, in a snug stateroom on one of those boats, with an air-conditioned wind coming in at the open porthole, and the wash of the paddle wheels beating a quiet rhythm in the darkness—and in the morning that boat came up the Detroit River, and the factories and pumping stations on the bank suddenly made you realize that man had taken over Nature and was trying to make something out of it. Then, a little after breakfast time, the boat docked along the Detroit water front, and no city in America offered a more thrilling or exciting entrance.

BRUCE CATTON

American Panorama, 1947

The picturesque natural wonders along the shores of Superior and Huron make a paradox of Michigan—contrasting sharply with the industrial complex growing on the Lower Peninsula

Michilimackinac! That gem of the Lakes! How bright and beautiful it looked as we walked abroad on the following morning. The rain had passed away, but had left all things glittering in the light of the sun as it rose up over the waters of Lake Huron, far away to the east. Before us was the lovely bay, scarcely yet tranquil after the storm, but dotted with canoes and the boats of the fishermen already getting out their nets for the trout and whitefish, those treasures of the deep. Along the beach were scattered the wigwams or lodges of the Ottawas who had come to the island to trade. The inmates came forth to gaze upon us. A shout of wecome was sent forth as they recognized Shaw-nee-aw-kee, who, from a seven years' residence among them, was well known to each individual.

JULIETTE KINZIE
Wau-Bun, 1840

ARCHED ROCK, NEAR MACKINAC

ROBINSON'S FOLLY

Up in the northern straits, between blue Lake Huron, with its clear air, and gray Lake Michigan, with its silver fogs, lies the bold island of Mackinac. Clustered along the beach, which runs around its half-moon harbor, are the houses of the old French village, nestling at the foot of the cliff rising behind, crowned with the little white fort, the stars and stripes floating above it against the deep blue sky. Beyond, on all sides, the forest stretches away, cliffs finishing it abruptly, save one slope at the far end of the island, three miles distant, where the British landed in 1812. That is the whole of Mackinac.

The wild, fascinating beauty of Mackinac Island and the surrounding regions were "one magnificent forest until the lumberjacks went to work and shaved the countryside"

ARCHED ROCK BY MOONLIGHT

CHIMNEY ROCK

The island has a strange sufficiency of its own; it satisfies; all who have lived there feel it. The island has a wild beauty of its own; it fascinates; all who have lived there love it. Among its aromatic cedars, along the aisles of its pine-trees, in the gay company of its maples, there is companionship. On its bald northern cliffs, bathed in sunshine and swept by the pure breeze, there is exhilaration. Many there are, bearing the burden and heat of the day, who look back to the island with the tears that rise but do not fall, the sudden longing despondency that comes occasionally to all, when the tired heart cries out. "O, to escape, to flee away, far, far away, and be at rest!" In 1856 Fort Mackinac held a major, a captain, three lieutenants, a chaplain, and a surgeon, besides those subordinate officers who wear stripes on their sleeves, and whose rank and duties are mysterious to the uninitiated.

CONSTANCE FENIMORE COOPER

Farthest North

Before the Soo Canals were opened, in 1855, it was necessary to haul vessels through the town's main streets—some schooners weighing fifty tons—in order to transport them from Lake Huron to Lake Superior

I subsequently looked into the different cabins and compartments of the boat not yet visited, and had reason to be gratified with the appearance of all; though the steamboat Michigan, which I have since visited at the docks here, puts me completely out of conceit of every part of the New-York, except her captain. The Michigan, machinery and all, was built at Detroit; and without entering into a minute description of it, I may say, that fine as our Atlantic boats are, I do not recollect any on the Atlantic waters, for strength and beauty united, equal to this. A great mistake, however, I think, exists here in building the boats for these waters with cabins on deck, like the river boats. In consequence of such a large part of the hull being above water, they are rendered dangerous during the tremendous gales which sweep Lake Erie, and are often compelled to make a port of safety several times during a passage.

CHARLES FENNO HOFFMAN
A Winter in the West, 1835

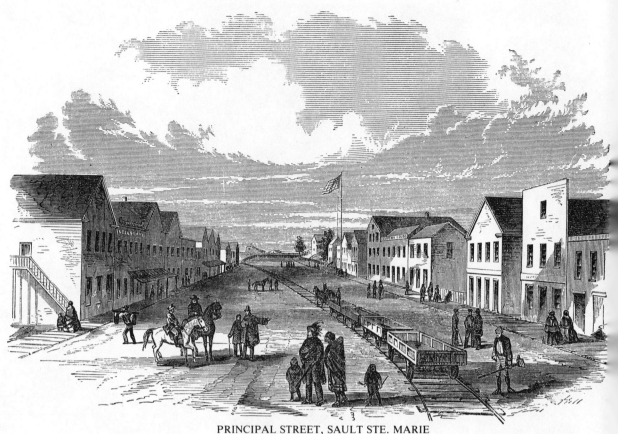

PRINCIPAL STREET, SAULT STE. MARIE

UPPER ENTRANCE TO SOO CANAL

Completion of the canals—boon to the heartland—was pushed through to meet a congressional deadline, requiring work round the clock, during the rigorous winter

LOWER ENTRANCE TO SOO CANAL

One of the interesting things to see up here is the canal at Sault Ste. Marie, whose big locks connect Lake Superior with the lower lakes. The Soo, as everybody calls it, is a lively little city during the eight months of the navigation season; it boasts that its canal handles more traffic than Panama and Suez combined. All day and all night the ships—enormous things, 500 and 600 feet in length—come majestically in from the upper lake, floating high above your head, sinking slowly as the water burbles out of the locks, and then gliding off for the great industrial region hundreds of miles to the south. In an average day, eighty or ninety of them will go through. Day and night, you are forever hearing the deep, haunting bass of their whistles—the inescapable, wholly characteristic and somehow deeply romantic noise of the Soo region. (Progress is taking a hand here, these immense boats are being equipped with air horns, which emit a blatting which carries a great deal farther than the traditional steam whistle but which is pure discord and nothing more.)

BRUCE CATTON
American Panorama, 1947

FORT BRADY, SAULT STE. MARIE

The passage of inland waters, from western Lake Superior to the Atlantic—a distance of over 2,300 miles—navigates a stairway of drops from lake to lake, including the sharpest drop at Niagara

SILVER CASCADE, LAKE SUPERIOR

There is more to Minnesota than just politics. Consider merely what Sinclair Lewis calls the "radiant, seafronting, hillside city of Duluth." I drove up to Duluth from Minneapolis, and in fact it was Mr. Lewis who was my host there. We looked at what is called Minnesota Point from a tall bluff, and watched the freighters come in with coal, and go out again with their mammoth burdens of ore, against the swelling blue backdrop of Lake Superior. Duluth is the end of the line. Here is the extreme westernmost tip of the Atlantic Ocean. Duluth, together with Superior (Wisconsin), *is* a seaport, though its shining water is fresh, not salt. But it is difficult, up in this piney stillness, to appreciate the well-known fact that this is the second biggest port in the nation; there is something incongruous about its comercial activity. "Port" connotes smoke and slums and men hurrying down greasy cobbled streets, whereas Duluth tingles with openness, the atmosphere of campfires, placid sunshine, and the free spirit of the viking north. Second busiest American port! But, if the local folklore is to be believed, Duluth is also a city where bears wander in from the woods every spring, push their way into back yards, and imperturbably invade the lobby of the chief hotel. Greatest iron ore city in the world! But the booster pamphlets call it "America's air-conditioned city, in the Hay Fever Haven of America."

JOHN GUNTHER
Inside U.S.A.. 1947

LA CROSSE HARBOR

The heartland regions on the Great Lakes were the source of myths and legends—some arising from the mysterious sinking of many ships, others from Indian lore

CLIFF NEAR BEAVER BAY

The blueness of the waters of the Great Lakes is remarkable; so unlike river water, or the colorless water of our mountain lakes. The vast expanse of the blue sky above them seems to have colored them; the heavenly blue is contagious and affects the water. There is a hint of the sea in the Great Lakes. In the smallest of them that I have seen (St. Clair) there is a strange, far-off, elemental look. Superior is the farther of it. You feel that that water has been somewhere, and has had unusual experiences.

JOHN BURROUGHS

The Heart of Burrough's
Journals, 1928

Not many years ago the shore bordering the head of Lake Michigan, the northern curve of that silver sea, was a wilderness unexplored. It is a wilderness still, showing even now on the school-maps nothing save an empty waste of colored paper, generally a pale, cold yellow suitable to the climate, all the way from Point St. Ignace to the iron ports on the Little Bay de Noquet, or Badderknock in lake phraseology, a hundred miles of nothing, according to the map-makers, who, knowing nothing of the region, set it down accordingly, withholding even those long-legged letters, "Chip-pe-was," "Ric-ca-rees," that stretch accommodatingly across so much townless territory farther west.

CONSTANCE FENIMORE WOOLSON

Castle Nowhere, 1875

DULUTH, HEAD OF LAKE SUPERIOR

*European visitors to America have always been intrigued with our fond-
ness for ice, iced drinks and ice cream—as far back as the early 1800s the
"musical tinkling" of ice water so typical, in hotels and restaurants*

Anyway, Michigan a cen-
tury ago was one magnifi-
cent forest, and even as
recently as the Civil War it
had hardly been touched.
But then the lumberjacks
went to work, and they
shaved the countryside the
way a razor shaves a
man's chins. Where there
had been wilderness, boom
lumber towns sprang up,
with rickety railroad lines
threading their way back
into the hills. In the
springtime, every stream
was clogged with logs,
with lumberjacks scamper-
ing across the treacherous
shifting carpet with peavy
and cant hook, mounds of
sawdust rising beside the
busy mills, and a mill town
with 1200 inhabitants nor-
mally supported from
twelve to twenty saloons.
For a time Saginaw was
the greatest lumber city in
the world, then Muskegon
had the title, and then
some other place; fresh-cut
boards were stacked in
endless piles by the railroad sidings or the lake-
side wharves . . . and then,
all of a sudden, it was all
over. The lumber was
gone, the mills were dis-
mantled, the booming
cities and towns lapsed into drowsiness, store-fronts
were boarded up—and the
razor which had done all
of this shaving had left a
stubble of stumps like a
frowsy three-day beard
across thousands of square
miles. Some towns died entirely, some almost died,
and the endless whine of
the gang saws became
quiet forever.

BRUCE CATTON
American Panorama, 1947

SAWING INTO LOGS.

BREAKING A JAM.

IN T

LANDING LOGS.

SILVER CASCADE.

ICE PLOWS.

HAULING OUT THE ICE BLOCKS.

FALLS OF MINN

WINTER SCENES IN MINNESOTA

This spurred a new refrigeration industry—the harvesting of ice cut from frozen lakes and rivers—shipped, for home consumption, to distant cities and warm climes as far away as the West Indies

UNLOADING LOGS.

LOGGERS' CAMP.

SAINT ANTHONY'S FALLS IN WINTER.

CAMP FOLLOWERS.

'Y MORNING.

BLOCKS OF ICE.

HAULING ICE.

The vast logging operation in the forests of Minnesota is best carried with a series of engravings based upon actual photographs taken by Whitney and Zimmerman, of St. Paul. As the great pine trees are felled, the loggers cut them into appropriate lengths and then these sections are hauled out by teams of oxen. Finally, the logs are "landed" on the frozen surface of a river or stream, in readiness for the spring freshet to sweep them down to a market. Though many of these streams are too shallow in summer to float an Indian in the lightest bark canoe, yet when swollen by spring freshets, each one becomes a wide and deep river. In some instances the pines grow near the streams, and the trouble hauling them is very slight; but often they grow four or five miles away, and the distance becomes greater every year, as the forests are gradually cut down, and with it the expense of logging. The camp followers are Chippewa Indians, who frequent the camps to get provisions and whiskey.

Harper's Weekly,
May 7, 1870

The long Northwest winters—along Lake Superior's frigid shores— tested the mettle of the hardiest trappers and fur traders

The glorious spectacle of the winter wonderland in Minnesota is illustrated with scenes of the Saint Anthony's Falls and the Silver Cascade, within sight of each other. The falls of Minnehaha on a frosty morning look more like a picture from Fairyland than an actual scene from nature. The sketches depicting actual scenes of the ice harvest were also rendered from photographs taken last winter. The thickness of the ice is well indicated, showing how great, almost transparent blocks are hauled out upon the banks, where they are chipped into shape for storage and transportation. As the temperature frequently drops to 40 below zero, the thickness of these blocks is not surprising. When the ice is of moderate thickness, it is cut by means of ice plows; but when very thick, hand saws are used for the purpose. In Minnesota, the ice crop has been so abundant that ice dealers will have no excuse for an exorbitant rise in the price of this commodity.

Harper's Weekly,
May 7, 1870

MID-WINTER, NORTHERN SHORE OF LAKE SUPERIOR

Chicago & Milwaukee...
Megalopolis on Lake Michigan

CHICAGO LAKEFRONT . . . LAKE STREET

. . . RANDOLPH STREET . . . CLARK

STREET BRIDGE . . . DEARBORN RAILROAD

STATION . . . RAILROAD BRIDGES . . .

SCENES IN CHICAGO STREETS . . .

SPRINGFIELD . . . STATE CAPITOL . . .

MILWAUKEE . . . RIVER AND LAKE FRONT

. . . MILWAUKEE RIVER . . . RACINE

. . . SUNSET ON LAKE MICHIGAN

CHICAGO, ON LAKE MICHIGAN'S SHORES

Chicago & Milwaukee...
Megalopolis on Lake Michigan

HOG BUTCHER, TOOL MAKER, Stacker of Wheat, Player with Railroads and Freight Handler to the Nation. So Carl Sandburg praised Chicago, the nation's second largest city, and the city which led in the explosive growth of the American frontier during the first half of the last century.

For almost fifty years after the founding of the nation, Chicago remained little more than a frontier settlement, inhabited chiefly by the fur traders and trappers who roamed the Great Lakes region, and by Indians, who lived in an uneasy peace with the newcomers.

As the new nation pushed its way west, it sought easier access to its Mississippi River ports, and so, in 1836, work on the Illinois and Michigan Canal began. This canal would allow boats to travel from the Chicago River into the Illinois and Mississippi rivers, thus providing means for continuous inland water navigation from the Erie Canal to the ports of St. Louis and New Orleans. As the canal neared completion, land speculation in Chicago grew to a fever pitch. For even if no one could predict Chicago's eventual size, it was easy enough to see that its geographical situation, at the heart of the great inland water system, would make Chicago a vital commercial center. For a quarter century or so, inland navigation fueled its growth, but by the 1860s vast rail linkages would assure Chicago's destiny.

When Chicago was incorporated in 1837, its population was a mere four thousand. By 1871 it had grown to almost three hundred thousand. Even the great fire in October 1871 could not slow Chicago's growth, though it consumed much of the city and left ninety thousand people homeless. By the turn of the century a population of over a million and a half had made Chicago America's Second City.

Despite its rampant expansion, Chicago remained a rough, pioneering sort of place well into the middle of the century. A visitor to the city in 1850 found that "the streets were abominably paved; the sidewalks, raised high above the level of the streets, were composed of rough planks, often out of repair so that one had to pick one's way carefully for fear of accidents. . . . The mud was so deep in bad weather that from side to side rickety boards served as unsafe bridges and the unfortunate hordes waded laboriously along as best they could." And the buildings? A correspondent of the London *Times* described them as "an extraordinary melange of the Broadway of New York and little shanties—of Parisian buildings mixed with backwoods life."

Led by inventors and engineers, such as George M. Pullman, Chicago tackled its mud by raising sidewalks and buildings and resurfacing almost the entire city. By the turn of the century, Chicago had solved its problems with architecture as well as with mud. Architects such as Louis H. Sullivan, D. H. Burnham, John W. Root, and Frank Lloyd Wright were transforming the cityscape from the "extraordinary melange" of crude copies into one that offered the world a bold, new, and characteristically American building—the skyscraper.

While men in Chicago were firing imaginations with the possibilities of industrial wealth, a man farther south would emerge to fire imaginations with another dream—Emancipation. Most of Illinois claims Abraham Lincoln for its own, but it was in Springfield, the state capital, that he first held office. It was

from Springfield that he would travel to Washington to lead a divided nation, and it was to Springfield the train bearing his body would end its long, slow journey.

Situated in the rich agricultural and coal region of central Illinois, Springfield is a city of broad lawns and tree-lined streets. Towns like Springfield—solid, dignified, with its Renaissance-style capitol building and large frame houses—can be found throughout the Middle West. Less glamorous perhaps than Chicago, their roaring and boisterous neighbor to the north, they are closer to the rich prairie culture that gave America its wheat, its corn, and its Lincolns.

The shipping industry that built Chicago was creating towns to the north of Chicago as well. Waukegan in Illinois, and Kenosha, Racine, and Milwaukee in Wisconsin all began to grow as the result of the heavy lake traffic. Waukegan, first settled around 1835 and called "Little Fort," provided an excellent harbor for Lake Michigan vessels. Since the 1850s it has shared in Chicago's industrial and shipping wealth. Kenosha and Racine profited from the lake traffic as well, and from the railroads, which reached these towns in the 1850s.

Milwaukee, situated at the point where the Milwaukee, Menomonee, and Kinnickinnic rivers enter Lake Michigan, stands as Chicago's sister metropolis to the north. Father Jacques Marquette visited the site in 1673, when it was still an Indian village. In 1795 the Northwest Trading Company established a fur trading post there, and Solomon Juneau, the famous fur trader, stopped there in 1818. Twenty years later the fur trade had made the area prosperous enough so that it was decided to merge several settlements and form the village of Milwaukee. Germans immigrating to the United States after 1848 found their way to Milwaukee. The city has retained its German character and, though it is a prosperous and diversified industrial and port city now, it is most famous for the breweries, which Milwaukee's German settlers brought to it over a century ago. Today, Milwaukee, as well as Waukegan, Kenosha, and Racine are all part of the virtually unbroken urban expanse that extends north from Chicago along Lake Michigan's western shore.

As the loneliest outpost, Fort Dearborn—a solitary trading post amidst wigwams of the unfriendly Potowatomis —slowly saw the surrounding wilderness disappear . . .

For years Fort Dearborn, built in 1803 at the river mouth, was the loneliest post in the West. When the Potowatomis burned it and massacred the garrison in the summer of 1812, there was no life there at all. But it was a strategic point where the Chicago River wound lakeward from the Des Plaines and the Illinois. In 1816 Fort Dearborn was rebuilt and a few huts sprang up on the riverbank. Two years later Illinois became a state. That summer 18-year-old Gurdon Hubbard, a trader for the American Fur Company, walked to Chicago from Mackinac. At the end of the journey he found the fort by the river, across from it the cabins of John Kinzie and a couple of other families, and the endless prairie beyond. It remained a lost place until 1830 when surveyors began running lines for the Illinois and Michigan Canal. The town of Chicago was incorporated in 1833; then the prairie silence gave way to a clatter of building and a clamor of men. In 1837 it became a city, with 4117 excited people.

WALTER HAVIGHURST

Romance of North America,
1958

LAKE STREET, CHICAGO

WESTERN MARKET, CHICAGO

LIGHTHOUSE AND SHOREFRONT, CHICAGO

. . . as endless prairies were conquered and forests felled, yielding millions of board feet of lumber to build the young city on the banks of Chicago River and Lake Michigan

CLARK STREET BRIDGE, CHICAGO

GRAIN STORAGE, CHICAGO

RANDOLPH STREET, CHICAGO

With sand bars dredged and the channel deepened the Chicago River was thronged with lumber schooners, grain schooners, passenger vessels. In 1839 when wheat fields were spreading over the prairies two grain merchants built the first Chicago elevator and the brig *Osceola* loaded the first cargo of grain for Buffalo. Railroads fanned into Chicago from six directions in the 1850's, linking the young city with the East and also with the Mississippi River; already the Illinois and Michigan canal was obsolete and Chicago was on its way to being the greatest railroad center in the world. Long trains of cattle cars brought western cattle to Chicago's growing stockyards. Down the lakes came endless cargoes of lumber, lumber to build the barns and houses of the prairie farms and to build the prairie cities. In 1870 Chicago was a wooden city with thirteen miles of wooden docks along the river and its branches, twenty-four wooden bridges, seventeen wooden elevators, miles of wooden warehouses, hundreds of livery stables, and long cliffs of lumber on the landings. Some men wondered what a fire would do.

WALTER HAVIGHURST
Romance of North America,
1958

*Transportation hub of the country's railroads, Chicago—
since its earliest lines were laid, girdling the heartland
—soon became the focal point for grain and lumber shipments . . .*

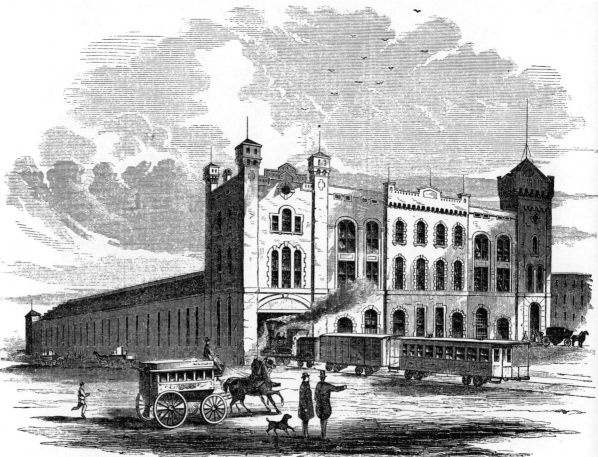

RAILROAD DEPOT, CHICAGO

Hog Butcher for the
   World.
Tool Maker, Stacker of
   Wheat
Player with Railroads and
   the Nation's Freight
   Handler;
Stormy, husky, brawling,
City of the Big Shoulders.

CARL SANDBURG

Chicago, 1914

Come all you bold sailors that follow the Lakes
On an iron ore vessel your living to make.
I shipped in Chicago, bid adieu to the shore,
Bound away to Escanaba for red iron ore.
   Derry down, down, down derry down.

In the month of September, the seventeenth day,
Two dollars and a quarter is all they would pay,
And on Monday morning in *Bridgeport* did take
The *E.C. Roberts* out in the Lake.
   Derry down, down, down derry down.

The wind from the south'ard sprang up a fresh breeze,
And away through Lake Michigan the *Roberts* did sneeze.
Down through Lake Michigan the *Roberts* did roar,
And on Friday morning we passed through death's door.

This packet she howled across the mouth of Green Bay,
And before her cutwater she dashed the white spray.
We rounded the sand point, our anchor let go,
We furled in our canvas and the watch went below.

Next morning we hove alongside the *Exile,*
And soon was made fast to an iron ore pile,
They lowered their chutes and like thunder did roar,
They spouted into us that red iron ore.

CARL SANDBURG

Red Iron Ore

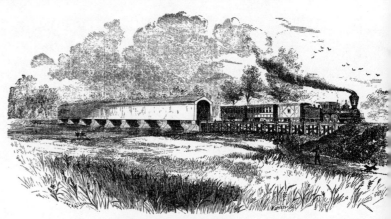

BRIDGE OVER ROCK RIVER

VIADUCT OVER THE ILLINOIS, LA SALLE

. . . connecting with heavily laden schooners along the lakefront where miles of warehouses and grain elevators handled, stored, and shipped the rich harvest to the East

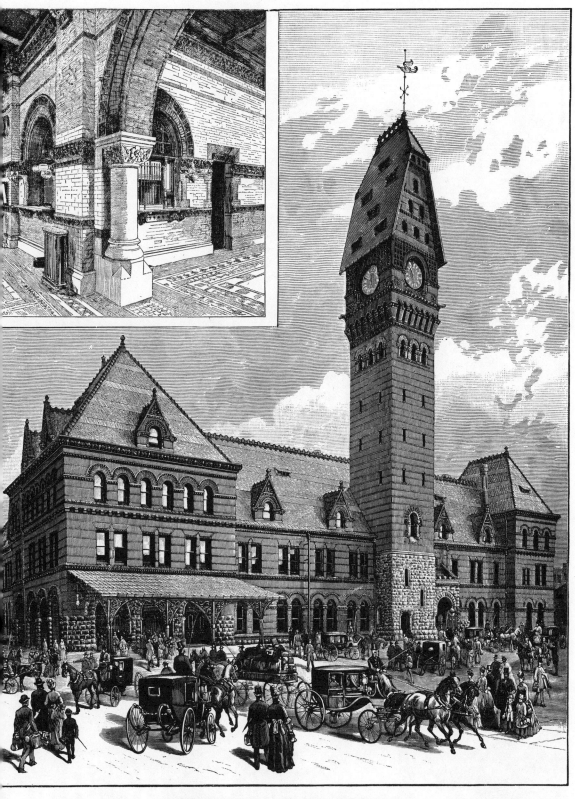

DEARBORN RAILROAD STATION, CHICAGO

Chicago, then, is the centre of a circle of 1000 miles diameter. If you draw a line northward 500 miles, you find everywhere arable land and timber. The same is true with respect to a line drawn 500 miles in a northwesterly course. For 650 miles westward there is no change in the rich and alluring prospect, and so all around the circle, except where Lake Michigan interrupts it, the same conditions are found. Moreover, the lake itself is a valuable element in commerce. The rays of spokes in all these directions become materialized in the form of the tracks of 35 railways which enter the city. Twenty-two of these are great companies, and at a short distance, sub-radials made by other railroads raise the number to 50 roads. As said above, in Chicago one-twenty-fifth of the railway mileage of the world terminates, and serves 30 millions of persons, who find Chicago the largest city easily accessible to them. Thus is found a vast population connected easily and directly with a common centre, to which everything they produce can be brought, and from which all that contributes to the material progress and comfort of man may be economically distributed.

JULIAN RALPH
The American City, 1968

I walked along Michigan Avenue and looked for hours to where for the first time in my life I saw shimmering water meet the sky. Those born to it don't know what it is for a boy to hear about it for years and then comes a day when for the first time he sees water stretching away before his eyes and running to meet the sky.

CARL SANDBURG

Chicago is stupefying . . . an Olympian freak, a fable, an allegory, an incomprehensible phenomenon . . . monstrous, multifarious, unnatural, indomitable, puissant, preposterous, transcendent . . . throw the dictionary at it!

JULIAN STREET

Chicago—"the Goliath of the corn-fed plains with various magnitudes and curiosities"—called the most American of our great cities . . .

But the visitor's heart warms to the town when he sees its parks and its homes. In them is ample assurance that not every breath is "business," and not every thought commercial. Once out of the thicket of the business and semi-business district, the dwellings of the people reach mile upon mile away along pleasant boulevards and avenues, or facing noble parks and parkways, or in a succession of villages green and gay with foliage and flowers. They are not cliff dwellings like our flats and tenements; there are no brownstone canons like our up-town streets; there are only occasional hesitating hints there are those Philadelphian and Baltimorean mills that grind out dwellings all alike, as nature makes pease and man makes pins. There are more miles of detached villas in Chicago than a stranger can easily account for. As they are not only found on Prairie Avenue and the boulevards, but in the populous wards and semi-suburbs, where the middle folk are congregated, it is evident that the prosperous moiety of the population enjoys living better (or better living) than the same fraction in the Atlantic cities.

JULIAN RALPH
The American City, 1968

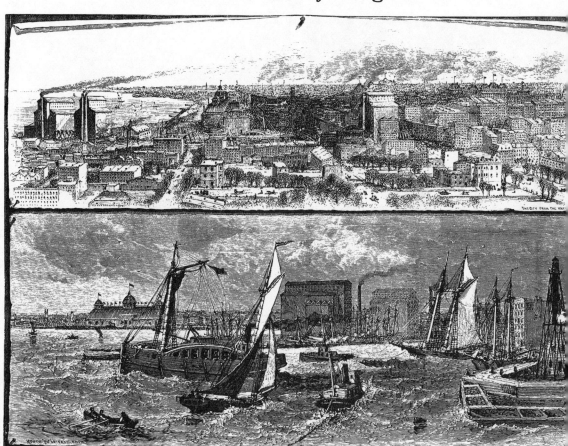

VIEW OF CHICAGO AND LAKEFRONT

SCENES IN CHICAGO

. . . a huge, brash, sprawling metropolis—the nation's leading railway and meat-packing center —its vastness extending in three directions

Chicago river.

Jefferson Park.

Madison Street

Chicago river from Clark St Bridge

West Side from Lake Street Bridge

PANORAMA OF CHICAGO, AND LAKEFRONT

I have struck a city—a real city—and they call it Chicago. The other places do not count. San Francisco was a pleasure-resort as well as a city, and Salt Lake was a phenomenon. This place is the first American city I have encountered. It holds rather more than a million people with bodies, and stands on the same sort of soil as Calcutta. Having seen it, I urgently desire never to see it again. It is inhabited by savages. Its water is the water of the Hughli, and its air is dirt. Also it says that it is the "boss" town of America. I do not believe that it has anything to do with this country. They told me to go to the Palmer House which is a gilded and mirrored rabbit-warren, and there I found a huge hall of tessellated marble, crammed with people talking about money and spitting about everywhere. Other barbarians charged in and out of this inferno with letters and telegrams in their hands, and yet others shouted at each other. A man who had drunk quite as much as was good for him told me that this was "the finest hotel in the finest city of God Almighty's earth." . . .

RUDYARD KIPLING
From Sea to Sea, 1914

In the middle of Illinois prairie lands, on the banks of the Sangamon River—Springfield, the state's capital —is renowned as the heart of Lincoln country where . . .

It is portentous, and a thing of state
That here at midnight, in our little town
A mourning figure walks, and will not rest,
Near the old court-house pacing up and down,

Or by his homestead, or in shadowed yards
He lingers where his children used to play,
Or through the market, on the well-worn stones
He stalks until the dawn-stars burn away.

A bronzed, lank man! His suit of ancient black,
A famous high top-hat and plain worn shawl
Make him the quaint great figure that men love,
The prairie-lawyer, master of us all.

He cannot sleep upon his hillside now.
He is among us:—as in times before!
And we who toss and lie awake for long
Breathe deep, and start, to see him pass the door.

His head is bowed. He thinks of men and kings.
Yea, when the sick world cries, how can he sleep?
Too many peasants fight, they know not why,
Too many homesteads in black terror weep.

The sins of all the war-lords burn his heart.
He sees the dreadnaughts scouring every main.
He carries on his shawl-wrapped shoulders now
The bitterness, the folly and the pain.

He cannot rest until a spirit-dawn
Shall come;—the shining hope of Europe free:
A league of sober folk, the Worker's Earth,
Bringing long peace to Cornland, Alp and Sea.

It breaks his heart that kings must murder still,
That all his hours of travail here for men
Seem yet in vain. And who will bring white peace
That he may sleep upon his hill again?

VACHEL LINDSAY,
Abraham Lincoln Walked at Midnight, 1914

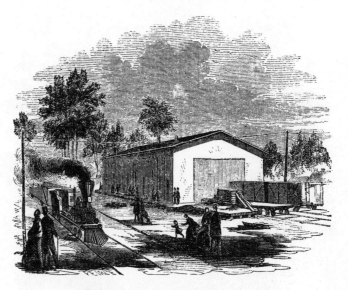

RAILROAD STATION, SPRINGFIELD

WASHINGTON STREET, SPRINGFIELD

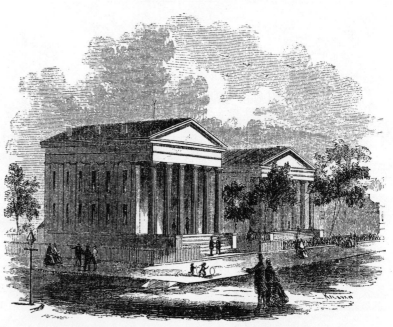

COURT HOUSE AND BANK, SPRINGFIELD

. . . the young lawyer tried cases before backwoods juries and judges, with wit and homespun eloquence that later were to serve him well as the wartime president

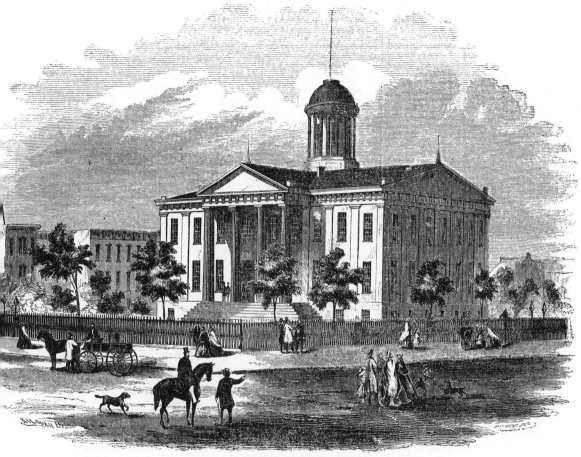

STATE HOUSE, SPRINGFIELD

The other way to Springfield is at the foot of the New Salem Hill, and leads along the river to the capital of Illinois, a city of over 70,000 people. It is the largest city of the Sangamon River valley. In his last years William H. Herndon lived on a farm just a few miles north of Springfield, and there struggled with his biography of Lincoln, while practicing law in Petersburg. At one time he had been mayor of Springfield, and a lawyer of fairly profitable business there. Toward the eighteen-seventies he went into bankruptcy. His farm did not pay, and in the nature of things could not. For he was in the fifties by this time, and his intemperate habits had reduced his vitality. I fancy him somehow sitting at the window of his little farm house, looking over the Sangamon River country and thinking of the days when he was in partnership with Lincoln, days that had unfolded to the incredible pageant that he saw passing before him, as America changed. He and his little son died the same day about 1891, there in the farmhouse. He was buried in Oakland Cemetery, a beautiful spot near Springfield.

EDGAR LEE MASTERS
The Sangamon, 1942

NEW STATE CAPITOL, SPRINGFIELD

Northward, along the sandy beaches of Lake Michigan—lured by opportunities of the burgeoning Midwest—sporadic settlements grew into the cities of Waukegan, Kenosha, Racine, and Milwaukee

Cities are the result of certain social necessities of civilized or semi-civilized Man,—necessities of Trade, of Manufacture, Interchange of Ideas, and of Government: they rest upon and are supported by the Country. Their support is of course mainly voluntary; its amount is controlled by the ability and desires of the rural population. Thus, while almost any farming County might give employment and ample subsistence to five or even ten times its present population, there is scarcely a city in the world whose population is not already quite as large as it has business to employ and income to sustain, while the greater number are constantly crowded with surplus laborers, vainly seeking employment and underbidding each other in the eager strife for it, until thousands can hardly sustain life on the scanty reward of their exertions, and other thousands are forced to live on public or private charity.

CITY OF MILWAUKEE

MILWAUKEE RIVER, MILWAUKEE

The thriving cities of the heartland brought reality to Father Hennepin's prediction that "an infinite number of considerable towns would establish an inconceivable commerce"

MILWAUKEE AND VICINITY

Many perish every year, not perhaps of absolute starvation, but of diseases induced by hunger, want and exposure, while a larger number are driven by destitution into evil courses, and close their brief careers of guilty mockery of enjoyment by deaths of shame and horror. Such are some of the dire consequences of the continual over-population of our cities, caused by the insane desire very generally felt to escape the ruder toils and tamer routine of country life. Until some marked change shall have been wrought in the general condition of our rural Industry, so as to render it less repulsive than it now is, our cities must continue over-crowded and full of misery. The naked truth that, as a general rule, no one lives by *bona fide* physical labor who can obtain a living without, and very few live by farming or the like who can live by what are esteemed the lighter and more genteel avocations mainly pursued in cities and villages, explains much of the misery so prevalent all around us.

HORACE GREELEY
Hints Towards Reform, 1850

The Indians called the land "Ouisconsin—where the waters meet—a richly endowed region of the Midwest where receding glaciers of the Ice Age scattered lakes and streams in profusion

RACINE

SUNSET ON LAKE MICHIGAN

The Mighty Mississippi...
above St. Louis to St. Paul

QUEEN'S BLUFF . . . TREMPEALEAU . . .

MUSCATINE . . . KEOKUK . . . BURLINGTON

. . . ROCK ISLAND . . . DAVENPORT . . .

BUENA VISTA . . . DUBUQUE . . . KELLY'S

BLUFF . . . MISSISSIPPI BRIDGE . . .

THE WISCONSIN . . . ST. PAUL . . .

THE CAPITOL . . . CITY HALL . . .

FULLER HOUSE . . . DAYTON'S BLUFF

. . . MINNEAPOLIS . . . .ST. ANTHONY'S

FALLS . . . MADISON . . . UNIVERSITY

OF WISCONSIN . . . CAPITAL HOUSE

. . . VALLEY OF THE UPPER MISS-

ISSIPPI . . . SUGAR LOAF . . . CHIMNEY

ROCK . . . THE NARROWS . . . DELLS OF

THE WISCONSIN . . . RAFTING LOGS

QUEEN'S BLUFF, BELOW TREMPEALEAU

The Mighty Mississippi...
above St. Louis to St. Paul

THE MISSISSIPPI—THE CHIPPEWA'S "Father of Waters," T. S. Eliot's "strong brown god"—begins as a ten-foot-wide stream in the pine forests of northern Minnesota. There, fed by cold, clear lakes, it runs first north, then east, and finally, augmented by runoff from the Mesabi Range, turns south and begins its journey through the forests and prairies of mid-America.

The Upper Mississippi has as many aspects as the civilization it nourishes; clear blue at its source, it quickly loses the blue of its origins as it begins to take in alluvial deposits. Flowing south, it carves out a varied bed of massive limestone palisades, gentle bluffs, and flat bottomland that gives way to forests and wheatfields.

In Minnesota it flows through swamps, lowlands, and lakes, grows to almost a quarter mile in width, plunges over rocks and boulders and creates the Falls of St. Anthony, near St. Paul. Then it plunges southward to receive the waters of rivers almost as famous as itself: the Minnesota, the St. Croix, the Wisconsin, the Rock, the Illinois, and the Missouri, whose muddy waters complete the transformation from blue to deep brown.

The earliest European settlers in the upper region of the river were the French. They hunted, trapped, mined copper, and dreamed of the treasures that could be wrested from the land for their king and for themselves: among them Joliet and Marquette, La Salle, Father Hennepin, Laclède and Auguste Chouteau. They opened the way for European settlement along the river.

The real bounty was to belong to the Scandinavians, who saw in the rich pine forests of Wisconsin and Minnesota land very like the land they had hungered for but could never own in the Old World. By the mid-nineteenth century, over two hundred thousand Scandinavians had come to the Upper Mississippi valley. They hacked away trees to build their farms and so created the lumber industry which, along with farming, first fulfilled the rich promise of the river valley. For decades, as the great pines in the north and the hardwoods farther south were exploited with a ferocity that led virtually to their extinction, the forests thundered with the sounds of falling trees and the river rang with the sounds of logs and loggers. Towns like Winona and La Cross grew rich from the timber which built the cities and farms of the central plains.

The Mississippi became the great highway down which the timber and farm produce of the North traveled to house and feed the burgeoning East and the growing West. But the timber and food stuffs came in such quantity and the demand for them was so voracious that the pioneer crafts of the Mississippi soon proved inadequate. They gave way to the steamboat, which provided the speed and car-

rying capacity necessary to satisfy America's endless appetite. By the 1830s the river and its great paddle-wheelers were synonymous, and the early prosperity and romance of the Mississippi are inextricably tied to those vessels.

As steamboats replaced the earlier river crafts, port towns grew into cities and new towns at or near the river sprang up. They were joined by a web of stagecoach lines. The Twin Cities of St. Paul and Minneapolis were already prospering from both the water power of the Falls of St. Anthony, which drove the grain and lumber mills, and their natural position as the point of departure for the Northwest and for the river traffic south. With the coming of the steamboat, however, they boomed and received wave after wave of European immigration.

Downstream, in Iowa and Illinois, lie Davenport, Bettendorf, Clinton, Rock Island, and Moline—towns which owe as much to the locomotive as to the steamboat. Here at the Quint Cities, as they are called, the first railroad bridge across the Mississippi was constructed in the mid-1850s.

Farther south lie Burlington, where steep bluffs replace the gentler Iowa hills, and, on the Illinois side of the river, the Mormon shrine of Nauvoo, where Joseph Smith died in 1844 in the bitter struggle over polygamy. From Nauvoo the Mormons began America's greatest peacetime migration, seeking, in the far West, an end to persecution.

Continuing into Missouri, the river flows by Hannibal, the birthplace of the Mississippi's great chronicler, Mark Twain, in whose books the legend was carried around the world.

Farther downstream lies the Mississippi's largest city, St. Louis. Founded as a fur-trading center by Laclède and his son, Auguste Chouteau, in 1764, St. Louis, perhaps more than any other city on the river, owes its prosperity and fame to the steamboat and the locomotive. In the early part of the nineteenth century it was already jammed with river traffic. In the 1860s it welcomed the railroad and quickly became a rail center second in size only to Chicago. Throughout the century St. Louis remained America's Gateway to the West.

To the Chippewa, the "Father of Waters," poetically called Mee-zee-see-bee—most lordly of living features of the vast heartland, a watershed of a hundred tributaries . . .

MUSCATINE, ON THE MISSISSIPPI

The Mississippi has served the nation as a highway, and as a battleground; it has been a road to opportunity, and a barrier to religion and the law; an international boundary, and a unifying force. It still remains the dividing line between "back East" and "out West." De Soto was the first white man to see the Mississippi nearly four centuries ago. Marquette and Joliet began the first real exploration of the river in 1673. Shortly after that, French-Canadian trappers, traders, and priests began nosing their canoes into every tributary of the river, searching for furs, or souls to be saved; seeking gold, or waterways to the Pacific. Villages slowly grew up along the routes of these explorers. The earliest permanent settlement was at Cahokia, Illinois, in 1699. During the following century other villages were established along the fertile banks all the way to New Orleans. For their settlers the only real link with each other and with the outside world was the river. The western farmers and merchants depended upon the river to get their produce to eastern or European markets, and by the thousands they loaded their grain, lead, cattle, salt, and furs onto to flatboats, and headed for New Orleans. Thus they saw more of the world than many of their descendants, and they came to know a national pride and solidarity.

PERRY T. RATHBONE
Mississippi Panorama, 1950

ALONG THE LEVEE, KEOKUK

ATHENAEUM, KEOKUK

. . . gave life and meaning to the inner continent, from its source in the dark wilderness of Lake Itasco, Minnesota— often snaking twenty miles to gain two—to reach its delta

BURLINGTON

FEMALE SEMINARY, KEOKUK

Those who made the first settlement in Burlington probably builded better than they knew, when they chose the only landing on the west bank of the Mississippi River, between New Madison and Muscatine, a distance of eighty-one miles. Burlington is well situated for becoming a great commercial and manufacturing city—with lines of railroad radiating in every direction, bringing to her warehouses the products of near and distant portions of the country; with the Mississippi River at her door ready to float upon its bosom such products as seek a Southern market . . . it does appear as if a promising future opened before the city.

The History of Des Moines County, Iowa 1879

GAS WORKS, KEOKUK

*Past endless prairies and pioneer settlements—wooded
riverbanks and shallow bottoms—lands of the Crow,
Minnesota, Chippewa, and Wisconsin tribes . . .*

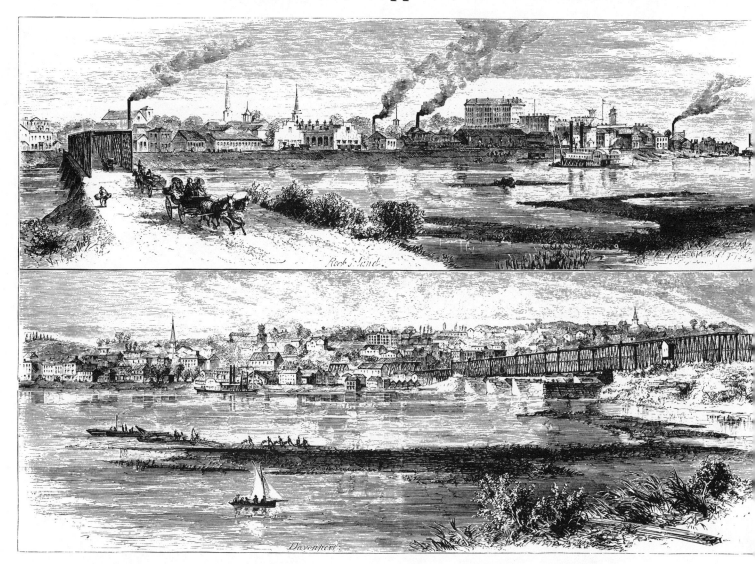

ROCK ISLAND, ILLINOIS AND DAVENPORT, IOWA

The first names on the prairie, before the
pioneer settlements dotted the map of Illinois,
were given to creeks and groves in the encircling
grassland. *Creek*, the Anglo-Saxon word for a
tidal inlet, a small arm of the sea, found a new
designation here, as the French *prairie* took on a
new spaciousness and wildness. Kickapoo Creek,
Sugar Creek, Beaver Creek, Rice Creek, Rock
Creek, Hay Creek, Horse Creek, Cow Creek,
Paint Creek, Smallpox Creek, Salt Creek, Ver-
milion Creek, Potato Creek, corrupted from
Petite Creek—they were frozen fast in winter,
alive and overflowing in spring, and all but
dried up by the end of summer. The islands of
forest—Buffalo Grove, Sugar Grove, Keg
Grove, Troy Grove, Dutch Grove, Deer Grove,
Fox Grove, Downer's Grove, Table Grove—
were the first sites of settlement in the country;
they offered wood and water at the edge of
farmland. Within the Great Prairie were lesser
prairies, bounded by marshy bottoms or timbered ridges, and their names were all inviting:
Cloud Prairie, Marine Prairie, Pretty Prairie,
Garden Prairie, Looking Glass Prairie, Blooming Prairie, Blowing Prairie, Rolling Prairie,
Fountain Prairie, Flower Prairie.

WALTER HAVIGHURST
The Heartland, 1965

BUENA VISTA

. . . the mile-wide tide is joined by yellow currents of the Missouri and the turgid waters of the Ohio— pushing southward in its flow to reach the Gulf

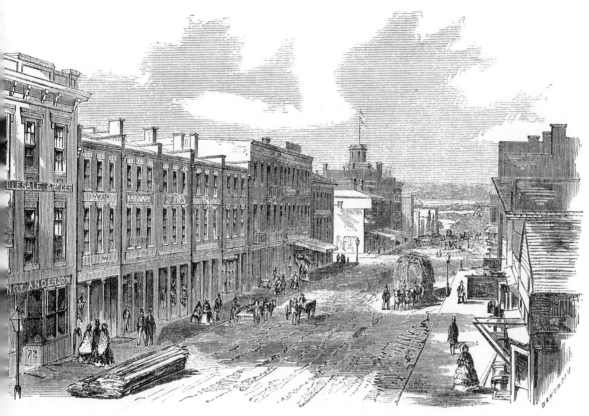

MAIN STREET, DOWN TOWN, DUBUQUE

Rail penetration of the far Northwest, improved agricultural machinery, the handling of grain in carload lots, trans-shipment to lake or ocean steamers by grain elevators, and a new milling process which ground the Northern spring wheat into superfine flour (much too superfine), were factors which combined to move the center of wheat production north and west from Illinois and Iowa into Minnesota, the Dakotas, Montana, Oregon, and the Canadian Northwest. In this new wheat belt the "bonanza" wheat farms, veritable factories for wheat production, were well established by 1890. The wheat crop increased from 152 to 612 million bushels between 1866 and 1891. With the low prices that prevailed after the panic of 1873, this meant disaster to competing farmers in the Middle West and the Eastern states; and, even more completely, to England. The silo which enabled dairy farmers to turn corn into milk, poultry raising, and the breeding of horses and cattle, saved Eastern farming from ruin; but enormous areas within a few hours of the great industrial centers on the Atlantic coast have reverted to forest.

UPTOWN ON MAIN STREET, DUBUQUE

America's heritage has been enriched by the endless ebb and flood of rivers draining a great empire— breadbasket of the nation—and even more . . .

We noticed that above Dubuque the water of the Mississippi was olive-green—rich and beautiful and semi-transparent, with the sun on it. Of course the water was nowhere as clear or of as fine a complexion as it is in some other seasons of the year; for now it was at flood stage, and therefore dimmed and blurred by the mud manufactured from caving banks. The majestic bluffs that overlook the river, along through this region, charm one with grace and variety of their forms, and the soft beauty of their adornment. The steep, verdant slope, whose base is at the water's edge, is topped by a lofty rampart of broken, turreted rocks, which are exquisitely rich and mellow in color—mainly dark browns and dull greens, but splashed with other tints. And then you have the shining river, winding here and there and yonder, its sweep interrupted at intervals by clusters of wooded islands threaded by silver channels; and you have glimpses of distant villages, asleep upon capes; and of stealthy rafts slipping along in the shade of the forest walls; and of white steamers vanishing around remote points. And it is all as tranquil and reposeful as dreamland, and has nothing this-worldly about it—nothing to hang a fret or a worry upon.

MARK TWAIN
Life on the Mississippi, 1874

MISSISSIPPI BRIDGES, DUBUQUE

DUBUQUE, FROM KELLY'S BLUFF

. . . giving the nation men to shape its destiny:
Abe Lincoln and Ulysses Grant, Mark Twain and
Carl Sandburg, Sinclair Lewis and the La Follettes

AT THE MOUTH OF THE WISCONSIN

LA CROSSE, ON THE MISSISSIPPI

The Twin Cities: St. Paul and Minneapolis—and nearby St. Anthony Falls—the entrepot at the head of northward navigation on the Mississippi . . .

Minneapolis is situated at the falls of St. Anthony, which stretch across the river fifteen hundred feet, and have a fall of eighty-two feet—a waterpower which, by art, has been made of inestimable value, businesswise, though somewhat to the damage of the Falls as a spectacle, or as a background against which to get your photograph taken. Thirty flouring-mills turn out two million barrels of the very choicest of flour every year; twenty saw-mills produce two hundred million feet of lumber annually; then there are woolen-mills, cotton-mills, paper and oil mills; and sash, nail, furniture, barrel, and other factories, without number, so to speak. The great flouring-mills here and at St. Paul use the 'new process' and mash the wheat by rolling, instead of grinding it. Sixteen railroads meet in Minneapolis, and sixty-five passenger-trains arrive and depart daily.

MARK TWAIN
Life on the Mississippi

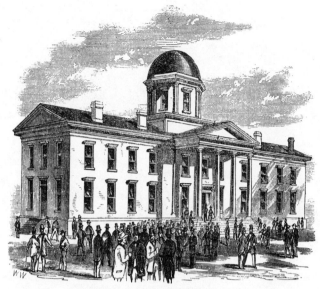

STATE CAPITOL, ST. PAUL

CITY HALL, ST. PAUL

FULLER HOUSE, ST. PAUL

ST. PAUL, ON THE MISSISSIPPI

*. . . owe their growth to the vast potential of the falls,
and the rich surrounding heartland of grain—producing
the largest flour-milling center in the world*

ST. PAUL, FROM DAYTON'S BLUFF

The Falls of St. Anthony
are not very imposing,
although not devoid of
beauty. You cannot see the
whole falls at one view, as
they are divided like those
of Niagara, by a large
island, about one-third of
the distance from the
eastern shore. The river
which as you ascended,
poured through a bed
below the strata of
calcareous rock, now rises
above the limestone formation; and the large masses
of this rock, which at the
falls have been thrown
down in wild confusion
over a width of from two
hundred to a hundred and
fifty yards, have a very
picturesque effect. The
falls themselves, I do not
think, are more than thirty
to thirty-five feet high; but
with rapids above and
below them, the descent of
the river is said to be more
than one hundred feet.

FREDERICK MARRYAT
A Diary in America, 1839

MINNEAPOLIS AND ST. ANTHONY'S FALLS

*In the rolling hills of southern Wisconsin's dairyland,
Madison—justly proud of its handsome capitol building
—dominates a region of hills and lakes . . .*

Madison is beautifully situated on an isthmus formed by Lakes Mendota and Monona, with Lakes Waubesa and Kegonsa joined by the Yahara River. The impressive Capitol rises 285 feet above the heights of the isthmus, its granite dome crowned by the gilt statue of "Forward" visible for miles. It is the seat of the State University which occupies the shores of Lake Mendota. Judge John D. Doty saw its beauty and realized the possibilities of making this "four lakes region" the capital when he first passed through in 1829. By 1836 he owned huge tracts of land on the isthmus and was able to persuade the legislature to choose it as a site of the capital and location of the University. From a "beautiful but uninhabitable" wilderness grew the present handome city. But development lagged and proceeded slowly until the arrival of the first railroad. When Jairus Fairchild from Milwaukee became mayor, in 1856, commercial and cultural interests vied with each other and public building went on furiously for a time. At this time Horace Greeley from the East visited and gave lectures—a further aid in the promotional development of the city.

The American Guide, 1949

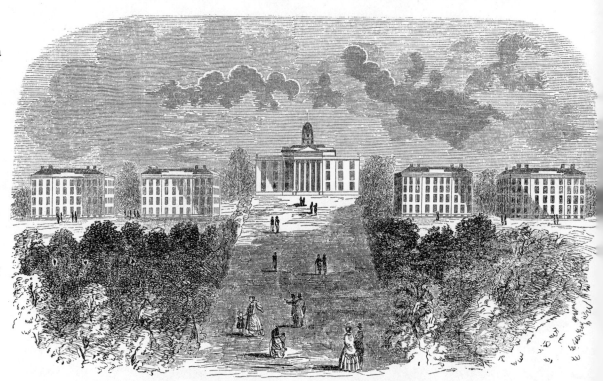

UNIVERSITY OF WISCONSIN, MADISON

MADISON, CAPITAL OF WISCONSIN

*. . . proclaimed, in the Badger State, to number ten thousand
—but actually numbering many more. In many ways Wisconsin
typifies the Midwest—its towns: Main Street, U.S.A.*

NEW MUSEUM BUILDING, MADISON

CAPITAL HOUSE, MADISON

The name Wisconsin is popularly thought to mean "a gathering of waters." Wisconsin is, indeed, a kind of peninsula: three of its four sides, notched and undulating, are determined by natural waterways— Great Lakes to the east and north, rivers to the north and west. The state is everywhere shot through with rivers, streams and lakes—there are over 8500 counted lakes, 10,000 miles of trout streams—and it is actually bisected from Lake Michigan to the Mississippi by the Fox and Wisconsin rivers. The peninsular character of the state suggests nearly every economic activity which has developed within it, beginning with Jean Nicolet, the first white man to step upon this ground. He was searching for the mythical northwest waterway to China, and landed near Green Bay in 1634, in the name of the governor of New France. He wore ritual robes to meet expected mandarins, but soon was shooting pistols from both hands when, instead, naked red men appeared.

WALTER HAVIGHURST

Romance of North America,
1958

The landscape of the Mississippi shores, in the remote northern regions—timbered with pine and tamarack—flashing past wooded bluffs where the Chippewa pitched their wigwams. . .

The river flows through three climates and three landscapes. It begins in a remote northern country, a land of pine and tamarack, where winter locks the lakes in ice from November until May. It is born out of the north end of Lake Itasca, in the Minnesota forests. Four inches deep and two steps across on the glacial boulders in its bed, the little stream flashes through the wild rice and curves under the birch-barred hill where a few Chippewas still live in these wigwams. It moves secretly through grassy swales and grows with the springs that flow down hidden in the horsemint. It keeps to the marshes and the lowland, often indeterminate in its flow as though it had no business with destiny and a nation. Bridges straddle it with a pair of ten-foot stringers. Blackbird and bright-eyed vireo sway on its reeds. Carelessly, without hurry, winding twenty miles to gain two miles of seaway, it sets out for the distant Gulf.

FLAT BOATS.

SUGAR LOAF.

THE VALLEY OF THE UPPER MISSISSIPPI

. . . a diversified countryside—plateaus that look down upon the silvery highway, or low-lying banks that seem to taper gently to kiss the eddying waters

MAIDEN ROCK.

LAKE PEPIN.

CHIMNEY ROCK, ON TURKEY RIVER.

It takes many streams to make a river. Out of those dark northern forests the tributaries flow, the Crow Wing, the Minnesota, the St. Croix, the Chippewa, the Wisconsin. And so, under the bluffs of Illinois the Mississippi is a mile-wide tide, moving through a prairie landscape where the cornfields lean upon the sky. The yellow current of the Missouri swings in from the far-distant Rockies and the darker waters of the Ohio bring the snows that fell in Appalachian valleys. Three great rivers have become one. Southward from a dark northern wilderness to a tropical sea the Father of Waters marks its road through a continent.

WALTER HAVIGHURST
Upper Mississippi, 1937

Between the long stretch of beaches bordering Lake Michigan to the western boundary along the Mississippi, Wisconsin's rolling country is endowed with innumerable lakes—happy haunts for outdoor recreation

And along with opportunity was the lure of equality and independence. From Wisconsin a Norwegian wrote home: "Here I take off my cap to no one—not even the minister—not even the President." A Swedish settler wrote: "Here a man can come to something by his own efforts." In Scotland after a visit to the Indiana frontier John Melish wrote of the western farmer: "None dare encroach upon him; he can sit under his own vine, and under his own fig tree, and none to make him afraid." Wrote a Welsh settler in Ohio to his brother in Glamorgan: "We have done very well in this country. Have a fine farm which would sell for about 6,000 dollars, and every other thing in proportion . . . . Thank God no orthodoxy, no tithes, no high church, no king but good and wholesome laws."

WALTER HAVIGHURST
Romance of North America, 1958

PARTED BLUFF.

STAND ROCK.

THROUGH THE NARROWS

LAKE OCONOMOWOC.

DELLS OF THE WISCONSIN.

SHOOTING THE RAPIDS.

SCENES IN WISCONSIN

Down the Mississippi...
from St. Louis to the Gulf

GRAND TOWER ROCK . . . LEVEE AT

ST. LOUIS . . . LOCUST STREET . . .

VERANDA ROW . . . COURT HOUSE . . .

MERCANTILE LIBRARY . . . ST. CHARLES

RAILROAD BRIDGE . . . STREET SCENES

IN ST. LOUIS . . . VICKSBURG . . .

MEMPHIS . . . PLANTER'S HOUSE ON

THE MISSISSIPPI . . . STEAMER WOODING

UP . . . COTTON BLOCKADE . . . MERIDIAN

. . . LOUISIANA SUGAR PLANTATION . . .

BATON ROUGE . . . SOUTHWEST PASS . . .

BAYOU OF THE MISSISSIPPI . . . NEW

ORLEANS . . . LEVEE SCENES . . . A

"CREVASSE" . . . NEW ORLEANS DOCKS

. . . THE BELIZE . . . CYPRESS SWAMP

. . . MOSS GATHERING

GRAND TOWER ROCK, BELOW ST. LOUIS

Down the Mississippi... from St. Louis to the Gulf

THE "MIGHTY MISSISSIPPI" REALLY begins where once it ended, in a great alluvial plain some thirty miles south of St. Louis, and over a thousand miles from its source. For it is here that the river, fed by the Missouri, Illinois, and Ohio, becomes the muddied, surging Mississippi of song and story.

Just as the New World had once beckoned immigrants from a crowded and exhausted Europe, so the Lower Mississippi valley offered its rich, dark soil to planters from the East. Intensive cultivation had worn out much of the Eastern cotton and tobacco lands, and productive land was growing scarce. But in the Lower Mississippi valley, men could dream once again of boundless riches. And for roughly half a century the dreams came true. England and America clamored for cotton. By the 1830s the seemingly inexhaustible soil of the Lower Mississippi valley and the easy access to the port of New Orleans offered by the river itself drew pioneers westward.

Travelers along the river in those years could see broad cotton fields stretching out beyond the riverbanks and, farther in the distance, the stately homes of the great planters. Closer to shore, they could see the wretched huts of the Mississippi woodcutters and squatters, and everywhere they could see the slaves.

The wealth of the Mississippi valley was indeed prodigious, but the river has always held claim against those who farmed its valley. Disastrous floods often took back all that the river had given, and more. So, from Illinois to the Gulf, great levees were built, in the endless struggle with the river.

Planters and slaves, roustabouts and dandies, riverboat gamblers and langorous belles thronged the streets of thriving river towns. The lore of the steamboats anchored in these towns excited generations of young boys, who dreamed of the romantic and often treacherous voyages up and down the river.

Cape Girardeau, in Illinois, may be considered the real gateway to the Lower Mississippi. It is here that the river has swollen to its full strength and the great levees begin. Downstream in Illinois lies Cairo, the staging area for the Union's forces in their conquest of the river. Farther south, in Tennessee, is Memphis, once cotton capital of the Lower Mississippi, and home to both Davy Crockett and W. C. Handy. It was just below Memphis that Hernando de Soto and his party first saw the Mississippi in 1541.

Arkansas's Helena, and Mississippi's Greenville and Vicksburg all shared as well in its destruction. Natchez, however, shared only the wealth. Unharmed by Union fire, Natchez retained its elegant antebellum homes and still remains a living monument to Southern culture before the Civil War. Indeed, no traveler along the river has failed to remark on the beauty of Natchez: situated high on a bluff at a bend in the river, its sloping streets are lined with gracious homes built more than a century ago.

As the river reached Baton Rouge it enters flatlands, where it spreads out into innumerable bayous and begins its final, three-pronged journey to the Gulf. Here at Baton Rouge, founded by the French in their earliest explorations of the river, moss, cane, and live oak, redolent of the town's quieter past, exist along with the throbbing machinery of the nation's largest oil refinery.

Below Baton Rouge the Mississippi flows through the gloomy bayous, swamps, cypress groves, and hanging moss of southern Louisiana, until it finally reaches New Orleans. Founded by Bienville in 1718, on orders from France, it was ceded to the United States in 1803 as part of the Louisiana Purchase. New Orleans, though renowned as French, has an architecture more unique to Spain. In 1788 much of the old wooden part of the town burnt and was replaced by the Spanish-style brick and plaster buildings which constitute the Vieux Carré.

Into New Orleans, and out again through its great port, poured the riches of the Mississippi: cotton, surely, but also corn, wheat, meat, fruit, and sugar. Its air of a gracious, somewhat quaint "ville de province"—as Mrs. Trollope remembered it—belie the tougher nature of this great port city, in which stevedores, boatmen, and pirates clustered, along with more genteel inhabitants. And here in New Orleans "Ol' Man River," silent witness of so much history, finally ends his long journey, as his mighty, brown waters pour slowly into the Gulf.

The levees along the St. Louis banks—jammed with hundreds of steamboats: from faraway Pittsburgh to the east; St. Paul to the north; New Orleans downriver, gateway to the Gulf and the seas . . .

At the crossroads of the Mississippi system St. Louis was able to levy a toll on the river trade in all directions. After the *Yellowstone's* pioneering trip up the Missouri in 1823, steamboats poked ever farther into the back country until in 1859 one vessel came within fifteen miles of Fort Benton, three thousand five hundred and sixty miles from the sea. Furs from the Northwest, annuities to the Indians, Mormon exiles, military personnel and supplies, emigrants, gold seekers— first California bound, then for Montana—all found space on the Missouri River boats; and St. Louis was the terminal of the traffic. Manufactures, hogs, grain, and other produce arrived from Ohio and Illinois river ports for transshipment. "All these advantages combine to make [St. Louis] a place of great trade," wrote F.B. Mayer in 1851. "It's inhabitants . . . all wear the anxious & care worn looks of 'men of business.' " Almost always, Mayer added, nearly one hundred steamboats could be counted on the levee, "taking in and discharging freight, letting off steam, & pushing out or arriving . . . .

ST. LOUIS ON THE MISSISSIPPI

MARINE HOSPITAL, ST. LOUIS

. . . pulsing with the heartbeat of the growing nation—
a scene of hectic activity—"for two miles a forest
of smokestacks . . . a dense mass of confusion and bustle"

THE LEVEE OR LANDING, ST. LOUIS

There is probably no busier scene in America in the same space. For two miles a forest of smoke stacks is seen towering above the 'arks' from which they seem to grow. All between this and the line of warehouses is filled with a dense mass of apparently inextricable confusion & bustle, noise & animation. More steamboats are probably seen here than at any port in the world . . . ."

MARSHALL B. DAVIDSON
Life in America, 1951

THE LEVEE AT ST. LOUIS

Midway along the length of the Mississippi—at its confluence with the Missouri, the thriving port of St. Louis grew as the great thoroughfare of western migration . . .

The appearance of St. Louis was not calculated to make a favorable impression upon the first visit, with its long dirty and quicksand beach, numbers of long, empty keelboats tied to stakes driven in the sand, squads of idle boatmen passing to and fro, here and there numbers pitching quoits; others running foot races, rough and tumble fights; and shooting at a target was one of their occupations while in port.

JAMES HEALEY WHITE
Early Days in St. Louis, 1819

LOCUST STREET, ST. LOUIS

By the mid-century there were probably a thousand boats operating regularly on the Mississippi. Even at the beginning of our period, in 1834, the steam tonnage on that river—39,000—was nearly half that of the whole British Empire, and it multiplied sixfold in sixteen years. Over the unknown spot where De Soto had been given his watery grave in the midst of a continental wilderness, there now raced against each other great boats, gleaming with lights at night, costing a hundred thousand dollars and more, carrying their picturesque hundred or two of passengers—gamblers, merchants, slaves and immigrants, fur traders, cotton planters, every imaginable type of humanity —and cargoes of every sort of merchandise. Of accidents there were plenty. Even when the fires were not being fed with resin or oil-soaked wood, while safety valves were illegally fastened down, in the races between steamers which were a favorite form of river sport, the snags, sand bars, explosions, and sudden conflagrations of the flimsy superstructures often resulted in heavy loss of life.

JAMES TRUSLOW ADAMS
Epic of America, 1933

VERANDA ROW, ST. LOUIS

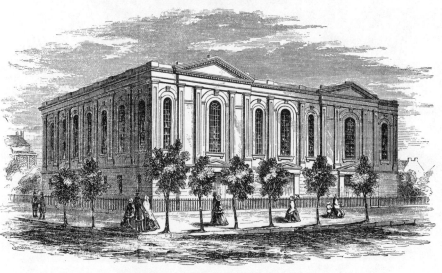

MEDICAL DEPARTMENT, ST. LOUIS

. . . where, in earlier days, emigrants and traders—in an endless caravan of wagons and coaches—purchased supplies for the journey west: in latter days, the hub for rail lines

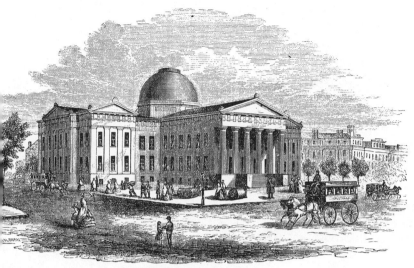

COURT HOUSE, ST. LOUIS

The cities of the West are all of them pre-eminently cosmopolitan cities. The Germans have their quarters there—sometimes half the city, their newspapers, and their clubs; the Irish have theirs; and the French theirs. The Mississippi River is the great cosmopolitan which unites all people, which gives a definite purpose of their activity, and determines their abode, and which enables the life of every one, the inhabitants themselves and their products, to circulate from the one end to the other of this great central valley.

FREDRIKA BREMER
America of the Fifties, 1933

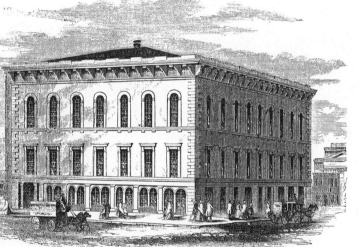

MERCANTILE LIBRARY, ST. LOUIS

BIDDLE MARKET, ST. LOUIS

ST. CHARLES RAILROAD BRIDGE, MISSOURI

When—between 1867 and 1874—James Eads threw his giant bridge across the Mississippi, Mark Twain predicted "the beginning of the end of the great age of steamboat navigation on the river"

As different railroads converged on the Mississippi and Missouri Rivers to take off across the rest of the continent, bridges sprang up to expedite the East-West traffic flow. The bridge at St. Louis, built by James B. Eads between 1867 and 1874, was the most costly and important of the early ones. Carriages and railroads traveled on separate levels sixty feet above the water. Revisiting St. Louis after the bridge had been built Mark Twain reviewed the melancholy and woeful sight of a half-dozen "sound-asleep steamboats" where once there had been a mile of wide-awake ones. "Remains of former steamboatmen told me," he wrote, " . . .that the bridge doesn't pay. Still, it can be no sufficient compensation to a corpse to know that the dynamite that laid him out was not as good quality as it had been supposed to be." Steamboating as Mark Twain remembered it was all but dead.

MARSHALL B. DAVIDSON
Life in America, 1951

ST. LOUIS

But what may have been lost in river traffic was more than compensated for in other directions, as buildings and institutions sprang up, at a great rate, in St. Louis

Entrance Shaw's Garden

Greenhouses Shaw's Garden

Mutile Ins. Bldg. Locust St.

Fourth St.

High School Olive Street

At the Waterworks.

The Elevator.

SCENES IN ST. LOUIS

St. Louis is ordained by the decrees of physical nature to become the great inland metropolis of this continent. It cannot escape the magnificence of its destiny. Greatness is the necessity of its position. New York may be the head, but St. Louis will be the heart of America. The stream of traffic which must flow through this mart will enrich it with alluvial deposits of gold. Its central location and facilities of communication unmistakably indicate the leading part which this city will take in the exchange and distribution of the products of the Mississippi Valley . . . . It is the geographical centre of a valley which embraces 1,200,000 square miles. In its course of 3,200 miles, the Mississippi borders on Missouri 470 miles. Of the 3,000 miles of the Missouri, 500 lie within the limits of our own State. St. Louis is mistress of more than 16,500 miles of river navigation. This metropolis, though in the infancy of its greatness, is already a large city. Its length is about eight miles, and its width three. Suburban residences, the outposts of the grand advance, are now stationed six or seven miles from the river.

ANSELM L. STRAUSS, ED.
The American City, 1968

Inland lifeline of the nation—highway for trade and travel —the river gave birth to a hundred towns and cities in ten states—some tiny hamlets, others giant sprawling cities

Mississippi begins in the lobby of a Memphis, Tennessee, hotel and extends south to the Gulf of Mexico. It is dotted with little towns concentric about the ghosts of the horses and mules once tethered to the hitch-rail enclosing the county courthouse and it might almost be said to have only two directions, north and south, since until a few years ago it was impossible to travel east or west in it unless you walked or rode one of the horses or mules. Even in the boy's early manhood, to reach by rail either of the adjacent county towns thirty miles away to the east or west, you had to travel ninety miles in three different directions on three different railroads. In the beginning it was virgin—to the west, along the Big River, the alluvial swamps threaded by black, almost motionless bayous and impenetrable with cane and buckvine and cypress and ash and oak and gum; to the east, the hardwood ridges and the prairies where the Appalachian Mountains died and buffalo grazed; to the south, the pine barrens and the moss-hung live oaks and the greater swamps, less of earth than water and lurking with alligators and water moccasins, where Louisiana in its time would begin.

WILLIAM FAULKNER

American Panorama, 1947

VICKSBURG, MISSISSIPPI

MEMPHIS, MISSISSIPPI

Along its banks lay virgin forests, alluvial swamps, quiet bayous, prairies of grazing buffalo—plantation homes in Louisiana and Mississippi built upon cotton and sugar profits

PLANTER'S HOUSE AND SUGAR PLANTATION, ON THE MISSISSIPPI

The whole of the steamboats of which you have an account did not perform voyages to New Orleans only, but to all points on the Mississippi, and other rivers which fall into it. I am certain that since the above date the number has increased, but to what extent I cannot at present say. When steamboats first plied between Shippingport and New Orleans, the cabin passage was a hundred dollars, and a hundred and fifty dollars on the upward voyage. In 1829, I went down to Natchez from Shippingport for twenty-five dollars, and ascended from New Orleans on board the Philadelphia, in the beginning of January 1830, for sixty dollars, having taken two state-rooms for my wife and myself. On that voyage we met with a trifling accident, which protracted it to fourteen days; the computed distance being, as mentioned above, 1650 miles, although the real distance is probably less. I do not remember to have spent a day without meeting with a steam-boat, and some days we met several. I might here be tempted to give you a description of one of these steamers of the western waters, but the picture having been often drawn by abler hands, I shall desist.

JOHN JAMES AUDUBON
American Scenery and Character, 1926

PLANTER'S HOUSE ON THE MISSISSIPPI

At many points along the snakelike course of the Mississippi, heavily laden steamboats on the river— at one time estimated to be well in the thousands . . .

Indeed there are solitary cabins of wood-cutters, who fix their dwellings on piles or blocks, raised above the inundation, who stay there to supply the steamboats with wood. In effect, to visit this very portion of the river in the autumn after the subsiding of the spring-floods, to see its dry banks, its clean sand-bars, and all traces of inundation gone, except its marks upon the trunks of the trees, one would have no suspicion of the existence of such swamp and overflow as it now exhibits.

TIMOTHY FLINT
*Recollections of
the Last Ten Years, 1826*

I suppose that St. Louis and New Orleans have not suffered materially by the change, but alas for the wood-yard man! He used to fringe the river all the way; his close-ranked merchandise stretched from the one city to the other, along the banks, and he sold uncountable cords of it every year for cash on the nail; but all the scattering boats that are left burn coal now and the seldomest spectacle on the Mississippi to-day is a wood-pile. Where now is the one wood-yard man.

MARK TWAIN
*Life on the
Mississippi, 1874*

STEAMER WOODING UP ON THE MISSISSIPPI

. . . Their high-pressure engines—gluttons for fuel—burning daily as much as thirty cords of wood, had to restock at least twice a day at wooding stations along the riverbanks

Negroes along the rivers are gorgeous romancers. They are full of stories of catfish as big as whales, of enormous snakes, and of incredible treasure finds. To the latter many look hopefully forward for the solution of all their difficulties in life. They put up with a miserable muddy existence year after year in the hope that floodwaters may bring some great prize which will enable them to satisfy all of their dreams. "Ole Man River" is for the colored children of his banks very much the measure of all things—he is fate, hope, and tragedy all in one. The most desirable job a river Negro can obtain is one on a boat which will take him to and from such legendary and inspiring river places as Cincinnati, St. Louis, Memphis, or New Orleans. The cook of a towboat on which I journeyed from Cairo to New Orleans was so proud of his position and his view of himself as a much traveled man that he could even speak of the sporty children of Beale Street as "dem niggahs." His lips curled scornfully about the "shiftless no-'count niggahs," who lived on the riverbanks waiting for flood riches and who "nevah got nuthin' but a mess o' catfish and a han'ful of ole boards."

THOMAS HART BENTON
An Artist in America, 1937

Throughout the vast regions of the South—where King Cotton reigned—the daily life of master and slave, the plantation system, and its effect, as an institution, on human freedom . . .

There were two other large plantations near him, in both of which the negroes were turned out to work at half-past three every morning—I might hear the bell ring for them—and frequently they were not stopped till nine o'clock at night, Saturday nights the same as any other. One of them belonged to a very religious lady, and on Sunday mornings at half-past nine she had her bell rung for Sunday school, and after Sunday school they had a meeting, and after dinner another religious service. Every negro on the plantation was obliged to attend all these exercises, and if they were not dressed clean they were whipped. They were never allowed to go off the plantation, and if they were caught speaking to a negro from any other place, they were whipped. They could all of them repeat the catechism, he believed, but they were the dullest, and laziest, and most sorrowful negroes he ever saw.

FREDERICK LAW OLMSTED

Seaboard Slave States, 1856

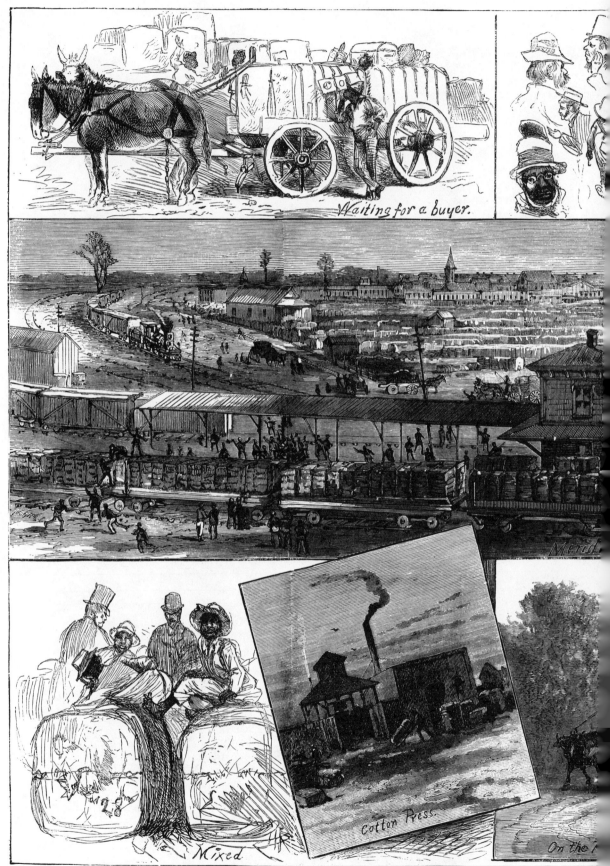

Waiting for a buyer.

Mixed

Cotton Press.

COTTON BLOCKADE, AT MERIDIAN, MISSISSIPPI

. . . varied little from state to state. In the days before improved agricultural equipment, the disgruntled labor force protested, setting up a blockade of rail shipments

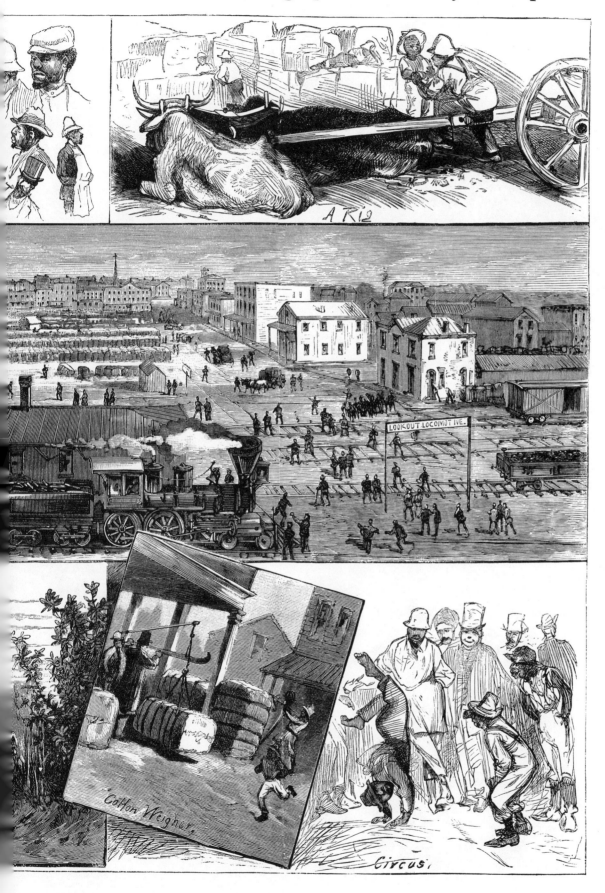

But what words shall describe the Mississippi, great father of rivers, who (praise be to Heaven) has no young children like him! An enormous ditch, sometimes two or three miles wide, running liquid mud, six miles an hour: its strong and frothy current choked and obstructed everywhere by huge logs and whole forest trees: now twining themselves together in great rafts, from the interstices of which a sedgy lazy foam works up, to float upon the water's top; now rolling past like monstrous bodies, their tangled roots showing like matted hair; now glancing singly by like giant leeches; and now writhing round and round in the vortex of some small whirlpool, like wounded snakes. The banks low, the trees dwarfish, the marshes swarming with frogs, the wretched cabins few and far apart, their inmates hollow-cheeked and pale, the weather very hot, mosquitoes penetrating into every crack and crevice of the boat, mud and slime on everything: nothing pleasant in its aspect, but the harmless lightning which flickers every night upon the dark horizon.

CHARLES DICKENS
American Notes, 1842

Typical of the great gentlemen of the lower South was John Hampden Randolph, who, in 1841 purchased a plantation in Iberville Parish, Louisiana—turning from cotton to sugar

In the moist, hot climate of the lower Mississippi sugar cane flourishes. What cotton has been to Alabama, sugar has been to Louisiana. Very early sugar mills appeared and sugar plantations were laid out. Neither the institution of slavery nor the plantation system required essential modification to fit the requirements of the crop. The pictures drawn herewith well represent the conditions of the old slave days, the drove of slaves—both men and women—the ubiquitous mules teams and carts, the broad open spaces, the simple mill and equipment for crushing and boiling, and the planter's house.

The Pageant of America, 1926

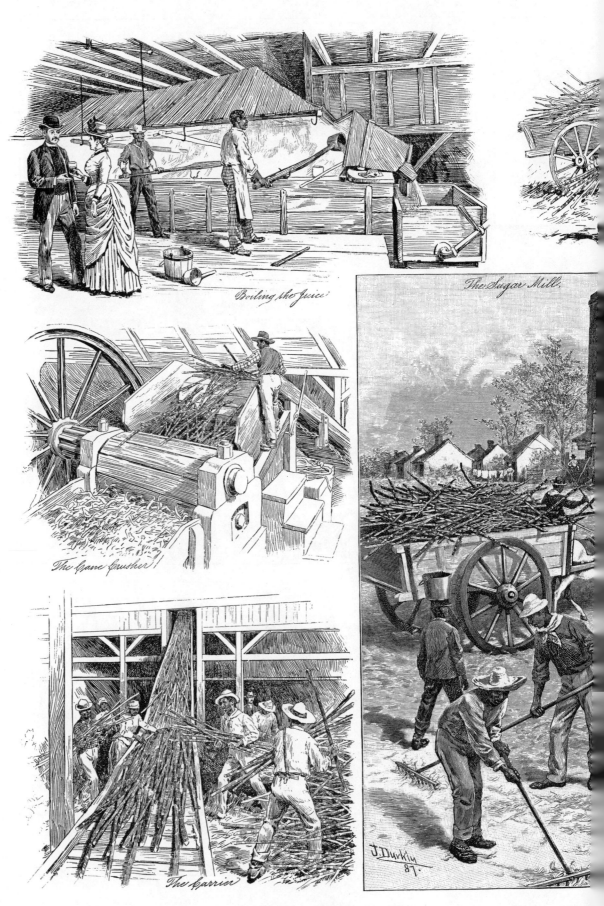

A LOUISIANA SUGAR PLANTATION

His land holdings increased to several thousand acres—his labor force from 23 to 195 slaves—becoming more profitable after the Civil War, as free Negro labor became available

A Sugar Cane Field

A Field Hand.

The Planters House.

White cotton fields and sugar plantations pushed westward into the black belt of Alabama, the lowlands of Mississippi and Louisiana, and on into the broad warm plains of Texas. With them went the negro and the plantation system. The new soil was fertile, cotton and sugar were profitable and labor scarce. Slavery which had seemed on the decline in the late eighteenth century sprang into new life. Even the ideal of aristocracy which had wavered in Jefferson's day was steadied by triumphant cotton and the expansion of negro slavery. Civilization in the heart of the South was based upon agriculture, and the planters, in the midst of smaller landholders, became a cultivated gentry worthy of the best traditions of aristocratic England. In their fine old homes moved a society out of which the crudities of the New World had been refined while much of its strength had been preserved. With dignity and courtesy they ruled the affairs of their local communities. How different from the hornyhanded folk north of the Ohio!

The Pageant of America, 1926

*Over two hundred miles upriver from New Orleans,
Baton Rouge—since 1849 the capital of Louisiana—its
deep-water port a rail hub and center of industrial activity*

Baton Rouge, capital and third largest city of Louisiana, overlooks the Mississippi River from Istrouma Bluff. It is a modern city bordered by great industrial plants and by tree-shaded reaches of the Capitol grounds. Residential streets are lined with oaks, elms, and magnolias. Here in 1719 the French built a fort to subdue the Indian tribes and gave it the name ("Istrouma" meaning "red stick" or in French, "baton rouge") derived from the reddened post that stood here to indicate the boundary between lands of two different tribes. Settlement was transferred, in 1763, along with other Louisiana territory ceded by the Treaty of Paris, to Great Britain, which made the port a point of origin for contraband commerce with Spanish Louisiana. During the American Revolution, the British garrison was defeated and forced to withdraw by the forces of Don Bernardo de Galvez, Spanish Governor of Louisiana, at the First Battle of Baton Rouge, September 21, 1779. The city remained under Spanish rule until American-born residents of the surrounding parishes rebelled and captured the fort— also the settlement that had grown around it—at the Second Battle of Baton Rouge, September 23, 1810. They raised the "Bonnie Blue Flag" of the West Florida Republic. In 1817 the town of Baton Rouge was incorporated and in 1849 it became the capital city.

The American Guide, 1949

BATON ROUGE, ON THE MISSISSIPPI

UNLOADING MILITARY STORES, BATON ROUGE LEVEE

Settled by "Cajuns"—Acadians who emigrated from French-Canada generations ago—the bayou country is formed of extensive lowlands bordering the Mississippi delta area

SOUTHWEST PASS

For miles before you reach the passes, you observe the muddy Mississippi water in great masses, rolling and tumbling unmingled with the briny blue sea. Gradually the dull hue assumes supremacy, and at last you are greeted by a simple object of beauty and practical interest, which has been erected by human hands. Rising up from the interminable level is a solitary light-house, built at the entrance of the Southwest Pass. This structure is the sentinel on guard—an immovable point, from the bearings of which the pilot is enabled to bring his ship to safe harbor. Just inside the Northeast Pass is a huge mud-bank, known as the Balize. Long years ago people, mostly of Spanish origin, who found it irksome to live under the restraints of settled communities, made a home at the Balize, tempted by the isolation, the abundance of game, and the occasional reward for acting as pilots or wreckers. Within a half century the growing demands of commerce have changed the rude huts of the settlement into pleasant residences.

T. B. THORPE
Picturesque America, 1872

A BAYOU OF THE MISSISSIPPI

*Black smoke belching from twin stacks of riverboats—
flags flying at jack staff—gang planks in the ready position
as passengers, heavily laden, scampered aboard*

It was always the custom for the boats to leave New Orleans between four and five o'clock in the afternoon. From three o'clock onward they would be burning rosin and pitch-pine (the sign of preparation), and so one had the picturesque spectacle of a rank, some two or three miles long, of tall, ascending columns of coal-black smoke; a colonnade which supported a sable roof of the same smoke blended together and spreading abroad over the city. Every outward-bound boat had its flag flying at the jack-staff, and sometimes a duplicate on the verge-staff astern. Two or three miles of mates were commanding and swearing with more than usual emphasis: countless processions of freight barrels and boxes were spinning, athwart the levee and flying abroad the stage-planks; belated passengers were dodging and skipping among these frantic things, hoping to reach the forecastle companionway alive, but having their doubts about it; women with reticules and bandboxes were trying to keep up with husbands freighted with carpet sacks and crying babies, and making a failure of it by losing their heads in the whirl and roar and general distraction; drays and baggage-vans were clattering hither and thither in a wild hurry, every now and then getting blocked and jammed together, and then . . .

ARRIVALS AT THE LEVEE, NEW ORLEANS

Such was the scene of helter-skelter confusion with every steamboat's departure—the chaos and turmoil reaching a crescendo of excitement as ''last bells'' clanged their final warning

LEVEE AT JACKSON SQUARE, NEW ORLEANS

. . . during ten seconds one could not see them for the profanity, except vaguely and dimly; every windlass connected with every forehatch from one end of that long array of steamboats to the other, was keeping up a deafening whizz and whir, lowering freight into the hold, and the half-naked crews of perspiring Negroes that worked them were roaring such songs as ''De Las' Sack! De Las' Sack!''—inspired to unimaginable exaltation by the chaos of turmoil and racket that was driving everybody else mad. By this time the hurricane and boiler decks of the steamers would be packed black with passengers. The ''last bells'' would begin to clang, all down the line, and then the powwow seemed to double; in a moment or two the final warning came—a simultaneous din of Chinese gongs, with the cry, ''All dat ain't goin', please to git asho'!''—and behold the powwow quadrupled! People came swarming ashore, overturning excited stragglers that were trying to swarm aboard. One more moment later a long array of stage-planks was being hauled in, each with its customary latest passenger clinging to the end of it with teeth, nails, and everything else, and the customary latest procrastinator making a wild spring shoreward over his head.

MARK TWAIN
The Gilded Age, 1873

COTTON BALES AND COTTON PRESS, NEW ORLEANS

Wharves of the Queen City of the South are lined with a congeries of keelboats, barges, river steamboats jostling with ocean-going schooners, five abreast at quayside

One hundred miles from the mouth of the Mississippi, and something more than a thousand from the mouth of the Ohio, just below a sharp point of the river is situated on its east bank, the city of New Orleans, the great commercial capital of the Mississippi valley. The position for a commercial city is unrivalled, I believe, by any one in the world. At a proper distance from the Gulf of Mexico,—on the banks of a stream which may be said almost to water a world,—but a little distance from Lake Ponchartrain, and connected with it by a navigable canal,—the immense alluvion contiguous to it—penetrated in all directions either by *Bayous* formed by nature, or canals which cost little more trouble in the making, than ditches,—steamboats visiting it from fifty different shores,—possessing the immediate agriculture of its own state, the richest in America, and as rich as any in the world, with the continually increasing agriculture of the upper country, its position far surpasses that of New York itself. It has one dreary drawback—the insalubrity of its situation. Could the immense swamps between it and the bluffs be drained, and the improvements commenced in the city completed; in short, could its atmosphere ever become a dry one, it would soon leave the greatest cities of the Union behind.

TIMOTHY FLINT
*Recollections of the
Last Ten Years, 1826*

THE MISSISSIPPI AT NEW ORLEANS

A "CREVASSE" ON THE MISSISSIPPI

From New Orleans to the delta . . . low-lying banks, sandbars, and marshes mark the channel to the sea—ideal habitat for migratory wildfowl—before reaching South Pass and the Gulf

TOWING ON THE MISSISSIPPI, FROM BELIZE TO NEW ORLEANS

That trip we went to Grand Gulf, from New Orleans, in four days (three hundred and forty miles); the *Eclipse* and *Shotwell* did it in one. We were nine days out, in the chute of 63 (seven hundred miles); the *Eclipse* and *Shotwell* went there in two days. Something over a generation ago, a boat called the *J.M. White* went from New Orleans to Cairo in three days, six hours, and forty-four minutes. In 1853 the *Eclipse* made the same trip in three days, three hours, and twenty minutes. In 1870 the *R.E. Lee* did it in three days and *one* hour. This last is called the fastest trip on record. I will try to show that it was not. For this reason: the distance between New Orleans and Cairo, when the *J.M. White* ran it, was about eleven hundred and six miles; consequently her average speed was a trifle over fourteen miles per hour. In the *Eclipse's* day the distance between the two ports had become reduced to one thousand and eighty miles; consequently her average speed was a shade under fourteen and three-eights miles per hour. In the *R.E. Lee's* time the distance had diminished to about one thousand and thirty miles; consequently her average was about fourteen and one-eighth miles per hour. Therefore the *Eclipse's* was conspicuously the fastest time that has ever been made.

MARK TWAIN

Life on the Mississippi, 1874

THE BELIZE, MOUTH OF THE MISSISSIPPI

The lush, semitropical climate of Louisiana—especially in its flooded swamplands—produces luxuriant forests where cypress trees and Spanish moss flourish

CYPRESS SWAMP

The first grand tree-development of the "swamps" is the tall and ghostly cypress. It flourishes in our semitropical climate of the South, being nourished by warmth, water, and the richest possible soil. The Louisiana product finds a rival in Florida; and in both places this remarkable tree is perfect in growth, often reaching the height of one hundred and thirty feet. The base of the trunk, generally covered with ooze and mud, conceals the formidable "spikes," called "knees," which spring up from the roots. These excrescences, when young, are sharp and formidable weapons, and, young or old, are nearly as hard as steel. To travel in safety through a flooded cypress-swamp on horseback, the greatest care must be taken to avoid the concealed cypress-knees; for, if your generous steed, while floundering in the soft mud, settles down upon one of them, he may never recover from the injury. The bark of the tree is spongy and fibrous; and the trunk of the tree oftens attains fifty or sixty feet without a branch. The foliage, as seen from below, is as soft as green silken fringe, and strangely beautiful and delicate, when contrasted with the tree itself and the gloomy, repulsive place of its nativity. The wood, though light and soft, is of extraordinary durability. It has been asserted, that cypress-trees which have been buried a thousand years under the solid but always damp earth, now retain every quality of the most perfect wood. At the root of the cypress the palmetto flourishes in vigor; and its intensely green spear-like foliage adds to the variety of the vegetable productions in the forest solitudes.

T. B. THORPE

Picturesque America 1872

MOSS GATHERING

Comparatively within a few years, the Spanish moss has become important as an article of commerce, for, when plucked from the trees, from which it is easily separated, and then thoroughly "cured" and threshed of its delicate integuments of bark and leaves, it is found that though the long, thready moss is a delicate fiber, as black as jet, and almost as thick as horsehair, which it strikingly resembles. For the stuffing of mattresses and cushions it is valuable, and the increasing demand for it has already opened a new field of enterprise among the denizens of the swamp.

T. B. THORPE

Picturesque America,

Over Plains & Prairies
... Ever Westward

OVERLAND MAIL COACH . . .

ATCHISON . . . DENVER CITY . . .

THE FIRST SPIKE . . .CROSSING

THE PLAINS . . . CAMP AT NIGHT

. . . PILGRIMS ON THE PLAINS . . .

COMPLETION OF THE UNION

PACIFIC RAILROAD . . . .PROMONTORY

POINT . . . DENVER AND RIO GRANDE

RAILROAD . . . CENTRAL PACIFIC

RAILROAD . . . TEN MILE CANYON . . .

GIANT'S GAP . . . AMERICAN RIVER . . .

DONNER LAKE . . . JOINING OF THE RAILS

. . . EN ROUTE BY RAIL . . . SCENES

ON AN IMMIGRANT TRAIN . . . AT

THE RAILROAD STATION . . . RED

RIVER . . . FARGO . . . CROW VILLAGE

CORN FARMING . . . CATTLE, ABILENE

. . . TEXAS SHEEP . . . THE ROUND-UP

COWBOYS ON THE PLAINS . . . BUFFALO

BULLS . . . HORSE AUCTION . . . CATTLE

COUNTRY . . . PRAIRIE FARM SKETCHES

Over Plains & Prairies
... Ever Westward

A TEXAN PONY

EVER SINCE THE EARLY YEARS OF THE nineteenth century, explorers had been venturing out beyond the Mississippi into the region now called the Great Plains. Their reports were not often favorable. Zebulon Pike, who traveled into the plains seeking the source of the Mississippi, declared the region to be "incapable of cultivation"; and Major Stephen H. Long, who followed the Platte River into Nebraska, gave the region a name it would bear for much of the century, "The Great American Desert."

Exploration by the white man began only in the early nineteenth century, with the appearance of French and, later, American fur trappers. As the fur trade grew, mountaineers blazed trails to the West. Jedediah Smith carved out the Overland Trail and demonstrated that it was possible to cross the mountains with wagons. William Becknell established the Santa Fe trail in 1821. By 1841, the first overland party was bound for California. These early pioneers, however, were entering a land that the federal government had reserved by treaty for the Indians, both for those native to the plains and for those who had been moved from their lands east of the Mississippi. In the 1830s and 1840s Plains Indians signed away much of their land, in return for outright payments in cash or goods, stipends, and guarantees of reserved land elsewhere.

Eventually sales and treaties gave way to bloody confrontation, as diseases brought by whites and the flight of the buffalo, caused by the settlers' frequent overland crossings, made life for the Indians unbearable. By the 1850s Indians began to actively harass white settlers and wagon trains, and the first of many legendary figures of the plains—the Warrior and the Indian Fighter—were born. In 1862, starvation among the Santee Dakotas led to serious warfare; hundreds of settlers were massacred and many towns were destroyed. Retaliation was swift and violent. In 1876, Custer's defeat by the Cheyenne and Sioux at Little Bighorn aroused a national fury. The Indians, decimated and starving and hopelessly outnumbered, faced the final slaughter. In 1881 Sitting Bull finally surrendered; the bloody saga was over.

Violence was everywhere in the Great Plains. The Indian wars raged for fifty years; and settlers fought equally bloody battles among themselves. Cattlemen and farmers fought bitterly over use of the land. Disputes over slavery led to outrageous acts of terrorism, even before the Civil War broke out. "Bleeding Kansas" was a battleground for partisans on both sides, before and during the war. After the war, guerilla action continued as attacks on railroads, stagecoaches, and banks were mounted by such legendary outlaws as Jessie James and the Dalton Boys.

Because the land of the Great Plains, and especially the southern parts of it, had never seemed hospitable to farming, many settlers had turned to grazing. But their great distance from the Eastern markets limited profits. By 1867, however, railroads reached out from St. Louis and across Missouri and Iowa, Kansas and Nebraska. The great cattle drives began. At Abiline, Kansas cattle pens were built along the tracks of the Kansas Pacific Railroad. And up from Texas, along the famous Shawnee and Chisholm trails, tens of thousands of cattle were driven along a route that took as long as forty days to travel. It was a rugged journey. Beset by Indian marauders and cattle rustlers, the men driving the great herds carved out their own legend in the harsh plains. By 1871 more than six hundred thousand head of cattle were moving yearly through Abiline. Elsewhere in the plains, the Sante Fe, Union Pacific, and Northern Pacific established other centers. These centers became the first cities of the Plains: Abiline, Wichita, Great Bend, Ellsworth, and Dodge City in Kansas; Ogallala in Nebraska; and Bismark in North Dakota.

While cattle herds were driven north and shipped east, another herd was being slaughtered—the buffalo. The Indians were dependent on this great beast for their very existence: they ate its meat and used its hide for clothing and shelter. It was clear that if deprived of the buffalo, the Indian would disappear. It became federal, state, and territorial policy to rid the plains of buffalo. Other pressures to kill the buffalo existed as well. Cattlemen wanted lands for grazing. The railroads wanted to encourage settlement by ranchers and farmers. Sportsmen simply wanted to hunt. So, by the 1870s, the slaughter of the buffalo became epic. Hundreds of thousands were killed every year, and by 1880 very few were left.

As the land was cleared of buffalo and Indians, and as the railroad spanned the continent, the population of the Great Plains soared. The number of farms doubled. Towns grew, and grew rowdier. Dodge City, prospering first from outfitting buffalo hunters and then from the railroads, became known as "Hell on the Plains," and its Front Street, Alhambra Saloon, Dodge City Opera, and Boot Hill became legends; as did its lawmen, Wyatt Earp and Bat and Jim Masterson.

There were many ways through the West: the Overland and Santa Fe and Chisholm and Shawnee trails; the Union Pacific, Northern Pacific, and the Santa Fe railroads; but the grandest, the busiest, was the Big Muddy—the "Wide Missouri." Long before the trails were blazed and the tracks laid, this river and its branches were moving men toward and through the West. The Missouri travels a course almost twenty-five hundred miles long, and with its branches it touches six of the seven plains states. A mighty and brutal river, it carries loam, marl, gravel, and sand. Floating islands of debris, and sandbars, and shifting currents make travel treacherous. Spring flooding and sudden, swift changes in its own bed maroon and often destroy whole towns. The Missouri could never be wholly tamed, but for some forty years, beginning in the 1840s, steamboats traveled its waters in a golden age of river commerce.

The Missouri was and is still a great travelway, but it has also nourished the Great Plains. The river itself and its tributaries flow through one of the most fertile areas on earth—the endless corn fields of Iowa and the wheat fields of Kansas, Nebraska, and North Dakota. To the farmers and the cattlemen who fought the river, the elements, the Indians, the outlaws, and each other, this land, "incapable of cultivation," has yielded an endless bounty.

"Westward the course of the empire takes its way"—the slogan stresses the need for news between the distant West and the rest of the nation, after the discovery of gold in California . . .

Prior to the discovery of gold in California there was no regular line of communication between the eastern United States and its Pacific territory. The steamers that sailed around the Horn constituted a very slow and intermittent contact. As a result of being cut off from the centers of trade and government Californians stirred up a great deal of agitation during the 40's and 50's. The governor and legislature pushed a vigorous program, not only for the building of railroads but for the regular schedule of an overland mail service to supplement the semi-monthly mails that arrived by slow boat. A monster petition bearing 75,000 signatures was sent to Washington in 1856, resulting in Congress' appropriation of $550,000 for three wagon roads. Finally, in 1857 a bill was passed authorizing a line "from such point on the Mississippi River as the contractors may select, to San Francisco in the State of California, for six years—cost not to exceed $300,000 per annum for a semi-monthly service, $450,000 for weekly and $600,000 for a semi-weekly service." The Post Office advertised for bids as prescribed and received nine, the successful bidders John Butterfield, William Fargo and others, all experienced in the express business. Postmaster Brown, from Tennessee, insisted upon a southerly route in spite of angry protests from many sections of the north. The final route formed a roundabout semi-circle from St. Louis, via El Paso and Fort Yuma, a distance of 2800 miles, favored over the northerly route via Salt Lake City.

CLARENCE P. HORNUNG

Wheels Across America,
1959

BUTTERFIELD'S OVERLAND MAIL, FROM SAN FRANCISCO FOR THE EAST

OVERLAND MAIL COACH LEAVING ATCHISON, KANSAS

. . . resulting, in 1858, in the inauguration of the overland stagecoach lines for delivery of mail, express matter, and passenger service—two years before the pony express

OVERLAND COACH OFFICE, DENVER, COLORADO

. . . On September 16, 1857, service was inaugurated on both east and western terminals, after a year of energetic preparations during which hundreds of way stations were built, wells sunk for water, teams procured and drivers trained. The first trips carrying only mail and papers, arrived ahead of the 25 day schedule. Both in St. Louis and San Francisco, the opening of the line was the occasion of much rejoicing—long parades, brass bands, salutes and unbridled jubilation were the order of the day. The famous Concord coaches, sturdily built spring wagons, stood up remarkably well under the continuous strain of the long journey. At first they carried few passengers but later on they were enlarged to accommodate up to nine inside and as many who dared cling to the outside seats were carried on top. Teams of four to six mustangs—"wild as deer"—sped the coaches over the usual 10 to 15 miles between stations. The fare from St. Louis was $100 to the east, $200 for the western trip, and meals were extra.

CLARENCE P. HORNUNG
Wheels Across America,
1959

EASTERN TERMINUS OF THE
OVERLAND ROUTE, ATCHISON

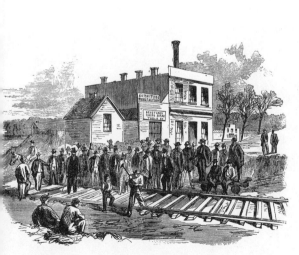

DRIVING THE FIRST SPIKE, ON
THE ATCHISON AND PIKE'S PEAK R.R.

"It is our manifest destiny to overspread and possess the whole of the continent which Providence has given us for the great experiment of liberty," said John O'Sullivan, in 1845

. . . our manifest destiny is to overspread and to possess the whole of the continent which Providence has given us for the development of the great experiment of liberty and federated self-government entrusted to us.

JOHN LOUIS O'SULLIVAN
New York Morning News,
December 27, 1845

PILGRIMS ON THE PLAINS

Not to-day, nor to-morrow, but this government is to last, I trust, forever; we may at least hope it will endure until the wave of population, cultivation, and intelligence shall have washed the Rocky Mountains and mingled with the Pacific. And may we not also hope that the day will arrive when the improvements and comforts to social life shall spread over the vast area of the continent? . . . It is a peculiar delight to me to look forward to the proud and happy period, distant as it may be, when circulation and association between the Atlantic and Pacific and the Mexican Gulf shall be as free and perfect as they are at this moment in England or in any other country of the globe.

HENRY CLAY
Speech of January 31, 1824

THE OLD BONE MAN OF THE PLAINS

The westward way pointed far beyond the reaches of the Mississippi—with crossings by long caravans of "prairie schooners"—handcart brigades of the Mormons, or by shank's mare

ARMY TRAIN CROSSING THE PLAINS

The *untransacted* destiny of the American people is to subdue the continent—to rush over this vast field to the Pacific Ocean—to animate the many hundreds of millions of its people, to cheer them upward . . . . to agitate these herculean masses—to establish a new order in human affairs . . . to regenerate the superannuated nations—to stir up the sleep of a hundred centuries—to teach old nations a new civilization—to confirm the destiny of the human race—to carry the career of mankind to its culminating point—to perfect science—to emblazon history with the conquest of peace—to shed a new and resplendent glory upon mankind—to unite the world in one social family.

WILLIAM GILPIN

A published letter, 1846

AROUND THE CAMPFIRE AT NIGHT

Journalists like John Soule and Horace Greeley, sensing the surging expansionist movement urged: "Go west, young man, and grow up with the country." The pressure of newspaper publicity . . .

On the morning of May 10, 1869, Hon. Leland Stanford, Governor of California and President of the Central Pacific, accompanied by Messrs. Huntington, Hopkins Crocker and trainloads of California's distinguished citizens, arrived from the west. During the forenoon Vice President T. C. Durant and Directors John R. Duff and Sidney Dillon and Consulting Engineer Silas A. Seymour of the Union Pacific, with other prominent men, including a delegation of Mormons from Salt Lake City, came in on a train from the east. The National Government was represented by a detachment of "regulars" from Fort Douglass, Utah, accompanied by a band, and 600 others, including Chinese, Mexicans, Indians, half-breeds, negroes and laborers, suggesting an air of cosmopolitanism, all gathered around the open space where the tracks were to be joined. The Chinese laid the rails from the west end, and the Irish laborers laid them from the east end, until they met and joined.

GREENVILLE M. DODGE
How We Built the Union Pacific Railway, 1869

What was it the Engines said,
Pilots touching, head to head
Facing on a single track,
Half a world behind each back?

You brag of the East! You do?
Why, I bring the East to you!
All the Orient, all Cathay,
Find through me the shortest way;
And the sun you follow here
Rises in my hemisphere!

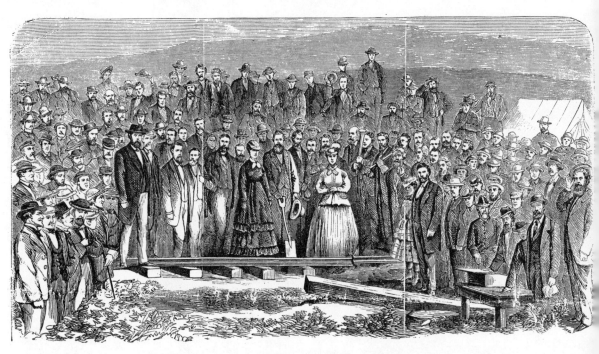

THE MEETING OF THE RAILS, PROMONTORY POINT, UTAH

THE GREAT LOOP OF THE DENVER AND RIO GRANDE R.R.

Colloquy by
BRET HARTE

. . . led to the Pacific Railroad Act of 1862—signed by President Lincoln during the Civil War crisis—to help speed army trains and forge a union of East and West

CENTRAL PACIFIC R.R., NEAR THE AMERICAN RIVER

DONNER LAKE

Each day taught us lessons by which we profited for the next, and our advances and improvements in the art of railway construction were marked by the progress of the work, forty miles of track having been laid in 1865, 260 in 1866, 240 in 1867, including the ascent to the summit of the Rocky mountains, at an elevation of 8235 feet above the ocean; and during 1868 and to May 10, 1869, 555 miles all exclusive of side and temporary tracks, of which over 180 miles were built in addition. The first grading was done in the autumn of 1864, and the first rail laid in July, 1865. When you look back to the beginning at the Missouri river, with no railroad communication from the east, and 500 miles of the country in advance without timber, fuel or any material whatever from which to build or maintain a road, except the sand for the bare roadbed itself with everything to be transported, and that by teams or at best by steamboats, for hundreds and thousands of miles; everything to be created, with labor scarce and high, you can all look back upon the work with satisfaction and ask, under such circumstances, could we have done more or better? The country is evidently satisfied that you accomplish wonders and have achieved a work that will be a monument to your energy, your ability, and to your devotion to the enterprise through all its gloomy as well as its bright periods; for it is notorious that, notwithstanding the aid of the Government, there was so little faith in the enterprise that its dark days—when your private fortunes and your all was staked on the success of the project—far exceeded those of sunshine, faith and confidence.

GREENVILLE M. DODGE
*How We Built the Union
Pacific Railway, 1869*

CENTRAL PACIFIC R.R., TEN-MILE CANYON, NEVADA

LABORERS, CENTRAL PACIFIC R.R.

GIANT'S GAP, CENTRAL PACIFIC R.R.

As Appomattox had reunited the North and South—
Promontary Point had joined the East and West—
a continent united—"one and indivisible"

I remember that the parties going to Salt Lake crossed the Wasatch Mountain on sledges and that the snow covered the tops of the telegraph poles. We all knew and appreciated that the task we had laid out would require the greatest energy on the part of all hands. About April 1st, therefore, I went on to the plains myself and started our construction forces, remaining the whole summer between Laramie and the Humboldt Mountains. I was surprised at the rapidity with which the work was carried forward. Winter caught us in the Wasatch Mountains, but we kept on grading our road and laying our track in the snow and ice, at a tremendous cost. I estimated for the company that the extra cost of thus forcing the work during that summer and winter was over ten million dollars, but the instructions I received were to go on, no matter what the cost. Spring found us with the track to Ogden, and by May 1st we had reached Promontory, five hundred and thirty-four miles west of our starting point twelve months before. Work on our line was opened to Humboldt Wells, making in the year a grading of seven hundred and fifty-four miles of line.

GREENVILLE M. DODGE

How We Built the Union Pacific Railway, 1869

THE LINKING OF EAST AND WEST . . . COMPLETION OF THE RAILS, MAY 10, 1869

The Golden Spike ceremony symbolizing the spanning of the continent, in 1869, brought the Union Pacific eastward, and the Central Pacific westward to join rails

The great Pacific railway,
  For California hail!
Bring on the locomotive,
  Lay down the iron rail;
Across the rolling prairies
  By steam we're bound
  to go,
The railroad cars are
  coming, humming
  Through New Mexico,
The railroad cars are
  coming, humming
  Through New Mexico.

The little dogs in dog-town
  Will wag each little tail;
They'll think that
  something's coming
  A-riding on a rail.
The rattle-snake will show
  its fangs,
  The owl tu-whit,
  tu-who,
The railroad cars are
  coming, humming
  Through New Mexico,
The railroad cars are
  coming, humming
  Through New Mexico.

CARL SANDBURG
*The Railroad Cars
Are Coming*

In 1882, the Southern Pacific in the Southwest extended its lines, forming a through passage from New Orleans to San Francisco. In 1883, the Northwest was joined from St. Paul to Portland

Immigrants reached the United States in extraordinary numbers during the early and mid '80's. In the fiscal year ending June 30, 1882, nearly 800,000 persons had arrived, about 35 percent of whom were English-speaking. England, Ireland, Scotland sent nearly 180,000; Canada over 98,000. Next in number were the Germans—nearly a quarter of a million. Sweden was represented with about 64,000; Norway with over 29,000; the Celestial Kingdom sent nearly 40,000; Italy over 32,000. All were said to be of excellent average character and many arrived, as *Harper's Weekly,* February 10, 1883, said: "with well-defined plans as to their places of destination, and for the most part provided with the railway tickets for their journey inland." Agents for the various railroads immediately took charge of these groups, placing the women and children—"with their natural protectors, if they have any"—in separate cars; keeping the "rougher persons" by themselves. A contemporary account says:

A BREAKDOWN ON THE ROAD

THE "MODERN SHIP OF THE PLAINS"

As railroads crisscrossed the nation in a network of trunk lines and branches to serve the ever wider areas, thousands of immigrants and travelers crossed the plains

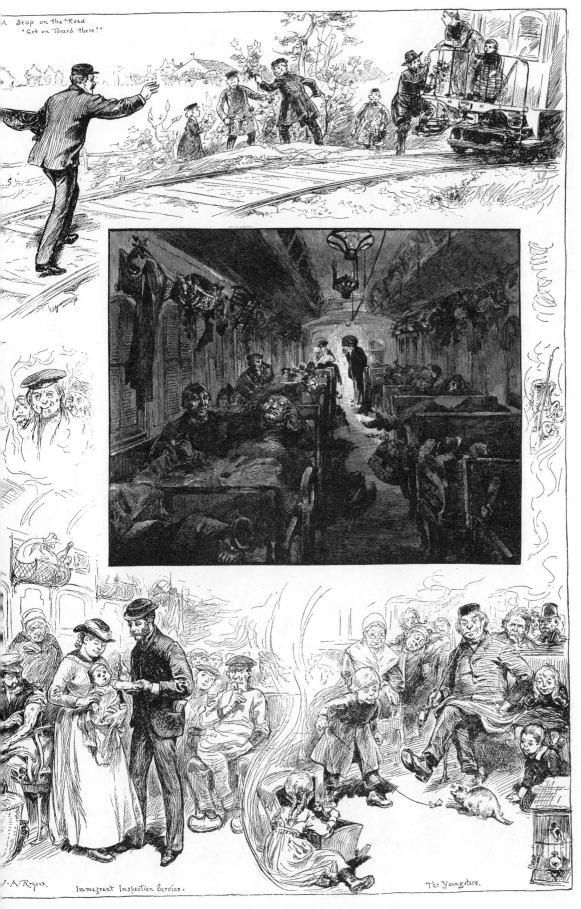

ABOARD AN IMMIGRANT TRAIN—WESTWARD BOUND

"At the start the cars are rude but cleanly. Plenty of fresh water is supplied. Some effort is made, too, to keep the air fresh and the car decent, but this is very difficult. . . . Pipes are lighted; meals are spread in which sausage, garlic and sauerkraut form prominent elements, and the mingled odors combine with the smoke of cheap tobacco to render the cars insupportable . . . . When the train stops, laden with its miscellaneous freight, the adults are glad to alight; the children rush eagerly about gathering the oddest mementoes of their journey. Occasionally a kitten is captured to the delight of the whole car-load . . . . It is petted, fed, put to sleep in dinner pails, and rarely abused." Before arrival at Chicago —which was the main point of distribution —sanitary inspectors came aboard the emigrant trains, conducting a very thorough inspection, prin-cipally with reference to smallpox. These men were under the direction of the National Board of Health. They inquired as to the general condition of the immigrants, then as to the date of vaccination, and its effectiveness. At Castle Garden, in New York—be-tween the arrival of the steamship and the evening departure of the West-bound trains—the colorful array of foreign costumes was described in *Frank Leslie's Illustrated Newspaper,* May 1, 1880: "The quaint costumes of Danish and German vil-lages, the rich colors of Connemara cloaks, the hues of the beribboned lassies from many climes, blend in glowing contrasts, while the immigrants sit or sprawl in indolent non-chalance in the Castle Garden rotunda."

CLARENCE P. HORNUNG
Wheels Across America, 1959

The railroads bound distant and diverse regions together—travel increased, building towns and creating new markets, exerting a unifying influence on our national life

Everywhere, the early railways acted like magnets; they drew people—idlers and busy alike—to the depot. From sleepy towns to quick-paced cities, the railway station could usually be counted on as the place where interesting things would be happening. The steam locomotives were exciting enough; and the welcomes to people arriving—the farewells to those departing—on a journey, were as good as a gossip column to keep one informed on the town's doings. Judge Gillis who, in 1835, took his first train ride behind the *"DeWitt Clinton,"* left additional notes on his experience. "The incidents off the train were quite as striking as those on the train; everybody, together with his wife and all his children, came from a distance with all kinds of conveyances, and being as ignorant of what was coming as their horses, drove as near as they could get, only looking for the best position to get a view of the train. As it approached, the horses took fright and wheeled, upsetting buggies, carriages, and wagons . . . and it is not now positively known in some of them have stopped yet." Now, around the seventies, the horses were less excitable, but the depot as a focus of local interest held an undiminished charm . . .

THE WAITING ROOM AT A COUNTRY DEPOT

THE RUSH FOR THE COUNTRY

Every town—even tiny hamlets on branch spurs—had its railroad depot, a new social center where arrivals and departures crammed waiting rooms with people and baggage

TRIALS OF THE BAGGAGE MASTER

. . . The old, bulging "balloon" or "diamond" shaped smokestacks were still in use, on locomotives during the Reconstruction era. Never designed for ornament, they served the utilitarian purpose of catching sparks and cinders from the wood-burning engines. When coal succeeded the use of wood as fuel, smokestacks were modified into a straight and narrow shape. Train conductors wore ordinary clothes and their attempts to collect fares were often resented by inexperienced travelers. A suspicion-ridden Senator from the West, on his first train journey, punched the conductor who tried to take his ticket. The Senator was determined not to be cheated by a railway "sharper." Soon, train employees were required to wear uniforms.

CLARENCE P. HORNUNG
Wheels Across America, 1959

HOME FOR THE HOLIDAYS

In the northern plains regions of the Dakota and Minnesota Territories—along the headwaters of the Mississippi, Missouri, Red, Platte, and Yellowstone rivers . . .

Out where the hand-clasp's a little stronger,
Out where the smile dwells a little longer,
  That's where the West begins;
Out where the sun is a little brighter,
Where the snows that fall are a trifle whiter,
Where the bonds of home are a wee bit tighter,
  That's where the West begins.

Out where the skies are a little bluer,
Out where friendship's a little truer,
  That's where the West begins;
Out where a fresher breeze is blowing,
Where there's laughter in every streamlet flowing,
Where there's more of reaping and less of sowing,
  That's where the West begins.

Out where the world is in the making,
Where fewer hearts in despair are aching,
  That's where the West begins;
Where there's more of singing and less of sighing,
Where there's more of giving and less of buying,
And a man makes friends without half trying—
  That's where the West begins.

ARTHUR CHAPMAN
Out Where the West Begins, 1911

RED RIVER, DAKOTA

THE HEAD OF NAVIGATION, RED RIVER, FARGO, DAKOTA

. . . fur traders and homesteaders learned to co-exist with natives of many tribes—the Assiniboin, Sioux, Mandan, Blackfeet, Dakota, Crow, and Cheyennes

LITTLE CROW VILLAGE, ON THE MISSISSIPPI

We've reached land of desert sweet,
Where nothing grows for man to eat,
The wind it blows with feverish heat
Across the plains so hard to beat.

We've reached the land of hills and
  stones
Where all is strewn with buffalo bones.
O buffalo bones, bleached buffalo
  bones,
I seem to hear your sighs and moans.

We have no wheat, we have no oats,
We have no corn to feed out shoats;
Our chickens are so very poor
They beg for crumbs outside the door.

Refrain:
O Dakota land, sweet Dakota land,
As on thy fiery soil I stand,
I look across the plains,
And wonder why it never rains,
Till Gabriel blows his trumpet sound
And says the rain's just gone around.

CARL SANDBURG
Dakota Land

INDIAN VILLAGE, DAKOTA

Throughout the Midwest, limitless prairie lands proved ideal for growing wheat, grains, and especially corn in Illinois, Indiana, Iowa, Kansas, and Missouri . . .

Corn is the greatest of all American crops; it grows in every state and in both value and production it outranks wheat, oats, rice, and rye combined. Glance at a Department of Agriculture map, showing the total American acreage of corn, with a black dot for every thousand acres. Parts of the map look like the ink blot tests used in psychiatry. The central puddle is Iowa—Iowa is so solid with black that you cannot see where the state begins or ends. Then smears and blobs drip over into adjacent areas, particularly in Nebraska and Illinois. Corn is everything in Iowa; it is eggs, milk, breakfast cereals, cattle, meal, chemicals, syrup, starch, liquor, and pork. But the chief thing to know about it is that it is not corn. It is hogs. The "corn-hog ratio," which can be worked out by a child on a blackboard, dominates corn as the formula $E = mc^2$ dominates the production of atomic energy. Corn grows on 11 million acres in Iowa, but only an infinitesimal fraction of these produce corn to be eaten as corn—in the shape of corn on the cob, popcorn or sweet corn. The enormous preponderance of production goes to "field corn," viz., corn fed to animals—chiefly hogs. Corn is not a corn problem at all. It is a pork problem and to some extent a beef and poultry problem.

JOHN GUNTHER
Inside U.S.A., 1937

PLANTING CORN.

BRE

FARM GANG.

SUNDAY IN "BURR OAK" GROVE.

A LARGE FARM IN THE WEST . . .

. . . the corn harvest, as autumn touched the long leaves with brown, called for large work gangs and teams of powerful oxen, used for heavy hauling in all seasons

CULTIVATING CORN.

HEDGE GANG.

The westward movement recovered momentum after the hard times of 1837-41. New Englanders, who a generation before had settled the interior of New York and Ohio, now pressed into the smaller prairies of Indiana and Illinois, where the tough sod taxed their strength but repaid it with bountiful crops of grain; where shoulder-high prairie grass afforded rich pasturage for cattle, and groves of buckeye, oak, walnut, and hickory furnished wood and timber. A favorite objective for Yankee settlement was southern Michigan, a rolling country of "oak openings," where stately trees stood well spaced as in a park. Others were hewing farms from the forests of southern Wisconsin, and venturing across the Mississippi into land vacated by Black Hawk's warriors—to Minnesota.

SAMUEL ELIOT MORISON
The Oxford History of the American People, 1965

I must soon quit the scene, but you may live to see our country flourish; as it will amazingly and rapidly after the war is over; like a field of young Indian corn, which long fair weather and sunshine had enfeebled and discolored, and which in that weak state, by a sudden gust of violent wind, hail, and rain, seemed to be threatened with absolute destruction; yet the storm being past, it recovers fresh verdure, shoots up with double vigor, and delights the eye not of its owners only, but of every observing traveler.

BENJAMIN FRANKLIN
Letter to Washington, March 5, 1780

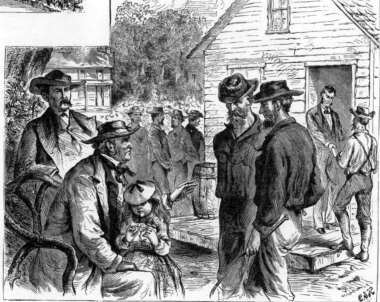

M. L. SULLIYANT AND HIS CAPTAINS AT EVENING.

THE GROWING, CULTIVATION, AND PICKING OF A CORN HARVEST, "BURR OAK" FARM, ILLINOIS

High drama on the range was the daily chore of the rancher— protecting the herds from rustlers, guiding half-wild longhorns or sheep on long drives to market, via rails to the north

There was commotion in Roaring Camp. It could not have been a fight, for in 1850 that was not novel enough to have called together the entire settlement. The ditches and claims were not only deserted, but "Tuttle's grocery" had contributed its gamblers, who, it will be remembered, calmly continued their game the day that French Pete and Kanaka Joe shot each other to death over the bar in the front room. The whole camp was collected before a rude cabin on the outer edge of the clearing. Conversation was carried on in a low tone, but the name of a woman was frequently repeated. It was a name familiar enough in the camp,—"Cherokee Sal." Perhaps the less said of her the better. She was a coarse and, it is to be feared, a very sinful woman. But at that time she was the only woman in Roaring Camp, and was just then lying in sore extremity, when she most needed the ministration of her own sex. Dissolute, abandoned, and irreclaimable, she was yet suffering a martyrdom hard enough to bear even when veiled by sympathizing womanhood, but now terrible in her loneliness. The primal curse had come to her in that original isolation which must have made the punishment of the first transgression so dreadful.

BRET HARTE

The Luck of the Roaring Camp, 1868

CATTLE DRIFTING ON THE RANGE

HERDING CATTLE INTO CHUTE

The cattle drove emerged as one of the most picturesque episodes enacted on the wide empire of grassland—the Great Plains of the West

ROUND-UP TIME

At last, after days of excitement and danger and after months of weary, monotonous toil, the chosen ground is reached and the final camp pitched. The footsore animals are turned loose to shift for themselves, outlying camps of two or three men each being established to hem them in. Meanwhile the primitive ranch-house, out-buildings, and corrals are built, the unhewn cottonwood logs being chinked with moss and mud, while the roofs are of branches covered with dirt, spades and axes being the only tools needed for the work. Bunks, chairs, and tables are all home-made, and as rough as the houses they are in. The supplies of coarse, rude food are carried perhaps two or three hundred miles from the nearest town, either in the ranch-wagons or else by some regular freighting outfit, the huge canvas-topped prairie schooners of which are each drawn by several yoke of oxen, or perhaps by six or eight mules.

THEODORE ROOSEVELT
Ranch Life and the Hunting—Trail, 1902

HERDERS DRIVING SHEEP BEFORE A PRAIRIE FIRE

The rugged life of the cowboy on the range, depicted in its varied phases and experiences by the great Western illustrator Frederick Remington, brought intimate details . . .

The round-up is the harvest of the range. Therefore it is natural that its customs should offer more of interest than those of any other part of the year. It were matter of course, also, that features so singular and stirring in their intense action as those of the cowman's harvest should be known and blazoned about for the knowledge of those living elsewhere than upon the cattle fields. Writers and artists have seized upon this phase of the cattle man's life, and given it so wide a showing that the public might well have at least a general idea of the subject. Yet perhaps this general idea would be a more partial and less accurate notion than is deserved by the complicated and varied business system of the cattle harvest. If we would have a just idea of the life and character of the man who makes the round-up, we should approach the subject rather with a wish to find its fundamental principles than a desire to see its superficial pictures . . .

MIDDAY MEAL

BUFFALO BULLS PROTECTING A HERD FROM WOLVES

*. . . of cowpunching, cattle droving, round-ups,
and rodeos to thousands of readers across the nation
—through the pages of the weekly and monthly journals*

. . . The system of the round-up, while it retains the same general features over the whole of the cow country, and has done so for years, is none the less subject to considerable local modifications, and it has in many respects changed with the years as other customs of the industry have changed; for not even the ancient and enduring calling of the cowman could be free from the law of progress. The Western traveller who first saw a round-up twenty years ago would not be in position to describe one of to-day. Sectional differences make still other changes which should be regarded. Yet all these round-ups, of the past and of the present, of the North and of the South, ground themselves upon a common principle—namely, upon that desire for absolute justice which has been earlier mentioned as a distinguishing trait of the cowman and the trade he follows.

EMERSON HOUGH
The Story of the Cowboy, 1897

CHUCK-WAGON ON "ROUND-UP"

ARIZONA COWBOYS WARNED BY A SCOUT

*The empire of the longhorn—of cattleman and nester,
of homesteaders and ranchers, miles of barbed-wire fencing to
keep cattle in and rustlers out—this was the cow kingdom . . .*

When the glow of fading sunlight,
　Gives way to gath'ring dark,
A lone campfire's glowing embers,
　Release gold-gleaming sparks;
A man sits in the deep shadows,
　In a posture of rest—
He's a man of rugged ranges,
　Man of the open West.

He's ridden atop the springtime,
　He's scorched in summer heat;
He has known Old Winter's
　　scourging,
　By frozen hands and feet,
Without a sign of a whimper,
　He long has faced the test;
He's a true son of the ranges,
　Man of the open West.

A face that is tan and freckled,
　Stubby beard on his chin;
A chest that is broad and muscled,
　And heart that's true within;
His legs are strong and sturdy built,
　Bowed a bit at the best,
This son of the rugged ranges—
　Man of the open West.

ARTHUR W. MONROE
The Man of the Open West

IN WITH THE HORSE HERD

AN EXPLORING OUTFIT

A BUCKING BRONCO

. . . where cowhands fought Indians and poachers, herdmen drove cattle on the long, long trails—the Chisholm Trail, the Western Trail, and the Shawnee Trail from lower Texas

CUTTING OUT A STEER

Night on the prairies,
The supper is over, the fire on the ground burns low,
The wearied emigrants sleep, wrapt in their blankets;
I walk by myself—I stand and look at the stars, which
   I think now I never realized before.

Now I absorb immortality and peace,
I admire death and test propositions.

How plenteous! how spiritual! how resumé!
The same old man and soul—the same old aspirations,
   and the same content.

I was thinking the day most splendid till I saw what the
   not-day exhibited,
I was thinking this globe enough till there sprang out so
   noiseless around me myriads of other globes.

Now while the great thoughts of space and eternity fill me
   I will measure myself by them,
And now touch'd with the lives of other globes arrived
   as far along as those of the earth,
Or waiting to arrive, or pass'd on farther than those of the
   earth,
I henceforth no more ignore them than I ignore my own life,
Or the lives of the earth arrived as far as mine, or
   waiting to arrive.

WALT WHITMAN
Night on the Prairies

AN EPISODE IN THE OPENING UP OF A CATTLE COUNTRY

The prairie was a boundless farmland—its rich soil of sand and gravel, clay and loam deposited by the broad glacier that overspread the continent—had to be tamed and worked from dawn to dusk

As I look back over my life on that Iowa farm the song of the reaper fills large place in my mind. We were all worshipers of wheat in those days. The men thought and talked of little else between seeding and harvest, and you will not wonder at this if you have known and bowed before such abundance as we then enjoyed. Deep as the breast of a man, wide as the sea, heavy-headed, supple-stocked, many-voiced, full of multitudinous, secret, whispered coloquies—a meeting place of winds and of sunlight—our fields ran to the world's end. We trembled when the storm lay hard upon the wheat, we exulted as the lilac shadows of noonday drifted over it! We went out into it at noon when all was still—so still we could hear the pulse of the transforming sap as it crept from cool root to swaying plume. We stood before it at evening when the setting sun flooded it with crimson, the bearded heads lazily swirling under the wings of the wind, the mousing hawk dipping into its green deeps like the eagle into the sea, and our hearts expanded with the beauty and the mystery of it—and back of all this was the knowledge that its abundance meant a new carriage, an addition to the house, or a new suit of clothes. Haying was over, and day by day we boys watched with deepening interest while the hot sun transformed the juices of the soil into those stately stalks. I loved to go out into the fairy forest of it, and lying there, silent in its swaying deeps, hear the wild chickens peep and the wind sing its subtle song over our heads.

HAMLIN GARLAND

A Son of the Middle Border,

1917

1. Turf House.—2. Claim Shanty.—3. Hay Stable.—4. Interior of Mud House.—5. Carrying Grain to Market.—6. Log and Mud House.—7. Breaking. 8. Cross Ploughing.—9. Seeding.—10. Dragging.—11. Spring Work Finished—Waiting for the Harvest.—12. Cutting.—13. Binding.—14. Loading.—15. Threshing.—16. Bagging the Grain.—17. The Grain Elevator.

SCENES ON A PRAIRIE FARM, MINNESOTA

From Yellowstone...
through the Rockies...
to the Sierras

THE LITTLE COLORADO . . . THE
YELLOWSTONE . . . YELLOWSTONE LAKE
. . . TOWER FALLS . . . THE LOWER FALLS
. . . HOT SPRINGS . . . GIANT GEYSER . . .
GREEN RIVER, BUTTES . . . ECHO CANYON
WEBER RIVER . . . BAD LANDS . . . SALT
LAKE CITY . . . MORMONS CROSSING PLAINS
. . . MORMON TEMPLE . . . THE TABERNACLE . . .
LARAMIE PLAINS . . . CHURCH BUTTE . . .
RED BUTTES . . . CHICAGO LAKE . . . PIKES
PEAK . . . GARDEN OF THE GODS . . . MOUNTAIN
OF THE HOLY CROSS . . . SILVER LAKE . . .
LEADVILLE, COLORADO . . . PARIS, TEXAS
. . . COLORADO IRRIGATION . . . BLACK
CANYONS . . . UTE RESERVATION . . . INGRAM
FALLS . . . MARSHALL BASIN . . . GRAND CANYON
. . . KANAB CANYON . . . INNER GORGE . . .
DEVIL'S GATE . . . DONNER LAKE . . . SAN
JOAQUIN RIVER . . . LAKE TAHOE . . .SUMMIT
OF THE SIERRAS . . . MINING CAMP LIFE,
COLORADO

From Yellowstone... through the Rockies... to the Sierras

AT THE MOUTH OF THE LITTLE COLORADO

FOR OVER A CENTURY AFTER ITS founding, America's story lay in its great move west. Down the Ohio, over the Appalachians, across the Mississippi, into the plains. With each succeeding decade it seemed that existing borders had grown too confining, and neither rivers, nor mountains, nor Indians, nor the untold hardships of a new, unbroken land could impede the progress west. James Clyman, wagon guide, wrote in 1846, "All ages and sects are found to undertake this long, tedious and even dangerous Journy, for some unknown object never to be realized even by the most fortunate. And why? Because the human mind can never be satisfied, never at rest, always on the stretch for something new."

Almost immediately after the Louisiana Purchase, Thomas Jefferson decided to discover what actually lay within and beyond the vast territory just acquired. Captain Meriwether Lewis and Lieutenant William Clark left St. Louis in 1804, under orders from the president to explore the territory, discover its western boundary, and then move on to the Pacific. By way of the Missouri River, through the Dakotas and Montana, and on to the Columbia River watershed in Idaho and Washington—guided through much of the journey by Sacajawea, their Shoshone guide—Lewis and Clark reached the Pacific in the fall of 1805. By the time they returned, they had covered over six thousand miles. At about the same time, the U.S. Army dispatched Lieutenant Zebulon Pike and a large party to explore the central Mountain West. Pike traveled past the

Colorado mountain that would eventually bear his name—Pikes Peak—almost to the source of the Arkansas River in the high Rockies. These expeditions provided the first sure knowledge that the Rockies really did exist, and they charted the western boundary of the Louisiana Territory—the Continental Divide.

More intimate topographical knowledge would be provided by the fur trappers, who began to enter the Rocky Mountains in the years following 1812. In 1824 trappers reached the Green River in Wyoming by crossing the south end of the Wind River Range at South Pass. This crossing revealed the only uninterrupted passage through the Central Rockies. It would become, for decades after, the great overland route to the West.

In the 1830s and 1840s the trappers' knowledge became vital, as the "manifest destiny" preached by politicians and journalists helped to encourage migration by thousands of farmers and missionaries. In the 1840s most immigrants—as pioneers were then called—were going into the Oregon Territory, which covered most of what is now Oregon, Washington, and Idaho. They started in Independence, Missouri, following the Oregon Trail to the Northwest, or the California Trail to Sacramento; some headed southwest along the Santa Fe Trail.

The years 1848 and 1849 were crucial for western migration. Great Britain had already ceded the southern portion of the Oregon Territory; in 1848 Spain relinquished Texas, the Mountain West, and California; and in 1849 James Marshall discovered gold in California's American River. Tens of thousands of immigrants flooded into the West. Most of them took the long, tedious journey by prairie schooner through the South Pass. For eleven years the Gold Rush continued, fueled by additional discoveries of gold in the Colorado Rockies and the Comstock Lode in Nevada. In the 1870s and 1880s the silver boom drove miners again into the western mountains. The Civil War did not interrupt the migration west.

In 1847, a group that was hungry, not for gold or fur, but for freedom from religious persecution, entered the West: the followers of the Church of the Latter-day Saints, the Mormons. Led by Brigham Young, they reached Emigration Canyon in Utah in July 1847. They settled in the valley below and found there the freedom to follow the precepts of their church —including the practice of polygamy for which they had been hounded out of the East. Only in 1896, after polygamy had been abandoned by the church, was Utah allowed to enter the Union. By then the Mormons had built a large and thriving community in the great salt desert.

As with all the westward migration that preceded it, the move into the Rockies and beyond entailed the subjugation of the Indians, many of whom were native to the West and many of whom had fled there when their eastern lands were taken from them. Alarmed by the extension of the railroads in the 1860s, forced into starvation by the slaughter of the buffalo, the Indians fought their last battles in the West. From the 1860s to the 1880s battles and massacres occurred from Montana to Arizona. Indian resistance was fierce and it was bloody—but it was also doomed. A destiny more contrived than manifest favored the Europeans.

The Rockies shelter innumerable streams and great forests. Mighty rivers, like the Arkansas and Colorado, have their source in the Rockies' highest reaches. Canyon walls, like those of the Grand Canyon, rise almost a mile high. Gold, silver, and copper are hidden beneath the soil. Its mountains reach over fourteen thousand feet. It was not an easy land to conquer, but by the turn of the century its peaks, its valleys, its streams, and its forests had been charted, and plundered.

In 1878 Major John Wesley Powell published a pamphlet, *Report on the Lands of the Arid Region*, in which for the first time the aridity, altitude, and climate of the Mountain West were described scientifically. He argued for conserving the vast potential of the mountains; and he could already see that this potential was being wasted. By the 1890s droughts, treeless forests, and grassless plains drove others to see what Powell meant. In 1891 the Forest Reserve Act was passed, putting some thirteen million acres into federal reserves to protect the western watershed. Some years later Theodore Roosevelt added almost one hundred fifty million acres of forest, and another eighty million acres of mineral land to the reserves. These were the first attempts to retrieve the land, not from the English, the Spanish, or the Indians, but from the settlers themselves. It seemed once that nothing could stop the move west and nothing could stem the flow of riches from the land so painfully won. But the Mountain West taught Americans the fragile nature of their mighty possession and showed them the limits of what could finally be grasped.

In the heart of the granitic Rockies—in Wyoming's northwest corner—lies the fabulous Yellowstone, a volcanic interlude between the sharp, serrated Grand Tetons to the south . . .

The Yellowstone River has occasion to run through a gorge about eight miles long. To get to the bottom of the gorge it makes two leaps, one of about one hundred and twenty and the other of three hundred feet. I investigated the upper or lesser fall, which is close to the hotel. Up to that time nothing particular happens to the Yellowstone—its banks being only rocky, rather steep, and plentifully adorned with pines. At the falls it comes round a corner, green, solid, ribbed with a little foam, and not more than thirty yards wide. Then it goes over, still green, and rather more solid than before. After a minute or two, you, sitting upon a rock directly above the drop, begin to understand that something has occurred; that the river has jumped between solid cliff walls, and that the gentle froth of water lapping the sides of the gorge below is really the outcome of great waves. I followed with the others round the corner to arrive at the brink of the canyon. We had to climb up a nearly perpendicular ascent to begin with, for the ground rises more than the river drops. Stately pine woods fringe either lip of the gorge, which is the gorge of the Yellowstone. You'll find all about it in the guide books.

RUDYARD KIPLING

American Notes, 1891

THE YELLOWSTONE

. . . Exploiters who followed the explorers have been busy both at home and abroad rooting up, exterminating or merely pushing to the wall species after species in order to make room for themselves and for "useful" products. The variety of nature grows less and less. The monotony of the chain store begins to dominate more and more completely. One must go farther and farther to find a window in which anything not found elsewhere is to be seen. More than a hundred species and subspecies of mammals are known to have disappeared from the face of the earth since the beginning of the Christian era. Along with them have gone perhaps as many birds and an unknown number of humbler creatures. How many plants have suffered extinction has not, so far as I am aware, been even guessed at.

JOSEPH WOOD KRUTCH

Grand Canyon, 1957

COLUMN ROCKS

. . . and the Montana Rockies' Beartooth and Gallatin Range to
the north—an area once the center of violent disturbance
where volcanos created natural wonders in infinite variety

447

TOWER FALLS

Tower Creek rises in the high divide between the valleys of the Missouri and Yellowstone, and flows about ten miles through a canyon so deep and gloomy that it has very properly earned the appellation of the Devil's Den. As we gaze from the margin down into the depths below, the little stream, as it rushes foaming over the rocks, seems like a white thread, while on the sides of the gorge the sombre pinnacles rise up like Gothic spires. About two hundred yards above its entrance into the Yellowstone, the stream pours over an abrupt descent of one hundred and fifty-six feet, forming one of the most beautiful and picturesque falls to be found in any country. The Tower Falls are about two hundred and sixty feet above the level of the Yellowstone at the junction, and they are surrounded with pinnacle-like columns, composed of the volcanic breccia, rising fifty feet above the falls, and extending down to the foot, standing like gloomy sentinels or like the gigantic pillars at the entrance of some grand temple. One could almost imagine that the idea of the Gothic style of architecture had been caught from such carvings of nature. Immense boulders of basalt and granite here obstruct the flow of the stream above and below the falls; and although, so far as we can see, the gorge seems to be made up of the volcanic cement, yet we know that, in the loftier mountains, near the source of the stream, true granitic as well as igneous rocks prevail.

O.B. BUNCE

Picturesque America, 1872

YELLOWSTONE LAKE

448 *The Yellowstone begins in the broad rolling highland known as the Absaroka, flowing north—creating the Great Falls, twice Niagara's height—to form the Grand Canyon with the steep, lava-sided walls . . .*

From the surface of a rocky plain or table [Yellowstone's Upper Geyser Basin], burst forth columns of water, of various dimensions, projected high in the air, accompanied by loud explosions, and sulphurous vapors, which were highly disagreeable to the smell. . . . The largest of these wonderful fountains, projects a column of boiling water several feet in diameter, to the height of more than one hundred and fifty feet . . . accompanied with a tremendous noise. These explosions and discharges occur at intervals of about two hours . . . . The Indians who were with me, were quite appalled, and could not by any means be induced to approach them . . . .They believed them to be supernatural, and supposed them to be the production of the Evil Spirit. One of them remarked that hell, of which he had heard from the whites, must be in the vicinity.

WARREN ANGUS FERRIS

Life in the Rocky Mountains,
1834

THE LOWER FALLS

. . . a thousand feet deep, which, for vivid and varied colorations and fantastic sculptured carvings, is second only to the glorious Grand Canyon of the Colorado

CLIFFS ON THE YELLOWSTONE

We drifted on, up that miraculous valley. On either side of us were hills from a thousand or fifteen hundred feet high, wooded from crest to heel. As far as the eye could range forward were columns of steam in the air, misshapen lumps of lime, mist-like preadamite monsters, still pools of turquoise-blue stretches of blue cornflowers, a river that coiled on itself twenty times, pointed boulders of strange colors, and ridges of glaring, staring white. A moon-faced trooper of German extraction—never was park so carefully patrolled—came up to inform us that as yet we had not seen any of the real geysers; that they were all a mile or so up the valley, and tastefully scattered round the hotel in which we would rest for the night. America is a free country, but the citizens look down on the soldier. I had to entertain that trooper. The old lady from Chicago would have none of him; so we loafed alone together, now across half-rotten pine logs sunk in swampy ground, anon over the ringing geyser formation, then pounding through river-sand or brushing knee-deep through long grass.

RUDYARD KIPLING
American Notes, 1891

Ancient geologic upheavals fired nature's forces, creating constant restlessness of "bubbling mud, boiling springs, erupting waterspouts, and subterranean fires"...

But the most remarkable of all the springs at this point are six or seven of a character differing from any of the rest. The water in them is of a dark blue or ultra-marine hue, but it is wonderfully clear and transparent. Two of these springs are quite large; the remaining five are smaller, their diameters ranging from eight to fifteen feet . . . . The largest two of these springs are irregular in their general outline of nearly an oval shape, the larger of the two being about twenty-five feet wide by forty long, and the smaller about twenty by thirty feet. Six miles above the upper fall we entered upon a region remarkable for the number and variety of its hot springs and craters. The principal spring, and the one that first meets the eye as you approach from the north, is a hot sulphur spring, of oval shape, the water of which is constantly boiling and is thown up to the height of from three to seven feet . . . . This spring is situated at the base of a low mountain and the gentle slope below and around the spring for the distance of two hundred or three hundred feet is covered from a depth of from three to ten inches with the sulphurous deposit from the over-flow of the spring. The moistened bed of a dried-up rivulet, leading from the edge of the spring down inside through this deposit, showed us that the spring had but recently been overflowing. Far-ther along the base of this mountain is a sulphurous cavern . . . out of which the steam is thrown in jets with a sound resembling the puffing of a steam-boat when laboring over a sand-bar, and with as much uniformity and intonation as if emitted by a high-pressure engine. From hundreds of fissures in the adjoining mountain from base to summit, issue hot sulphur vapors, the apertures through which they escape being encased in thick incrustations of sulphur, which in many instances is perfectly pure. There are nearby a number of small sulphur springs, not especially remarkable in appearence.

NATHANIEL P. LANGFORD

Diary of the Washburn Expedition to the Yellowstone and Firehole Rivers, 1871

HOT SPRINGS

MUD SPRINGS

. . . but the most spectacular sight is the action of "Old Faithful"—a geyser which performs its awe-inspiring eruption with regularity, reaching a height of 250 feet

THE GIANT GEYSER

Old Faithful geyser, when all is said, must remain the traveler's favorite. It is beautiful and faithful and perfect and very venerable. It is the first to welcome his arrival. It performs a miracle every sixty-five minutes of his stay. It is the last to speed him onward. And it would have performed the same good offices, back there in the small hours of history, for the same traveler's inarticulate ancestors, when they were still swinging from branch to branch,—provided they had had the good sense to swing in his direction. Every evening a search-light on the Inn roof is trained upon one of Old Faithful's performances. One does not forget a scene like that. We were sitting there, perhaps a hundred pilgrims of us, as Old Faithful once more took its famous leap and spread itself out on the breeze. The searchlight casually regarded the spectacle, and instantly there came upon the wall of steam and spray a circular rainbow surrounded by an aureole of misty gold. Then the lens was thrown out of focus, and one could distinctly catch the thrill which ran through the crowd as purple, then emerald, then violet overspread the base of that miracle of cloud soaring up through the fiery rain. One could feel the common human heart throb faster as at the climax of some supreme symphony or drama.

ROBERT HAVEN SCHAUFFLER
Romantic America, 1913

Eons ago, deep beneath an inland sea that covered the region, the Rockies slowly pushed their way to the surface, erupting in jagged peaks and vast plateaus . . .

BUTTES, GREEN RIVER

Near the head of Echo Canyon stands Castle Rock, one of the noblest of the great natural landmarks that are passed in all the route—a vast and ragged pile of massive stone, fantastically cut, by all those mighty forces that toil through the centuries, into the very semblance of a mountain-fortress. A cavernous opening simulates a giant door of entrance between its rounded and overhanging towers; the jagged points above are like the ruins of battlements left bristling and torn after combats of Titans; the huge layers of its worn sides seem to have been builded by skilful hands; and the great rounded foundations, from which the sandy soil has been swept away, would appear rooted in the very central earth. It surmounts a lofty, steep-sided eminence, and frowns down with an awesome strength and quiet on the lonely valley below it.

All Sunday and Monday we travelled through these sad mountains, or over the main ridge of the Rockies, which is a fair match to them for misery of aspect. Hour after hour it was the same unhomely and unkindly world about our onward path; tumbled boulders, cliffs that drearily imitate the shape of monuments and fortifications—how drearily, how tamely, none can tell who has not seen them; not a tree, not a patch of sward, not one shapely or commanding mountain form; sage-brush, eternal sage-brush; over all, the same weariful and gloomy colouring, grays warming into brown, grays darkening towards black; and for sole sign of life, here and there, but at incredible intervals, a creek running in a canyon. The plains have a grandeur of their own; but here there is nothing but a contorted smallness. Except for the air, which was light and stimulating, there was not one good circumstance in that God-forsaken land.

ROBERT LOUIS STEVENSON
Across the Plains, 1879

MONUMENT ROCK, ECHO CANYON

. . . where sculptured gardens and impregnable rocky fortresses reveal "an epic written by Mother Nature in her most ecstatic humor—in her most majestic manifestations"

WEBER RIVER, ENTRANCE TO ECHO CANYON

TERRES MAUVAISES, UTAH

Beyond it the road enters the Echo Canyon itself. It is a narrow gorge between rocky walls that tower hundreds of feet above its uneven floor, along which the river runs with a stream as bright and clear as at its very source. Not simply a straight cut between its precipices of red-and-dark-stained stone, but a winding valley, with every turn presenting some new variation of its wonderful scenery. On the mountains that form its sides there is little verdure —only a dwarfed growth of pine scattered here and there, leaving the steeper portions of the rock bare and ragged in outline. Now and then there are little openings, where the great walls spread apart and little glades are formed; but these are no less picturesque than the wilder passages. There are memorable places here. Half-way down the gorge is Hanging Rock, where Brigham Young spoke to his deluded hundreds after their long pilgrimage, and pointed out to them that they approached their Canaan—preached the Mormons' first sermon in the "Promised Land." Full of all that is wild and strange, as is this rocky valley, seen even from the prosaic window of a whirling railway-car, what must it have been with the multitude of fanatics, stranger than all its strangeness, standing on its varied floor and looking up at the speaking prophet, whom they half believed, half feared? The weary multitude of half-excited, half-stolid faces turned toward the preacher; the coarse, strong, wild words of the leader echoing from the long-silent rocks—why has no one ever pictured for us all of the scene that could be pictured?

OLIVER B. BUNCE
Picturesque America, 1872

Fleeing religious persecution in Nauvoo, Illinois, thousands of Americans—members of the Church of the Latter-day Saints, known as Mormons—journeyed west to distant Deseret . . .

SALT LAKE

Salt Lake City wears a pleasant aspect to the emigrant or traveler, weary, dusty, and browned with a thousand miles of jolting, fording, camping, through the scorched and naked American desert. It is located mainly on the bench of hard gravel that slopes southward from the foot of the mountains toward the lake valley; the houses— generally small and of one story—are all built of adobe (sun-hardened brick), and have a neat and quiet look; while the uniform breadth of the streets (eight rods) and the "magnificent distances" usually preserved by the buildings (each block containing ten acres, divided into eight lots, giving a quarter of an acre for buildings and an acre for garden, fruit, etc., to each householder) make up an ensemble seldom equaled. Then the rills of bright, sparkling, leaping water which, diverted from the streams issuing from several adjacent mountain canyons, flow through each street and are conducted at will into every garden, diffuse an air of freshness and coolness which none can fail to enjoy, but which only a traveler in summer across the Plains can fully appreciate. On a single business street, the post office, principal stores, etc., are set pretty near each other, though not so close as in other cities; everywhere else, I believe, the original plan of the city has been wisely and happily preserved. Southward from the city, the soil is softer and richer, and there are farms of (I judge) ten to forty or sixty acres; but I am told that the lowest portion of the valley, nearly on a level with the lake, is so impregnated with salt, soda, etc., as to yield but a grudging return for the husbandman's labor. I believe, however, that even this region is available as a stock range—thousands on thousands of cattle, mainly owned in the city, being pastured here in winter as well as summer, and said to do well in all seasons.

HORACE GREELEY
An Overland Journey, 1859

NEW MORMON TEMPLE, SALT LAKE CITY

Who cares to go with the wagons?
    Not we who are free and strong;
Our faith and arms, with right good will,
    Shall pull our carts along.

A Mormon Song, 1856

. . . plodding on foot, pushing handcarts, guiding ox-drawn supply wagons, they finally attained the "Promised Land" in 1870. Their leader, Brigham Young declared, "This is the place!"

MORMONS CROSSING THE PLAINS

VIEWS ON MAIN STREET, SALT LAKE CITY

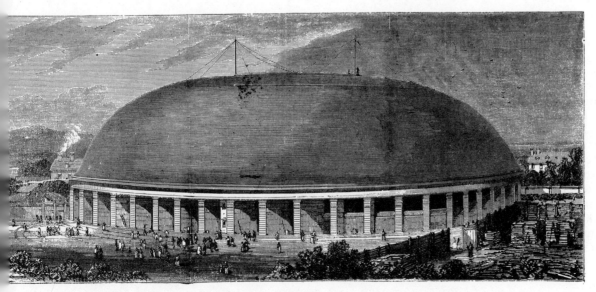

MORMON TABERNACLE

The American frontier never before beheld a movement quite like that of the Mormons. The authority of the Church was absolute. This discipline, when coupled with the wise leadership of Young, made the Mormon experiment a success. More than fifteen thousand people made their way to Utah from Nauvoo. The numbers in the mountain settlement steadily increased as converts poured in, coming particularly from England. The opportunity for material success and for independence on the American frontier was a powerful aid to the Mormon missionaries preaching to impoverished and despairing folk of the British Isles. Nor did the control of the Church end with the completion of the trek from Illinois. In Utah, Church and State were practically one and through the political as well as spiritual power of the Church controlled the economic and social life of the community. Natural leaders who arose among the people were rewarded by ecclesiastical office. Dissension was negligible. Only a community so disciplined and so forgetful of the individualistic characteristics of the American frontier could have established itself in the semi-arid edge of the Central Basin. The Mormon settlement is an illustration of the power of religion in moulding society.

Pageant of America, 1926

Picturesque buttes, carved cliffs, and monolithic canyons of vivid colors—created by emerging rivers of the Utah landscape plunging through shales and sandstones . . .

RED BUTTES, LARAMIE PLAINS

Only with the approach to Green River does the verdure come again—and then only here and there, generally close by the river-bank. Here the picturesque forms of the buttes reappear—a welcome relief to the monotony that has marked the outlook during the miles of level desert that are past. The distance, too, is changed, and no longer is like the great surface of a sea. To the north, forming the horizon, stretches the Wind-River Range—named with a breezy poetry that we miss in the later nomenclature of the race that has followed after the pioneers. To the south lie the Uintah Mountains.

The Church Butte is the grandest of the groups that rise in this singular and striking series of tower-like piles of stone. It lies somewhat further on, beyond the little station of Bryan, and forms a compact and imposing mass of rock, with an outlying spur that has even more than the main body the air of human, though gigantic architecture. It "imposes on the imagination," says Mr. Bowles, in one of his passages of clear description, "like a grand old cathedral going into decay—quaint in its crumbling ornaments, majestic in its height and breadth." And of the towering forms of the whole group, he says: "They seem, like the more numerous and fantastic illustrations of Nature's frolicsome art in Southern Colorado, to be the remains of granite hills that wind and water, and especially the sand whirlpools that march with lordly force through the air—literally moving mountains—have left to tell the story of their own achievements. Not unfitly, there as here, they have won the title of 'Monuments to the Gods.' "

E. L. BURLINGAME

Picturesque America, 1872

CHURCH BUTTE, UTAH

PLAINS OF THE HUMBOLDT

. . . evolved in "Monuments of the Gods"—the scenic wonderland where the plateau country is dotted with natural masterpieces in eerie formations

CLIFFS OF GREEN RIVER

DIAL ROCK, RED BUTTES, LARAMIE PLAINS

The route of the Pacific Railway is not only that which for many years will be the most familiar path across the Plains, and not only that which passes nearest to the well-known emigrant-road of former days, but it is also the road which, though it misses the nobler beauties of the Rocky Mountains, shows the traveller the prairie itself in perhaps as true and characteristic an aspect as could be found on any less-tried course. It passes through almost every change of prairie scenery—the fertile land of the east and the alkali region farther on; past the historic outposts of the old pioneers; among low *buttes* and infrequent "islands;" and over a country abounding in points of view from which one may take in all the features that mark this portion of the continent. To the south, the great level expanse is hardly interrupted before the shore of the Gulf of Mexico is reached, and the Mexican boundary; to the north, the hills and high table-land of the Upper Missouri are the only breaks this side of the Canadian border. Through almost the middle of this vast and clear expanse the Union Pacific Railway runs east and west—a line of life flowing like a river through the great plain— the Kansas Pacific joining it at the middle of its course, a tributary of no small importance.

E. L. BURLINGAME
Picturesque America, 1872

*In the 1830s and 1840s, exploring expeditions were
fortunate to have among them artists like Samuel Seymour,
George Catlin, Carl Bodmer, and Alfred Jacob Miller*

That grandeur was still to be found in the Far West; and as the explorer, the frontiersman, the hunter, the road builder, the homemaker pushed into the vast region beyond the Mississippi, many an American artist went along with his sketchbook to record the appearance and habits of the vanishing redskin. George Catlin journeyed from St. Louis up the Missouri River. His subjects ranged from prairie fires to a buffalo hunt on snowshoes, and his observation and daring broke through the limitations of his technique. Audiences here and in Europe marveled at Catlin's traveling exhibition, which included not only his many canvases but also a group of live Indians. Many others followed Catlin: John Mix Stanley painted from Texas to Oregon; Alfred J. Miller made fresh and brilliant water colors of the Rockies; Seth Eastman illustrated the six volumes of Henry Schoolcraft's work on the Indian tribes; a German-born artist named Albert Bierstadt joined the surveying expedition of General Lander and made the first of those great panoramic pictures of towering canyons, mighty waterfalls, redwood forests, and stupendous mountain peaks for which American millionaires were to pay fantastic prices. Thus was the natural setting of America presented in fresh, bold colors to its inhabitants.

OLIVER W. LARKIN
*The Artist in the 19th
Century, 1949*

CHICAGO LAKE

PIKES PEAK, FROM GARDEN OF THE GODS

Later, the illustrated weeklies, and their staffs of graphic artists, did much to acquaint a nation hungry for information—with words and pictures of the fabulous West

MOUNTAIN OF THE HOLY CROSS

Not a great distance from here, leading down the mountain from Elk Lake, is a picturesque cascade, that finds its way through deep gorges and canyons to the Rio Grande. The Mountain of the Holy Cross is next reached. This is the most celebrated mountain in the region, but its height, which has been over-estimated, is not more than fourteen thousand feet. The ascent is exceedingly toilsome even for inured mountaineers, and I might give you an interesting chapter describing the difficulties that beset us. There is a very beautiful peculiarity in the mountain, as its name shows. The principal peak is composed of gneiss, and the cross fractures of the rock on the eastern slope have made two great fissures, which cut into one another at right angles, and hold their snow in the form of a cross the summer long.

W. H. RIDEING
Picturesque America, 1872

Main Street in the frontier towns: boxlike shanties and false fronts reflecting the slapdash haste of construction, a mix of saloons and hardware stores, bakeries and bordellos . . .

SITE OF SILVERTON R.R.

SILVER LAKE, COLORADO

BEAR CREEK FALLS

DONKEY PACK HAULING RAILS

. . .dominated by congested traffic churning helter-skelter: covered wagons and stagecoaches creating scenes of frenzied activity

Going to town, by carriage or buggy, was a deeply ingrained American custom throughout the past century. In thousands of villages and towns, the highlight of the week was the family shopping trip on Saturday. Often the farmer, on such a visit, would trade his produce like eggs, fruit or vegetables for dry goods or household items needed at the general store . . .

. . . On Main Street U.S.A., the grain dealer's was a very important stop on the visiting farmer's busy schedule. His store was generally built around a wide driveway to allow hand-trucking of bags, barrels and bales. To one side of the entrance was usually a crudely improvised office, with a window for the display of grain samples. The simple placards told their story: "No. 1 Yellow corn"; "No. 2 White oats"; or "Fancy white middlings." His walls were often decorated with colorful lithos of famous race horses, agricultural calendars, black and white broadsides of a coming Fair, plus a sprinkling of patent feed posters. Over the owner's cluttered rolltop desk, there hung, more than likely, *The Horse Fair* . . . certainly a few *Currier and Ives* featuring the latest in horse-drawn carriages. The town livery stable was a scene of hectic activity. Here, while Farmer Jones did his trading, he also parked his horse and buggy, where for the sum of twenty-five cents his horse would be fed and watered. In the more progressive towns public tie-racks with feed troughs were provided, especially for those who arrived early.

CLARENCE P. HORNUNG
Wheels Across America, 1959

MAIN STREET, LEADVILLE, COLORADO

MARKET SQUARE CONGESTION, PARIS, TEXAS

Many gold seekers—whose luck did not pan out— returned home or took to farming, irrigation projects helping to enrich the arid soil

"Those whom we meet here coming down confirm the worst news we have had from the Peak. There is scarcely any gold there; those who dig cannot average two shillings per day; all who can get away are leaving; Denver and Auraria are nearly deserted; terrible sufferings have been endured on the Plains, and more must yet be encountered; hundreds would gladly work for their board, but cannot find employment—in short, Pike's Peak is an exploded bubble, which thousands must bitterly rue to the end of their days. Such is the tenor of our latest advices. I have received none this side of Leavenworth that contradict them. My informant says all are getting away who can, and that we shall find the region nearly deserted."

HORACE GREELEY

An Overland Journey, 1859

Soon the sun rose bright and clear; but the air was keen, with a stiff breeze eastward in our teeth. We were down in a wide depression of the Plains: but presently we rose up out of it, and as we struck the summit of the 'divide,' lo, the Rocky Mountains were before us in all their grandeur and sublimity. To the north rose Long's Peak, fourteen thousand feet above the sea, heaven-kissing, but with his night-cap still on; to the south, was Pike's Peak, eleven thousand feet above the sea, snow-crowned; while between, a hundred miles or more, swelled and towered the Mountains—at the base mere foot-hills, then ridge mounting on ridge and peak on peak, until over and above all the Snowy Range cropped out sublime.

JAMES F. RUSLING

Across America, 1874

RESULT OF IRRIGATION.

MAKING A START.

LIFTING WHEELS ON THE GUNNISON.

THE BAD LANDS.

IRRIGATION IN COLORADO

High up in the San Juan Mountains of southwestern Colorado —the nations's most mountainous state—gold, silver, lead, and other ores lured miners into almost impassable terrain

Burnett's Burro Camp.
(Ore Express Train)

Bridal-Veil Park—Telluride.

Black Cañon,—Gunnison River.

Ingram Falls.

Bridal-Veil Falls.

Ouray.

Marshall Basin.

San Juan Mountains.

THE OLD UTE RESERVATION, COLORADO

Such was the actual state of things when the first flood of gold-seeking immigration began to pour in upon Auraria and Denver two months or more ago. Many of the seekers had left home with very crude ideas of gold-digging, impelled by glowing bulletins from writers who confounded sanguine expectations with actual results, and at best spoke of any casual realization of five to ten dollars from a day's washing as though it were a usual and reliable reward of gold-seeking industry throughout this region. Many who came were doubtless already wearied and disgusted with the hardships of their tedious journey—with sleeping in wet blankets through storms of snow and hurricanes of hail, and urging hollow and weary cattle over immense, treeless plains, on which the grass had hardly started. Coming in thus weather-beaten, chafed and soured, and finding but a handful of squalid adventurers living in the rudest log huts, barred out from the mountains by snow and ice, and precluded from washing the sands of the streams on the plains by high water, they jumped at once to the conclusion that the whole thing was a humbug, got up by reckless speculators to promote selfish ends.

HORACE GREELEY

An Overland Journey,

1859

Six to eight million years ago, when the Colorado River snaked its way across a sea-level plain, a giant upheaval of the land caused the waters to rush in . . .

KANAB CANYON, NEAR THE JUNCTION

Clouds are playing in the canyon to-day. Sometimes they roll down in great masses, filling the gorge with gloom; sometimes they hang a loft from wall to wall and cover the canyon with a roof of impending storm, and we can peer long distances up and down this canyon corridor, with its cloud-roof overhead, its walls of black granite, and its river bright with the sheen of broken waters. Then a gust of wind sweeps down a side gulch and, making a rift in the clouds, reveals the blue heavens, and a stream of sunlight pours in. Then the clouds drift away into the distance, and hang around crags and peaks and pinnacles and towers and walls, and cover them with a mantle that lifts from time to time and sets them all in sharp relief. Then baby clouds creep out of side canyons, glide around points, and creep back again into more distant gorges. Then clouds arrange in strata across the canyon, with intervening vista views to cliffs and rocks beyond. The clouds are children of the heavens, and when they play among the rocks they lift them to the region above.

JOHN WESLEY POWELL

Canyons of the Colorado, 1895

THE GRAND CANYON

The walls now are more than a mile in height—a vertical distance difficult to appreciate. Stand on the south steps of the Treasury building in Washington and look down Pennsylvania Avenue to the Capitol; measure this distance overhead, and imagine cliffs to extend to that altitude, and you will understand what is meant; or stand at Canal Street in New York and look up Broadway to Grace Church, and you have about the distance; or stand at Lake Street bridge in Chicago and look down to the Central Depot, and you have it again. A thousand feet of this is up through granite crags; then steep slopes and perpendicular cliffs rise one above another to the summit. The gorge is black and narrow below, red and gray and flaring above, with crags and angular projections on the walls, which, cut in many places by side canyons, seem to be a vast wilderness of rocks. Down in these grand, gloomy depths we glide, ever listening . . .

JOHN WESLEY POWELL

. . . granular sand and silt chiseled deeply into Archean rock strata of shale and limestone to form the Grand Canyon— the most spectacular gorge in the New World—217 miles long

THE INNER GORGE

Whenever the brink of the chasm is reached the chances are that the sun is high and these abnormal effects in full force. The canyon is asleep. Or it is under a spell of enchantment which gives its bewildering mazes an aspect still more bewildering. Throughout the long summer forenoon the charm which binds it grows in potency. At midday the clouds begin to gather, first in fleecy flecks, then in cumuli, and throw their shadows into the gulf. At once the scene changes. The slumber of the chasm is disturbed. The temples and cloisters seem to raise themselves half awake to greet the passing shadow. Their wilted, drooping, flattened faces expand into relief. The long promontories reach out from the distant wall as if to catch a moment's refreshment from the shade. The colors begin to glow; the haze loses its opaque density and becomes more tenuous. The shadows pass, and the chasm relapses into its dull sleep again. Thus through the midday hours it lies in fitful slumber, overcome by the blinding glare and withering heat, yet responsive to every fluctuation of light and shadow like a delicate organism. As the sun moves far into the west the scene again changes, slowly and imperceptibly at first, but afterwards more rapidly. In the hot summer afternoons the sky is full of cloud-play and the deep flushes with ready answers. The banks of snowy clouds pour a flood of light sidewise into the shadows and light up the gloom of the amphitheaters and alcoves, weakening the glow of the haze and rendering visible the details of the wall faces. At length, as the sun draws near the horizon, the great drama of the day begins.

CLARENCE E. DUTTON

its own aloof, almost contemp-
ous, way it is nevertheless ex-
ordinarily beautiful—nature's
timate achievement in that
uthwestern Style which surpris-
gly executes great monolithic
rms, sometimes sculptural and
metimes architectural, in bright,
ultihued sandstone. About the
yle there is nothing to suggest the
arm of the landscape which
elcomes man; instead, there is
ly the grandeur of something
werfully alien, indifferent, and
during, as though it had been
ade to please the eye and perhaps
en to soothe the spirit of some
eature older, as well as less tran-
ory, than . . .

JOSEPH WOOD KRUTCH
Grand Canyon, 1957

GRAND CANYON OF THE COLORADO, WITH AMPHITHEATRE AND SCULPTURED BUTTES

The unsurpassed beauty of the High Sierras, the enchantment of nature's monuments, were lost to overland travelers trudging through dangerous mountain passes of the Great Divide

In this region of hidden grandeur lies the ground of hope for those cosmopoltan tourists who complain that the world is a small place, full of hackneyed scenes, after all. So long as there is locked up here in our great mountain-chain such a glory as the few who have penetrated into its fortresses have described, even the mountaineer who fancies he has exhausted two continents, need never despair. One noble feature of the whole Sierra—of all of it save that which lies above the level of any vegetable life—is its magnificent forest-covering. It may well be doubted if the growth of forests of pine is ever seen in greater perfection than is found here. These tall, straight, noble shafts are the very king of trees. Covering the great slopes with a dense mantle of sombre green, they lend a wonderful dignity to the peaks, as one looks upon them from a distance; and, to one already in the forest, they seem the worthy guardians of the mountain-sides. They are magnificent in size, as they are admirable in proportion. No mast or spar ever shaped by men's hands exceeds the already perfect grace of their straight, unbroken trunks. They are things to study for their mere beauty as individual trees, apart from their effect upon the general landscape, which even without them would be wild and picturesque enough.

E. L. BURLINGAME

Picturesque America, 1872

DEVIL'S GATE, WEBER CANYON

Bound for California, in the winter of 1846-1847, the Donner Party— 467
three family groups with sixteen children—suffered a gruesome tragedy:
snowed-in, hunger-driven, the survivors resorted to cannibalism

DONNER LAKE, NEVADA

Nov. 20 [1846]

Came to this place [now called Donner Lake] on the 31st of last month. It snowed. We went on to the pass. The snow is so deep we were unable to find the road, when within 3 miles of the summit. Then turned back to this shanty on the Lake. . . . We now have killed most part of our cattle having to stay here untill next spring & live on poor beef without bread or salt. It snowed during the space of eight days with our little intermission, after our arrival here. . . .

[December] 25th

Snowed all night & snows yet rapidly. Great difficulty in geting wood. John & Edwd. has to get it. I am not able. Offered our prayers to God this Cherimass morning. The prospect is apalling but hope in God. *Amen.*

PATRICK BREEN

Diary of a member of
the Donner Party

The loss of the Donner Party—within sight of their goal just west of the Nevada Territory—illustrated the terrors of travel through the High Sierras

Bring me men to match
   my mountains,
Bring me men to match
   my plains,
Men with empires in their
   purpose,
And new eras in their
   brains.

The plain man is the
   basic clod
From which we grow the
   demigod;
And in the average man
   is curled
The hero stuff that rules
   the world.

SAM WALTER FOSS

The Coming American,
                    1897

SAN JOAQUIN RIVER

LAKE TAHOE

Descending from the mountain passes, the fertile fields of the Golden State appear: orchards, citrus groves, vineyards, and farms—outpacing the nation in growth and vitality

SUMMIT OF THE SIERRAS

The machine has divorced man from the world of nature to which he belongs, and in the process he has lost in large measure the powers of contemplation with which he was endowed. A prerequisite for the preservation of the canons of humanism is a reestablishment of organic roots with our natural environment and, related to it, the evolution of ways of life which encourage contemplation and the search for truth and knowledge. The flower and vegetable garden, green grass, the fireplace, the primeval forest with its wondrous assemblage of living things, the uninhabited hilltop where one can silently look at the stars and wonder—all of these things and many others are necessary for the fulfillment of man's psychological and spiritual needs. To be sure, they are of no "practical value" and are seemingly unrelated to man's pressing need for food and living space. But they are as necessary to the preservation of humanism as food is necessary to the preservation of human life.

HARRISON BROWN

In 1859, ten years after California's gold strike, the new diggings at Gregory Gulch came in "with a whoop and a holler" as thousands struck it rich in Colorado's golden era of mining

And the Rocky Mountains, with their grand, aromatic forests, their grassy glades, their frequent springs, and dancing streams of the brightest, sweetest water, their pure, elastic atmosphere, and their unequalled game and fish, are destined to be a favorite resort and home of civilized man. I never visited a region where physical life could be more surely prolonged or fully enjoyed. Thousands who rush hither for gold will rush away again disappointed and disgusted, as thousands have already done; and yet the gold is in these mountains, and the right men will gradually unearth it. I shall be mistaken if two or three millions are not taken out this year, and some ten millions in 1860, though all the time there will be, as now, a stream of rash adventurers heading away from the diggings, declaring that there is no gold there, or next to none. So it was in California and in Australia; so it must be here, where the obstacles to be overcome are greater, and the facilities for getting home decidedly better. All men are not fitted by nature for gold-diggers; yet thousands will not realize this until they have been convinced of it by sore experience.

HORACE GREELEY
An Overland Journey, 1859

Making ready to leave the Winter camp.

Camp on the Mountains.

A Find.

Arrival of the first Stage.

MINING LIFE IN COLORADO

Golden California...
Gateway on the Pacific

BRIDAL VEIL FALLS . . . EMIGRANTS'
LAST DAY ON THE PLAINS . . . GLACIER,
MTS. RITTER AND LYELL . . . SAN
LORENZO CREEK . . TOLTEC GORGE . . .
TUOLUMNE RIVER . . . MT. SHASTA . . .
"WILDCAT CASCADES" . . . SUTTER'S MILL
. . . COLOMA . . . AMERICAN RIVER . . .
CALIFORNIA GOLD DIGGERS . . . SAN
FRANCISCO . . . CENTRAL PACIFIC R. R.
TERMINUS . . .MARKET STREET . . . SANSOME
STREET . . . NEW CITY HALL . . . MARIN
COUNTY COAST . . . MENDOCINO . . . SEAL
ROCKS . . . MOUNT TAMALPAIS . . . MONTEREY
. . . HOTEL DEL MONTE . . . CYPRESS DRIVE
. . . CARMEL MISSION . . . SEQUOIA TREES . . .
MARIPOSA GROVE . . . YOSEMITE FALL . . .
CATHEDRAL SPIRES . . . GORGE OF THE
MERCED . . . HALF DOME . . . SENTINEL ROCK
AND FALLS . . . LOS ANGELES . . . STREETS AND
RESIDENCES . . . SANTA BARBARA MISSIONS

BRIDAL VEIL FALLS

Golden California...
Gateway on the Pacific

URING THE GREAT AGE OF EXPLORA-
tion in the sixteenth century,
Europeans were beguiled with tales
of exotic and fabulously rich lands
on the other side of the globe. One such land
was an island of rocks and gold ruled by an
Amazon queen, Califía. Her realm was
described in a popular novel of the 1530s, and
despite its clearly fictional existence, the island
did resemble lands real, imagined, and a little
of both, which were rumored to have been
sighted across the seas. In 1535, Hernán Cortés
landed on a rugged peninsula off the Mexican
coast which reminded him of Queen Califía's
island. He named the land "California"; and
so, long before it would actually be explored

or settled, this rich and beautiful land had
found its name in the sort of legend that for
three centuries would draw people to her.

California has always inspired the wildest
dreams, and its reality has always exceeded
those dreams. The land was richer and far
more awesome than Califía's fabled island,
and the miners' gold would seem trifling compared to the fortunes that were made after the
gold gave out.

California has been described as a "sudden
land," where the mountains meet the sea and
do not slope down gently to it as they do on
the East Coast. Below Monterey the Santa
Lucia Mountains rise some eight hundred feet
above the water at Big Sur, and at sunset these

cliffs become a sheer plate of golden rock.

It is also a land of superlatives. Just east of Los Angeles is the highest peak in the continental United States, Mount Whitney, and the lowest point, Death Valley. South of the Oregon border stand some of the oldest and tallest trees on earth, the redwoods; while to the east lies the desolate lava country of the Modoc Plateau. Between the lofty Sierra Nevada and Coastal ranges lies the great Central Valley—four hundred fifty miles of flat farm land.

The Spanish came first to California in the 1540s, but did not find the gold they sought. More than two and a half centuries would pass before they would return in earnest. In 1770, Gaspar de Portolá established a garrison at Monterey, the city that would eventually become the Spanish capital of California. Just a year before, a lame and aging friar, Junípero Serra, had set off on muleback up the Baja peninsula to establish missions. Within a few years he had established twenty-one of them, all along the coast.

In 1821, after a protracted struggle, Spain granted Mexico its independence. The new republic included California, and since it was virtually uninhabited, the Mexican government awarded large tracts of land there to retired soldiers. The romantic era of the "ranchos" was extravagant, but short-lived. In 1846-1847 the war between Mexico and the United States, fought chiefly over possession of Texas, resulted in American acquisition of California. Still there were few inhabitants in the American settlements.

In 1848 James Marshall, working at Sutter's Mill, a small settlement in the north, discovered gold in the American River. Gold fever swept the East. Within four years the population of California increased sixfold, and regular steamship service between Boston and New York and San Francisco had begun, using the Isthmus of Panama as a transshipment point for passengers. San Francisco, up until then a small village called Yerba Buena, became something close to a metropolis. In 1849 alone, some five hundred fifty vessels arrived at her port, carrying some forty thousand passengers. The overland route, despite its hardships, became so popular that guidebooks were published for travelers along its two-thousand-mile route. By 1850 California had become a state, America's thirty-first.

The gold-digging in California lasted only some five years, but discoveries in the Northwest and in Nevada throughout the 1850s continued to draw prospectors and others to the port of San Francisco. In these years San Francisco was a lawless and raucous town. But as the population grew and settled, and as fortunes accumulated, it developed worldly amenities to accompany the more boisterous attractions of its Barbary Coast dancehalls and saloons. Comfortable, cosmopolitan, and cultured, San Francisco became America's Western capital. Frequently hidden in fog, but sometimes bathed in a light of Mediterranean clarity, its wind-shaped pines and gingerbread Gothic houses follow the angle of hills that dip gracefully toward the bay and the sea. San Francisco burned to the ground twice in the 1850s and again after an earthquake in 1906. But it always recovered, rebuilt more splendidly, and attracted a steady migration from Europe, the Orient, and the American East. Shaped by the wide-open, flamboyant spirit of its Gold Rush heritage, San Francisco calls itself "the city that knows how." By common assent, it does.

Dreams of gold first drew people to San Francisco. Dreams of agricultural riches drew people south, to Los Angeles. Its growth was slower than San Francisco's, but wild speculation in land—much of which was only desert—increased Los Angeles's population from the fifteen hundred counted in the census of 1850 to over eleven thousand by 1880. By the end of the 1880s, however, speculation faltered and thousands of disappointed migrants turned back east, or traveled north. Still, growth continued, if at a slower rate. Some came to farm, but many more came to enjoy a climate reputed to cure almost any ill. Los Angeles, San Diego, Santa Barbara, San Bernardino were already established towns by the turn of the nineteenth century, and they shared the influx of health-seekers with newer spas like Palm Springs, Pasadena, and Santa Monica.

Within half a century after its founding the United States stretched from the Atlantic to the Pacific. The destiny sought in the West was achieved by hardship, cruelty, and a perseverance that has always defied complete comprehension. But standing on Yosemite's snowy peaks, or looking out over a glistening San Francisco Bay, it is possible to glimpse the vision that lured a people west.

*California . . .El Dorado . . .land of golden promise—
hope and heartbreak of many, from the argonauts of '49
to the many millions who followed, by land and sea . . .*

They came by wagon and by horseback. Some 16,000 sailed around the Horn, a six months' voyage considerably longer than halfway around the world. Others—the more energetic —sailed to Chagres, threaded the Panamanian jungles by foot or mule-back, and completed the six weeks' journey by ship. They arrived singly and in companies, with or without guidebooks, these young men from China, Peru, Mexico, and Europe; from the neat little towns of New England and the farm lands of Ohio. Most of those who came by ship were city men, described by Bancroft as "editors, ministers, traders, the briefless lawyer, starving student, the quack, the idler, the harlot, the gambler, the henpecked husband, the disgraced . . ." Among them were also many honest men and devoted women. Those who made the 2000 mile journey westward from the marshaling points in Missouri were largely farmers and mechanics— experienced frontiersmen. By the end of 1849 the population of California had skyrocketed to 100,000 exclusive of native Indians. Of this number the vast majority were somewhere between Sutter's Fort and the various mines at such places as Red Dog, Poker Flat, Rough and Ready, or Hell's Delight. They were in possession of what remained of the $10,000,000 pried from the earth that year. With the arrival of the bulk of those who had left home in '49, the value of the pannings jumped to $41,000,000—to double that amount in 1851.

SCOTT O'DELL

*The Romance of North
America, 1958*

CALIFORNIA EMIGRANTS' LAST DAY ON THE PLAINS

. . . making their arduous way across the continent, the Isthmus of Panama, or around the Horn—lured by the magnetic pull of land gracious in climate, rich in resources

Even on a map the state looks odd. Four of the boundary lines are as straight as a surveyor's eye can make them. The fifth is the huge wriggling gorge that the Colorado has cut for itself. The sixth boundary is stupefying. It is the Pacific Ocean. The California Current and millions of years of savage storm waves and winds have worked at the western edge of California. This line is made up of jagged inlets, irregular sandbars, unlikely harbors, long white beaches. It changes constantly; every year some of the tall soft cliffs tumble into the ocean and part of California is gone. Most rates are fairly uniform in climate and terrain, and this tends to make their citizens somewhat similar. California has few uniformities— and fantastic differences. Part is white, hot desert, part perpetual snow, part subtropical and part heavily wooded with pine and oak and redwood. It has an active volcano. It has a place called Bagdad where a man looked into the sky for 767 days for rain and was rewarded by a touch of wet on the 768th day. This was the longest unofficially recorded dry period in America. But another man, at Hoegees Camp, stood unbelievingly as it rained twenty-six inches in a single day and watched the deluge melt mountains into soft mud. Huge redwoods slid down slick canyons, and enormous boulders came loose with a large suck and ponderously, surrounded by tons of mud, crashed down on the redwoods.

EUGENE BURDICK

"Gold from the American River" was President Polk's message to Congress, December 5, 1848—electrifying news that changed the life of a nation, as eager adventurers came from all points of the compass

One morning in January [1848]—it was a clear cold morning; I shall never forget that morning—as I was taking my usual walk along the race, after shutting off the water my eye was caught by a glimpse of something shining in the bottom of the ditch. There was about a foot of water running there. I reached my hand down and picked it up; it made my heart thump, for I felt certain it was gold. The piece was about half the size of the shape of a pea. Then I saw another piece in the water. After taking it out I sat down and began to think right hard. I thought it was gold, and yet it did not seem to be of the right color; all the gold coin I had seen was of a reddish tinge; this looked more like brass. I recalled to mind all the metals I had ever seen or heard of, but I could find none that resembled this. Suddenly the idea flashed across my mind that it might be iron pyrites. I trembled to think of it! This question could soon be determined. Putting one of the pieces on hard river stone, I took another and commenced hammering it. It was soft and didn't break; it therefore must be gold, but largely mixed with some other metal, very likely silver; for pure gold, I thought, would certainly have a brighter color . . . .

SUTTER'S MILL, COLOMA

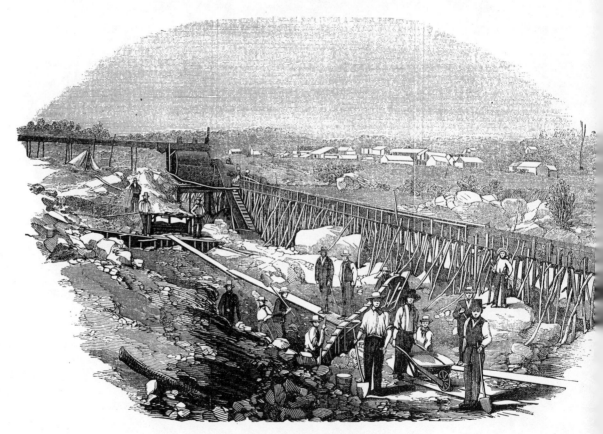

PARKS' BAR COMPANY WORKS AND FLUME

Gold fever swept the nation. Wrote Walter Alton: ''The blacksmith dropped his hammer, the carpenter his plane, the mason his trowel, the farmer his sickle, the baker his loaf. All were off for the mines''

. . . When I returned to our cabin for breakfast I showed the two pieces to my men. They were all a good deal excited, and had they not thought that the gold only existed in small quantities they would have abandoned everything and left me to finish the job alone. However, to satisfy them, I told them that as soon as we had the mill finished we would devote a week or two to gold hunting and see what we could make out of it. While we were working in the race after this discovery, we always kept a sharp lookout, and in the course of three or four days we had picked up about three ounces—our work still progressing as lively as ever. JAMES MARSHALL

Account of the Discovery of Gold, 1848

NORTH FORK, AMERICAN RIVER

CALIFORNIA GOLD DIGGERS

San Francisco—frontier fort, presidio, and mission, surrounded by a village of friendly Indians—visited by Richard Dana in 1835—gave promise of becoming "a place of great importance"

The city of San Francisco is built along the eastern base and up the side of a row of high sand hills, which stretch southwardly from the Golden Gate, between the Pacific Ocean on the west and the bay of San Francisco on the east. The city has been built out into the bay some fifty to a hundred rods by carting in sand from the eastern slope of the hills, which are thus left more abrupt than they originally were. The compactly built district seems rather more than two miles north and south, by somewhat less east and west. I judge that the city is destined to expand in the main southwardly, or along the bay, avoiding the steep ascent toward the west. The county covers 26,000 acres, of which one-half will probably be covered in time by buildings or country seats. I estimate the present population at about 80,000. It seems not to have increased very rapidly for some years past, and this is as it should be. San Francisco has the largest trade of any city on the Pacific; but as yet she is the emporium of California and Oregon only. A railroad communication with the Atlantic states would make her the New York of this mighty ocean—the focus of the trade of all America west of the Andes and Rocky Mountains, and of Polynesia as well, with an active and increasing Australian commerce . . .

WESTERN TERMINUS, CENTRAL PACIFIC RAILROAD, SAN FRANCISCO

MARKET STREET, SAN FRANCISCO .

*Dana's vision materialized with news of gold's discovery—
an instant metropolis mushroomed, devastated many times by fire,
rebuilt each time as soon as flames died and embers cooled*

NEW CITY HALL, SAN FRANCISCO

. . . Without an inter-oceanic railroad, she must grow slowly, because the elements of her trade have been measured and their limits nearly reached. The gold product of this region has for years averaged about fifty millions per annum, and is not likely soon to rise much above that amount. That sum does not require, and will not create, a larger mart than San Francisco now is.

HORACE GREELEY
An Overland Journey, 1859

San Francisco has some fine buildings, but is not a well-built city—as, indeed, how could she be? She is hardly yet ten years old, has been three or four times in good part laid in ashes, and is the work mainly of men of moderate means, who have paid higher for the labor they required than she ever paid elsewhere for putting so much wood, stone, brick and mortar into habitations or stores. Her growth for the first five years of her existence was very rapid; but Pottsville, Chicago, Liverpool have also had rapid growths, and St. Louis is now expanding faster than this city has done since 1852. Cities are created and enlarged by the wants of populations outside of their own limits; San Francisco will take another start when she shall have become beneficent if not indispensable to a much larger radius than that now buying and selling mainly through her. In the hope that the time for this is not far distant, I bid her God speed.

HORACE GREELEY
An Overland Journey, 1859

SANSOME STREET, SAN FRANCISCO

John Charles Fremont, flamboyant freebooter and explorer, precipitated the seizure of Spanish California, acquiring, without bloodshed, the regions then loosely held by Mexico

The Bay of San Francisco is separated by the sea by low mountain ranges. Looking from the peaks of the Sierra Nevada, the coast mountains present an apparently continuous line, with only a single gap, resembling a mountain pass. This is the entrance to the great bay, and is the only water communication from the coast to the interior country. Approaching from the sea, the coast presents a bold outline. On the south, the bordering mountains come down in a narrow ridge of broken hills, terminating in a precipitous point, against which the sea breaks heavily. On the northern side, the mountain presents a bold promontory, rising in a few miles to a height of two or three thousand feet. Between these points is the strait—about one mile broad in the narrowest part, and five miles long from the sea to the bay. To this Gate I gave the name of *Chrysopylar,* or GOLDEN GATE; for the same reasons that the harbor of Byzantium (Constantinople afterwards), was called *Chrysoceras,* or GOLDEN HORN. Passing through this gate, the bay opens to the right and left, extending in each direction about thirty-five miles, having a total length of more than seventy, and a coast of about two hundred and seventy-five miles . . .

PACIFIC COAST SCENE, MARIN COUNTY

COAST OF MENDOCINO

He described the Golden Gate and California coastline:
"a varied character of rugged and broken hills, rolling land,
and rich alluvial shores backed by fertile and wooded ranges"

SEAL ROCKS, SAN FRANCISCO

. . . It is divided, by straits and projecting points, into three separate bays, of which the northern two are called San Pablo and Suisoon Bays. Within, the view presented is of a mountainous country, the bay resembling an interior lake of deep water, lying between parallel ranges of mountains. Islands, which have the bold character of the shores—some mere masses of rock, and others grass-covered, rising to the height of three and eight hundred feet—break its surface, and add to its picturesque appearance.

JOHN CHARLES FREMONT
A Year of American Travel,
1878

MOUNT TAMALPAIS AND RED PORCH

Every day of my life at Big Sur I had before me the incomparable vista of the Pacific. Its everchanging aspects offered me alternately peace and stimulation. I had to learn to live with this overwhelming force which is hidden within its obvious grandeur.

HENRY MILLER
My Life and Times, 1971

*Monterey—secure fort, presidio, and provincial capital of the
California area since its founding in 1770—grew in importance
after Mexican Independence, in 1821, luring settlers and traders . . .*

In Monterey there are a number of English and Americans (English or "Ingles" all are called who speak the English language) who have married Californians, become united to the Catholic Church, and acquired considerable property. Having more industry, frugality, and enterprise than the natives, they soon get nearly all the trade into their hands. They usually keep shops, in which they retail the goods purchased in larger quantities from our vessels, and also send a good deal into the interior, taking hides in pay, which they again barter with our vessels. In every town on the coast there are foreigners engaged in this kind of trade, while I recollect but two shops kept by natives. The people are naturally suspicious of foreigners, and they would not be allowed to remain were it not they they become good Catholics, and by marrying natives and bringing up their children as Catholics and Spaniards and not teaching them the English language, they quiet suspicion and even become popular and leading men. The chief alcaldes in Monterey and Santa Barbara were both Yankees by birth.

RICHARD HENRY DANA, JR.

Two Years before the Mast,
1840

THE OLD CUSTOM HOUSE.

CLIFF NEAR CYPRESS DRIVE.

CHINESE FISHING BOAT.

THE "ARGUS" OFFICE.

MONTEREY, CARMEL AND VICINITY

*. . . who sailed up and down the Pacific coast, visiting settlements,
—offering a wide assortment of household goods and knickknacks
to Californios, hungry for more of life's amenities*

ARIZONA GARDEN — CACTI 13 FT HIGH.

HOTEL DELMONTE.

CHINESE FISHING VILLAGE.

CARMEL MISSION—EST. 1770.

Four generations have seen few changes in the Spanish quarter of the town; yet, in the last decade, Monterey has become one of the great popular resorts of the Pacific coast, and every year sees thousands of tourists enjoy its varied scenery and its equable climate. It boasts of one of the finest hotels in the country; it prides itself on the magnificent seventeen-mile drive which has been laid out through the dark pine woods and along the shore of the Pacific. After the scenery—which seems to possess a perennial charm, giving the visitor fresh surprises every morning—there is nothing more attractive about Monterey than this dreamy Spanish life that takes no count of time or progress, the changes of governments or the new discoveries of science. Sleepy as the old town looks in its mid-day siesta, it has had a stirring history. It was founded by Junipero Serra, the leader of the Franciscan monks who established the chain of missions along the California coast, and for fifty years created there the idyllic pastoral life, now seen only in the poet's dream of Arcadia. The Bay of Monterey witnessed the arrival of stout Spanish troopers from Mexico, the building of a rude fort on the hill that overlooks the town, and the establishment of the seat of government of Alta California.

J. R. FITCH
Picturesque California, 1888

"Great trees and groves," declared John Muir, one of America's revered naturalists, *"need to be venerated as sacred monuments and halls of council and worship . . .*

The Big Tree *(Sequoia gigantea)* is nature's forest masterpiece, and, as far as I know, the greatest of living things. It belongs to an ancient stock, as its remains in old rocks show, and has a strange air of other days about it, a thoroughbred look inherited from the long ago, the auld land syne of trees. Once the genus was common, and with many species flourished in the now desolate Arctic regions, the interior of North America, and in Europe; but in long eventful wanderings from climate to climate only two species have survived the hardships they had to encounter, the *gigantea* and *sempervirens:* the former now restricted to the western slopes of the Sierra, the other to the Coast Mountains, and both to California, excepting a few groves of redwood which extend into Oregon. The Pacific coast in general is the paradise of conifers. Here nearly all of them are giants, and display a beauty and magnificence unknown elsewhere. The climate is mild, the ground never freezes, and moisture and sunshine abound all the year. Nevertheless, it is not easy to account for the colossal size of the Sequoias. The largest are about three hundred feet high, and thirty feet in diameter.

JOHN MUIR

My First Summer in the Sierra, 1911

THE SEQUOIAS—GIANT TREES OF CALIFORNIA

*"but soon after the discovery of the Calaveras Grove,
one of the grandest trees was cut down by laborious vandals
for the sake of the stump—to be used as a dance floor!"*

No description can give any adequate idea of their singular majesty, much less of their beauty. Excepting the sugar pine, most of its neighbors with pointed tops seem to be forever shouting "Excelsior!" while the Big Tree, though soaring above them all, seems satisfied, its rounded head poised lightly as a cloud, giving no impression of trying to go higher. Only in youth does it show, like other conifers, a heavenward yearning keenly aspiring with a long quick-growing top. Indeed, the whole tree, for the first century or two, or until a hundred to a hundred and fifty feet high, is arrowhead in form, and, compared with the solemn rigidity of age, is as sensitive to the wind as a squirrel tail. The lower branches are gradually dropped, as it grows older, and the upper ones thinned out, until comparatively few are left. These, however, are developed to great size, divide again and again, and terminate in mossy rounded masses of leafy branchlets, while the head becomes dome-shaped. Then, poised in fullness of strength and beauty, stern and solemn in mien, it glows with eager, enthusiastic life, quivering to the tip of every leaf and branch and far-reaching root, calm as a granite dome,—the first to feel the touch of the rosy beams of the morning, the last to bid the sun good-night.

JOHN MUIR
My First Summer in the Sierra, 1911

BIG TREES, MARIPOSA GROVE

FALLEN SEQUOIA

It is a curious fact that all the very old Sequoias have lost their heads by lightning. "All things come to him who waits;" but of all living things Sequoia is perhaps the only one able to wait long enough to make sure of being struck by lightning. Thousands of years it stands ready and waiting, offering its head to every passing cloud as if inviting its fate, praying for heaven's fire as a blessing; and when at last the old head is off, another of the same shape immediately begins to grow on. Every bud and branch seems excited, like bees that have lost their queen, and tries hard to repair the damage. Branches that for many centuries have been growing out horizontally at once turn upward, and all their branchlets arrange themselves with reference to a new top of the same peculiar curve as the old one.

JOHN MUIR

Yosemite—land of enchantment, and a botanist's paradise—with peaks and precipices of infinite immensity, Yosemite Falls, with a drop of almost fifteen hundred feet, a height nine times that of Niagara . . .

We set out from Yosemite about the end of August, and our first camp was made in the well-known Mariposa Grove. Here and in the adjacent pine woods I spent nearly a week, carefully examining the boundaries of the grove for traces of its greater extension without finding any. Then I struck out into the majestic trackless forest to the southeastward, hoping to find new groves or traces of old ones in the dense silver fir and pine woods about the head of Big Creek, where soil and climate seemed most favorable to their growth; but not a single tree or old monument of any sort came to light until I climbed the high rock called Wamellow by the Indians. Here I obtained telling views of the fertile forest-filled basin of the upper Fresno. Innumerable spires of the noble yellow pine were displayed rising one above another on the braided slopes, and yet nobler sugar pines with superb arms outstretched in the rich autumn light, while away toward the southwest, on the verge of the glowing horizon, I discovered the majestic dome-like crowns of Big Trees towering high over all, singly and in close grove congregations.

JOHN MUIR
The Yosemite, 1912

CATHEDRAL SPIRES

. . . owes its establishment as one of the nation's most popular parks largely to the voice and efforts of John Muir— naturalist, explorer, and environmentalist extraordinaire

YOSEMITE FALLS

Then your eye is smitten by the marvel of Yosemite Falls. You stand entranced while a river rushes out of the blue in great spurts like the throbbing of the heart of the earth. You see it fall half a mile in a rock-shaking torrent into a land of soft beauty that differs from the snowy regions of the Valley's rim as Italy differs from Norway. One never wearies of watching the comets or rockets of water whitened by the friction of the air. They are continually forming, shooting downward and either exploding or fading into mist-wraiths before the end of the first clear plunge of twenty-six hundred feet. These rockets descend much faster than the main masses; and when the air is filled with them, one might almost imagine oneself witnessing the collapse of some roof-ful of gypsum flowers and alabaster stalactites in one of the "cities" of Mammoth Cave. On certain heavy days this fall is peculiarly effective, as when a broad white wreath of cloud festoons itself along the top of the crag, and the torrent, alike in hue, gushes out of it like a vast beard gushing down from a huge mustache. Or, to vary the figure, one might fancy that some cyclopean distillery were busy condensing that cloud and pouring the product immediately into the vat of the Valley. It is as though nature were giving so simple a laboratory demonstration of her methods that every child might grasp the workings of her divine chemistry.

ROBERT HAVEN SCHAUFFLER
Romantic America, 1913

The battle, in 1854, to protect Yosemite's renowned scenic wonders from the cattleman's invasion and public abuse—later led by John Muir —halted the encroachment of lumber and logging interests, and . . .

GORGE OF THE MERCED,
FROM GLACIER POINT TRAIL

I cannot stop to give my impressions of Yosemite here, further than to say that, as contrasted with the Grand Canyon, one could live in Yosemite and find life sweet. It is like a great house in which one could find a nook where he could make his nest, looked down upon by the gods of the granite ages. The floor of the Valley really has a domestic, habitable look, with its orchards and ploughed lands, its superb trees, and its limpid, silently gliding river; and above all, its waterfalls fluttering against the granite precipices. The ethereal beauty of waterfalls, and the genial look of the pure streams, make almost any place habitable.

JOHN BURROUGHS

The Writings of John Burroughs, 1904-1

HALF DOME

I shall not multiply details, nor waste paper in noting all the foolish names which foolish people have given to different peaks or turrets. Just think of two giant stone towers, or pillars, which rise a thousand feet above the towering cliff which form their base, being styled the Two Sisters! Could anything be more maladroit and lackadaisical? The Dome is a high, round, naked peak, which rises between the Merced and its little tributary from the inmost recesses of the Sierra Nevada already instanced, and which towers to an altitude of over five thousand feet above the waters at its base. Picture to yourself a perpendicular wall of bare granite nearly or quite one mile high! Yet there are some dozen or score of peaks in all, ranging from three thousand to five thousand feet above the valley, and a biscuit tossed from any of them would strike very near its base, and its fragments go bounding and falling still further. I certainly miss here the glaciers of Chamonix, but I know no single wonder of nature on earth which can claim a superiority over the Yosemite. Just dream yourself for one hour in a chasm nearly ten miles long, with egress, save for birds and water, but at three points, up the face of precipices from three thousand to four thousand feet high, the chasm scarcely more than a mile wide at any point, and tapering to a mere gorge, or canyon, at either end, with walls of mainly naked and perpendicular white granite, from three thousand to five thousand feet high, so that looking up to the sky from it is like looking out of an unfathomable profound—and you will have some conception of the Yosemite.

HORACE GREELEY

An Overland Journey, 1859

. . . became a landmark victory of the conservationists, establishing a national park of infinite natural resources, as a legacy for the enjoyment of future generations

nd here let me renew my tribute to the
rvelous bounty and beauty of the forests of
s whole mountain region. The Sierra Nevadas
k the glorious glaciers, the frequent rains, the
h verdure, the abundant cataracts of the Alps;
t they far surpass them—they surpass any
er mountains I ever saw—in the wealth and
ce of their trees. Look down from almost any
their peaks, and your range of vision is filled,
unded, satisfied, by what might be termed a
npest-tossed sea of evergreens, filling every
and valley, covering every hillside, crowning
ry peak but the highest, with their unfading
uriance. That I saw during this day's travel
ny hundreds of pines eight feet in diameter,
h cedars at least six feet, I am confident; and
re were miles after miles of such a smaller
es of like genus standing as thick as they
ild grow. Steep mountainsides, allowing them
grow, rank above rank, without obstructing
h other's sunshine, seem peculiarly favorable
the production of these serviceable giants. But
Summit Meadows are peculiar in their heavy
nge of balsam fir of all sizes, from those bare-
one foot high to those hardly less than two
ndred, their branches surrounding them in
lars, their extremities gracefully bent down by
weight of winter snows, making them here, I
confident, the most beautiful trees on earth.
e dry promontories which separate these
adows are also covered with a species of
uce, which is only less graceful than the fir
resaid. I never before enjoyed such a tree-
st as on this wearing, difficult ride.

SENTINEL ROCK AND FALLS

FOOT OF SENTINEL FALLS

It is not the Merced River that makes this fall,
but a mere tributary trout brook, which pitches
in from the north by a barely once-broken descent of two thousand six hundred feet, while the
Merced enters the valley at its eastern extremity,
over falls of six hundred and two hundred and
fifty feet. But a river thrice as large as the Merced, at this season, would be utterly dwarfed by
all the other accessories of this prodigious
chasm. Only a Mississippi or a Niagara could be
adequate to their exactions. I readily concede
that a hundred times the present amount of
water may roll down the Yosemite Fall in the
months of May and June, when the snows are
melting from the central ranges of the Sierra
Nevada, which bound this abyss on the east; but
this would not add a fraction to the wonder of
this vivid exemplification of the divine power
and majesty. At present, the little stream that
leaps down the Yosemite, and is all but shat-
tered to mist by the amazing descent, looks like
a tapeline let down from the cloud-capped
height to measure the depth of the abyss. The
Yosemite Valley (or Gorge) is the most unique
and majestic of nature's marvels, but the
Yosemite Fall is of little account. Were it absent, the valley would not be perceptibly less
worthy of a fatiguing visit.

HORACE GREELEY

An Overland Journey, 1859

The Sierra Nevada—backbone and chain of mountains endowing California with picturesque and dramatic natural spectacles, endless in variety and richness . . .

Once in a lifetime, if one is lucky, one so merges with sunlight and air and running water that whole eons, the eons that mountains and deserts know, might pass in a single afternoon without discomfort. The mind has sunk away into its beginnings among old roots and the obscure tricklings and movings that stir inanimate things . . . . one can never quite define this secret; but it has something to do, I am sure, with common water. Its substance reaches everywhere; it touches the past and prepares the future; it moves under the poles and wanders thinly in the heights of air. It can assume forms of exquisite perfection in a snowflake, or strip the living to a single shining bone cast up by the sea.

LOREN EISELEY

MOUNT LYELL GROUP, FROM TUOLUMNE RIVER

The home ranch from which we set out is on the south side of the Tuolumne River near French Bar, where the foothills of metamorphic gold-bearing slates dip below the stratified deposits of the Central Valley. We had not gone more than a mile before some of the old leaders of the flock showed by the eager, inquiring way they ran and looked ahead that they were thinking of the high pastures they had enjoyed last summer. Soon the whole flock seemed to be hopefully excited, the mothers calling their lambs, the lambs replying in tones wonderfully human, their fondly quavering calls interrupted now and then by hastily snatched mouthfuls of withered grass. Amid all this seeming babel of baas as they streamed over the hills every mother and child recognized each other's voice. In case a tired lamb, half asleep in the smothering dust, should fail to answer, its mother would come running back through the flock toward the spot whence its last response was heard, and refused to be comforted until she found it, the one of a thousand, though to our eyes and ears all seemed alike.

JOHN MUIR

MOUNT SHASTA

. . . a gentle wilderness, made accessible through decades of persistent efforts of dedicated conservationists, led by the energy of John Muir and the Sierra Club he founded, in 1892

In the great Central Valley of California there are only two seasons—spring and summer. The spring begins with the first rainstorm, which usually falls in November. In a few months the wonderful flowery vegetation is in full bloom, and by the end of May it is dead and dry and crisp, as if every plant had been roasted in an oven. Then the lolling, panting flocks and herds are driven to the high, cool, green pastures of the Sierra. I was longing for the mountains about this time, but money was scarce and I couldn't see how a bread supply was to be kept up. While I was anxiously brooding on the bread problem, so troublesome to wanderers, and trying to believe that I might learn to live like the wild animals, gleaning nourishment here and there from seeds, berries, etc., sauntering and climbing in joyful independence of money or baggage, Mr. Delaney, a sheepowner, for whom I had worked a few weeks, called on me, and offered to engage me to go with his shepherd and flock to the headwaters of the Merced and Tuolumne Rivers—the very region I had most in mind. I was in the mood to accept work of any kind that would take me into the mountains whose treasures I had tasted last summer in the Yosemite region. The flock, he explained, would be moved gradually higher through the successive forest belts as the snow melted, stopping for a few weeks at the best places we came to. These I thought would be good centers of observation from which I might be able to make many telling excursions within a radius of eight or ten miles of the camps to learn something of the plants, animals, and rocks; for he assured me that I should be left perfectly free to follow my studies. I judged, however, that I was in no way the right man for the place, and freely explained my shortcomings, confessing that I was wholly unacquainted with the topography of the upper mountains, the streams that would have to be crossed, and the wild sheep-eating animals, etc.; in short that, what with bears, coyotes, rivers, canyons, and thorny, bewildering chaparral, I feared that half or more of his flock would be lost.

JOHN MUIR

"WILDCAT CASCADES," NEAR BERKELEY

A tiny pueblo founded by the Spanish in the late 18th century, Los Angeles—its Church of Our Lady the Queen of the Angels built 1818-1822—is one of the oldest settlements on America's West Coast . . .

California, the most spectacular and most diversified American state, California so ripe, golden, yeasty, churning in flux, is a world of its own in this trip we are beginning. It contains both the most sophisticated and the most bigoted community in America; it is a bursting cornucopia of peoples as well as of fruit, glaciers, sunshine, desert, and petroleum. There are several Californias, and the state is at once demented and very sane, adolescent and mature, depending on the point of view. Also, it is blessed by supernal wonders in the realm of climate, and a major item controlling its political behavior is the Pacific Ocean. The story of California is the story of migrations—migrations both into and within the state. The intense fluidity of America, its nomadism, is a factor never to be discounted.

JOHN GUNTHER
Inside U.S.A., 1947

SCENES IN LOS ANGELES

. . . yet one of its youngest and most vital—bursting out, amoeba-like in all directions, extending from the sea to the foot of coastal ranges—a melting pot for peoples of every continent and state

Los Angeles has been called every name in the book, from "nineteen suburbs in search of a metropolis" to a "circus without a tent" to "less a city than a perpetual convention." Frank Lloyd Wright, the architect, is supposed to have said once, "If you tilt the whole country sideways, Los Angeles is the place where everything loose will fall." And listen to Westbrook Pegler: "It is hereby earnestly proposed that the U.S.A. would be much better off if that big, sprawling, incoherent, shapeless, slobbering civic idiot in the family of American communities could be declared incompetent and placed in charge of a guardian like any individual mental defective." Freakishness, however, is not the characteristic that makes the town most interesting. What distinguishes it more is *(a)* its octopuslike growth, and *(b)* the way it lives on climate, mobility, and water . . . In general what is going on is a spreading out of the *city* of Los Angeles to a point where it will some day be coterminous with the county.

JOHN GUNTHER
Inside U.S.A., 1947

Father Junipero Serra started the chain of Franciscan missions— first building San Diego in 1769, Monterey in 1770, San Juan Capistrano in 1776—and is reputed to have planted the first California vineyard.

Of grapes, it is hardly yet time to speak so sanguinely as many do; for years will be required to render certain their exemption from the diseases and the devastators known to other lands of the vine. But it is certain that some kinds of grapes have been grown around the old Jesuit Missions for generations, with little care and much success; while it does not appear that the more delicate varieties recently introduced are less thrifty or more subject to attack than their Spanish predecessors, and vineyards are being multiplied and expanded in almost every farming neighborhood; single vines and patches of choice varieties are shooting up in almost every garden throughout the mining regions; and there can be little doubt that California is already better supplied with the grape than any other state of the Union. That she is destined soon to become largely and profitably engaged in the manufacture and exportation of wine is a current belief here, which I am at once unable and disinclined to controvert.

HORACE GREELEY

An Overland Journey, 1859

The mother vine, *vinta madre,* was also found at San Gabriel. To it the fathers had brought vine slips of a Spanish variety, known universally as the Mission grape. While these were growing, *aguardiente* was manufactured from the wild grapes of the country. In 1831 this pioneer vineyard contained 50,000 vines, and 50,000 more had been distributed along the Indian *rancherias.*

JOHN MUIR, ED.

Picturesque California, 1888

SANTA BARBARA AND VICINITY

1. City Hall and Hall of Records.   2. A Street.   3. Rose Cottage.   4. Roses in Private Grounds.   5. Ruin near the Mission.   6. The Beach and Bath-House.   7. In the Garden of the Mission.   8. The Old Mission.   9. Private Residence.   10. The Cliffs and Sea-Shore.

The Pacific Northwest

COLUMBIA RIVER . . . CAPE

HORN . . . MOUNT HOOD . . .ROOSTER

ROCK . . . PORTLAND . . . MOUTH OF

THE COLUMBIA . . . ASTORIA . . .

LOGGING AND LUMBERING SCENES . . .

TACOMA . . . PACIFIC AVENUE . . .

MOUNT TACOMA . . . THE WHARVES . . .

SEATTLE . . . SNOQUALMIE FALLS . . .

OLYMPIC MOUNTAINS . . .LAKE

WASHINGTON . . . MOUNT BAKER . . .

PUGET SOUND . . . SPOKANE FALLS . . .

RIVERSIDE AVENUE

COLUMBIA RIVER

The Pacific Northwest

THE PACIFIC NORTHWEST WAS America's "last frontier." Two centuries after New England saw its first permanent settlement, the Northwest still had only a few isolated fur-trading posts. It was not until late in the eighteenth century that Europeans took any interest in this land of mountains, rain forests, and fog-hung cliffs. Virtually unexplored beyond its rocky coast, it was known then only through rumor and myth.

In 1792 Robert Gray, captain of the American brig *Columbia,* entered and explored the mouth of the Columbia River and named it after his ship. His reports of the voyage served to end the centuries-old speculation about a Northwest passage. Late in 1805 Lewis and Clark reached the Pacific and wintered on the banks of the Columbia. Their detailed description of the topography, the resources, and the natives of the region west of the Continental Divide gave the West to Americans "as something their minds could deal with," in Bernard de Voto's words. This unknown and uncharted land finally became real, visible, and desirable. Within a few years it would become a land to settle in and, if necessary, to fight for.

The rich trade in the skins of sea otters first drew Europeans to the region. The Spanish had withdrawn their claims to the Northwest in 1793, and the British looked to be its heirs. The Northwest Company and the Hudson Bay Company were already actively engaged in fur trading, as was John Jacob Astor's Pacific Fur Trading Company. In 1812, at the start of the war with the British, Astor withdrew briefly from the territory, but reentered it after the war. The terms of the Treaty of Ghent, which ended the war, guaranteed joint British-American control of the region. But the growing American migration into the Northwest would shortly make this unworkable.

In 1840 the Reverend Jason Lee, who had lived in the the Northwest for some time, traveled east to petition Congress for a territorial government for Oregon. He then returned to Oregon with fifty-one settlers, who called themselves "The Great Enforcement." They settled in the Willamette Valley, south of the Columbia River. Lee's migration inaugurated the Great Migration that began in 1843. Thousands of pioneers traveled the Oregon Trail in covered wagons, suffering the intense heat of the desolate land east of the Cascade Range, and risking the winter hardships of the mountain crossing. They came in such large numbers that for a century after it was possible to follow their trail by the deep ruts cut by the wagon wheels.

The Great Migration of 1843 worried the British, who sent warships to the mouth of the Columbia. In 1844 James Polk was elected president on the platform "fifty-four forty or fight"—a slogan reflecting the extreme demand of the expansionists to extend American authority up to Russia's Alaskan holdings at 54.40 degrees north latitude. The question was settled peacefully; the British withdrew to the forty-ninth parallel, below Vancouver Island.

Congress and most Easterners then relaxed into indifference regarding the newly acquired land. It was still a long way away: over two thousand miles overland from the Midwest frontier or a sea voyage from New York or Boston that meant two or three years away

from home. The "Whitman Massacre" reawakened Congress and the public. In 1847 a Presbyterian missionary, Marcus Whitman, and his wife Narcissa, along with twelve others, were murdered by Cayuse Indians in the Walla Walla region of what is now Washington State. The provisional government then operating in the territory hunted down and executed the Indians, and dispatched a messenger to Washington to relate the news. They sent Joe Meek, a huge, buckskinned mountaineer, whose sensational appearance with news of the massacre stirred renewed interest in the Northwest. Within the year the region became a territory. Oregon and Washington were officially divided in 1853. In 1859 Oregon became the thirty-third state; in 1889 Washington became the forty-second state.

Most settlers made their way across eastern Washington and Oregon, over the Cascade Range, and into the heavily forested western region. East of the Cascades the land is desolate and brutally dry, but just at the crest of the mountains the climate suddenly changes, and the land to the west is some of the wettest in the nation. This is the land of the massive Douglas fir and Sitka spruce, trees that became the basis of the Northwest's economy for most of the century.

Despite the migration of the 1840s, the Northwest remained geographically and economically isolated for the next thirty years. In 1870 there were more people in the city of San Francisco than in all of Washington and Oregon. The region's isolation ended, however, with the arrival of the railroads in the 1880s. Between 1880 and 1890 the population of Oregon doubled and Washington's population grew fourfold. Tacoma, Seattle, and Portland thrived on lumber wealth, as rail connections to the East vastly expanded the market. Then, in 1897, the *SS Portland* docked in Seattle's harbor. It was reported that she carried a ton of solid gold found in Alaska. In fact, it was a ton of gold dust, found not in Alaska but in the Canadian Yukon. These details troubled no one. Americans, suffering a severe economic depression, reacted wildly to the news and the Gold Rush of '98 brought thousands to Washington's ports. The population swelled. America's "last frontier" became the jumping-off place for a journey into a new, harsher frontier—Alaska.

*The vast Oregon Territory, extending to Washington and Idaho:
rich in luxuriant forests, fertile soil, rivers abounding in
salmon, and with notably large beaver colonies . . .*

On the Olympic Peninsula in Washington, the wilderness stands unchanged since the first dawn. On the windward side of the mountains, 150 inches of rain will fall in an average year, and these primitive rainforests are rank and dark, full of wild beasts and twenty-foot ferns that grow in Pleistocene silence from the forest floor. The Olympic Mountains, a miniature Himalaya, rise sharp and snow-capped from the center of this low arboreal jungle. Saturated clouds obscure the peaks a good part of the year, casting a mood of Kieregaardian introspection over the entire massif. You could circle the peninsula for days on end and never know those mountains were there, yet sometimes they will stand out crisp and wild from the sea. . . . Now the Columbia is a commercial thoroughfare of vast international importance, and if you follow it upstream towards The Dalles, you will see its banks change before your eyes in a few minutes, from the lush, rain-blessed slopes of the windward side of the mountains to the sere plateau. It's like moving from the Garden into the desert wilderness.

CALVIN KENTFIELD

CAPE HORN

. . .attracted a flood of fur traders and pioneer-farmers, especially after the government-sponsored expeditions of John C. Fremont—the "pathfinder"—and his reports, in 1845

ROOSTER ROCK

Serene, indifferent of Fate,
Thou sittest at the Western Gate.

Upon the heights so lately won
Still slant the banners of the sun;
Thou seest the white seas strike their tents,
O Warder of two Continents!

And scornful of the peace that flies
Thy angry winds and sullen skies,
Thou drawest all things small or great
To thee, beside the Western Gate.

When forms familiar shall give place
To stranger speech and newer face;
When all her throes and anxious fears
Lie hushed in the repose of years;
When Art shall raise and Culture lift
The sensual joys and meaner thrift,
And all fulfilled the vision we
Who watch and wait shall never see,
Who in the morning of her race
Toiled fair or meanly in our place,
But, yielding to the common lot,
Lie unrecorded and forgot.

BRET HARTE

MOUNT HOOD

The cities of the Northwest burgeoned at a great rate—reflecting the wealth of coastal fisheries, valuable timber, and farmland yielding apples, pears, sugar beets, and truck vegetables . . .

First to define terms. It would seem that we have been in western regions a long time already, but actually in one sense California, Oregon, and Washington are not "the West" at all. In Portland I actually heard a lady say that she was "going West" on a brief trip—and she meant Utah! People on the Pacific Coast think of themselves as belonging to the "coast"; the "West" is quite something else again. Let us, however, be more inclusive. Of course the West comprises all the eleven states that lie wholly or in part west of the Continental Divide from any national point of view. But of these the three fronting the Pacific are a special case.

JOHN GUNTHER

Inside U.S.A., 1947

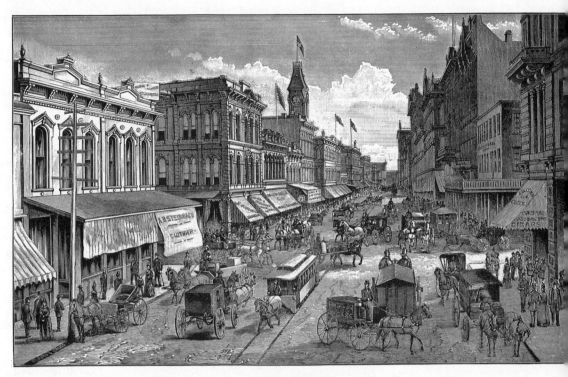

PORTLAND, OREGON

VIEW OF ASTORIA.

TILLAMOOK LIGHT.

SALMON FISHING NEAR PILLAR ROCK.

MOUTH OF THE COLUMBIA RIVER

In Paul Bunyan's Washington realm—truly the Evergreen State—were millions of acres of Douglas fir, hemlock, ponderosa and sugar pine: a land of Indian names—Skookumchuk, Dosewallips, and Puyallup

The most attractive sight which we had yet met with upon this voyage, now presented itself to our view. The steam-boat lay too close to the willow thicket, and we saw, immediately before us, the numerous, motley, gaily painted, and variously ornamented crowd of the most elegant Indians on the whole course. The handsomest and most robust persons, of both sexes and all ages, in highly original, graceful, and characteristic costumes, appeared, thronged together, to our astonished eye; and there was, all at once, so much to see and observe, that we anxiously profited by every moment to catch only the main features of this unique picture. . . All these Indians were dressed in their very finest clothes, and they completely attained their object; for they made, at least upon us strangers, a very lively impression. Many of them were distinguished by wearing leather shirts, of exquisite workmanship, which they obtain by barter from the Crows. Several tall, athletic men were on horseback, and managed their horses, which were frightened by the noise of the steam-boats, with an ease which afforded us pleasure.

MAXIMILIAN, PRINCE OF WIED

Travels in the Interior of North America, 1843

LOGGING SCENES—FROM FOREST TO RAFT

PUYALLUP HOP RANCH, TACOMA, WASHINGTON TERRITORY

John Muir observed: "The forests of America, however slighted by man, must have been a great delight to God, because they were the best He ever planted"

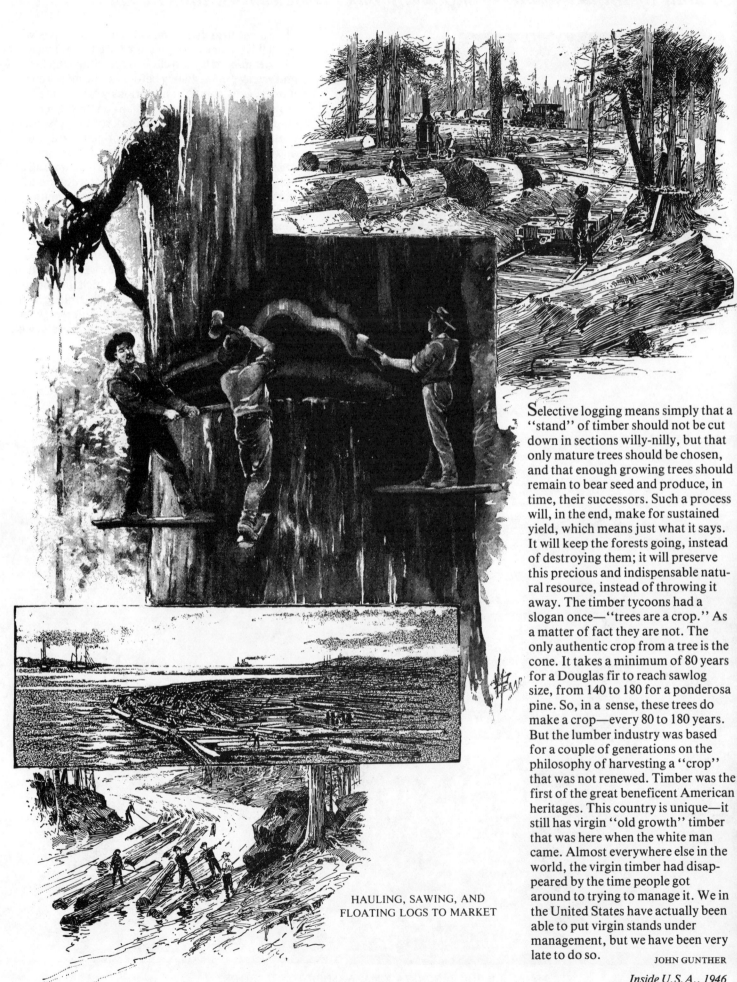

HAULING, SAWING, AND FLOATING LOGS TO MARKET

Selective logging means simply that a "stand" of timber should not be cut down in sections willy-nilly, but that only mature trees should be chosen, and that enough growing trees should remain to bear seed and produce, in time, their successors. Such a process will, in the end, make for sustained yield, which means just what it says. It will keep the forests going, instead of destroying them; it will preserve this precious and indispensable natural resource, instead of throwing it away. The timber tycoons had a slogan once—"trees are a crop." As a matter of fact they are not. The only authentic crop from a tree is the cone. It takes a minimum of 80 years for a Douglas fir to reach sawlog size, from 140 to 180 for a ponderosa pine. So, in a sense, these trees do make a crop—every 80 to 180 years. But the lumber industry was based for a couple of generations on the philosophy of harvesting a "crop" that was not renewed. Timber was the first of the great beneficent American heritages. This country is unique—it still has virgin "old growth" timber that was here when the white man came. Almost everywhere else in the world, the virgin timber had disappeared by the time people got around to trying to manage it. We in the United States have actually been able to put virgin stands under management, but we have been very late to do so.

JOHN GUNTHER

Inside U.S.A., 1946

A century ago, the timber barons and their loggers—assuming the forests to be inexhaustible—cut great swaths of "old growth" acreage, before conservationists enforced selective logging

CUTTING AND TRANSPORTING LOGS TO MARKET

The loggers arrived in the Northwest still cherishing the idea they had held for nigh three hundred years: There was always timber, plenty of timber, just over the next hump. They had already cut a swath of it from eastern Maine through the lake states, and some had moved south to do as much for the timbered states bordering the Gulf of Mexico. The rest loaded their gear and themselves into the steam cars for Oregon and Washington. Loggers never looked backward, eastward. Had they done so, the more reflective among them might have seen what was happening—that as fast as they abandoned their old works a horde of farmers, traders, and city promoters moved in to grub stumps, plat towns, and make highways of the grass-grown logging roads. It was the loggers' ancient enemy, Civilization, following hard in their wake, and they wanted none of it. Yet here on the west coast, loggers and lumbermen were in their last stronghold, their backs to the sea. There was no hump to go over from here. Civilization had at last caught up with them; and it was going to tame them, too. Time out of mind their war cry had been to let daylight into the swamp, then to move on West. And now there was nothing west of the continent's west shore.

STEWARD HOLBROOK

The Romance of North America, 1958

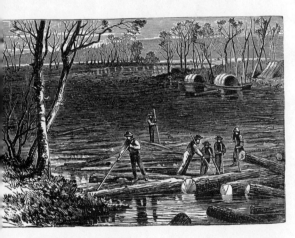

Tacoma—at the head of navigation on Puget Sound, with two hundred miles of waterfront, built upon the prosperity of lumber reserves and sawmills—typifies the mushroom growth of Northwest frontier towns

Here is the city of Tacoma, one of the very latest creations of the modern pioneer. The peculiar advantages of its site have been known ever since Puget Sound was discovered, and yet the march of civilization would not be there now if the modern pioneer had not pushed it to the head of Commencement Bay and left it there. He could not very well have pushed it farther, because Tacoma is absolutely the last trench of the march of empire. In Tacoma there is no West. The pioneer in this case was the Northern Pacific Railroad. There came a time in the construction of this great steel throughfare when a definite limit had to be placed upon its westward progress—when some spot should be picked out and called the end of the road. The managers of the road picked out the head of Commencement Bay, and put it down on their maps as Tacoma, the western terminus of the Northern Pacific Railroad. There was a sort of sawmill community there at the time, but the able-bodied men in it would hardly have made a corporal's guard; and when it heard that it was to become one of the important cities of the American continent it simply gasped in awe and wonder. . . .

1. A Bit of Ninth Street. 2. Wheat Warehouses. 3. Pacific Avenue. 4. Elevator and Coal-Bunkers. 5. A View from Railroad Bridge. 6. Mount Tacoma, fr

TACOMA AND ENVIRONS

Majestic Mount Rainier dominates the scenic splendor of the environs—but more important are the hustle and bustle of this seaport: shipping wheat, lumber, canned fish, fruits, and vegetables

The soil that is favorable to the growing of hops is rich enough for almost anything else, which is fully shown in the variety and excellence of other things that thrive in the new State. The people assert that they can raise better fruit than California can, and more of it, with the exception of oranges and lemons and other tropical fruits. As the State is new and undeveloped, the agricultural possibilities are as yet hardly appreciated. The climate is unusually well adapted to fruit-culture, and, in fact, to the growing of all manner of grains, vegetables, and grasses. The winters are mild and equable, with a temperature like that of Tennessee. The summers are long and cool. In winter-time one would naturally expect at Tacoma the climate of the Arctic circle, but the geographical position is here at fault, at least so far as practical results are concerned. Were there no such thing as the warm current of Japan beating against the Pacific coast, the chief winter feature here would be the ice palace. As a result Tacoma has more rain than snow. Much of the rain in Tacoma is little more than a sort of Scotch mist and people get accustomed to that sort of thing in time.

Harper's Weekly, June 20, 1891

the Union Club.   7. Along the Wharves.   8. A Tacoma Saw-Mill.   9. A Typical Home.   10. The oldest Bell Tower in America.   11. The Tacoma Theatre.

Seattle—a remote village with a handful of settlers, when founded in 1851; with a few thousand in 1880—soon expanded, as it became the gateway to the Northwest and distant Alaska . . .

The sounds that have influenced us in the Northwest are the crash of timber and the savage music of the whining headsaws on the sandspits of Puget Sound, on the banks of the Columbia, and elsewhere in the two states. The aroma that stirs us most is that of fresh sawdust wild on the wind. Roughly sixty cents of every dollar in the region derives from forest products. There are two distinctive forests in the region. West of the Cascades is the forest dominated by the massive Douglas fir, with which is mixed hemlock, and where, in the coastal strip called the Rain Forest, stands the gigantic Sitka spruce. East of the Cascades are the immense timber stands of pine bordering the grasslands and deserts. Logging here was not of major importance until the arrival of the several transcontinental railroads. Rain is the great tree maker, and rain up to the extreme measure of 130 inches a year falls in the coastal region of the two states. At the summit of the Cascades, however, the moisture lessens markedly, and presently all but disappears. It is here that the Douglas fir forest begins to diminish and the pine takes over. This is the dividing line between two vastly different climates. It often divides the political thought of both states. Perhaps nowhere else in the United States is the transition from one climate to another so sharp and sudden as in the Cascade Mountain passes, including the Columbia River highway. Less than half an hour takes you from one to the other. The change can be felt and seen . . .

SEATTLE AND VICINITY ON PUGET SOUND

1. View of Seattle and Mount Tacoma from Hotel Denny.   2. Snoqualmie Falls, 286 Feet High.   3. Distant View of th

. . . Klondike gold fields boomed; Alaska's timber crop and fisheries flourished; steamship lines and trading companies developed; all home-based in progressive Seattle

. . . In contrast to the standard type of city boomer, talking shrill and fast of projected railroads, gaslights, and streetcars, the Puget Sound region attracted an extraordinary number of settlers who were seeking not the conventional metropolis, but the ideal community symbolized in the anagram of "nowhere" which Samuel Butler, an Englishman, used as title for his celebrated philosophical novel. *Erewhon* had no slums. It had no poor. It had a great deal of milk and no little honey. All hands lived on the sunny side of the street. Later and still more influential came a book called *Looking Backward*, by Edward Bellamy, an American, who also seemed to think the future of man lay in cooperative effort. Because the Northwest corner was a new region and not yet wholly corrupted by materialism, it seemed—in the eighties and nineties to thousands of Americans— that this was the place to establish the perfect Erewhon. So they came, the idealists, to found their Edens, under various names, mostly on the bays of Puget Sound and adjacent waters. There was the Puget Sound Colony, or Model Commonwealth, near present Port Angeles; the Glennis Socialists near Tacoma; the Co-operative Commonwealth of Equality, near Edison; the Co-operative Brotherhood of Burley; the Freeland Association on Whidby Island; and the Mutual Home Colony Association of Home, on Joe's Bay.

STEWART HOLBROOK

The Romance of North America, 1958

tains.   4. View of the City from the Bay.   5. Lake Washington.   6. View of Mount Baker.   7. On the Sound.

Spokane Falls—four hundred miles east of the Pacific, on the fringe of Washington Territory—grew from frontier hamlet to boom town, with valuable mines, horses and cattle, and luxuriant grazing land

It is the street of a town. It is quiet, almost as quiet as the woods, the hill crest, and the pond that can be reached in ten minutes from the center. The town has no vision of becoming a city. None of its inhabitants expects to become a millionaire. The basis of its vigor and its magnetism is quite simple and it is also quite real. One is freer here than elsewhere to be oneself. there are space, leisure, and freedom for personality to develop. One may follow his calling and raise his family in decent self-respect with less pressure to conform to the prepossessions or timidity of others, with more immunity from the dictation of fashion or belief or group passion or group orthodoxy.

BERNARD DE VOTO

The Romance of North America, 1958

Riverside Avenue

SPOKANE FALLS, WASHINGTON TERRITORY

No, the American dream that has lured tens of millions of all nations to our shores in the past century has not been a dream of merely material plenty, though that has doubtless counted heavily. It has been much more than that. It has been a dream of being able to grow to fullest development as man and woman, unhampered by the barriers which had slowly been erected in older civilizations, unrepressed by social orders which had developed for the benefit of classes rather than for the simple human being of any and every class. And that dream has been realized more fully in actual life here than anywhere else, though very imperfectly even among ourselves. It has been a great epic and a great dream.

JAMES TRUSLOW ADAMS

The Epic of America, 1933

Howard Street

List of Authors

Artists & Engravers

Abbey, Edwin A., 108, 124
Andrew, John, 18, 19, 26, 31, 33, 44-46,
    83, 96, 252-53, 404, 405, 474, 475,
    479
Birch, H., Jr., 250, 251
Bobbett, Albert, 271, 423
Bogert, J.A., 268, 269, 297, 459
Bonwill, C.E.H., 130-31, 154
Bross, R.S., 280, 355
Brown, S.E., 10, 12, 13, 100, 101, 241

Champney, W.L., 23, 26-29
Chapin, John R., 82, 158, 176, 177, 202
    274
Crane, W.T., 276-77

Damoreau, 28, 29, 292, 315, 366, 383,
    386
Davis, Theodore, R., 150, 151, 421, 422,
    429, 434, 435, 486
Devereux, George Thomas, 210, 214,
    215, 218, 219-23
Durkin, John, 291, 408, 409, 412

Fenn, Harry, 2, 4, 14, 66, 104, 106, 107,
    122, 128, 135, 136, 140, 142-45,
    156, 159, 161-67, 170, 178, 179,
    184, 185, 188-90, 236, 237, 264,
    266-69, 272, 273, 279, 284,
    288-90, 296-99, 301, 322-25,
    328, 330, 331, 446-51, 463
Filmer, J., 7, 183, 192, 204, 206, 233,
    257, 259, 266, 290, 331, 384, 448,
    449, 453, 456, 457, 466
Fitler, W.C., 496, 508
Frost, Arthur B., 138, 224-25, 428, 430

Gibson, William H., 78, 80, 81, 84, 97,
    98, 132
Gifford, R. Swain, 482, 483, 498, 499
Goater, Walter, 266-67, 280-81
Graham, Charles, 111, 116, 118, 126,
    286-87, 291, 326-28,362, 375,

390-92, 412, 424, 433, 462, 484,
    485, 492-94, 500, 501, 504-07
Gray-Parker, 123

Harley, 134, 156, 186, 201, 237, 279,
    281, 289, 296, 299, 330, 343, 354
Hart, William, 358, 359
Hawley, Hughson, 102, 295, 508
Hill, A.H., 18, 19, 22-25, 31-33, 336,
    352, 356, 357, 388, 389
Hogan, Thomas, 84, 117, 126, 197

Karst, John, 248, 256, 272
Kilburn, S.S., 10, 12, 13, 172, 180-81,
    332, 333, 336, 337, 346, 353,   396-99

Lagarde, 112-13
Lauderbach, James W., 271, 240, 242,
    243
Leslie, Frank, 40, 49, 55, 65, 148, 176,
    177, 221, 364
Linton, William James, 5-7, 376, 447,
    451

Measom, A., 200, 201, 212, 262
Meeder, 199, 246
Merrick, William M., 212, 420
Miller, W.R., 62, 91, 101, 146-48, 150,
    160, 174, 175, 241
Moran, Thomas, 75, 444, 452, 453, 456-
    59, 465-69
Moser, J.H., 406, 407

Nast, Thomas, 152-53

Orr, John William, 386, 389
Orr, Nathaniel, 60, 81, 204, 205, 387

Palmer, W.J., 106, 107, 159, 160, 166
Peirce, 22-25, 28, 29, 38, 131, 147, 150,
    176, 177, 180, 181, 183, 202, 203
Perkins, Granville, 192, 204-07, 212,
    213, 216, 219, 226, 228, 232-35,

238, 239, 258-62
Pierson, R.B., 80, 396
Pilliner, 43, 160, 183, 195, 214, 282
Pranishnikoff, Ivan, 108

Quartley, F.W., 140, 145, 184, 255, 258,
    272, 273, 328, 452

Remington, Frederic, 418, 436-41
Richardson, James H., 205, 235, 258,
    358, 370
Rix, Julian, 477
Roberts, G., 60, 469
Rogers, William A., 110, 115, 123, 432,
    439, 470

Schell, F.H., 84, 117, 126, 203, 216,
    217, 230, 245
Sheppard, W.L., 248, 256, 257, 430
Smillie, James D., 156, 487-91
Snyder, W. P., 120-21

Tarbell, Edmund C., 21, 50, 130, 182,
    244, 353, 386
Tavernier, Jules, 112-13, 200, 201
Thomson, E.T., 476, 477
Thulstrup, Thure de, 116

Wade, 43, 176, 177, 250, 251, 318, 396
Warren, A. Coolidge, 21, 23, 38, 40, 41,
    46, 374, 380
Waud, Alfred R., 304, 306, 307, 312,
    313, 316, 317, 320, 371, 374, 378,
    382, 384, 387, 394, 397, 400, 401,
    403, 411, 414, 416
Waud, William, 11, 386
Williams, G. P., 428, 430
Wolf, Henry, 418, 440
Woodward, J. Douglas, 9, 16, 52, 53,
    68, 86, 88-95, 133, 183, 186, 187,
    208, 340, 342-45, 348-51, 354,
    355
Zogbaum, Rufus F., 168, 422, 428

I N D E X

514

518